THE AIR WA
1939-1945

This is the first *general* history of the air war, 1939–45, to appear in English.

This is not a "blood and guts" book; it is a general history in the sense that it covers the whole war period and all the warring powers, and in that it covers not just the military campaigns and oft-recounted battles, but the grand strategy, economic mobilization, the recruitment of science, production, and the nature and training of leadership.

This book shows two things. First, why the Allies won the air war, in the narrower sense of the contest between air forces. Second, that strategic bombing really was much more important to the achievement of overall victory than most post-war histories have been prepared to concede.

Examining the conflict from the points of view of both the Allies and the Axis, and buttressed with extensive new evidence, this book deepens our understanding not only of the Second World War, but of military history in general.

"Entirely unique....This book is important."   *—Best Sellers*

"A solid recommendation for serious military collections."
—Library Journal

"Exceptional....Honest, broadly informed and well-stocked with useful data."   *—Kirkus Reviews*

"Solid, authoritative, and thought-provoking. A good, thick chunk of history."   *—St. Louis Post-Dispatch*

"Excellent....Sound and balanced....Highly recommended."
—A.L.A. Booklist

THE AIR WAR
1939 - 1945

R. J. OVERY

5B

A SCARBOROUGH BOOK
STEIN AND DAY/*Publishers*/New York

For my parents

FIRST SCARBOROUGH BOOKS EDITION 1982
The Air War, 1939–1945 was originally published in
hardcover by STEIN AND DAY/*Publishers* in 1981.

Copyright ©1980 by R. J. Overy

Printed in the United States of America
STEIN AND DAY/*Publishers*
Scarborough House
Briarcliff Manor, N.Y. 10510

Library of Congress Cataloging in Publication Data

Overy, R. J.
      The air war, 1939–1945.

      Bibliography: p.
      Includes index.
      I. World War, 1939–1945—Aerial operations.
2. Military history. Modern—20th century.   I. Title.
D785.9   1981   940.54′4   80-6200
ISBN 0-8128-6156-6   AACR2

Contents

List of Illustrations   vii

List of Tables   viii

Abbreviations   ıx

Preface   xi

Introduction   1

1. Preparing for War   5
(i)   Aircraft and Sea Power   6
(ii)   Armies and Air Power   8
(iii)   Strategic Bombing   12
(iv)   Aerial Defence   14
(v)   Air Power and Strategy   18

2. The European Air War: September 1939–1941   26
(i)   From Poland to the Blitz   26
(ii)   The RAF, Bombing and the War at Sea   37
(iii)   The Struggle for the Mediterranean   40
(iv)   Air Power and War 1939–41   44

3. The European Air War: 1941–1945   47
(i)   Air War on the Eastern Front   47
(ii)   The United States and the War in Europe   60
(iii)   Air Power in the Mediterranean and Atlantic   64
(iv)   From Casablanca to Victory   73
(v)   The Collapse of the Luftwaffe   78
(vi)   Air Power and the War in Europe   82

4. The Air War in the Far East   85
(i)   The Victory of Japanese Air Power   85
(ii)   The Allied 'Defensive-Offensive'   90
(iii)   Bombing and the Collapse of Japan   97

5. The Strategic Bombing Offensives   102
(i)   Preparation and Purpose   102
(ii)   Problems of Execution: Technology and Intelligence   108

(iii) The Strategic Argument   115
(iv) The Impact of Bombing   119

6. Leadership, Organization, and Training   127
(i)   Leadership in the Air War   127
(ii)   Organization in the Armed Forces   131
(iii) The Air Force Officer Corps   134
(iv)   Recruitment and Training   138
(v)   Morale and the Military Tradition   145

7. The Aircraft Economies   149
(i)   Production and Strategy   151
(ii)   The Organization of Aircraft Production   155
(iii)   Industry, Bureaucracy and Administration   159
(iv)   The Mobilization of Industry   162
(v)   The Efficiency of Aircraft Production   168
(vi)   Labour and Raw Materials   171
(vii)   The Quality of Aircraft   177
(viii) Finance, Capitalism and the War Effort   180

8. Science, Research, and Intelligence   185
(i)   Science and the Air War   186
(ii)   Research, Development and the Quality of Weapons   191
(iii) Intelligence and the Air War   196
(iv)   Scientific Intelligence   200

9. Conclusions   203
Notes   212
Bibliography   240
Index   257

Illustrations

Between pages 148 and 149

A WWI Italian biplane fighter in use during WWII
British "Swordfish" biplanes with modern rocket
    weaponry
A German "Stuka"
Soviet "Yak-9" fighters
American "Hellcat" carrier fighter-bombers
Italian "Cant Z506" naval aircraft serving with the
    Allies
Three views of the Luftwaffe's He 177 heavy bomber
Cant Z1007 bombers dropping bombs over Malta
Female ground crew worker loads a Lancaster with an
    8000 lb. bomb
Czech mechanics servicing a Spitfire during Battle of
    Britain
A pilot
Female aircraft factory workers in Britain, the United
    States, and Russia
German radar installation
British mobile radar and communications unit
Manufacturing "Window," a jamming aid against
    German radar
A German V-2 rocket

(photos courtesy of the Imperial War Museum)

Tables

1 Aircraft Production of the Major Powers 1932–39   21
2 Air Strength of Allies and Germany September 1938 and September 1939   23
3 Single-engine Fighter Statistics for the Battle of Britain   33
4 German Air Force Strength March 1940–March 1942   50
5 Production, Strength and Losses of Britain, United States and Germany 1942–44   77
6 American and Japanese Strength and Losses in the Pacific War   94
7 Japanese Warship and Merchant Losses and Cause 1941–45   96
8 Sorties by Suicide Pilots October 1944–August 1945   99
9 Comparative Bomber Performance, United States, Britain and Germany   113
10 Bomber Production and Bomb Tonnages Delivered, Germany, Britain and the United States, 1940–45   120
11 Air Force and Army Maximum Size during World War II   139
12 Aircraft and Aero-engine Production of the Major Powers by Number and Weight 1939–45   150
13 Comparative Economic Statistics, Allied and Axis Powers in 1938   151
14 Floorspace for Aircraft and Main Components Manufacture in the United States 1939–44   164
15 Output of Aircraft in Pounds per Man-day in Japan, Germany and the United States 1941–45   168
16 Labour in the Aircraft Industry at Selected Dates 1940–45   171

Abbreviations

In the text:

AAF Army Air Forces (United States)
ABC America, Britain, Canada (Staff talks)
ADD Aviatsiya dal'nevo deistviya (long-range air arm)
AWPD Air War Plans Division
CBO Combined Bombing Offensive
He Heinkel
MAP Ministry of Aircraft Production
Me Messerschmitt
OR Operational Research
RAF Royal Air Force

In the bibliography and footnotes:

BA Bundesarchiv
BIOS British Intelligence Objectives Sub-committee
CIOS Combined Intelligence Objectives Sub-committee
FIAT Field Intelligence Agencies Technical
HMSO Her/His Majesty's Stationery Office
IMT International Military Tribunal
IWM Imperial War Museum, London
JRAeI Journal of the Royal Aeronautical Institute
JRUSI Journal of the Royal United Services Institution
NA National Archives, Washington, D.C.
RDGM Revue d'histoire de la Deuxième Guerre Mondiale
SAOG Strategic Air Offensive against Germany
UP University Press
USSBS United States Strategic Bombing Survey

Preface

This is not a 'blood and guts' book about the air war. It is a general history of the air war. General in the sense that it covers the whole war period and all the warring powers; and general in the sense that it covers not just the military campaigns but the wider strategic, economic and scientific world that encompassed the air war. The purpose of the book is to show two things. First of all why the Allies won the air war, in the narrower sense of the contest between air forces. Secondly, to show how important air power was to the achievement of overall victory. The answer to both questions lies not so much in the battles, whose details have been retold many times before, but with what went on in the background. There is as a result much less on battles and air fighting and much more on strategy, tactics, training and production. The air war had its limits set by decisions of government, by the economic environment, and by the level of scientific and technical achievement. Only by understanding this wider historical context can the familiar aerial battles themselves be understood.

There are a number of obvious pitfalls in attempting such a history. From its very nature the book appears perhaps too general. I am well aware that topics to which I have devoted a paragraph are the subject of a dozen books. The very size of the task is perhaps an explanation of why no general academic history of the air war has yet appeared. Another pitfall lies with the nature of comparative analysis. It is a difficult task to compare the economic and scientific systems of the major warring powers without, albeit sometimes unconsciously, producing some scale of values in making comparative judgements. In war this is perhaps inevitable. One side lost the war; another side won it. It would be plausible to argue that the Allies made better use of their resources for war than did the Axis powers, but this was not always so. A comparative view allows a more critical approach to the waging of war on both sides. In some cases the Allies won their battles through the possession of huge resources rather than through the efficient use of those resources. It was possible for Axis forces to be used with great efficiency from a military point of view but for these forces to be overwhelmed by sheer numbers. A comparative approach is indispensable in illuminating such perspectives.

It is important to state at this point that the book has a historical rather than a polemic purpose. The war itself raises the temptation for the historian to be continually passing judgement on military decisions knowing as he does the final outcome of the battles for which such decisions were made. The danger here is that military history turns into mere argument with the figures who made it. In the air war the danger is perhaps more obvious with the debate about the efficacy of bombing still warm. I have tried to avoid this kind of argument. I have concentrated instead on trying to establish the historical context within which such decisions were taken. That the war did raise important ethical questions, particularly in the context of bombing, is clear. This account is not about the history of post-war recrimination. It is about the war as it was understood, however imperfectly or unethically, at the time. This of itself involves a great deal of historical judgment in analysing motives, purposes and choices. Moreover in the course of reconstructing that historical context many of the myths sustained since the Second World War can be shown to be just that; myths created for a special purpose but uncorroborated by the evidence. In this respect history itself is the harshest judge of yesterday's errors and the sternest critic of man's unfailing propensity to see things as other than they are.

The final problem in so general a book as this is the source material. Even were it not for the fact that much of the necessary documentation has been destroyed or is closed to researchers, the sheer volume remaining would barely be covered in a lifetime and could not then be compresssed into a book of 90,000 words. Much of the material used is therefore published, either as official histories, volumes of documents or memoirs. My own work on the Luftwaffe has proved invaluable as so little has been written on the German air force from original sources and it still lacks even an official history. This book is offered as an introduction to the general history of the air war and will, I hope, in its turn prompt more research in those areas still starved of scholars. Most of my work has been done at the University Library in Cambridge and at the Imperial War Museum in London. I should like to thank the staff of the War Museum reading room and documents department for their assistance over the last ten years. I should also like to acknowledge advice kindly given in the preparation of the book by Professor N. Gibbs, Professor F. H. Hinsley and Mr. C. Trebilcock. Any remaining errors and misjudgements are my own. I should finally like to thank my wife and large family for a variety of inspiration and encouragement.

R. J. Overy
Oakington, Cambridge 1980

Introduction

By itself the air war does not make much sense. There were few battles in the Second World War fought only by aircraft. Even fewer can be said to have had any decisive strategic effect. This is not to say that aircraft were not important in the war. Each of the combatant powers wanted to gain command of the air—an overwhelming supremacy designed to neutralize and destroy enemy air power while subjecting the enemy to continuous air attack. Yet such command was not expected to bring the war to an end by itself. Command of the air was a necessary component in the successful execution of naval and military strategies. But it was these strategies, involving the movement of ships and men and the occupying of land, that won the day. Air power had a complementary rather than an autonomous role to play. As a result the air war also lacks historical autonomy. Any attempt to impose it on the evidence necessarily exaggerates the significance of aircraft and distorts the view of military strategy during the war itself. The first purpose of any history of the air war is to avoid overemphasizing the role of air power. The air war must remain a component of the wider war and can only be fully understood in a strategic context of which it forms only a part.

It could be argued that strategic bombing is the exception. The bombing offensive, the one ostensibly independent air operation, was regarded by some of its supporters as capable of winning the war on its own. For Britain bombing was the sensible successor to the old policy of naval blockade. Unable to challenge the Axis powers in Europe with large land armies, it was tempting to see strategic bombing as a way to destroy the German and Italian will-to-war without having to set foot on the Continent. A group of senior American soldiers subscribed to the same view. The other fighting powers, despite the popular attraction of the theory of the 'knock-out blow' from the air, remained sceptical and never seriously contemplated a strategic bomber campaign designed to do what armies and navies had done hitherto. In the end neither the British nor the American supporters of bombing could provide convincing evidence that the war in Europe could be ended from the air. Pressure from the Russians and the Joint Chiefs of Staff persuaded the Allied leaders that only a large-scale invasion of mainland Europe would achieve the desired strategic goal of defeating Hitler and liberating Europe within a reasonable length of time. In the Pacific the bombers had a better case. Japan's economy was weaker and her air resistance much poorer. Bombing would avoid the needless loss of life that an invasion of the Japanese mainland would predictably produce. Yet the American defeat of Japan was a combined operation in every sense. Naval power cleverly combined with air power helped to back up and protect the long haul of the American and

Commonwealth armies into the land perimeter of the Japanese Empire. Only when bases sufficiently close to Japan had been won could bombing come into its own, and only the use of the atomic bomb, which air strategists could not have counted on when making their original calculations, brought the war to an abrupt halt, with the conventional bombing debate unresolved.

It is obvious that the air war raises more questions than its place in military strategy. One of the most significant things about air warfare was its close correlation with a certain level of economic and technical achievement. Only the most advanced industrial powers could afford to run a large air force and undertake the research and development necessary to maintain the technological momentum associated with such an advanced weapons system. Hence the ability to wage a successful war in the air did not depend just on the heroism and tenacity of pilots or the tactical inspirations of air force leaders, but to a large extent on economic and technical factors. As the Germans were to discover in Russia and the Japanese in the Pacific, quality could not forever make up for inadequate provision of aircraft from the factories. As the numerical gap widened sheer quantity became a factor capable of achieving domination in the air. Fortune smiled on the big battalions no less in the air battles than elsewhere. Hence aircraft production assumed a great importance in the warring economies and became a real test of how successfully modern industrial economies could be converted to war purposes. The German and Japanese economies were conspicuously less successful at this conversion than those of the Allies. Not that the fascist powers could ever hope to produce as many aircraft as Russia, Britain and the United States together. Nevertheless aircraft production rose to great heights in Germany and Japan in 1944 when it could be used with very much less effect. Had both countries been able to produce what was demanded from an early stage of the war, when its provision might have proved decisive, then they would have posed a very much greater military threat in 1941 and 1942. Nor is this an argument from hindsight. Both in Germany and Japan great plans were laid for aircraft output. The problem arose between the plan and fulfilment, the explanation for which lies in the way in which the war economies were administered, as well as in a wide range of resources difficulties which for political and economic reasons could not be solved until the war was well under way. Whether these difficulties had been overcome or not there still remained the problem of an overwhelming economic advantage to the Allies. If air supremacy depended to an increasing extent on the numbers produced then the Allies were assured of a permanent superiority.

It was at this point that the question of research and development became so important. The superiority gained through quantity depended on the average performance of aircraft on both sides being more or less similar. A really major shift in quality, such as that implied with the jet aircraft or rockets, might in itself have led to a shift in the balance of air power. Hence the powers had to be prepared not only to produce large quantities of aircraft but at the same time to assure the maintenance of at least an approximate technical parity. The 1935-45 period saw a rapidly accelerating rate of technical change in aircraft and equipment which placed a great premium on scientific and engineering skills and necessitated the close co-operation of scientific and military establishments. Some powers, like Japan, depended to a large extent on successful imitation and were hampered by a lack of sufficient native engineering skill to keep up the technological race. Only in America and Britain was enough attention paid to the fact that air planning had to take full account of change over time. Forward planning was one of the most important tasks of any air staff and one which had to be fully and carefully integrated into the administrative apparatus in such a way that there would always be better weapons in the pipeline and a strategy to use them. Germany arguably enjoyed a technical lead in 1938–39. Japan certainly had close to parity at the same time, yet in both cases that lead was squandered through poor development procedures and wrong strategic decisions. With the exception of the German jet fighter—which itself suffered in development from Hitler's intention to use it as a bomber—the Axis powers fell further behind not just in quantity but in quality too. There were certainly German scientists capable of keeping Germany at the forefront of research. What failed to materialize was an entirely satisfactory way of integrating such research into industrial and military planning. The air war was won and lost not only in the skies but in the factories and research establishments.

No study of the air war would be complete without taking some account of the personnel involved. In the case of the air forces this raises some interesting questions. In most cases air forces emerged as independent services. In some cases they were subordinate to the army and navy. The different constitutional position was often dictated by the nature of the emergence of early air forces, the strength of opinion among the other two services and the nature of recruitment and leadership. In Germany the Luftwaffe achieved significance as the specifically Nazi arm and was led by men who were both committed Nazis as well as airmen despite the resistance of the Prussian army to an independent air service. In Japan there had never been the same problem. The air forces were branches of both the Army and Navy, and formed an important part of both traditional establishments. To a certain extent actual performance in war was conditioned by problems of organization, personality and leadership. There was no question of a shortage of recruits, although pilot training was an important factor in the air war. But there were questions associated with the leadership corps that sometimes produced fundamental differences between air forces and in many cases actively contributed to military success or disaster.

There was also a more general social background to the air war. The air forces were all new. Around them developed the special *mentalité* of air power, an 'airmindedness' that affected populations deeply in the inter-war period. Few people remained ignorant of the supposed threat of air power, and air raid precautions became a part of everyday life. Air power carried with it a kind of mystique which made it both threatening and exhilarating at the same time. Some of the mystique has contributed to that tendency to exaggerate the role of aircraft in the war itself. Many of the heroes of the period were air pioneers and air aces. Secret weapons were often seen as a potential product of the air war. The nature of warfare itself and the relationship of civilian populations to war were all believed to have changed irreversibly as a result of aircraft. Air power raised new moral issues and challenged old military values. In the end, however, the air forces turned out to be much like the other services. Many more were butchered through political calculation than through bombing; no knock-out blow proved to be decisive, with the unique exception of the atomic bombs at the end of the war. Despite contemporary alarm, both air power and civilization survived the conflict.

1

Preparing for War

By 1939 it was widely believed that the air weapon was coming of age. The experience of the First World War, when advanced technology had already suggested the changing contours of modern warfare, persuaded many, politicians and generals among them, that the next war would be an air war. This was partly founded on the uncritical expectation that science was now harnessed sufficiently closely to military life to produce a stream of new weapons; of secret devices from the air whose nature could only be guessed at. It was founded too on the more critical scrutiny of what aircraft had actually done in the First World War. In reconnaissance work, in support of troops on the ground, in co-operation with the navy on the first clumsy aircraft carriers and primarily in the carrying out of bombing campaigns independent of surface forces, the aircraft threatened to dwarf the contribution of the other services or even to supplant it altogether. Yet by 1939 a combination of military conservatism and technical impoverishment had produced air forces that could do little more than the air forces of the First World War. Certainly the quality of aircraft had changed over the period but only dramatically in the last two or three years of peace before 1939 and then at too short notice to allow strategic and operational planning to catch up with it before war actually broke out. The development of air doctrine during the intervening period concentrated much more on what it was already known that aircraft could do. It was as much recapitulation as vision. Even if air power could be exercised with greater intensity and better techniques during the second war these were changes of degree rather than kind. The impact of jet aircraft, rockets and nuclear power came too late to substantially change this fact, and were brought into none of the early strategic calculations of the major air powers before 1939. Preparations of a strategic, doctrinal and technical character were related closely to the world of 1914–18.

By the 1930s the lessons of the earlier conflict had been turned from a hasty empiricism into a refined doctrine. By 1939 even the refined doctrine was becoming obsolescent, overtaken by scientific and strategic events. But even though doctrine was sometimes inappropriate to the circumstances of war, the formulation of air theory before 1939 was crucial in understanding the actual development of air forces and the choices made about how they should be used. It is possible to distinguish four separate, though not mutually exclusive, areas of strategic thinking on air power: co-operation between ships and aircraft; co-operation between armies and aircraft; 'independent' or 'strategic' bombing; and aerial defence.

(i) Aircraft and Sea Power

It was already clear by the end of hostilities in 1918 that aircraft had added a new dimension to naval warfare. The first converted aircraft carriers had been used at the Battle of Jutland for reconnaissance and other navies rapidly imitated their use. Britain, Japan and the United States took the lead, a fact largely dictated by geography and naval tradition. The first purpose-built carriers were constructed in Britain between 1918 and 1923; the first Japanese carrier in 1922.[1] Considerable dispute existed over how they were to be used. Aircraft at sea could be used for the bombing of other ships; the bombing of land targets from the sea; the aerial defence of the surface fleet; and for reconnaissance. For most of the interwar period the British navy favoured the last of these. Until the outbreak of war itself it was naval policy to store all aircraft and drain their petrol tanks to avoid the risk of fire during an enemy air attack in the belief that a barrage of anti-aircraft fire would provide a ship with adequate protection.[2] The naval authorities remained sceptical of the ability of aircraft to sink large ships so that little effort was directed to producing aircraft capable of doing so. Even when they became more sympathetic to air power during the 1930s the naval air arm remained relatively deprived of resources.[3]

Japanese naval leaders happily embraced all aspects of combined naval-air strategy. This was partly a result of rivalry with the Japanese army over air force development. A large carrier force gave the navy an argument for retaining its own air service. It was also a result of the Washington Naval Agreement which restricted the construction of certain classes of heavy warship and compelled the Japanese to increase fleet striking power through the intelligent use of aircraft. As there was no restriction on ships of less than 10,000 tons the Japanese navy designed small aircraft carriers whose effectiveness against larger warships more than compensated for restrictions in size.[4] The aircraft carrier lay at the centre of Japanese Pacific strategy. It was to be used for fleet protection, for destroying enemy ships and for bringing air reinforcements quickly to distant land battles. It was thus an ideal instrument for any planned programme of expansion to the southern island complex and south-east Asia, and was used with great effect in the fighting with China in 1937. Moreover the discovery that aircraft could destroy large warships provided the Japanese armed forces with a means of narrowing the gap that existed between Western and Japanese power in the Far East. The dive-bomber and torpedo-bomber aircraft on which development was concentrated in the 1930s were essential to the success of any imperial expansion which might bring an armed clash with American or British naval power.[5] In 1936 Commander Genda completed the development of Japanese carrier power by getting the navy to adopt his theory of the mass carrier strike-force. By concentrating carriers in one large fleet, instead of using them singly with other capital ships, a very much more decisive attack could be launched at any one time. Although other naval commanders argued that such a fleet would be very vulnerable to submarine attack, it was agreed that the risk was worth taking.[6] Such concentrated use of naval air power brought the victory at Pearl Harbor and in southern Asia at the beginning of the war in the Far East.

Outside Japan it was necessary to overcome the conservatism of traditional navies before aircraft could be given a place in naval strategy. In the United States General Mitchell predicted in 1920 that air attack would 'render surface craft incapable of operating to the same extent that they have heretofore, if it does not entirely drive them off the surface of the water'.[7] The naval response was divided. Until late into the 1930s individual naval commanders refused to accept that aircraft could achieve what their champions expected. The naval high command was less inflexible, though its attitude fluctuated with the personalities in command. On balance the American navy met the challenge instead of ignoring it. As early as 1919 the General Board called for 'a naval air service [to] be established capable of accompanying and operating with the Fleet in all waters of the globe'.[8] If such a service was slow to develop it was due more to the policy of isolationism than to reluctance on the part of the navy to accept aircraft into naval thinking. By the 1930s the use of aircraft carriers to attack the enemy fleet, to protect the American fleet and to give flexibility to the defence of Pacific possessions was fully accepted. Because only limited intelligence existed on Japanese preparations the total number of carriers and naval aircraft available failed to match those of the Japanese navy in the Pacific; but the naval commitment to a carrier strategy bound the government to an expansion of naval aviation in the event of a deterioration in the military situation of the United States in the Far East.[9]

In Europe the attitude towards naval aviation and to carriers in particular was unenthusiastic. In Germany and Italy the carrier had no role at all. In Germany this was partly because of Luftwaffe claims to be able to attack ships at sea with shore-based aircraft under its own command and partly because of rivalry between the services. The Luftwaffe was reluctant to pass control over any air forces to the navy, whose aviation accordingly got the lowest priority.[10] In Italy the lack of aircraft carriers stemmed from Mussolini's mistaken belief that Italian bombers and torpedo-bombers could operate from land bases against potential French or British naval targets. It was only after the battle of Matapan that Italy began seriously to consider a carrier programme but with little success.[11] What was more surprising was the weakness of the senior naval powers, Britain and France, in naval aviation and aircraft carriers. France possessed one converted carrier by 1939 and had one major carrier under construction but uncompleted by the armistice. Britain, although possessing the largest carrier force on paper, had failed to develop a doctrine for its offensive use, had too few trained naval pilots and carrier and naval aircraft considerably inferior to those of America and Japan.[12] Two factors explained the situation in Europe. First of all the distances to be covered were small; the seas in which carriers were to operate were narrow and subject to air attack from land-based enemy aircraft, or from submarines. The second factor was the generally poor relationship between air force and navies during the inter-war period. Naval conservatism was hard to overcome. Most emphasis in the 1930s was placed on the construction of fleets of new capital ships which were still widely believed to be unsinkable from the air. Even in Britain it was still maintained in 1939 that aircraft from carriers could only slow down large ships leaving them to be sunk by other ships rather than by aircraft. Even in those cases where naval commanders were willing to adopt naval aviation more enthusiastically the air forces themselves, particularly if they were independent services as in Britain and Germany, were reluctant to divert air resources to navies or to work in co-operation with naval forces.[13] The land-based bomber was seen to be the key to sea power in any future war and naval air arms, with their unfulfilled demands for high-performance special-purpose aircraft, became so many Cinderellas.

The independent air forces instead brought their own doctrine for use in aero-naval strategy; the blockade from the air of the enemy's sea-borne trade. This could be carried out by using conventional land-based bombers of long range with special armament. For Britain aircraft complemented a traditional strategy of naval and diplomatic activity to cut off supplies to a European enemy. The attack on trade was introduced during the 1930s as one of the roles assigned to bomber forces on the outbreak of a war. The only restriction imposed upon it was the need to avoid civilian casualties in carrying out such attacks, making it almost impossible to plan attacks on ports or food stocks. Merchantmen at sea were given as the prime targets.[14] For Germany a blockade of Britain had become a real possibility by combining aircraft and submarine warfare. Yet preparations for such a contingency lagged considerably behind the idea. Not until 1939 did the German navy begin making plans for combined naval-aerial attacks on British shipping lanes beyond the range of British shore-based fighters. The Luftwaffe had itself only begun to plan attacks against coastal shipping and ports in 1938 and even by the outbreak of war had not yet produced special-purpose anti-shipping aircraft fitted with torpedoes. Nor did the air force and navy work well together on the planned mining campaign because of the diversion of insufficient aircraft for the task, and the refusal of Goering to give it any priority or to train the crews required for the specialized work.[15] Raeder believed that the blockade strategy properly applied was 'capable of exerting a decisive influence'.[16] Even Hitler himself approved 'of the view always held by the Navy, namely, that only that naval and air activity which is concentrated on cutting off supplies will help to bring about the defeat of Great Britain'.[17] But lack of preparation, poor co-operation with the jealous Luftwaffe, and the failure to produce a satisfactory long-range bomber all prevented the aero-naval strategy from being applied with any vigour at all after 1939. The early successes enjoyed in the trade war were a reflection not of large-scale German preparation but of the fact that British preparations were even poorer.

(ii) Armies and Air Power

The second role assigned to air power, co-operation with the army, was similarly influenced by the relations between the two services, and by the strength of the army tradition in national military life. Although there existed fundamental differences at a tactical and command level between air forces on the question of co-operation with armies, there was never any question about the necessity of air support for ground forces. Such support was both offensive and defensive. In the first place an air force was expected to seek out the enemy air force in the skies and at its air bases in order to eliminate it as a threat to the army. Secondly an air force was expected to attack enemy ground formations and to harass the movement of his troops and supplies to the front, and to undertake tactical bombing attacks of rear depots and bases to speed up the progress of an attacking army, or to strengthen the resistance of a defending one. The defensive role, which relied in most cases on offensive tactics, lay in the protection of ground troops and rear areas from enemy air attack. The best means of defence was regarded as offence, the ability to knock out an enemy air force before it arrived at its target, so that the tactics for either role tended to blur together. The winning of air superiority over an enemy air force was achieved when it was forced back permanently on the defensive; command of the air was won when the enemy could no longer undertake air sorties. In either case once the enemy air force was neutralized or defeated the task of the air force switched to supporting ground troop attacks by air-to-ground combat instead of air-to-air combat, the characteristic of the early stages of a battle.

Most of the air power theorists between the war failed to stress two points sufficiently. The first was the need to make generous provision for reserves, for air forces deteriorated at a steady but largely unknown rate. Even numerous and well-armed air forces found air superiority difficult to maintain in the war when reserves and production were lacking. The second was the fact that air activity was continuous. Air 'battles' in the conventional sense in which armies and navies fought battles could not be fought because air forces apparently defeated could be reconstituted within days by new production, repair or re-siting. Moreover in order to help a land battle materially it was necessary for air forces to be engaged on a wide number of tasks over a considerable period of time and although superiority might be gained at one moment or in one place it was often to prove during the war that this was at the expense of superiority somewhere else. It is perhaps not surprising that such points were not emphasized enough. They depended upon combat experience. What combat experience there was during the inter-war period tended to be between enemies of very unequal resources which gave few clues as to how an air war was to be fought between large air powers with a greater parity of striking-power. Moreover air doctrine, being drawn closely into the general battle doctrine of the army leadership, was still over-influenced by Clausewitzian thinking from which it was slowly disentangled as the war progressed.

No army disputed the fact that air power was an important part of its armoury. Dispute arose over how the part was to be used. In those countries with an independent air force and a less influential army the tactical use of air forces was less constricted by army requirements. Where the air forces had relatively little independence or were tied to armies with powerful combat traditions, tactics were subordinate to the army view. This was the case even in those countries where the air force itself wished to play a more autonomous role but was denied this by the influence of the army. Armies began from the premise that the main function of air power was to give support to the ground forces in the destruction of the enemy army. In the United States the air forces were restricted by the regulations laid down in 1926 in the 'Fundamental Principles of Employment of the Air Service' which directed that air forces should be organized 'on the fundamental doctrine that their mission is to aid the ground forces to gain decisive success'. The fact that the air forces were constitutionally subordinate to the army command and the army-dominated War Department confirmed the auxiliary function.[18] In Germany the independent Luftwaffe was strongly influenced by the traditional army thinking of the air force staff which had been largely recruited from the army in the first place. The principles governing air force use were laid down in 1936. It was emphasized that 'the decision in war can only be achieved by the co-operation of the three services' for 'the foremost goal in war is to destroy the enemy armed forces . . . it is the task of the air force in leading the war in the air within the wider framework of the whole war, to serve this goal'.[19] Since the strategy favoured by the army was the swift blow with armoured forces against the main weight of the enemy army, air forces were built up to complement it. The small medium bombers, dive-bombers and heavy attack fighters were all developed with the support of the German army in mind.[20] The same was the case in Russia and Japan.

In all these cases the control over the air forces exercised by the army ground commanders was the essential instrument in tying aircraft to the requirements of the army. In Russia the 'attack doctrine' of Tuchachevski developed in the mid-1930s combined with Soviet combat experience in Spain convinced Stalin of the need for largely tactical air forces.[21] The Red Air Force was accordingly organized along close-support lines. In the spring of 1939 special mixed air divisions (*smeshannaya diviziya*) were created, composed of a complement of fighters, bombers and reconnaissance aircraft to be attached to each army group, while certain army corps kept their own squadrons of aircraft for reconnaissance and communications work. The new mixed divisions were subordinate to the needs of the individual army divisions, each of which was expected to be given close support on the battlefield by particular air squadrons. Even the long-range bomber aircraft were split up between the army groups for use on mainly tactical missions close behind the front.[22] This integration of air forces with small land units was practised in America and France as well, as a means of checking what would otherwise have amounted to a claim for operational independence by the air forces. Although German command and organization was more flexible that was largely because both sides agreed on the basic role the air force should be performing in helping the army.

In both France and the United States the air forces forcibly expressed the need for greater independence and operational flexibility in the face of army opposition. In the United States the air force leaders favoured independent command over air forces on the battlefield for they argued that this would allow more latitude in deciding the crucial areas for air support as well as giving greater freedom to choose whether to protect troops in the field or combat enemy aircraft and troops away from the battle itself. In addition the American air theorists developed the view that strategic bombing, carried out independently of the army, was a more useful way of making a contribution to eventual victory.[23] On both points the army disagreed. The problem of air force command and battlefield doctrine was not resolved until the middle of the war when combat experience demonstrated the shortcomings of the army view. In France there was too little time for combat experience to provide lessons in air force use. Despite the fact that the French air force had won the battle for constitutional independence from the army in 1933, the unity of command over the armed forces remained, as did the predominant position of the army in French military life. Air force demands for an independent air strategy and for more tactical freedom in support of ground troops were both effectively combated by the over-representation of the army on the Commission du Conseil supérieur de la Guerre and the Section de la Défense nationale du Cabinet. By the outbreak of war French aircraft were to be used like French tanks, in close support of front ground units and tied to the commands of the ground forces themselves.[24] Even attacks in the rear areas on supplies and troops, although planned for, were regarded askance by the army commanders. General Weygand told a British audience in May 1939 that 'Douhet has no partisans in France. . . . There is something in these bombardments of defenceless people behind the front that smacks of cowardice which is repugnant to the soldier'.[25]

The attitude in Britain was, however, very different. The fear of a new continental commitment and the renewed horrors of army warfare along the lines of the First World War reduced army influence in favour of an air force capable of carrying out independent tasks through blockade and bombing. This did not blind the RAF to the need for army support, but it gave it a different character. The difference was that the RAF insisted on remaining constitutionally distinct and on retaining command over air forces rather than giving it up to the army commanders in the field. Moreover air doctrine stressed that aircraft should be used in as flexible a way as possible and should not be parcelled out to each small army unit for its own protection.[26] The best method of defence against an enemy air force and the best method of assisting the ground forces was thought to be the attack on the enemy economy and rear areas, in which case the army units would be unlikely even to see a British aircraft for they would be engaged on tasks elsewhere. Resistance to such a view persisted, although it was to be finally vindicated in North Africa and Europe after 1942. As a result of such resistance the air forces that faced the German attack in 1940 were used hesitatingly in a role that fluctuated between the French view of aircraft use and that of the RAF against an air force large enough to be able to do both.

Although army conservatism at times compelled air forces to adopt a restrictive operational framework, most armies agreed that if aircraft were to make a full contribution to defeating the enemy ground forces then tactical bombing attacks on rear areas, sources of supply, bases and equipment were equally as important as attacks on the battlefield itself. Although tactical bombing was operationally independent, targets were usually designated by army commanders while it was made clear that such bombing attacks were designed only to speed up the process of defeating an enemy army. This was not 'independent' or 'strategic' bombing in the sense in which its proponents understood it, since it was undertaken in immediate conjunction with a land battle and was concerned not with long-term targets such as economic collapse or morale-breaking but with short-term objectives designed to hinder the direct deployment of troops or material in a particular battle. The most important target was enemy air power itself, in particular air bases and air supply depots in the immediate rear of operations. By 1939 the RAF was committed to carrying out 'the attack on the German Air Striking Force and its maintenance organisation' as a first priority in tactical support.[27] The Luftwaffe was similarly instructed to protect the land advance 'by an offensive use of air forces against the opponent's air force in enemy territory'.[28] In addition to such attacks bombers were also expected to attack stocks of military materials, supply lines and communications to the front and other military targets whose destruction would lead to the reduction of enemy fighting capabilities. This extended too, to attacks on aircraft factories where such attacks were likely to lead to decisive shortages for the enemy in the battle itself. Some air forces, in particular the Soviet and French air forces, favoured limited tactical bombing in the immediate vicinity of the front. The British, German and Japanese air forces all favoured more adventurous tactical bombing but in all cases such bombing was planned as an integral part of the general land battle and was subordinate to the needs of the army commanders and the immediate battle objective.

(iii) Strategic Bombing

The third element in air doctrine, strategic or 'independent' bombing differed from tactical bombing because it was operationally distinct from the actions of the ground forces. It did not aim at the direct destruction of the enemy's forces but at the undermining of a war capability by continuous and long-term attacks on non-military targets. The overall strategic objective remained the same as the objective of tactical air power; to bring about the eventual defeat of enemy armed forces. But in the case of strategic bombing this was through starving them of economic resources and undermining national morale. Even the supporters of strategic bombing doctrines during the inter-war period hesitated to see it as a war-winning weapon on its own. Lord Trenchard, one of the foremost champions of independent air operations, qualified his support by not wishing 'for a moment to imply that the air by itself can finish the war. It will materially assist, and will be one of the many means of exercising pressure on the enemy, in conjunction with sea power and blockade and the defeat of his armies . . .'.[29] Even General Douhet, whose work was not widely known outside Italy in more than a vulgarized form, was primarily interested in how air forces could contribute to the combined efforts of the services in overwhelming enemy forces. He emphasized that air power properly used 'should lead armies and navies to reorganise on a new basis', not that air power should replace them altogether. The winning of command in the air was a condition which could only be fully exploited by the other services.[30] In this sense strategic and tactical bombing became blurred together. Strategic bombing was tactical bombing on a grander, more expensive and longer-term scale.

Not all airmen, however, shared this view. The doctrine of strategic bombing thus fluctuated from time to time and place to place according to the influence of those who supported it as an extension of combined operations and those who saw it as an independent war-winning weapon. Because the means of waging a bombing campaign were the same in either case a considerable degree of uncertainty of purpose was characteristic of bombing forces before 1939 and remained so when neither one side nor the other was proved conclusively right under combat conditions. The championship of bombing as a war-winning weapon had a partly political explanation. In Britain it gave added weight to the demand for an independent air force. Once such a force had been achieved the bombing strategy was used as a shield to protect the RAF from any further attempt to compromise its autonomy. Bombing was championed as a strategy peculiarly suited to Britain as an island power anxious to avoid army commitments in Europe again, and traditionally attached to blockade strategies. To achieve such a campaign it was always argued that the independence and intergrity of the RAF were essential.[31] In the United States bombing was used for the same purpose. General Mitchell's attempts to secure an independent air force in the 1920s was underpinned by his argument that strategic bombing had revolutionized war, made armies redundant and overthrown 'The old theory that victory meant the destruction of the hostile main army . . .'. The air forces' failure to achieve any independent status led to a continued defence of the strategic bombing argument in order to show that an independent strategy required an independent force.[32] Elsewhere the dominant position of the army excluded the use of air forces on strategic tasks, partly because air power was subordinate to land power and partly because other air forces believed it to be operationally impossible to achieve the decisive results by bombing that its adherents claimed. The Luftwaffe, although intended by Hitler and Goering from the start to have a strategic capability, developed an independent bombing doctrine only slowly and never subscribed to the more optimistic expectations of the British and American airmen for whom the effectiveness of strategic bombing remained an act of faith.

The objective of strategic bombing, whether of a more limited character or not, was to undermine morale in the enemy territory on the one hand and to destroy vital economic targets on the other. Morale was a difficult target to define. Its definition for operational purposes depended on a highly subjective assessment of the political or moral character of an enemy state. The RAF interest in the attack on morale stemmed from Trenchard's often repeated assertion that the moral effect of bombing was twenty times greater than the material, a fact that could not be verified quantitatively but which nevertheless attracted the more enthusiastic bombing theorists to morale as a potentially decisive target.[33] Moreover the choice of morale served the political aims of those who defended independent bombing doctrines because it was an objective easily understood by the political leadership, which was itself under pressure in the 1930s from an anxious public fearful of the impact of terror bombing. The political decision to build up a large strategic bombing force was partly based on the belief that it might serve as a substitute for armed continental intervention through terrorising a European enemy from the air, and partly on the grounds that the existence of a terror bombing capability might deter a prospective enemy from aggressive acts. Most major air powers were aware of the terroristic nature of bombing but only the RAF believed that it would seriously act as a deterrent or, in the event of its use, so undermine enemy morale that it would force capitulation or the demoralization of enemy armed forces.[34] Although Hitler used the terror bombing threat to gain diplomatic concessions, neither he nor the Luftwaffe staff planned seriously for its use against a major military power once war had actually broken out.

Instead those air forces that planned for strategic action at all, and including the RAF, argued that the most important target was the economy. By destroying its key areas the armed forces of the enemy would be so weakened as to leave only token resistance to an advance by ground troops; or it might lead in certain cases to the enemy government giving up the struggle altogether. Both the British and United States air forces favoured attacks against crucial economic and military targets. The British air staff saw such attacks as a means of reducing the offensive capability of an enemy air force and of producing 'an adverse effect on the German war effort and German economic life generally'.[35] Not until 1936, with the establishment of an Air Targets Sub-Committee of the Industrial Intelligence Centre, was a priority of essential targets worked out. An obvious choice was the enemy aircraft industry, on the basis that aircraft factories were 'large, distinctive and vulnerable targets'.[36] But the main argument concerned the relative merits of attacks on electricity, communications and oil. By the outbreak of war oil was chosen as the single most important target.[37] In the United States, under the influence of General Mitchell, the air force developed a theory of striking at the 'vital targets', one of which was oil. Mitchell's supporters argued that an air force should attack 'the whole of the "enemy national structure" and in particular the "industrial web" '. 'A nation', the Air Corps claimed, 'may be defeated simply by the interruption of the delicate balance of this complex organization. . . . It is possible that a moral collapse brought about by the disturbances in this close-knit web may be sufficient to force an enemy to surrender, but the real target is industry itself, not national morale'.[38] At the Air Corps Tactical School throughout the 1930s the doctrine of strategic bombing of vital industrial targets was elaborated and strengthened by further research although no decision was made until 1941 about what the most vital targets actually were.[39]

No other air force became committed to the idea of long-range bombing of strategic objectives as a prime function of air forces. The Luftwaffe prepared target folders on all important British and French industrial installations without committing the air force in advance to any particular bombing strategy.[40] The Soviet Union, which had at first favoured long-range bombing, abandoned the pursuit altogether after 1938 in the wake of experience in the Spanish Civil War.[41] In fact all those who participated in the war in Spain emerged with considerable support for tactical air forces and a certain scepticism over the probable effect of an independent bombing campaign.[42] By contrast, British experience of aircraft use in colonial crises in India or Iraq tended to confirm the importance of independent action, for aircraft on their own had proved capable of subduing rebel tribesmen through terror bombing tactics. Only when the RAF began to make serious operational surveys of the likely effect of a bombing campaign in the late 1930s did it become aware of the shortcomings, both technical and tactical, in carrying such an offensive out.[43] By that time the air force was already too committed to the plan and, like its United States counterpart, too anxious to preserve for itself an area of action independent of that of the other services to be very disturbed by the obvious gap between strategic intention and the operational possibilities.

(iv) Aerial Defence

The irony of the situation was that at the very time that the RAF re-emphasized its commitment in the mid-1930s to a strategic bombing force, other British airmen were at the forefront in the development of a theory of air defence. The bomber theorists of the 1920s had rested much of their case on the belief that there was little effective defence against bombing. Douhet wrote that 'the aeroplane is not adaptable to defence' and that 'nothing man can do on the surface of the earth can intefere with a plane in flight'.[44] By the time Baldwin made his remark that 'the bomber will always get through', the disparity in performance between fighter and bomber aircraft was still so low that the prospect of a successful fighter defence seemed correspondingly unlikely.[45] Anti-aircraft defences and passive defences were developed only slowly in the 1930s as public concern at the threat of a bombing attack became more acute. America relied on distance as an immunity against such attacks; France on the fact that French industry was so dispersed as to discourage enemy air forces from seeking targets behind the front. Policies of active air defence remained half-hearted as long as the technical means of combating bombers was lacking. Two things revolutionized the doctrine of air defence and gave it a new strategic significance. The development of the fast monoplane fighters gave a growing performance superiority to the fighter, particularly when equipped with heavy armament. Secondly the long search for effective ways of predicting where bomber aircraft were coming from and at what height was finally resolved by the invention of radar and the development of an operational organization to use radar information effectively.

The shift towards a mixed air doctrine of defence and offence was met with some reluctance by those in the RAF who favoured the bombing strategy. To admit that there was a defence against the bomber was to question the whole basis upon which an independent air force had been built up. That the bombing role did not suffer as much as it might have done was due in part to the growing preference for night-bombing over day-bombing, against which it was thought there was still no satisfactory defence, and in part to the hope that British efforts in radar and co-ordinated fighter defence would not be imitated abroad, or not until it was too late.[46] In 1935 the RAF, under pressure from politicians and senior soldiers, accepted the Re-orientation Plan under which greater emphasis than hitherto was placed on air defence and on the production of defensive fighters and anti-aircraft weapons. A defensive belt was formed from the River Tees to the Solent, which was supplemented over the four years between 1936 and 1940 by the establishment of the Chain Home radar stations giving early warning of approaching enemy aircraft.[47] One of the key points of the scheme was communication; between radar stations and fighter controllers, between the controllers and aircraft in the air, between the stations and central Fighter Command. By centralizing the system it was hoped that intelligence could be disseminated much more rapidly and that operations could be mounted with much more effectiveness. Although tactics were to wait upon combat experience, one tactical principle was firmly understood before 1939; the object of the defending fighters was to destroy enemy bombers, not to engage in combat with escorting fighters. Since the objective of the enemy was to drop bombs to cause destruction and dislocation to military and economic targets the objective of a defending fighter force was to deny the bombers the opportunity to do so.

The RAF was the only air force before 1939 to place such reliance on the defensive capabilites of the fighter. This fact was dictated partly by strategic priorities. The British government concentrated efforts on being able to retain Britain's position of geographical immunity from large-scale invasion by adding air-power to sea-power as a means of defence. For European countries the threat of large scale invasion by armies across land frontiers was the more immediate, and air-power was primarily to be used in assisting armies to carry out or prevent successful invasion. Some means of air defence was certainly created but with less urgency and fewer resources than in Britain. In Germany a chain of radar stations was also established by the outbreak of war, though the intelligence from it was less detailed and was not disseminated through a central control body.[48] The defensive network remained decentralized, each air district being responsible for the defence of its own vulnerable targets. Before 1939 two special defence zones were created, the Ruhr/Rhineland zone and the Berlin zone, which were given extra resources in guns and searchlights for anti-aircraft defence but few aircraft.[49] Russia and Japan also had a system of decentralized defence districts with little or no advance warning of attacking aircraft and only a relatively small number of fighter aircraft reserved for defensive work. The United States, Italy and France had by the outbreak of war only the most rudimentary means of air defence.[50]

One reason for the slow spread of the doctrine of air defence and of preparations to meet it was the continued acceptance of an offensive strategy for aircraft and the belief that all the advantages lay with the attacker. French air force leaders stressed the importance of surprise in making air attacks.[51] In Italy Mussolini remained committed to Douhet and the doctrine of attack as an Italian idea expressing the spirit of the new fascist Italians.[52] In the United States the Air Corps was still under the influence of Mitchell's assertion that 'to sit down on one's own territory and wait for the other fellow to come is to be whipped before any operation has commenced'.[53] In 1936 Arnold, the future chief of the air forces, wrote that the 'whole concept in the Air Force is offence: to seek out the enemy; to locate him as early and as far distant from our vital areas as we can . . .'.[54] Even Bomber Command of the RAF, in the face of British efforts to arm for aerial defence, still maintained that the primary role of any air force should be offensive.

The second factor that affected the development of defence doctrines outside Britain was the reliance based on anti-aircraft fire as a defence against attacking aircraft. In Germany, Russia and France in particular the massed use of heavy-calibre guns against bomber attack was stressed at the expense of fighter defence. In Italy and Japan even this was lacking for it was hoped that pre-emptive strikes against enemy air forces would make expenditure on anti-aircraft defences unnecessary. A final factor lay with the slow spread of radar and good communications equipment. Fighter Command relied on the most modern technical means for air defence and felt under no compulsion to spread the technical secrets until obliged to do so to the French in 1939 and the United States in 1940, by which time it was too late for either to establish a satisfactory air defence system before the onset of hostilities.[55] Only the Luftwaffe approached the technical competence of British air defence even though research resources were diverted to other tasks of greater urgency. The fact that British strategy increasingly relied on sophisticated defensive technology had brought about a corresponding concentration of British scientific resources upon this critical area.

The main areas of strategic air doctrine were not mutually exclusive, nor did they remain constant over the inter-war period. But even though all the major powers took an interest in each of the major strands of air doctrine and recognized to some degree their complementarity, there was already discernible before the

16

outbreak of war a division between those armed forces that favoured a limited as distinct from a general exercise of air power. The former comprised those forces in which the doctrine of army co-operation was most fully developed to the practical exclusion of other alternative uses for air power. The latter were those forces in which all the areas of air power were pursued simultaneously and in an inter-related way. Under conditions of war the distinction between the two became clear. Before 1939 it was obscured by doctrinal instability. This was a product both of inter-service rivalry and of the rapid rate of technical change. Inter-service rivalry encouraged air force leaders to search for strategies peculiar to the air force in defence of its independence and operational integrity, even when their military value was questionable. The guardianship of strategic prerogatives by the navy and the army encouraged the air force to think of prerogatives for itself. In some cases changes in army doctrine occasioned changes for the air force too, particularly in the area of tactical support where there were few doctrinal fixed points until battle experience determined what they should be. Another factor was technical change. Air strategy was closely related to technical changes and the rate of technical change was unpredictable and accelerating by the end of the 1930s. The ability to cope with technical change was in itself an important component of air strategy. An obsolete air force, however numerous its aircraft, was of considerably less strategic value than a smaller but technically superior force. Changes in aircraft performance or equipment could also alter doctrinal priorities. The shift towards fighter defence before 1939 depended entirely on new fast fighters, good radio and radar. The strategy could not be successfully supported without them. Similarly the possibilities of carrying out an effective bombing strategy depended on aircraft range, bomb-load, bombing accuracy and the effectiveness of bombs, all of which were altering rapidly over the 1930s.

Above all the instability of air doctrine lay in the fact that air forces were compelled to make guesses about how aircraft would be used once war had actually broken out. There was little experience to draw on about the kind of air war most powers expected to fight, so that much air doctrine was an act of faith that the guesses of one particular air force were the right ones. As powers became more aware of what potential air enemies were preparing to do the initial guesswork was often modified or abandoned. The large quantity of conflicting and uncertain doctrine contrasted sharply with the small quantity of practical experience. When this experience was widened in exercises and manoeuvres to test out particular doctrines it was discovered that there had been too little preparation and too much theory. The practical capabilities of aircraft had been prone to much exaggeration. Bombing and blockade were not as simple as Douhet's paradigm has suggested. Moreover the emergence of fighter defence had, in a relatively short space of time, rendered much of the thinking on bombing obsolete. A new bombing technology was needed before bombing could hope to match the expectations held out for it between the wars. Such ambiguities were made more complicated still by the encroachment of political affairs. Politicians wanted aircraft to be able to fulfil the maximum that air theory promised, and themselves promised the maximum without a sufficiently critical assessment of the practical possibilities. Nor were the air forces, doctrinally divided themselves and uncertain of future trends, in a position to moderate the politicians intemperate emphasis on air power. Part of the confusion demonstrated in the public debate on air power during the 1930s was due to the sources of instability within the generation of air strategy itself.

(v) Air Power and Strategy

The development of theories of air power, while themselves constantly under review, called for much re-thinking of grand strategy as well. No power ignored, or could afford to ignore, the advent of air power. In fact the very novelty of the weapon encouraged governments and military staffs to devote more efforts to incorporating air power into strategy than to more traditional strategic considerations. In some respects air power did offer substantial changes. Those countries that had been protected by a natural sea barrier were no longer immune from the direct threat of attack. Even in the United States this fact had become obvious and prompted Roosevelt in 1941 to remind his audience that Americans could no longer 'measure [their] safety in terms of miles on any map'.[56] As long as aircraft range continued to increase the number of countries that could be reached effectively for attack from another became greater. At the height of the Abyssinian crisis there were real fears that Italy would undertake a bombing strike against London in retaliation for British intervention in the dispute.[57] Many such fears were exaggerated for they ran considerably ahead of the technical capabilities of bombing aircraft currently in use. They were nevertheless important as a measure of public concern at the changes air power promised to bring about in warfare. It was this same public concern that spurred governments on to carry out rearmament schemes and civil defence measures in France and Britain and later in the United States.[58] It was concern over the political effects of bomb attack that prompted the Axis powers to build up large active and static defences and to boast that fascist armed strength would forestall the enemy from the air. If military leaders were uncertain about the prospects of a future war in the air, governments were compelled for political as well as military reasons to assume the worst. So much was this the case that by 1938 Hitler was able to brandish the threat of bombing as a diplomatic weapon, using it to put pressure on the western powers at Munich and successfully intimidating the Czech government in the spring of 1939.[59]

The response of all the major powers to the new threat from the air was to embark upon a policy of air rearmament and a new arms race, while preparing the civil population to meet air attacks and, half-heartedly, exploring the possibility of outlawing air terrorism by international agreement. The scope of air rearmament was conditioned by the extent of the perceived threat and by the nature of military ambitions. Those countries more committed to air warfare gave greater prominence to schemes for air expansion. Where the army or navy had a large claim on military resources the opposite was the case. The influence of the more senior services in the military and political establishment ensured that politicians did not neglect the interests of military preparation in general in favour of an uncritical and panic-ridden growth of air forces. That such a danger was never far removed was shown by the clash of priorities in Germany in 1938–39, Britain in 1935–37 and the United States in 1940–41.[60]

The threat for which such preparations were put in hand had become clear only by the mid-1930s. The growing threat of Japan to British and United States interests in the Pacific, the fear in Russia that at any time the capitalist west or east might try to destroy the Bolshevik state, and the growing instability of Europe with the rise of fascist military power all contributed to the desire to arm in strength everywhere. For France and Britain there was an additional strain on military resources in policing and keeping together empires that were larger in extent than they had been in 1914. During the 1930s the arms race was largely confined to Europe. Japan was only in the process of creating a large-scale air force and an industry to support it and remained consistently weaker than any of the other major air powers before 1939; the United States sanctioned large-scale rearmament only when the crisis in Europe had reached a crucial stage in 1939. Within Europe the powers were more aware of where their interests and loyalties lay. Britain and France armed for a possible war with Germany and Italy. Germany re-armed to fulfil Hitler's opaque ambitions in the east and west. The Soviet Union, maintaining the largest air force in Europe in the 1930s, prepared for the immediate problem of Japanese imperialism in the Far East and the revisionism of German fascism.[61]

One of the main problems of air rearmament was knowing what to produce. This posed two questions: what it was necessary to produce for carrying out air strategy; and what an enemy or group of enemy powers was capable of producing. Rearmament programmes were constructed to some extent on the intelligence available of preparations elsewhere. But there was no real way of knowing whether an enemy had got the guesses right on questions such as the right proportion of bombers to fighters, the right number of reserves, the likely rate of combat attrition. As a result aircraft programmes were conditioned more by domestic circumstances, in particular the size of the aircraft industry, its expected rate of expansion and the amount of money available to finance it. In Germany the difficulty in securing raw materials was used to moderate what German industry regarded as over-optimistic planning by the Luftwaffe.[62] In Britain, finance was a constraining factor.[63] In all cases the difficulties experienced by air forces were compounded by the competition for resources with the other services. Although the army and navy regarded the air force as an auxiliary service it was the most expensive of the three, and such large expenditures had to be justified in the face of naval or army shortages. In Germany the air force consumed some 36 per cent of all military expenditure between 1934–35 and 1938–39. In Britain the RAF took 36 per cent of expenditure in 1938, rising to 41 per cent in 1939.[64] In both cases efforts were made to force the air service to take smaller funds; in the German case successfully. In the American rearmament programme of 1939 the air forces were also compelled to reduce the large allocation given to them by the President in favour of the demands of the army.[65]

Nevertheless such constraints only imposed temporary limits; expansion was constantly revised upwards in the face of mounting international insecurity. All powers planned within such limits to build large air fleets. Rearmament accelerated after the Abyssinian crisis and the formal remilitarization of Germany in 1935, though in the British case it had begun even before Hitler came to power. A second expansion came in the wake of Munich, particularly for the non-fascist powers. In reply to this crisis Roosevelt announced that 'neither we, nor any nation, will accept disarmament while neighbor countries arm to the teeth'. His immediate response was to authorize in November 1938 the beginnings of American rearmament with a provisional programme of 30,000 aircraft, a figure subsequently reduced because of the hostility of Congress.[66] The Soviet Union, alarmed more seriously by Japanese expansion, introduced plans early in 1939 to expand air forces to over three times their size in 1933.[67]

Air rearmament was, however, a more complicated affair than simply expanding numbers. Numbers had to be related to performance, and a balance kept between quantity and quality. Technical changes in aircraft had reached a critical point by the mid-1930s, reflected in the symbolic switch from biplanes to monoplanes. This change was reflected in the rearmament programmes. Germany planned a special stage of conversion (*Umbau*) for the air force in 1938–39 that temporarily reduced the number of aircraft and left the Luftwaffe weaker in early 1939 than it had been in early 1938 as older aircraft were scrapped from the squadrons.[68] The RAF began a similar phase of conversion between 1938 and 1941, again with the effect of temporarily weakening defences by too great a reliance on old models while the new ones were being tested and phased in. For much of this period combatant powers everywhere progressively removed more obsolescent aircraft from the front-line and put them into reserve or in training schools. Front-line aircraft of the most modern quality were small in number in most air forces even by 1939 and an air war fought in the early part of the year would have found most air forces poorly prepared in terms of reserves and in terms of aircraft quality. Another problem was that of deciding the right proportion between aircraft of different types in an air force. This depended on changes in air doctrine. For example the interest of the French army in ground-support aviation meant that 37 per cent of the production planned in the first rearmament 'Plan I' was made up of reconnaissance aircraft.[69] In Britain, on the other hand, the central position of bombing in RAF strategy gave a preponderant position to bomber production. Between 1936 and 1939 2.3 bombers were produced for every fighter. The Luftwaffe too began by planning a ratio of two bombers to every fighter in 1936 but by 1939, with the growing emphasis on tactical air striking forces, the ratio had dropped to 1.3 : 1, a little lower than that in the RAF after 1939.[70] The trend towards greater fighter production reflected the increasing technical superiority of fighters over bombers and the growing realization that the potential of bomber aircraft had been exaggerated.

It is difficult to compare figures for aircraft rearmament in simple numerical terms, for the quality of aircraft differed so much from country to country. What was a front-line aircraft in one air force was obsolescent in another. Moreover the effectiveness of an air force depended on which enemy it was fighting. A comparatively obsolescent aircraft of the Polish air force would, for example, have been of little value in a combat with the Luftwaffe but would have been more than equal to a war with Finland or Hungary. Nor do simple current output figures indicate long-term plans or the ability of an aircraft industry to convert to war production after mobilization. With such qualifications borne in mind Table 1 gives figures for aircraft production, where known, of the major powers before 1939.[71]

Nor was rearmament confined simply to aircraft. Static defences also consumed considerable production and planning effort, particularly in Germany where greater emphasis was placed on anti-aircraft artillery. By 1939 Germany had available some 650 heavy batteries with 2,600 guns and 560 light batteries of anti-aircraft guns with 188 searchlight batteries of 3,000 lights, quantities

Table 1: Aircraft Production of the Major Powers 1932-39

	1932	1933	1934	1935	1936	1937	1938	1939
France	–	–	–	785	890	743	1,382	3,163
Germany	36	368	1,968	3,183	5,112	5,606	5,235	8,295
Italy	–	–	–	–	–	–	1,850	–
Japan	691	766	688	952	1,181	1,511	3,201	4,467
U.K.	445	633	740	1,140	1,877	2,153	2,827	7,940
U.S.A.	593	466	437	459	1,141	949	1,800	2,195
U.S.S.R.	2,595	2,595	2,595	3,578	3,578	3,578	7,500	10,382

considerably in excess of those of any other power.[73] In Britain and France production difficulties, due partly to the greater effort and urgency devoted to aircraft, held up the expansion of static defences. By spring of 1939 only 570 heavy guns were available in Britain, some 45 per cent only of the Ideal Plan formulated in 1937 for 1,264 heavy guns and 4,700 lights. In fact the 1937 plan was not fulfilled until the Battle of Britain by which time even higher plans had been laid.[74] The French situation was the same. Equipment was old and in small numbers with only a few hundred, mainly light, anti-aircraft guns available by 1939.[75] With the sudden and rapid need to produce more military goods after 1938 there were bound to be some casualties. Static defences came well behind other means of air defence, notably fighter aircraft, when the money and resources were distributed. In addition more and more targets for protection were added to the lists of vital targets, constantly inflating the demands for guns and lights beyond initial expectations. Even in Germany production ran considerably behind the swollen plans despite Goering's personal enthusiasm for the anti-aircraft gun.

One factor was common to nearly all the expansion plans in the 1930s; they could not be fulfilled with the available industrial and administrative resources. This was perhaps to be expected. Aircraft were large and complicated pieces of engineering and were becoming more so as the air forces demanded the most advanced aviation equipment. By 1939 the Spitfire took two and a half times the man hours that it took to produce a Hurricane fighter.[76] Moreover those countries that had allowed air forces to decline numerically or, like Germany, had been prohibited from keeping large air forces, had the task of building up a large industrial and organizational structure for air rearmament in a very short space of time. Only the Soviet Union had been building up continuously a large aircraft industry since the 1920s and although backward in some respects industrially, was the largest air power in the world throughout the 1930s. Moreover central control over the industrial system made it easier to integrate military and economic planning than in western countries where a balance had to be struck between war preparation and commercial expansion. In the west large plans were laid either to allay public fears or to exaggerate military preparedness and such plans ran invariably ahead of the ability to fulfil them. In fact the anxiety of governments chasing a quick air capability led to a temptation to put everything into the 'shop window'. Both Baldwin and Chamberlain found themselves in that situation, forced on occasion to go against the interests of the air staff to appease the voters. So much so that the Air Member for Supply complained in September 1938 that 'We had during the past few years been building up a front line Air Force which was nothing but a façade.

We had nothing in the way of reserves or organization behind the front-line with which to maintain it'.[78] Hitler, too, in order to gain the maximum effect abroad of the German rearmament drive, created an air force that appeared numerically strong on paper but still lacked by 1938–39 much of the essential material and organizational background and whose numbers were swollen by including transport, trainer and converted aircraft of doubtful usefulness. The 'Risikoluftwaffe' was always in fact weaker than its enemies believed.[79] After the war Erhard Milch, head of the German air ministry, complained that 'the Luftwaffe was not prepared for a major war in 1939 . . . the plans envisaged were scheduled for completion in six or eight years . . . about 1944–46'.[80] Such a view was confirmed by the German air leaders themselves in 1938 and 1939 when active preparation for a future war was undertaken and the shortcomings of the air force made more public.[81] The value of the German air force, like that of most other air forces, was as a deterrent rather than as a weapon ready for major strategic operations against strong enemies.

Another problem with rearmament and strategy was the extent to which the decisions taken in both depended upon intelligence of enemy intentions. Except in areas such as anti-aircraft defences where requirements were self-evident, much of the arms effort and the strategy that accompanied it depended on what one power believed another to be doing or planning to do. Before 1939 the western allies tended to overestimate German strength, the Germans to underestimate that of the allies. Fear of German rearmament produced a popular belief that Germany already possessed an air force larger than Britain by 1935, a view fed by uncritical intelligence to politicians such as Churchill and civil servants such as Vansittart who used the information to turn the British government to a policy of rearmament directed against Germany.[82] Although the figures used about Luftwaffe strength were considerably exaggerated, failing to take account of the large number of training aircraft currently in production in Germany or of the number of obsolescent civilian aircraft converted to war use, even the RAF expected the German air force to be expanded faster and further than was in fact the case. This view was not based on poor information on current production, which tended to be accurate enough before 1939, but on what Germany might produce when mobilized.[83] British and French air planning took place on the basis that German aircraft production would expand enormously on the outbreak of war, while the belief that Germany had a large fleet of bombers ready to attack by 1938 and 1939 confirmed the RAF in the wisdom of continuing to build up a large bombing strike force of its own.[84] Yet by late 1939 British output passed that of German aircraft industry and by 1940 the Allies between them were producing two aircraft to every German one.

One of the main explanations for this disparity lay in the German failure to discover the true state of Allied preparations. Believing the Allies to be producing far fewer aircraft than was in fact the case encouraged a complacent belief that German plans were more than sufficient for the immediate future. Intelligence reports in 1938 and 1939 dismissed French and Soviet air forces on the one hand because production was too small, on the other because they were believed to be technically and tactically inferior.[85] The British air force was seen as the greatest threat, but British industrial potential and defensive capabilities were both considerably underrated. As late as May 1939 German air intelligence believed Britain capable of producing only 3,000 aircraft during the next year, when the true figure was over three times as great.[86] Such over-confidence tended to undermine further attempts to strengthen the Luftwaffe at just the time that its likely enemies were renewing efforts to erode its lead.

Germany was in fact relatively weaker in the air than her enemies believed in 1939, and the Allies correspondingly stronger. The balance of forces shifted somewhat in Germany's favour with the conquest of Czechoslovakia, many of whose aircraft were brought into the Luftwaffe in subsidiary roles, freeing production resources in the Reich for combat production. But at the time of Munich and at the outbreak of war in September 1939 the Allies had more first-line aircraft than Germany and considerably larger reserves.[87] German first-line aircraft were of a higher technical quality than those of the Allies, but the great disparity of forces believed to have existed in the air was a myth (see Table 2).

Table 2: Air Strength of Allies and Germany September 1938 and September 1939[88]

	September 1938			September 1939		
	A	B	C	A	B	C
Germany	2,847	1,669	n.a.	3,609	2,893	900
Britain	1,982	1,642	412	1,911	1,600	2,200
France	1,454	n.a.	730	1,792	n.a.	1,600
Czechoslovakia	600	n.a.	n.a.	–	–	–
Poland	–	–	–	397	n.a.	n.a.
Total Allied	4,036			4,100		

A First-line strength
B Serviceable first-line aircraft
C Reserves

During 1939 the plans laid for the future expansion of air forces in the event of war continued to favour the Allies. German air staff planning was based on the belief that war would not break out until at least 1942 and was circumscribed by the amount of industrial capacity still left for use after the outbreak of war, which was believed to be little, given existing raw material difficulties. Even when war broke out the Luftwaffe remained trapped in the planning schedules produced by Milch in 1936 which were little above peace-time levels of output.[89] The RAF, by contrast, still in the expectation that German output would similarly expand during the war, planned to increase production 100 per cent in the first year of war, and another 100 per cent the following year. Where the British 'War Potential' programme projected an output in 1940 of 16,000 aircraft, the first German wartime plan, Plan 16, called for 11,000.[90] Had the Luftwaffe been brought more fully into Hitler's confidence the level of preparation would perhaps have been higher. As it was throughout the summer of 1939 there prevailed uncertainty about the kind of war to prepare for and if war would break out at all, made more uncertain by Goering's personal conviction that Hitler would not dare to risk war against the western powers under the conditions of 1939.[91] Yet it was as a result of Goering's own uncritical optimism, and his desire to please Hitler by representing the Luftwaffe as a force much stronger than was the case, that Hitler moved one step nearer to accelerating his foreign policy initiatives, confident himself of the superiority of his arms.

The Allies might have been more powerful still in the air in 1939 had it not been for the fact that the French air force, like the Luftwaffe, faced a number of special circumstances in 1938–39 that made it difficult to fulfil plans. The difficulties experienced in nationalizing the aircraft industry and by decentralizing its operations, although gradually overcome by 1940, held up production in the crucial years of preparation.[92] So, too, did the conflict within French strategy between army and air force views of air power which made it difficult to select weapons and held up the introduction of aircraft of the highest quality. Further delays in development occurred as a result of the decision to separate air force procurement from design and development, giving the air force little say in choosing its weapons and antagonizing both manufacturers and professional airmen.[93] These were problems not unknown elsewhere but coming as they did together with a more deep-rooted military and political crisis, French efforts at air rearmament were continuously frustrated by events. Even then the three powers that found themselves at war with Germany in 1939 were much closer to German air power than the outcome of the Battle of France might suggest. It was the German army more than the German air force that exposed the very considerable gap in military capability that separated Germany from the Allies.

At the time, however, many of the weaknesses of both sides were unknown to the other. In the hope that an air war might not break out at all, and the untried weapon not be tested, efforts continued throughout the 1930s at reaching agreement on multilateral air disarmament.[94] Nor was such an effort confined just to the democracies. Hitler, anxious to make every effort to avoid the bombing of German civilians which he feared might bring a second 'stab-in-the-back', expressed to Eden and Simon in 1935 his view that 'the German government particularly liked the idea of the prohibition of indiscriminate bombing of densely populated regions'.[95] In March 1936 the German government indeed set about planning for a conference on air arms limitation which found echoes of sympathy among the British Chiefs of Staff, similarly anxious about the effects of bombing on morale.[96] Yet the plans came to nothing. The Malkin Committee set up in Britain in 1938 to study the possibility reached the conclusion that any *quid pro quo* demanded by other powers would be too costly to Britain's strategic position.[97] Germany felt too insecure in the face of the Soviet presence to risk disarming. Von Ribbentrop told the British ambassador in 1938 that 'even if the Soviet Union declared itself ready to refrain from the use of bombs, it would be impossible to place any faith in such a declaration'.[98] Thus by 1939 the situation had been reached where both sides possessed considerable bombing forces to deter the other from using them for terror bombing attacks. On the eve of war Hitler announced that he would restrict bombing to military targets only, and Goering asked Dahlerus to convey to the British that if the RAF would do the same the Luftwaffe would 'limit aerial attacks to aerodromes and fortifications. Will make no attack on civil population'.[99] Unknown to Goering, Chamberlain had already intervened to force the RAF to confine its targets to 'legitimate military targets' which 'must be capable of identification'.[100] In the wake of Hitler's appeal Chamberlain announced that 'Britain will never resort to the deliberate attack on women and children, and other civilians for the purpose of mere terrorism'. In such a climate Roosevelt's appeal on 1 September for all the belligerents to restrict their bombing met with general approval.[101]

Nevertheless governments prepared for the worst. In case the bomber did get through large-scale programmes of civil defence were established in order to prepare populations for emergencies brought about by bombing, including chemical and biological warfare. Plans were elaborated for the evacuation of urban areas and the dispersal of industry. A general programme of education in air raid protection was begun all over Europe.[102] In Russia a policy was followed from the 1920s of creating cadres of trained men and women capable of restraining panic in the face of attack and of restoring essential services. Each cadre was based on an individual factory or residential block.[103] In Germany the Reich's Air Defence League (*Reichsluftschutzbund*) trained some 12 million Germans in elementary passive air defence, and provided advanced courses of 26 weeks training to those entrusted with civil defence organization.[104] By 1939 the British Government, while providing free air raid precaution information and training, became the only government to supply every member of the population with a gas mask.[105] Air raid shelters were built in all major cities and air raid building regulations became statutory requirements in most major European countries during the 1930s. The enthusiasm for civil defence preparations reflected a general fear that however good the active defences or however powerful the deterrent quality of bomber fleets, a policy of unrestricted bombing would be too tempting a weapon for any combatant to lightly abandon it. The experiences of Abyssinia, Spain and China were seen as pointers to the effects of an air war between even more powerful air rivals. If air commanders were more critical of airpower than the public, sufficient uncertainty existed as to the scope of the air force in war to warrant both anxiety and optimism at the same time when that war finally broke out in September 1939.

2

The European Air War
September 1939-41

When war finally broke out at the beginning of September 1939 the expected knock-out blow from the air did not materialize. Both sides scanned the skies expecting such action. Civil defence measures went into immediate activation. Operational preparations went ahead for an active air defence against bombing attack. But in fact the 'knock-out blow' could not be delivered by either side. There had been little planning preparation for such action and both sides went to great lengths to ensure that they should not be seen to be the ones initiating unrestricted air warfare. It was one thing to threaten the use of air power for diplomatic advantage; quite another to use air power directly on its own in wartime. For Hitler as for the Allies it was the very fact that the effect of air war was an unknown quantity that discouraged adventurism in using aircraft. Yet it was precisely that element of the unknown that had made the air weapon an instrument of international politics between the wars. When more detailed operational preparations demonstrated the hollowness of the threat of air power, used on its own, the politicians' reluctance to strike the first blow was given a pragmatic justification. Not only were the technical means to hand unsuitable for a sustained and effective bombing campaign, but the air crews lacked training; and the air staffs had not yet prepared a strategy in detail for the independent use of aircraft. As a result aircraft remained at first, for both sides, auxiliary to the army and navy, while retaining the promise that technical improvements would give air power a more decisive role at a future date. This situation worried Hitler less than the Allies because co-operation with the army, with its emphasis on dive-bombing and battle aircraft, remained central to his strategy. There was no question, despite Goering's boasts, that a German strategic bombing campaign could be launched in 1939 with any prospect of success. In the event co-operation between the Luftwaffe and the army proved to be a vital factor in German victory.

(i) From Poland to the Blitz

Once Hitler had announced his intention of preparing for a likely war against Poland in April 1939, the Luftwaffe was, together with the rest of the armed forces, instructed to carry out the annual exercises on the assumption of a state of war with Poland. The manoeuvres, while exciting a considerable amount of anxiety among the air staff as to the poor state of training and operational preparedness, were carried out along the lines predicted in earlier contingency planning. The Luftwaffe was to destroy the Polish air force by attacks against air fields and then turn to give close tactical support to the attacking armies. This intention was given substance in Hitler's first war directive.[1] Hitler also asked that operational preparations for attacks by air against England should be worked out but the result was disappointing. It was concluded that there would be great difficulty and little chance of success in waging an independent air war against Britain in the immediate future.[2]

The same conclusion had been reached by a different route in the Western Allies' planning. Direct preparations for a possible war against Germany had been begun after the occupation of rump Czechoslovakia. Uppermost in the minds of both the French and British supreme commands was the desire not to initiate anything that could be interpreted as unrestricted bombing. The major task of the bomber forces was to help as far as was possible in the event of attack by Germany over land or in retaliation for air attacks by enemy bombers but at all events to try to conserve and expand forces that were ill-prepared for such a campaign in September 1939.[3] French leaders remained consistently opposed to the use of bombers on strategic tasks, particularly the attack against the Ruhr, and insisted that bombers be used to attack enemy columns and hold up the enemy advance.[4] The RAF retained in its planning the use of bombers in strategic attacks with a maximum striking force only if there appeared to be imminent danger of total defeat. For the carrying out of these and other priorities the RAF had produced by the end of 1939 a list of fourteen tasks under the Western Air Plans which were sufficiently flexible to allow rapid switch of priority should the need arise. The major task was defensive.[5] The French air force on the other hand had no other plan except for the use of aircraft with armies in close co-operation or for bombing the battle area. In order to co-ordinate the different aspects of allied air strategy an Allied Central Air Bureau was established designed to work closely with the supreme command organization under Gamelin who was able to insist that air forces should follow the French interest rather than the British in any effort to repulse a German attack. Preparations of a broad strategic nature were finalized in November 1939 under the heading Plan D, the plan to move French and British armies as quickly as possible into Belgium to form a defensive line on the rivers that would link up with actual fortifications in France. This was effectively the plan that was to go into operation in the battle for France six months later.[6]

Two factors governed the operational decisions taken by Germany and the Allies. The first was the state of air technology, which conditioned the strategic choices open to both sides. The lack of heavy bombers, or of bombers fast enough to avoid fighter defences, or of bombing aids accurate enough for economic warfare restricted air forces, and particularly the RAF, to carrying out very little. The second factor was the supply of aircraft. Of the Western powers' aircraft a large proportion were obsolete or becoming so and were to be replaced by newer types still at the testing stage or only coming in small quantities from the factories. British planning assumed the need for the eventual production of 2,000 to 3,000 aircraft a month after 18 months of war. The first year of war under the Harrogate programme published in January 1940 was to aim for 1,700 aircraft a month by September 1940, sufficient to meet the needs of a wartime establishment of 360 squadrons.[7] French intentions were much more modest. Plan V, the past pre-war programme, had called for an output of 330 aircraft a month by early 1940. When war broke out the war mobilization plan aimed for 780 aircraft a month by the seventh month of war, although more ambitious plans were laid for a war of longer duration.[8] The immediate mobilization plans for the Luftwaffe did not reflect the same sense of urgency as those of the Allies, partly because of industrial restrictions and unsatisfactory planning, partly because of the over-confidence of the leadership secure in possessing in 1939 the larger and more effective air force. The first mobilization plan aimed for a production of 1,040 aircraft per month of all types by the end of the first year of war, with a long-term aim of producing an average of 1,100-1,200 a month for a war of three years duration. Successive plans revised these totals downwards to a planned monthly production of 1,000 a month until 1942.[9]

British monthly production thus began to exceed that of Germany in the course of 1939. French production totalled 2,113 aircraft for the first five months of 1940, giving the Allies an advantage in the supply of aircraft of almost two to one.[10] Moreover Britain and France were able to call on the aircraft manufacturing capacity of the United States, which, despite the political arguments over the question of neutrality, proved willing to supply large quantities of aircraft. By September 1939 orders for 1,500 had been given to American industry; by December for 2,500. By August of the following year Britain alone had outstanding orders for 14,000 aircraft and 25,000 aero-engines. Once Roosevelt had persuaded Congress to lift the Neutrality Ban in November 1939, the Air Corps sanctioned the sale not only of trainers and obsolescent aircraft but of more advanced combat types as well, arguing that the American aircraft industry would grow faster using European rather than American investment and orders and that the American public would be spared the expense.[11] The Allied advantage in numbers was tempered by the fact that the Allies had smaller high-quality forces to start with and were still achieving parity rather than a substantial lead. Both Britain and France were in the process of changing over from obsolescent to more modern aircraft types, building up new units from scratch and sending the older aircraft back into the reserve parks and training schools. The German change-over to modern types, although by no means complete in 1939, was considerably further advanced when war broke out.

The war opened with the successful invasion and deafeat of Poland. The strategy worked out earlier in the year was put into operation with the maximum effect. The Polish air force was overcome rapidly, many of the aircraft being destroyed on the ground. The Luftwaffe then moved on to attack communications and troop movements and to work closely in co-operation with the armies in the field as aerial artillery. The campaign provided few lessons other than those already known, since the main enemy was to the west. The one lesson that the campaign might have taught was the need for making generous provision for wastage. Even against the Polish air force the Luftwaffe had lost 285 aircraft with 279 damaged against a loss of 333 Polish aircraft.[12] Between the defeat of Poland and the campaign in France there was relatively little air activity. Hitler directed that the air force limit its operations to attacks on shipping and reconnaissance work in order to conserve forces for the major offensive and to reduce the risk of starting an unrestricted air bombing war. Plans were laid in reluctant co-operation with the German navy for attacks on Britain's trade and ports but the attack was postponed until after the Western army offensive.[13] Allied air activity confined itself to intelligence work and propaganda from the air.

The campaign in Norway and Denmark marked the first real air activity of the war in the west although the commitment of air forces was limited, particularly for the Allies, by the demands in the main theatre of war. The Luftwaffe gained air superiority by virtue of the larger numbers diverted to the operations and the advantage, after the occupation of Denmark, of internal lines of communication over land with good air bases against the Allies' difficulty in flying from distant bases over sea in hazardous conditions. If the campaign demonstrated anything it was the failure of both sides to prepare for effective air-sea co-operation, symbolized by the sinking of two German destroyers by the Luftwaffe. Both sides were persuaded of the importance of air support for ground forces, if such persuasion were needed. On observing German success with close-support aircraft the British air minister commented that 'strong air power must be met by stronger air power' while, as in Poland, the German army was confirmed in the wisdom of tying the aircraft to a tactical role with the army. Again Luftwaffe losses, against light opposition, were high: some 242 aircraft were lost, many of them transport aircraft, a large number simply due to non-combat attrition. Allied losses were much lower only because so few aircraft were committed. The RAF kept aircraft at home for air defence, the French for the expected attack in the west.[14]

When the attack in the west finally came it followed lines already familiar to both sides. Using air forces in conjunction with the main weight of the army with its mobile spearhead gave the German armed forces a major tactical advantage. To this was added the advantage of starting with larger air numbers, while the British were reluctant to commit their main forces to the land battle and the French had too few modern aircraft to carry out an effective defence for very long. On 10 May 1940 the RAF had only 416 aircraft in France, which together with the 1,200 aircraft of the French air force on the eastern borders was a considerably weaker force than the 2,750 German aircraft assigned to the campaign. The Luftwaffe was able to protect its own troop movements as well as attack the enemy air force both at its bases and in the skies. Air supremacy was achieved rapidly even if the Allied air forces were never completely destroyed. But for the purposes of the battle plan the air force was designed to do no more than this. No bombing campaign in the rear ensued and it was always clear that the main purpose of the air force was to help ease the path of the advancing armies rather than to provide decisive action of its own. It was the main thrust of the heavily armoured mobile divisions that broke the Allied armed forces. To this end the Luftwaffe played an important but auxiliary role.[15]

In the face of the overwhelming success of the German combined offensive the Allies' air strategy, that had always been far from clear, became yet more confused. The RAF stationed in France and the French air force concentrated on attacking troop movements and the battle areas as well as protecting the Allied troops from attacks by the Luftwaffe. The RAF stationed in Britain, however, had a different role. The French wished the British to use as much of this force as possible to help in the battle. Some bombers were used on the southern front for that purpose while others were sent from southern bases in England to harass German communications and concentrations with little success.[16] Bomber Command itself was anxious to be allowed to turn to bombing Germany since the decisive moment of the land battle seemed to have arrived with the rapid collapse of Allied resistance at the end of May. On 15 May the first strategic bombing operation against the Ruhr was carried out to attack oil and railway installations. The Allied air effort was thus dispersed over a number of objectives with little effect. The conflict between French and British opinions on bombing targets left a situation in which what little air support there was was frittered away in a vain attempt to find some target to which the Germans would be particularly vulnerable. Attacks on the Ruhr in fact were few because of the insistent needs of the French forces and when Germany was attacked oil installations proved very difficult to hit.[17] Very quickly Bomber Command changed its objectives. Portal instructed pilots that efforts should be made 'to bring about continuous interruption and dislocation of German war industry', in particular aircraft factories. In the event that neither oil nor aircraft installations could be seen then 'any self-illuminating target or targets which are otherwise identifiable' were to be attacked. Despite its ineffectiveness Bomber Command had taken the opportunity of the defeat of France to begin to launch a strategic air offensive along the lines planned in the preceding years.[18]

The first period of the war had not seen the great bombing offensives that had been predicted in the period of preparation. All the combatant powers made great efforts to avoid initiating such a campaign and when the British finally did so it was in an act of desperation to help stem the flow of German forces and in the face of government opposition to what threatened to become a war against civilians. Even this campaign when it began was of little military value and posed no threat either to German morale or German industry. Air forces had primarily proved their worth in land campaigns. The Blitzkrieg strategy relied on aircraft co-operating with the army for its maximum effect. One reason why Hitler had no need of independent strategic operations was the expectation that victory could be achieved more economically and more rapidly by using forces in a combined way. Under the circumstances of general strategic air weakness in 1940 this was a sensible choice. In every other department aircraft performed in a very limited way. In the trade war submarines were clearly more important than aircraft and very little work had been done on co-ordinating air-sea operations. In bombing it was clear that under the technical conditions of 1940 the amount of damage that could be inflicted and the accuracy of bomb-aiming left much to be desired. Even the relentless bombing of the Dunkirk evacuation did little substantial damage and proved indecisive. All the evidence tended to point to the fact that air power had been greatly exaggerated and that denying air space over the battlefield to the enemy was, as in the First World War, the most important contribution that air forces could make.

The defeat of France was expected to lead to the British capitulation. The fact that it did not left Hitler with two alternatives, either to blockade the British into surrender by intensifying the trade war or to attempt the actual invasion of England. Both strategies were soon to be subordinated to the new goal of moving east against Soviet Russia, a decision that Hitler reached before he knew finally whether or not the British would seek a peace.[19] Both the alternatives against Britain necessitated the use of air forces as an anti-trade weapon in co-operation with the Navy or in preparing the ground for any invasion by defeating the RAF. There was, of course, another possibility, that Britain could be bombed into submission through indiscriminate terror attacks but in the preparatory period before the Battle of Britain such a possibility was not accepted either by Hitler or the Luftwaffe staff. By 2 July Hitler asked the services to provide contingency plans for the invasion of Britain but made no final decision. The most definite direction that German strategy seemed to be taking was in pursuing the blockade and trade war which was now made possible by establishing bases in the Low Countries and Norway. In late May Keitel had ordered the Luftwaffe to attack stocks of British food, public services and the aircraft industry 'in order to deprive the English Air Force, the last weapon that can be directly used against us, of the basis of its existence'.[20]

On 16 July, however, Hitler finally decided to go ahead with a direct invasion of Britain and issued a directive to that effect. The essential precondition was that the Luftwaffe should win mastery in the air without which no invasion would be possible. For the first time the air forces were to be launched on a major strategic operation for which there had been little preparation and little experience. The plan was not, however, to win the war with the air force alone. The battle for which Hitler was preparing was an enlarged version of the attack on France. The invasion was to be carried out by the Army and Navy and most of the tasks of the Luftwaffe were defined as support tasks again—to prevent interference by enemy planes, to attack coastal defences and troop concentrations, and reserves and communications in the immediate rear of the English armies. 'In carrying out this task', insisted Hitler, 'the closest liaison is necessary between individual Air Force units and the Army invasion forces.'[21] However, one of the conditions for the invasion at all was that the Luftwaffe should guarantee that the RAF could not operate effectively over southern England, at least for the period of successful army invasion, and it was to that end that Goering directed his forces throughout August and early September. On 1 August the Luftwaffe was ordered to 'overpower the English Air Force ... in the shortest possible time. The attacks are to be directed primarily against flying units, their ground installations, and their supply organizations, but also against the aircraft industry.'[22] This was in addition to the tasks of helping the naval war against trade and preparing for the active assistance of the invasion itself. The Battle began sporadically in early August and continued until mid-September during which time Hitler finally recognized that air superiority of the kind required could not be achieved and postponed the invasion indefinitely.[23]

For the British the situation that developed after the fall of France was exactly the contingency for which preparations had been in hand since 1937. If the Battle of Britain tested the German ability to undertake a strategic air campaign it was also a test of the major strand of British air doctrine, the provision of adequate aerial defence against the air attack. The advantage lay very much with the defender since the equipment and organization of Fighter Command was for the express purpose of preventing enemy air attack. The equipment and preparation of the Luftwaffe was hardly adequate since such a campaign had not been an important part of German air planning. There was no heavy bomber capable of carrying large loads over long-range. Fighters were not long-range and the heavier fighters and dive-bombing aircraft were produced for the main purpose of supporting ground troops in battle, not guarding bomber groups or attacking well-defended airfields. Finally, there was no real operational experience of combating an enemy equipped with a comprehensive early warning system and centralized communications and command systems. The technical and organizational advantages enjoyed by the RAF could only have been overcome by massive bomber attacks for which the Germans were ill-prepared or by overwhelming numerical superiority, which the Luftwaffe lacked.[24]

It was on this question of numbers that the Luftwaffe made its major mistakes, both in estimating the strength of the British air forces and in deciding the necessary level of supply for its own forces. Goering relied on information from his chief of intelligence, Josef Schmid. It was this source that was largely responsible for creating Goering's own massive over-confidence in the superiority of his air force. In his report issued in mid-July on comparative British and German strength Schmid concluded that 'the Luftwaffe is clearly superior to the RAF as regards strength, equipment, training, command and location of bases'. German air intelligence credited Britain with an aircraft output of only 180–300 first-line fighters a month and 150 first-line bombers and assumed that under conditions of war these figures would decrease rather than increase.[25] This margin of error was significant. Actual British fighter production in July was 496, in August 476, in September 467. Overall production rose from 1,279 (all types) in May to 1,601 in August. Schmid then heavily overestimated German successes. The High Command was informed on 20 August that 644 British aircraft had been destroyed between 12–19 August and 11 airfields permanently destroyed when the true figure was only 103 and one airfield temporarily put out of action.[26] In fact it was the Luftwaffe that failed to expand during the period, both in terms of aircraft and in terms of pilots.

Without adequate supply the kind of superiority needed in the face of well-organized fighter defence could not be achieved. At the end of the Battle of France the Luftwaffe had suffered heavy losses and needed time to rest and regroup. Deliveries of new aircraft were insufficient to meet the continuing drain on resources. This was partly because air strategy had not anticipated such a campaign when production plans were laid in 1939. Even though aircraft production was given priority in the summer of 1940 the army held up the transfer of resources and the air ministry failed to press for them. In fact the new air plans worked out in June and July gave smaller totals for the crucial months of the Battle of Britain than the plans published in September 1939. The number of fighter aircraft planned for production dropped from 227 in July to 177 by September 1940.[27] British fighter plans for the period were exceeded by 43 per cent where German plans were 40 per cent behind target by the summer of 1940.[28] This situation gave real respite to the RAF, which despite heavy and continuous attacks over the period from July to September, emerged with a fighter strength actually larger than had existed when the battle began (see Table 3). The same was true of pilots. British training programmes ran at full stretch to make up for past deficiencies, concentrating mainly on producing fighter pilots to meet the emergency. German programmes were less urgent and less relevant to the battle. Of the large stock of pilots available many were trained as bomber pilots and could not be quickly retrained to fly fighters. As the battle progressed it became obvious that the number of pilots was barely adequate to cover the first five or six weeks. Moreover the Luftwaffe suffered from a problem to which the RAF was immune. Where British pilots parachuted to safety, Luftwaffe pilots were lost for the duration of the war. By the end of September the Germans had suffered not only a sharp decline in fighter numbers but also heavy attrition of the men to fly them.

Table 3: Single-engine Fighter Statistics for the Battle of Britain[29]

	Luftwaffe			RAF	
	Strength	Serviceable		Strength	Serviceable
1 July	893	725	6 July	871	644
1 August	860	n.a.	3 August	1,061	708
1 September	680	438*	7 September	1,161	746
1 October	700	275	28 September	1,048	732
1 December	680	n.a.			

*Figure for 7 September.

	Production	
	German	British
May		325
June	164	446
July	220	496
August	173	476
September	218	467
October	144*	469
Total fighters 1940	1,870	4,283

*Figure for October is that for acceptances rather than production.

Such advantages made it unnecessary for aircraft from central and northern England to be drawn into the battle. The Luftwaffe was prevented from achieving its object by those aircraft fighting in southern England alone whose losses were made good by large efforts in production and well-organized repair facilities co-ordinated by the Nuffield motor-car corporation.[30] Concerted Luftwaffe attacks were certainly a major hazard for Fighter Command but even at the most dangerous moments the German air forces were little closer to achieving the aim of air supremacy for long enough to permit a successful invasion than they had been at the beginning of the battle. Moreover the very strategy of overwhelming an air force in a single 'battle' betrayed the Luftwaffe's failure to grasp that air superiority could not be absolute against a well-armed enemy with large economic resources, a fact that had been widely misunderstood amongst the pre-war air powers. It was impossible under the conditions of the summer of 1940 for the Luftwaffe to eliminate the RAF because it lacked the operational and material means to destroy the British aircraft industry—in fact air attacks spurred on the industrial effort—or to prevent the RAF from re-grouping again for renewed combat over the contested area. Poor German intelligence coupled with a complete lack of urgency in the question of production and repair had a crucial part to play in the failure of the Battle of Britain. Douhet's contention that air command could be considered won when one side was forced on to a permanent defensive in air warfare was finally confounded.

The Luftwaffe was, of course, able to inflict heavy losses on the RAF in both pilots and aircraft. Lack of combat training and the inadequacy of early British fighter tactics contributed to this. But it should be remembered that the RAF sustained higher losses in the seven weeks of the Battle of France than in the whole period of the Battle of Britain. In many ways the battles in May and June were more critical for the survival of the RAF than the attacks in August and September 1940. In these attacks the Luftwaffe was caught in an operational cleft stick. Attacks by bombers by day had to be escorted by large numbers of fighters. The early attacks by fighter-bombers and dive-bombers from June onwards had shown how ineffective they were against good modern fighters. Essentially the Battle of Britain had to be fought with medium bombers too slow and vulnerable to defend themselves accompanied by fast fighters with short-range, even from French bases, which were given little freedom of action because of the need to guard the bombers. It was the bomber that was supposed to do the damage and strategy dictated that the fighters be used to protect them rather than being able to hunt and pursue enemy fighters as in a combined land offensive. The RAF, on the other hand, had the main task of breaking up and dispersing bomber formations and was expressly forbidden to take up major combat with enemy fighters. This gave the RAF the chance to do what fighters were good at, shooting down slower and less well-defended bombers but it gave the Luftwaffe the task of using fighters where they would be least effective and most vulnerable. Hence the large disparity in losses. British losses from 10 July to 31 October totalled 915 aircraft. German losses totalled 1,733.[31]

The failure in the Battle of Britain left German strategy in some confusion. No invasion could be attempted and it was indefinitely postponed. Some senior officers doubted whether Hitler had ever intended to attack at all as preparations were simultaneously in hand for the war against the Soviet Union for which Hitler was now much more committed.[32] Clearly, however, the only way to continue hostilities against Britain was to carry on with air attacks, and according to Hitler's earlier directives, the war against the British economy was still a priority. In the middle of September, therefore, Hitler instructed Goering to make one last attempt to bring Britain to defeat in 1940. For the first time the Luftwaffe was to be given the task of bringing the war to an end by the exercise of air power alone through a policy of night bombing against industry, trade, and administration. However, the circumstances surrounding such a decision were confused and the Luftwaffe was left with an increasingly aimless strategy for which the technical and tactical means of fulfilment were even less promising than in the initial Battle of Britain.

There was not one but several reasons why the Luftwaffe changed to the Blitz. One factor was the continuing need to create suitable conditions for invasion should that suddenly become a possibility—however remote—during 1940. The Supreme Command staff assumed for some time that the change in targets was simply a tactical switch, as Goering claimed.[33] Hitler, on the other hand, was faced with two further problems. First of all Germany was itself being bombed more and more regularly by Bomber Command, at night and with increasing lack of discrimination in choosing targets. Hitler took the opportunity of a heavier raid on Berlin to announce in the Reichstag on 4 September 'Just now . . . Mr. Churchill is demonstrating his new brainchild, the night air raid. . . . When they declare that they will increase their attacks on our cities, then we will raze their cities to the ground. We will stop the handiwork of these night air pirates, so help us God!'[34] His mounting concern at the kind of war that was developing and which he, among other war leaders had sought to avoid before 1939, persuaded him of the need for reprisals and inclined him towards the night air raid, an inclination confirmed by the disastrous results of the early attempts to bomb London by day. Hitler's second problem was the need to bring some decision in the west before turning towards Russia. The use of the terror weapon, which he now considered to be under no moral imperative to withhold, was a final gamble in the search for a quick end to the first stage of the war. By 14 September he claimed that the air attacks 'could work decisively for the war'. As a general solution to these several problems the Luftwaffe proposed to end the war by bombing alone, the dream of the air theorists of the 1920s.[35]

The equivocal way in which the Blitz began was reflected in the actual campaign itself. Once it became clear that no decision could be reached that would make an invasion possible in 1940, and plans were being tentatively drawn up for a similar attempt the following year, the enthusiasm of the air force for its task began to diminish. The obvious failure of the Blitz to do more than temporarily dent British production and the favourable effect that it had on British morale and will-to-resist was soon clear to the German leadership. The Ministry of Home Security was, with some justification, able to announce that 'effective damage has not been serious in relation to the national war effort'. Good dispersal policies helped industry and rapid repair work ensured that no railway or port facilities were inoperable for any length of time, including the Port of London on which many of the German attacks were specifically directed.[36] The major problem facing the Luftwaffe during the Blitz period was a technical and tactical one. The difficulty lay in trying to get a large enough bomb-load with sufficient accuracy to have any real impact. From July the Germans had been bombing ports and military targets with precision attacks by day. The bombing of London was to be conducted along similar lines with precision attacks on installations vital to the life of the city and its industry. When the daylight bombing was ended precision bombing became much harder. There was little training in such attacks and the main medium bombers carried too small a load to be destructive enough against targets that could not always be seen. Once the German navigational beams were finally combated by British air intelligence, the prospects for such bombing became even less satisfactory.[37]

The lack of a German heavy bomber was a result of the specific decision taken in 1937 not to concentrate on strategic bombing but to concentrate on the Blitzkrieg air force. This decision created two distinct miscalculations. First of all the air planners genuinely believed that Hitler did not intend war with England and concluded that the medium bomber would suffice for all strategic contingencies. Secondly Hitler believed that the destructive power of the medium bomber was greater than it actually was and that the bomber fleets he possessed in 1940 were capable of carrying out such a campaign without the need for heavy bombers.[38] The Blitz was to disprove both points Even against almost non-existent defences against night attack the campaign produced very little of real strategic advantage, and in the encouragment that it gave to the RAF to produce counter measures promised positive disadvantages. As a battle the bombing became less and less attractive to the Germans. The rate of combat attrition was still high, though much lower than during the daylight battles. Over 600 aircraft were lost and the Luftwaffe emerged with fewer aircraft available in March 1941 than in March 1940. The tonnage of bombs dropped, which had reached a peak of 9,000 tons in October 1940, dropped to 6,500 tons in November and 1,100 tons by February 1941. These figures represented a mere fraction of the monthly totals dropped by the Allies in 1943 and 1944.[39] Moreover the conflict among the German air leaders as to what targets to attack most profitably dispersed these modest bomb-loads over a wide area. Priority was given to aircraft production targets, but public services, communciations and administrative centres were also attacked. The resistance among the Luftwaffe junior officers to mere terror raids meant that unless Hitler or Goering specifically asked for retaliation, the bombing campaign was directed against military and economic targets as originally intended. Hitler himself complained later of the ineffectiveness of such a programme. 'The munitions industry . . .' he said 'cannot be interfered with effectively by air raids. We learned that lesson in the autumn of 1940 . . . usually the prescribed targets are not hit; often the fliers unload their bombs on fields camouflaged as plants; and in both countries the armaments industry is so decentralized that the armament potential cannot really be interfered with . . .'.[40]

The Blitz finally ended in the spring of 1941. Nothing had changed since 1940 as a result of the campaign except that the Luftwaffe were more than ever persuaded of the advantages of a tactical role for air forces. The theories of Douhet seemed doubly confounded. Fighter defence had proved an active and effective deterrent by day. Technical shortcomings and poor planning had contributed to the failure to achieve any decisive result through bombing alone. The Blitz had anyway long dropped out of Hitler's main strategic thinking. Aircraft needed to be conserved for the coming attack against Russia, for the problem of aircraft supply had not yet been solved and the winter and spring of 1940–41 still found the Luftwaffe producing well below its planned output. In January aircraft production sank to 635 for all types, just over 50 per cent of the planned number. Moreover the temporary priority won by aircraft production in the armaments economy after June was rescinded by Hitler in late September 1940 and a renewed effort made with army armament to meet the requirements for the campaign of the following spring.[41] Despite Goering's demands to double aircraft production as quickly as possible actual production stagnated. Had Hitler been fully aware of the supply situation he might have prohibited the continuation of the Blitz altogether. As it was he began to insist that the Luftwaffe use its resources in the most economical way from the point of view of current and expected strategy.

The end of the Blitz coincided, too, with the increased prosecution of the attack against British imports for which the German navy demanded much greater air support. Hitler had been persuaded by Raeder that such a strategy of blockade was more likely to bring strategic results, if more slowly, than the attack from the air. Blockade became the major strategy employed against Britain until the decision to invade could again be taken. In a directive issued in February Hitler directed the Luftwaffe to reduce air attacks on the British mainland and to concentrate efforts on helping the naval war. 'Only by these means', he directed, 'can we expect a decisive end to the war within the foreseeable future'.[42] Air force co-operation with the navy had never been good, however. The naval air forces were small and poorly equipped and Goering jealously guarded his command over all Luftwaffe units that might be compelled to support naval operations. Nevertheless the far-ranging Kondor aircraft in co-operation with submarines achieved remarkable successes in the early stages of the campaign,[43] partly because the British convoy system had not yet been fully organized; partly because Coastal and Bomber Command had not prepared for a major air-navy war of the kind now required. But once such preparations were in hand it became a relatively easy matter to restrict the impact of German aircraft on British shipping; with the improved weapons of Coastal Command the threat from the submarine and surface raider was also substantially (if temporarily) reduced. The German navy remained starved of enough resources in aircraft. The mine-laying campaign which promised considerable success ground to a halt because Goering would not release enough aircraft for the task. Torpedo development was well behind that of the other combatants because of the lack of interest shown in naval co-operation during the 1930s. No delayed fuse torpedoes were available in 1940 and fuses had be purchased from Italy. Conventional bombers had to be converted to the task and such a conversion took time. Not that conventional bombers had a sufficient range, for the Navy needed a long-range heavy bomber built for the purpose. The Kondor was in fact a converted airliner and transport plane and could not hope to compete with the modern fighter aircraft it opposed. Finally the German Navy possessed no aircraft carriers that would have allowed greater tactical flexibility in choosing where to concentrate the aerial attacks on shipping.[44]

Blockade failed like the Blitz and the Battle of Britain through the lack of preparation for such strategic employment and the rapid ability of the British air forces to produce an effective enough defence against the rapidly switched and increasingly half-hearted strategies of the *Wehrmacht*. The failure of the Luftwaffe in the autumn and winter of 1940-41 marked the high-watermark of German air strategy. Thereafter the air force was to play a vital but mainly tactical role. In this capacity it had more than proved its value, justifying the faith in the dive-bomber and the tactics of close support for ground troops championed by Jeschonnek and the German air staff. The lesson that the German high command drew from the experience of 1940 was that 'air strategy' as distinct from a 'combined strategy' was a delusion. From that period onwards Hitler insisted on tying aircraft more rigidly to the purposes of the army, preferring to ignore the fact that other air forces might draw different conclusions from the air operations of 1940 and that a more general German air strategy might be needed at a later date.

(ii) The RAF, Bombing and the War at Sea

The German rejection of a more general air strategy coincided with shifts in the war itself that made such a strategy more rather than less necessary. The strategic initiative that had lain with the German forces began from the middle of 1940 to be taken out of Hitler's hands. In the first place the RAF, even while engaged upon the defensive battle, had launched from May 1940 onwards a continously expanding, if rather ineffective, bombing campaign. Secondly the war was no longer a war simply against Hitler but became in June 1940 a Mediterranean war and threatened in the near future to become a war in Asia as well. The attractiveness of the bombing offensive lay in the fact that war could be continued while preparations were in train for an invasion of the continent, a task that was well beyond Britain's immediately foreseeable military capability. 'The Air Force and its action,' said Churchill, 'on the largest scale must therefore claim the first place over the Navy and the Army'.[45] There still remained the division over how such action should be taken. Churchill and some of the Air Staff favoured an indiscriminate offensive, partly in retaliation, partly because it was by no means clear that night attacks could be made with enough precision to ensure that targets could be hit, let alone destroyed. But throughout the summer of 1940 the Air Staff stuck rigidly to the target plans laid down before the war and elaborated in directives in June and July 1940. These targets were the German aircraft industry, oil and communications. While the Battle of Britain threatened, the attack against the aircraft industry was paramount. By September the Air Staff had returned to the view that attacks on oil were 'the basis of our longer term offensive strategy'.[46] In fact the selection of a satisfactory target system was constantly postponed both by the technical and operational difficulties experienced and by the more pressing needs of bombing Hitler's invasion build-up and the need to divert resources to help with the crucial Atlantic Battle.

The operational difficulties were similar to those experienced by the Luft-waffe—difficulty of locating target, little experience of night-flying, shortage of crews. The technical problems were also considerable. The large four-engined bombers were not yet ready and would not be ready in quantity until 1942. The existing bombers were inadequate for the major tasks, although efforts were made to improve the bomb itself. Finally there were no effective navigational aids introduced even though scientific intelligence had already located and described the German aids and prepared ways of defeating them. Despite these drawbacks the Air Staff continued to press for precision bombing and concentration on synthetic oil plants.[47] The Prime Minister and Cabinet took a different view. On the basis of the evidence that targets could not be easily destroyed by night bombing, the War Cabinet insisted that 'whilst we should adhere to the rule that our objectives should be military targets, at the same time the civilian population around the target areas must be made to feel the weight of the war'.[48] Such an ambiguous statement emerged as a directive to the Commander of Bomber Command to start 'harassing the enemy's main industrial towns and communications' when the attack on oil could not be carried out. As it happened a general harassment was all Bomber Command had been operationally capable of. Photographic evidence showed that the targets claimed as destroyed were often not hit at all. These were all lessons which were easily available from the failure of German night bombing.

During the first six months of 1941 the Government's growing concern with the ineffectiveness of bombing and the indecisiveness of its strategy coincided with the gradual acceptance by the airmen that they lacked the operational means to do more than simply bomb cities and communications more or less indiscriminately. Such a situation paved the way for the development of area bombing, a strategy arrived at by a process of elimination. Only Churchill seemed genuinely convinced that area bombing would be capable of cracking German morale based, among other things, on the ill-founded assumption, summarized by the Ministry of Information in December 1940, that 'all the evidence goes to prove that the Germans, for all their present confidence and cockiness will not stand a quarter of the bombing that the British have shown they can take.'[49] Such views blinded many politicians to the inescapable conclusion that bombing policy whether British or German, was not capable on its own of achieving anything decisive under the conditions of warfare in 1941. But whereas the Luftwaffe accepted this fact and moved away from bombing plans, the RAF and the British government took precisely the opposite course. Assuming that the German failure in 1940 had been caused by poor preparations rather than a wrong strategy, plans moved ahead for the development of a massive heavy bomber force designed to raise the bomb war to a new level of strategic significance.

Until then, however, aircraft production had to be geared to other, more urgent tasks of defence. Of these the most vital was the Battle of the Atlantic. Although the German effort here was itself rather half-hearted and ill-prepared Raeder had been able to persuade Hitler to devote some resources to exploring the possibility of starving Britain into surrender. For this the German navy needed aircraft, not only to bomb incoming shipping but for reconnaissance purposes in guiding submarines to the vulnerable ships. The exploratory campaign was a considerable success. The Focke-Wulf Kondor long-range aircraft itself sank 150,000 tons of shipping a month during the first half of 1941 although it was slow and very vulnerable to fighter attack. Shipping losses through air action were 580,000 tons in 1940 and over one million tons in 1941, almost half the total sinkings for the North Atlantic theatre.[50] Only Goering's refusal to divert more aircraft to the war at sea and the failure to produce a satisfactory long-range bomber built for the purpose prevented aircraft from achieving an even higher degree of destruction. The navy was consistently starved of resources. In January 1939 it had been agreed with the Luftwaffe that the navy should control its own air force of 492 aircraft. At the outbreak of war it possessed instead only 120 mainly obsolescent aircraft for the war in the west.[51]

The success of the Kondor and the submarine was exaggerated by the conspicuous failure of the British forces to prepare for just such an attack, reflecting a more general failure to give sufficient urgency in Britain too to the fusing of air power with traditional naval power. That the preparation had been trivial was made the more obvious when Coastal Command and the Fleet Air Arm were compelled to call in the assistance of the other branches of the RAF, which, with limited resources, were able to halt the aerial blockade within a few months. There was less success with the war against the submarine even after air command had been won over the sea because of the need for advanced radar detection equipment, but even in submarine warfare a temporary fall in shipping losses was secured by better patrolling of the seas within aircraft range which forced the submarines to shift the battleground to the mid-Atlantic.[52]

In these changes in the Atlantic battle the use of bombers and carriers was crucial. The diversion of sufficient heavy aircraft from bombing Germany to bombing German naval targets and for patrolling purposes, while it led to a reduction in the bombing attacks on Germany itself, provided a weapon against which the German navy and air force were themselves ill-prepared. The same was true of the introduction of escort carriers. An ambitious carrier programme was begun when it was realized that aircraft would be needed to help protect the large convoys. They were brought into operation from September 1941 and within a short period of time eliminated the threat from the Kondor aircraft which had no long-range supporting aircraft to give them protection.[53] In response to these changes in organization and weapons the German navy demanded throughout 1941 that the Luftwaffe provide more assistance in mine-laying and in general support of naval operations. The stumbling block to this policy was not a shortage of resources, as Goering argued, but the fact that Goering would not relinquish control over the Luftwaffe in the way that operational control over Coastal Command in direct support of naval activity had been granted in March 1941. Since Hitler agreed with Goering over the question of indivisibility and since Goering gave little credence to the view that the air war at sea could achieve anything decisive, the German navy was starved of resources that might otherwise have been used to great effect in the spirit of Hitler's rather hollow directive 'to concentrate all the weapons of air and sea warfare against enemy imports' and 'to destroy the most important English harbours'.[54]

(iii) The Struggle for the Mediterranean

The opening of the Mediterranean theatre also took the initiative out of Hitler's hands. Mussolini's ambitions ran considerably ahead of those of his ally, and indeed considerably ahead of his military potential. Spurred on by the imminent collapse of France and the expected capitulation of Britain, Mussolini had hoped to be able to create his Mediterranean empire out of the ruins of Allied control of the Middle East and North Africa. There was the additional problem of Ethiopia as well. Sooner or later Italy might be called upon to defend her colony and the ill-defended routes to it. The collapse of the Allies in June 1940 provided as good a time as any to consolidate what Italian empire there already was. For Mussolini—who was also head of the Italian Air Force—air power was to play an important part in overall strategy. In the first attacks against southern France by Italian bombers some vindication was sought for the strategic bombing theory claimed as Italian in origin.[55] Mussolini also hoped to be able to dominate the sea through the use of aircraft based in southern Italy and to roll up the British colonies and protectorates in the Middle East through a combination of bombing and army attacks. For such tasks considerable Italian air forces were already in existence. There were some 313 aircraft in Libya and the Dodecanese and 325 aircraft in East Africa and a numerically significant home air force, which had already begun some desultory attacks against British shipping from the onset of hostilities.[56]

The nature of the Italian strategy was dictated largely by the mistaken belief that Britain was now no longer an effective enemy. Even in September Mussolini was trying to force Graziani to begin the attack on Egypt prematurely, to coincide with the first steps taken by German soldiers on British soil.[57] The entry of Mussolini into the war had, of course, substantially changed the condition of British strategy. Although it was not an altogether unexpected eventuality, the entry of Italy turned the war from one in defence of the motherland into an imperial war. This was one kind of war for which Britain was ill-prepared in mid-1940. Although likely to be a predominantly naval war, the fleets were required for the protection of trade across the Atlantic and the defence of Home Waters against the possibility of German attack. For the same reasons the air force had to be retained for war at home. British resources were stretched to the limit by Italian intervention, but due to the lack of preparedness on the part of the Italian armed forces, the limit proved to be enough.

Italy's problems were obvious to many within Italy itself. Aircraft production was poorly co-ordinated and stifled by lack of raw materials and poor administration. Over the three years of Italian intervention in the war only 7,183 new aircraft were built, producing in a year what the British economy was producing in a month by 1943.[58] Most Italian aircraft were obsolete or obsolescent by the new standards of 1940, there being only two fighter groups armed with modern monoplanes. Although the Italian air force was alleged to possess 4,900 aircraft in mainland Italy, almost half were trainer aircraft and almost all the remainder biplanes. When the figures of first-line aircraft available were separately investigated by the Italian navy it was discovered that in fact only 454 serviceable bombers and 129 serviceable fighters were ready for use at the outbreak of war.[59] There were too few pilots; few effective repair and maintenance facilities; and barely any anti-aircraft defences. The early attempts at bombing proved ineffective as there had been little active staff preparation in training, selection of targets and tactical research. Although Mussolini saw the importance of mounting attacks against the Suez Canal and its shipping, neither the air forces in the eastern Mediterranean or in North Africa attacked it with any sustained vigour or success. Other bombing attacks against Egypt produced the same result and produced disillusionment to the Italian advocates of strategic air power. Tactical support of ground and naval forces proved to be more effective, though not much more. Influenced by German experience, Mussolini himself limited the activity of the Regia Aeronautica by directing it 'to conform its activities to that of the other services'.[60] Italian use of the Blitzkrieg tactics, of massive air force cover over advancing columns of troops, depended on the possession of large numbers of dive-bombers and effective pursuit aircraft to guarantee air superiority on the battlefield. There were not enough of either type. Instead the air force was composed of aircraft designed for a multiplicity of roles, without sufficient numbers or advanced enough technology to really fulfil them. What air advantages the Italians had—in North Africa it was estimated at 4 : 1 in fighters—was frittered away.

For Britain the prime task was to defend Egypt and the Suez Canal, first of all by arranging smaller combat aircraft in defence of the threatened territory, secondly by using medium bombers to harass the enemy's troop formations, supply depots and shipping. As had been shown in the skies over England defence was the easier strategic option where air forces had a rough parity. Although Italian strength on paper looked impressive, Britain had by May 1940 205 aircraft in Palestine and Egypt and a further 154 in East Africa, including 15 Junkers and 86 aircraft of the South African Air Force. From June onwards anything that could be spared was pressed into service in the Middle East.[61] Not until October, however, could the government comply realistically with the demands for reinforcement, particularly re-equipment with modern types, and not until the middle of 1941 was the help sustained and significant. Before then the valuable resources of modern aircraft that were released to the Middle East were used in a primarily defensive and reconnaissance role. There were not enough aircraft available to do more. The only independent operations were carried out by bombers and torpedo-bombers against Italian shipping, which, despite their small numbers, were able to cripple the Italian fleet at Taranto due to good use of intelligence and poor Italian defences.

The combined use of aircraft with the other services gave the British the first real opportunity of testing the tactical use of air power. The naval war, and in particular the use of aircraft carriers, anticipated the experience of successful aero-naval co-operation in the Atlantic and the Pacific.[62] Fewer mistakes were made than had been exhibited in the Norwegian campaign or the early stages of the northern naval war. The early use of aircraft in the desert and the East African campaign anticipated the use to which tactical air power was to be put in the campaigns from 1942 onwards. In both cases, however, the tactical achievement was compromised by poor supply and poor maintenance. Any appearance of success came through the greater weakness of Italy's colonial and naval forces rather than through the strength and organization of the British. Because of this weakness Italian ambitions, against the expectations of both sides, were not only thwarted but turned upside-down. East Africa was lost, with the loss of almost all Italy's colonial air forces of over 400 aircraft. The initial thrust by Graziani along the road to Egypt was repulsed and a successful British counter-offensive drove the Italians out of Cyrenaica. It was only at this point that Hitler was forced to commit German air forces to a second front to redeem the disasters of his ally's independent policy.[63]

The British reaction to the new threat was to build up the supply of aircraft and equipment to produce an aerial defence similar to the one that had worked so well in England in the autumn of 1940. By September 1941 more fighters were available in Egypt than had been available in England at the beginning of the Battle of Britain. Moreover the Italian and German air forces continued to be considerably under-supplied. For East Africa only 75 additional aircraft were made available for the Italian air forces in the period from June 1940 to the end of the campaign. Some 250 aircraft were destroyed in the area and the remaining 200 were unserviceable owing to a shortage of parts, fuel and trained maintenance men.[64] In North Africa on the eve of Graziani's offensive, General Porro had approximately 300 serviceable combat aircraft of all types which were rapidly whittled away through poor supply, maintenance and non-combat wastage.[65] Very little new material was made available from Italy. The disparity in numbers also rendered the impact of the Luftwaffe Fliegerkorps X increasingly half-hearted and ineffective. The British emphasis on supply and material superiority was underlined by the importance in overall strategy attached to the long air supply route to the Middle East and to the improvement in the maintenance of those aircraft that arrived at their destination. In both respects the RAF emerged in 1941 with a considerable advantage over the Axis powers that laid the foundation for the successful capture of air superiority in 1942. A special route for aircraft deliveries was established across Africa from Takoradi in the Gold Coast, a route that provided a defensible lifeline for the Egyptian air forces and released valuable shipping space for the supply of valuable fuel and spare parts by the longer route around the Cape.[66] The realization that many of the new aircraft remained grounded for want of parts or proper maintenance prompted the RAF to establish a Maintenance Group responsible directly to the area commander-in-chief, in charge of maintenance, repair, salvage and stores. The group was given wide responsibilities along the lines of the Maintenance Command set up in Britain to such good effect. As a result not only were more aircraft available to the RAF than to the enemy, but the level of serviceability was also much higher.[67]

Yet despite the success in building up supplies, in containing the Luftwaffe in the Mediterranean and in breaking Italian air power, the British were unable to bring about the speedy defeat of Rommel. His success in the desert was certainly not due to air supremacy; far from it. The Luftwaffe had had little time to plan for a southern campaign and few resources could be diverted to it away from the main campaign in Russia. Ground organization was poor in the Balkans. There were very few long-range bombers, which were essential to bring effective damage to the British military build-up in Egypt. Hitler's enthusiastic directives to the Luftwaffe betrayed an ignorance of its true capability.[68] Nursing wounds from the failure of the Blitz, and engaged from June onwards in Russia, the bomber forces were in no condition to provide large numbers of pilots or aircraft for hurried strategic tasks in the south. The main aircraft, the Ju 88, was unsuitable for long-range operations and was a fairly limited weapon against small and scattered targets which were increasingly well-defended by modern fighter aircraft. This was certainly the case in the attacks on Malta which took a heavy toll of Luftwaffe aircraft for little military advantage.[69] There were other problems too, not least being the need to co-ordinate Italian and German air planning as well as to integrate air activity into the wider campaign. Neither enterprise was particularly successful, partly because the German and Italian commanders had different priorities. Hitler had achieved his minimum aim in the south with the final explusion of British forces from Crete. Italian commanders wanted to drive the British out of North Africa and recapture the empire, and although resentful of having to co-operate with German forces were also anxious that Germany should divert more effort southward. Instead Hitler took a new initiative, as he had intended, and moved eastwards.

Hitler's seizure of a fresh initiative, determined upon even before the Battle of Britain had begun, had substantial repercussions on the air war. The main task in 1941 for the Luftwaffe was the winning of supremacy over the Russian battlefront. The Mediterranean front was a subsidiary and diversionary campaign. Britain could not strike effectively at Hitler in isolation in Egypt or from the British mainland in the foreseeable future. Hitler intended to return to the destruction of British resistance after the short and successful campaign planned for the east. He also intended that the main weight of the attack on Britain should be borne by the air forces, centred around a new force of heavy bombers planned for 1942.[70] The attack on Russia was planned according to the experiences of 1939 and 1940 and almost all aircraft were diverted to tactical support of the German armies. The German strategic view was a gamble that Britain would be unable to interfere with German plans in any important way before German forces were once again able to concentrate in the west. Yet this gamble overlooked the fact that Britain's own war effort in 1941 depended upon the degree to which Hitler was occupied elsewhere. The Russian invasion made it clear that Hitler would not turn west in 1941 and freed British forces for reinforcement in the Middle East and for the build-up of large offensive and defensive air forces at home.

The British emphasis on air power in general in fact coincided with a shift on the German side to an emphasis on armies and the growth of a purely tactical air force, and further strengthened, in a relative sense, the one weapon for blockade and attack which British forces were able to use at that stage of the war. In the Middle East air supremacy passed to the RAF not long after the invasion of Russia and little effort was made to recapture it. Britain was able to draw more extensively on American aid as well. By July 1941 Britain was planning for an air force of 62½ squadrons in the Middle East with initial equipment of 1,046 aircraft. By mid-October 52 of the squadrons were already in being with a strength of 846 aircraft and substantial repair and maintenance facilities. Fliegerkorps X, on the other hand, was starved of aircraft as the Russian front expanded. Total strength varied between 400 and 450 aircraft, of which only about 250 were serviceable at any one time—a figure that included only about 30 single-engined fighters.[71] This situation was due not just to production priorities in the Reich. The German maintenance network was improvised, and the crews under a heavy strain of fighting throughout the summer of 1941 with insufficient replacements. The Italian commitment was even more meagre. Having lost all the aircraft in East Africa, the North African air force contained only 210 aircraft by the late summer of 1941. There were in addition some 83 Italian aircraft in the Aegean area with a low rate of serviceability.[72]

The only thing that prevented the RAF from exploiting the local advantage was the fact that the loss of Greece, Crete and Cyrenaica had reduced the number of good air bases from which to be able to strike effectively at the Axis powers from the air. A large number of aircraft helped to safeguard Egypt and the Canal but did not necessarily make it possible to accelerate the return to the offensive in North Africa and the seizure of the new air bases. Only the army could do this and until better co-ordination had been established between army and air force the amount of aid that the RAF could directly bring to bear on army operations was also limited. Nevertheless the time allowed to Britain to reinforce and prepare for taking the initiative meant that when Hitler had defeated Russia, as he expected, he would be compelled to act defensively in the west against the bombing offensive and against British forces in the Mediterranean before being able to complete the air attacks which he still believed held the key to forcing Britain's surrender.

(iv) Air Power and War 1939–41

The impact of aircraft on the war in the first two years was both less decisive and less terrible than had been expected before 1939. In combination with the army the Luftwaffe had confirmed that tactical support was an essential component for ground offensives. If there had been any doubt about such a conclusion it was dispelled in 1939 and 1940. But in many other respects the impact of air power was disappointing and the air theory out of touch with operational reality.

The early air campaigns showed that the exercise of air power was subject to a number of specific constraints. First of all the amount of actual preparation for air operations, particularly with aero-naval warfare or with independent bombing, was well below what was required for their successful prosecution. The same was true of air defence; whether in France in 1940 or in Italian

Africa in 1941 it was generally deficient. A second constraint was a technological one. To carry out what air doctrine required involved a degree of scientific advance and of quality in design not yet available. This was true for those air forces without advanced fighters and radar and for those air forces, like the RAF, that would have liked to bomb more effectively but were unable to because of poor bomber performance, poor navigation and a lack of long-range fighters. Technical improvements were certainly taking place all the time but not at a sufficient pace to overcome the operational difficulties.

Another constraint was the supply of aircraft. Pre-war air theory had largely avoided the difficult questions concerning the appropriate level of supply to sustain air power. Yet it was this question that proved to be vital in the first years of war. This was not a question of sheer numbers alone, but also of aircraft quality, and of repair and maintenance as well. Thus the RAF, although numerically smaller, had a defensive system advanced enough in 1940 to prevent the Luftwaffe from using its large size to advantage. But on the whole it was numbers of aircraft that counted. This was even true for the Battle of Britain where the British concentration on aircraft production, and fighter production in particular, produced not only a qualitative but also a quantitative advantage by the end of the battle. It was obviously true in the Battle of France, the battles in Africa and the campaign at sea. The RAF in particular relied on numerical superiority. Other virtues such as good training and high courage were also necessary but they were by no means confined only to the RAF. British production plans gave a guaranteed supply of the most modern aircraft running for much of the period at a rate almost twice that of Germany. German plans remained not only underfulfilled but at a level not far above the level achieved in peace-time at least until the end of 1941. Nor did Italian production help. It was heavily reliant on unwilling German assistance and was frustrated by a higher degree of economic backwardness. Nor, it should be added, was British aircraft production at the expense of other kinds of war production. In almost all the major weapons categories Britain produced more than Germany.[73] This situation helped to achieve some degree of air superiority and to immunize Britain from Axis invasion, even it it could not yet produce air strategies for successful offence.

It was on the question of what was an appropriate strategy for air power that the early experience of war had the greatest impact. It has already been shown that before 1939 a dichotomy was developing between those air forces favouring limited, tactical air power and those favouring a more general air power.* Such a dichotomy became explicit in the first two years of war. The reasons for such a dichotomy were to be found in the different expectations of air power and in different strategic circumstances. In Germany the army had considerable influence over strategy and the Luftwaffe was obliged, and not unwillingly, to relate air doctrine and air operations to the needs of the army. The actual course of the war did nothing to alter this emphasis, but only to confirm it. During the brief period between August and October 1940 when the Luftwaffe attempted to carry out an air strategy on its own the results were disappointing enough to return the air force to its subordinate role once again for the invasion of Russia. In the other main strategic areas, in air defence and the war at sea, the

*See above pp. 16–18.

Luftwaffe was also influenced strongly by strategic circumstances. There was little serious attempt by the British to breach German defences before 1941 and so little effort was devoted to building up such a defence. In the war at sea the lack of clear objectives and Goering's personal hostility towards it combined to reduce the air component of the campaign to a mere fraction of what the navy wanted. Moreover Hitler's whole strategy was centred on the army and the continental war. An independent air force campaign against Britain was seized upon only briefly as a panacea for the strategic impasse of late 1940, but on the whole air power remained of secondary importance in Hitler's calculations and suffered as a result in the amount of strategic energy that was devoted to its problems.

In Britain, on the other hand, air power was a central feature of strategy. There were certainly disappointments in the way in which air power performed in the first eighteen months of war, but these were used to inspire the RAF to greater efforts rather than to persuade the Chiefs of Staff to abandon the general exercise of air power. British strategy had different conditions from that of Germany. The importance of air defence was obvious. The need for aircraft for the war at sea in ever-increasing numbers was again apparent from an early stage of the war. But the central decision to retain a strategic bombing capability as the only way to strike back at Germany for several years, was not compromised either by the failure of German bombing or the poor operational performance of Bomber Command. Finally the lesson drawn from the battle of France and the campaigns in Norway and the Balkans was not that the RAF should simply become an adjunct of the army, but that the RAF should be allowed to expand numbers greatly to cope with all the general requirements of air strategy at the same time. Thus a combination of strategic circumstance and the doctrinal legacy of the Trenchard period brought the RAF to a realization of the character of a general air strategy, and of the interdependence of its component parts.

The existence of a general air strategy side by side with the more limited air strategy of the Axis powers by no means suggested that the former was superior to the latter. In fact the limited use of air power, with its concentration of large forces on a limited objective, was conspicuously more successful in Continental warfare than its general counterpart in the period up to 1941. But what it did mean was that limited air power could not easily be adapted to the defeat of general air power. This meant that Britain could not be defeated in 1940 because the Luftwaffe could not eliminate its air force. It meant that the air blockade of British trade could not be successfully carried on in the face of British counter-measures in the air. Finally it meant that the Luftwaffe was forced to abandon any serious long-term effort to mount a bombing offensive. Even if a general air strategy had not yet been produced capable of any decisive effect it did not mean, as the period after 1942 was to demonstrate, that a general strategy could never be made to work.

3

The European Air War 1941–45

The year 1941 was a watershed for the development of the air war in Europe. Before that date there had already been several major battles fought with aircraft and the expectation from the exercise of air power had been high. By early 1941 it was obvious that air power had been greatly exaggerated. Not only had no knock-out blow been successful, no combatant had yet produced an air force equal to the task of inflicting it. All the significant gains in the war had been the result of conventional land warfare. The difficulties experienced in waging the kind of air war that both sides wanted to wage were compounded with shortages of supply on the one hand and technical shortcomings on the other. This was the explanation for the sustained development of the limited use of air power by both German and Soviet forces on the eastern front. Since both sides agreed that little more could be gained by using aircraft in different roles the air war was confined to the massive support of ground offensives. The problem for Germany was that the Allied forces did not agree to a limited view of air warfare. From 1941 onwards the Axis powers were fighting two different air wars, and to the general air war in the west they paid too little attention until it was too late to convert their own air forces to a general strategy too. Luftwaffe co-operation with the army was still of great significance for the land war, but the lack of attention in doctrine, strategy and preparation given to air defence, bombing and the naval war paved the way not only for the Allied victory in the air but for the land victory as well.

(i) Air War on the Eastern Front

On the eastern front the exercise of air power was confined on both sides to the limited role in support of ground armies. In Hitler's case this was a result of his conviction that the Luftwaffe was only capable of working decisively in co-operation with the army. In Soviet Russia it was because the use of tactical air power was Stalin's own brainchild, brooking no rivals. Although both sides had prepared in a limited way for some long-range bombing activity the bulk of air operations were in direct support of ground forces and in the winning of air superiority over the battlefield. For the Luftwaffe this made the task of preparation relatively straightforward. In the attack on Russia it was intended to use the same combination of air and tank power that had been used in the West.

An additional advantage was to be won by achieving an element of surprise against forces that German intelligence continually underrated numerically. So much so that Hitler ordered part of the air force to remain on the defensive in the Reich, and part to continue the attack on English trade at the same time as the attack on Russia.[1] Added to the expanding air commitment in the Balkans and North Africa, Hitler was prepared to undertake an assault in the east with heavily dispersed air forces fighting on three or four fronts at once. In the attack itself the air force was ordered to support the Central and Southern sectors and to eliminate the effectiveness of the Red Air Force there. German confidence lay not only with their own battle experience but with estimates that total Red Air Force strength was only 5,500 aircraft of poor quality; that pilot training was well below standards set in the Luftwaffe; and that the Soviet aircraft industry was small, strategically vulnerable and relatively inefficient.[2]

Some of these impressions of the Soviet Air Force were, to be sure, not unfounded. It was known that large formations of uncamouflaged and undispersed fighter aircraft were stationed on often inadequate airfields close to the frontier openly inviting the kind of massive first strike that the Luftwaffe planned. These represented fundamental tactical errors on the Soviet side.[3] It was also known that the quality of Russian aircraft was well below that of Germany, although Russian air forces were in the process of being converted to more modern types as the Luftwaffe had itself been converted in 1939-40. What was underestimated was the production and technical potential of the Soviet aircraft industry and the Russian ability to improvise and reorganize the structure of air forces under the circumstances of a sudden and devastating attack.

The first miscalculation was the more serious one. The Luftwaffe wanted to win supremacy over a wide and increasingly deep battle zone through operations 'to paralyse and eliminate the effectiveness of the Russian Air Force as far as possible'.[4] The directives to the Luftwaffe, however, failed to include any instructions for follow-up attacks to deny the Red Air Force the opportunity to mount a counter-offensive or to continue to reinforce itself from internal supply lines. The 'paralysing' of the Red Air Force was only a short-term objective. The longer-term objectives remained undefined. All subsequent directives indicated Hitler's failure to understand that the winning of air mastery was a continuous operation and that against an enemy like Soviet Russia the 'knock-out blow' was as inappropriate as it had been against Britain in 1940. Hitler obviously hoped that air command would last long enough to allow the army's Blitzkrieg to succeed, but such success was not strategically inevitable. As a result of his exaggerated belief in the invincibility of German forces insufficient attention was paid to longer-term strategy or to other contingencies. Since Soviet air strength had been underestimated the need for alternative air strategies was all the more pressing. When it came to the air force, however, Hitler lacked strategic imagination, preferring to use it in close support of the army whose strategy he more fully understood and even to the extent of denying the air force the same degree of freedom in choosing objectives not directly related to the battlefield than it had had in the battle of France and the preparations for Sealion.[5]

Had the true state of Russian air preparation been known, German air strategy might have been different. Even without this knowledge Hitler was placing undue faith in the ability of air forces to inflict a knockout blow against the Red Air Force, given the size of the Luftwaffe in the East. As it was Russian air rearmament had expanded rapidly. German intelligence estimated that some 5,000 aircraft per annum were produced in 1939 and 1940. In fact Russian sources show that 10,382 were produced in 1939 and 10,565 in 1940.[6] In 1941 Russian air forces in the west, including reserves, probably numbered up to 10,000 aircraft, supported by an average monthly production in 1941 of 1,311 aircraft.[7] By mid-1941 some 3,700 of the new aircraft models had been produced and the conversion from existing obsolescent types was well under way, although most of the aircraft stationed at the frontier were older types. The new fighters, Yak-1, MiG-3 and LaGG-3, were technically a significant improvement on the I-153 and I-16 and they were produced in large quantities in the early months of the campaign. In the period up to June some 1,946 were produced. From July to December some 5,173 of the new fighters were produced. These figures compared very favourably with the 1,619 Luftwaffe fighters produced over the same period for all fronts, or even the 4,408 produced for the RAF. These fighters were supported in addition by the new Il-2 ground-attack aircraft of which 1,293 were produced in the second half of 1941 and which proved to be a very effective dive-bomber kept in production for almost the whole of the war. The bulk of the very many Russian aircraft destroyed in June 1941 were therefore already obsolete, the Luftwaffe simply completing a job that was already being carried out by the Red Air Force itself. For the later desperate defence of Moscow and around Smolensk the Russians were able to call on largely new types produced at the rate of four aircraft for every one German.[7]

For the early stages of the war in the east the supply situation did not, admittedly, seem critical for the Luftwaffe. The air force did exactly what was expected of it. Huge numbers of Russian aircraft were destroyed on the ground. German estimates claimed the destruction of 4,017 Russian aircraft in the first week of operations. The Russians themselves admitted total losses of 5,316 by 5 October.[8] Having achieved initial mastery over the frontier area Luftwaffe units were sent to help the main army offensives and in particular the central and southern fronts. The Luftwaffe did not regard Soviet air tactics as more than rudimentary. Hitler's gamble appeared to have paid off. By October an apparently demoralized and ineffective Red Air Force could do little to prevent the progress of German armies. Yet by the end of the year a combination of an early winter and growing Red Army and Air Force resistance brought the wide offensive to an end. Not only did the failure to defeat Russia in three months leave the German armies unprepared for winter fighting, it left the Luftwaffe in great difficulties too. There had been little effective strategic appreciation of what should be done beyond the immediate plan; little or no operational preparation for such a contingency; and—having regard to the expected conditions of a Russian winter—incomprehensibly few technical preparations for fighting in sub-zero temperatures. No amount of good training or tactical superiority could make up for poor planning and preparation. By the end of 1941 the Luftwaffe was actually being held before Moscow as were the German armies, and the relief of the Demyansk pocket from the air, although ultimately successful, was a Pyrrhic victory, for the Luftwaffe had to overstrain and waste resources that were needed for more vital strategic tasks elsewhere.[9]

By December it was clear that the initial demands made of the Luftwaffe in

Hitler's strategy were far greater than its resources could bear. By Dec. 1941 the serviceable strength of all Luftwaffe units in Russia amounted to 500 aircraft. Russia still had over 1,000 aircraft on the Moscow front alone.[10] One basic reason why the German air force failed to achieve decisive air supremacy in 1941 lay in the problems of supply and maintenance. Not that this was a new problem. During the attack on England in 1940 there had been a growing shortage of aircraft. Even though the strategic demands expanded continuously, throughout the first half of 1941 aircraft production remained at the same level. Luftwaffe strength actually declined from a peak reached in March 1940 as the following table indicates.

Table 4: German Air Force Strength March 1940—March 1942[11]

Date	Strength	Date	Strength
March 1940	3,692	June 1941	3,451
June 1940	3,327	September 1941	3,561
September 1940	3,015	December 1941	2,561
December 1940	3,050	March 1942	2,872
March 1941	3,583		

Moreover German air resources had to be divided between three combat fronts. Those in the west and the Mediterranean faced a numerous and technically well-armed opponent and required that sufficient forces be kept for meeting the British threat. By contrast Soviet units could be used almost exclusively for the crucial battles on the eastern front.

There were a number of reasons for the poor supply situation. Part of the problem stemmed from the fact that Hitler gave economic priority to the army. When he finally directed that the war economy be re-orientated to meet the needs of the Luftwaffe and navy this was to begin only after the achievement of 'military mastery of the European continent'.[12] The failure to gain such mastery by the end of 1941 thus postponed the strategic conversion of the economy to air force tasks. The problems went deeper than that, however. Even during the period when the air force had economic priority, after the fall of France, nothing was done to switch actual production to air force requirements. In fact production went down.[13] The main problem lay at the planning stage. Every major combatant laid down high targets for aircraft production from the early stages of the war except Germany who for two years produced at only just above peace-time levels. A failure to co-ordinate military and industrial strategy combined with excessive overconfidence on the part of Goering and woefully inadequate technical staff at the Air Ministry produced a situation in which only modest targets were set. These in turn failed to be met by the producers because of poor preparation and formulation of demands from the Luftwaffe staff. Instead of setting high targets and then developing the industry and resources to meet them, Udet and Goering asked industry what it could currently produce and then tailored demands to meet these calculations.

In addition the communications gap between Hitler and his air force was extraordinary. Only a low-ranking air force officer worked at the Supreme Headquarters and co-operation between the three services at the highest level was often non-existent.[14] Had air production been set more firmly into a wider organizational or political framework such difficulties might have been avoided.

Its relative isolation under the jealous guardianship of Goering led to a growing gap in the early years of war between Hitler's demands and actual air strength. Hitler had demanded a fivefold increase in the air forces in 1938 but had not pursued his demand which in consequence went largely ignored. When Hitler returned to the question of air force supply in mid-1941 he demanded to know what had happened in the interval. The fact was that Goering told Hitler one story and his staff another; boasting of production successes to Hitler but recognizing with his technical staff the impossibility of meeting requirements in the existing economic circumstances. It was not until 1941 when the Luftwaffe was demonstrably under-supplied that Hitler intervened to turn the problem into a crisis.[15] By then, however, it was too late to do anything effective for at least a year. New production capacity would take time to set up. In fact Germany was not to start producing at the same rate as Russia until mid-1944 by which time the additional aircraft were of much less strategic use. Had Hitler's initial requirement been met, however, then the Luftwaffe would have been a much more formidable enemy both in the Battle of Britain and on the eastern front.

As it was the situation of regular battle attrition that set in from June onwards was precisely the sort of situation that the Luftwaffe needed to avoid. The Russians were particularly anxious to conserve where possible and deliberately put up a weak defence in some places in the knowledge that a particular area or battle was not likely to be decisive. Even by the end of July the Luftwaffe was reduced to 1,045 serviceable machines on the whole of the eastern front.[16] By December this was reduced to 500 machines. The supply of the Demyansk pocket promised by Goering although successful swallowed valuable air resources at this critical moment in air supply. During this operation some 262 Ju 52 transport and supply aircraft were lost at a time when annual production was running at just 500 a year, and in addition training schools and factories in the Reich had been combed for pilots and transport aircraft for the emergency.[17]

The difficulty in the supply of German aircraft was made worse by the fact that even those aircraft that were available to the Luftwaffe could not be used because of poor servicing and repair. There were a number of reasons why the Luftwaffe found itself in such difficulties. First of all the front changed so rapidly and the Russians destroyed installations so systematically that it was difficult to provide adequate maintenance facilities near the front. In fact many of the damaged aircraft had to be transported back to Germany to await repair by an aircraft industry already overstrained by shortages of labour. Secondly the temporary airfields that had to be constructed were often based simply on rough grassland which proved as hazardous to aircraft as enemy action, particularly as there was often poor communication due to the enormous demands made on the signals regiments in getting radio and telephone links set up in sub-zero temperatures.[18] Moreover the sheer number of such airfields constituted a major task in itself. One *Luftgau* (air administrative district) completed 105 airfields in the course of the 1941 campaign. Another problem was an organizational one. The job of supply and maintenance was given to Air Administrative Commands (*Luftgaukommandos*) that were run by low-ranking ex-First World War officers (*Ergänzungsoffiziere*) brought back into active service in a reserve capacity. They had little technical training or aptitude for the tasks but much enthusiasm.[19] The problem was exacerbated by the creation of Special Duty staffs recruited from among these ex-officers to act as mobile units to help 'maintain and supply Luftwaffe units, equip the Luftwaffe ground organization, provide for initial repair of captured airfields . . .'. All air stations were required to provide one or two of its officers for such special duties and the temptation was to rid the station of unpopular and unwanted men whose technical competence for such a crucial task was often very low.[20] State Secretary Milch helped to ease the situation a little by insisting that groups of skilled engineers be recruited for the maintenance part of the task, but this meant denuding aircraft firms in the Reich of personnel and led to pressure from these firms for their return.[21] Not until much later in the war did the repair and maintenance programme receive the same priority it enjoyed in Britain and Russia.

The final problem was a thoroughly self-made one. Just as the Battle of Britain had suffered from the shortage of operational preparation and planning and the strategic miscalculations of the Luftwaffe high command, so the preparations for fighting a protracted war in Russia were conspicuously inadequate. Admittedly Milch and Seidel, the Luftwaffe Quartermaster-General, had made preparations to provide the air force alone of all the services with winter clothing.[22] But proper preparations or appreciation of a situation of fighting in sub-zero temperatures had not been done, nor had the supreme command provided a satisfactory strategic framework within which such preparations could be properly anticipated. The Luftwaffe, like the army, finally ground to a halt in late 1941 because of the technical shortcomings in coping with cold. Cold-start methods proved entirely inadequate so that by January 1942 only 15 per cent of the Luftwaffe's 100,000 vehicles at the front were in use while many aircraft were grounded for lack of the parts and equipment that such vehicles should have carried.[23] The complicated cold-start equipment could not be operated in such low temperatures and more practical methods first pioneered by the Luftwaffe some years before were only first publicized in October 1941 and did not become War Office policy until November. The Quartermaster-General was still issuing explanatory leaflets as late as February 1942 while aircraft were being flown straight from the Mediterranean theatre to Russia without winter protective equipment.[24] This was still happening the following winter, too, despite the experience of the first. At one of the key airfields supplying Stalingrad the only vehicle available for heating up engines was used instead to thaw out mechanics frozen fast to the machinery on which they were working.[25] Under circumstances such as these serviceability was bound to fall off. By January 1943 the serviceability rate in the east was below 25 per cent.[26]

By contrast with production and supply, Luftwaffe military organization had been relatively successful. The absence of sufficient aircraft had been compensated for in part by the good tactical use to which supplies had been put on the battlefield. This meant that the considerable numerical advantage enjoyed by the Red Air Force could not be fully exploited. It also meant that as neither side could achieve mastery over the battlefront, the war in the east became primarily a struggle between opposing armies supported to a rather poor degree by air forces, at least until conditions changed and Russian numbers finally overwhelmed those of the Luftwaffe.

The situation was the reverse with the Russian air force. Supply and maintenance were better than could have been expected under the circumstances but tactical deployment and military organization had been shown to be deficient. The winter of 1941-42 saw substantial reforms. The reforms began right at the top in the creation of the State Committee for Defence on which Malenkov represented air affairs. Below this committee, whose work, like the British cabinet, combined military, political and civil affairs, was a new supreme command (*Stavka*) that was directly responsible for authorizing the strategic use of aircraft. At a lower level the close and often inflexible organization of army and air force units was replaced by a new system of air armies consisting of mixed aircraft types with an air army commander directly subordinate to the army group commander at the front on major questions of tactical deployment, and to the C in C and *Stavka* for the strategic movement of air armies from one situation to another as the course of fighting dictated. Where previously each army had had its own air division and an inadequate hierarchy of command between the front and Moscow, a satisfactory way had been found to move aircraft quickly to where they were wanted and to guarantee a high degree of co-operation with army groups once they were there.[27] To facilitate such co-operation even more a system was finally developed in which each air-army commander placed a deputy commander and staff at the front to work closely with the army units whose headquarters would be either the same or be close enough to ensure constant direct contact.[28]

In addition to the reorganization of tactical air forces, *Stavka* created three strategic forces and a service maintenance command directly subordinate to the central command. The first was a strategic reserve consisting of special corps of one type of aircraft (fighter, ground-attack, etc.) which could be switched from one front or battle to another as need arose. This reserve in fact constituted some 43 per cent of all available tactical air forces by the end of the war. The second was a long-range bomber arm (ADD) set up in April 1942 for special strategic tasks on the battlefront and the third was a fighter defence force (PVO) modelled on the fighter defences set up in Britain before 1940.[29] These arrangements avoided the difficulty of having an army air force primarily concerned with army support and so unable to see aircraft use in a wider strategic context.

The Red Air Force also tried to solve the problem of maintenance that had plagued the Luftwaffe. First of all a senior officer was given the main task of coping with the necessary administration. Under commander-in-chief Novikov, who was appointed in early 1942, were seven major deputies one of whom was designated Head of Rear Services and another Head of the Engineering-Technical Service.[30] This gave a necessary prominence to questions of supply in the overall command structure. These deputies set up special staffs to cope with servicing and supply and both had to co-operate in establishing Air Basing Regions (RAB). Each RAB served the equivalent of an air corps in size and contained six to eight airfield servicing battalions. These would also work closely with the mobile repair workshops set up under the Head of the Engineering Service. The job of these groups was simple; to keep as many aircraft as possible operational and to report on the effectiveness of all newly supplied equipment. By integrating the organization into the overall military structure and by giving top priority ranking to those who headed the supply services the Red Air Force avoided the danger of losing initiatives through poor serviceability.[31]

The most important reforms came, however, in the sphere of strategic and tactical doctrines of aircraft use. While continuing to support the principle of giving priority to the tactical support of the army, even subordinating the long-range bomber force to this aim, the Red Air Force staff placed great emphasis on the need for operational flexibility and concentration of forces. These were traditional principles of warfare but airmen needed to learn them. Instead of dispersing effort, forces were conserved and concentrated before being used in the main offensive. Instead, too, of committing all units to a fixed position at the front, *Stavka*'s control of a large reserve gave flexibility in placing operational priority at certain points along the front. This did not necessarily guarantee permanent air supremacy but it would help to give local and temporary supremacy for a particular battle.[32] These were lessons that could have been learned from the Luftwaffe in 1940, though the growing dispersion of German air forces compelled the Luftwaffe itself to abandon the degree of concentration that had been possible in the early Blitzkrieg and eventually to sacrifice flexibility as well. Other lessons were well-learned too. Steps were taken to ensure that Russian air bases were sufficiently camouflaged while the rear areas contained a system of staggered airfields consisting of hundreds of small temporary air strips near the front with larger operational bases some 40–60 kilometres behind the front, well dispersed to avoid enemy action.[33] As the war drew on the Soviet Air Force elaborated its flexible concentration of air forces into a doctrine of the 'air offensive'.

The air offensive had two purposes. The first was to prepare the way for a ground attack by massive preparatory strikes against enemy airfields and supplies. The second was to give immediate support in large concentrations of aircraft to the ground armies, accompanied where necessary by attacks on tactical targets in the enemy rear. The tactics were designed specifically for aircraft. The fighters were given 'their choice to attack targets in whatever manner they wished', and were not confined to the direct battle area. In fact the fighter aircraft were encouraged to carry on the combat with the enemy air force over the enemy bases and before enemy aircraft reached Soviet lines. The balance between attacks on the enemy air force and defence of Soviet ground troops in the advance was to be decided through a highly centralized control of operations.[34] Soviet sources after the war calculated that some 35 per cent of all sorties were flown for the purposes of achieving control over the battlefield, 46.5 per cent in support of ground troops. Of those sorties flown by the long-range bombers operating near the front, some 43 per cent were flown against enemy troop formations on the battlefield.[35] This huge concentration of effort on the battlefront complemented the strategic aim of the Red Army, i.e. the destruction of enemy armed forces on the battlefield, a task that was helped considerably by the fact that the eastern combat zone was a shallow one, allowing maximum effect for the kind of air war that the Soviet supreme command chose to wage.

It took much longer for levels of training to be improved and for air force morale to be restored, although by the middle of the winter of 1941–42 morale on both sides was low. The Luftwaffe had suffered the additional problem of losing a very large number of the skilled and experienced pilots of 1939 and 1940 often through accident—Mölders, hero of the 1940 battles, was killed flying back to Ernst Udet's funeral—and at such a rate that by the summer of 1942 flying instructors and test pilots were being drafted in to work at the front. Soviet aircraft losses had been high but because so many aircraft had been hit on the ground, their crews had survived. During the early months of the summer campaign of 1942, however, the Luftwaffe, though now considerably inferior in numbers, was able to continue to operate successfully due to better training and marginally better aircraft.[36] This was not, of course, an advantage that was likely to last. Tactical and technical superiority was slowly eroded by improvements in Russian aircraft and tactics. Luftwaffe successes reflected, too, the fact that the German army offensive towards the Caucasus was regarded by Stalin and his staff as a diversion and that the main offensive of 1942 would be launched in the centre. Thus in accordance with Soviet strategy army and air force units were kept back in reserve and the minimum forces necessary kept in the south.[37] Even though this mistake was realized in the end and the German advance finally halted, the delay in deploying all available units in the south played into Russian hands. The Luftwaffe continued to be heavily undersupplied and wore out what supplies there were in the southern attack. The assault on Sevastopol, for example, saw the loss of 300 German aircraft for the loss of 77 Soviet.[38] Elsewhere, however, the Luftwaffe was facing heavy Soviet concentrations of aircraft in readiness for the expected renewed German attack on Moscow and Leningrad and had to disperse its own forces in case of a Russian counterstrike. During the course of 1942 Russian control of the air was achieved over the Leningrad-Bryansk front and when a Soviet counter-offensive was successfully launched to create the Kursk salient there were 2,000 Russian aircraft massed against 400 German.[39] By this time, however, the German forces were heavily committed in the Stalingrad region. Of the 3,950 aircraft with which the Luftwaffe had begun the summer campaign in 1942 only 1,600 were left by the end of the year for the whole front.[40]

When the Soviet counter-offensive was finally launched it was to prove the first vindication of the new Soviet doctrine of the air offensive. The 8th Air Army supporting Stalingrad had a total of 1,414 aircraft for the attack and inflicted heavy losses on an already tired and increasingly demoralized German force. The relief of Stalingrad from the air, a promise made by Goering for political rather than strategic reasons, proved to be the disaster that the air commanders on the spot had predicted. The 490 transport and bomber aircraft lost in the operation represented a rate of attrition that could only be supported by a very significant increase in aircraft production at home.[41] But whereas Russia was able to produce 25,000 aircraft in 1942 for one main front, Germany only produced 15,000 for three major fronts, including a growing number of defence aircraft for the Reich itself. By the winter of 1942-43 the question of numbers had once again become a vital one. In the Russian attack at Kursk the Soviet armies enjoyed at times a superiority in fighter aircraft of as much as 10 : 1. Moreover it was precisely at this time that improvements in Soviet tactical training were reaching fruition. Methods copied from the Germans were adopted for fighter and ground-attack aircraft. A special *Guide for Interceptor Operations* was published in December 1942 and the final form of the 'air offensive' was published in the *Infantry Military Manual* for November.[42] It was also the time when the qualitative gap was finally closed. The less successful MiG-3, Pe-8, Yak-4 and Su-2 went out of production in order to concentrate on the Il-2, Il-4, Pe-2 and the improved LaGG and Yak fighters. The temporary improvement of the Luftwaffe's position with the introduction of the Me 109G and FW 190 was finally eroded in the course of 1943.

The task of the German air force in Russia would have been made considerably easier had it not been for the fact that the Western Allies, in lieu of a second front, promised to divert the Luftwaffe by air attacks in the west. Churchill tried to reassure Stalin from the start of the German invasion that bombing could have important strategic implications for the war in the east. On 28 June he wrote to Stalin that 'a terrible winter of bombing lies before Germany. No one has yet had what they are going to get'. In September the same commitment was given; the best way to help Soviet forces was to tie down German air power in the west and to bomb the industrial sources of German war material.[43] Stalin and the Soviet commanders retained a strong scepticism about the possibilities of doing anything decisive with bombing, particularly as the British placed greatest emphasis on the prospect of an internal German political collapse. Churchill was writing to Roosevelt at the same time that 'we must subject Germany and Italy to a ceaseless and ever growing air bombardment. These measures may themselves produce an internal convulsion and collapse.'[44] When America entered the war in 1941 strategic assistance from air activity in the west became a central part of Anglo-American strategy. The British resolved early in 1942 that in the absence of any ability to open a second land front in Europe air activity in the west would help 'in taking the weight off Russia during the summer'.[45] Churchill even promised to open a gas bombing campaign against the Reich if a single gas attack were carried out on the Soviet Union, backing up his promise with the secret information that 'I have been building up an immense stock of gas bombs for discharge from aircraft . . .'.[46] Despite Stalin's protests the air initiatives remained the major contribution made to aiding Russia between June 1941 and the final invasion of Italy in late 1943. At Casablanca the final reports directed that help for Russia was of top priority in the course of 1943 and the western air forces were directed to 'take every opportunity to attack Germany by day, to contain German fighter strength away from the Russian and Mediterranean theatres of war'.[47] The result was that Germany was forced to keep large air defence forces in the Mediterranean and in defence of the Reich from bombing. Between February 1943 and February 1944 the ratio of fighters between the western and eastern fronts rose from 2:1 to 3.5:1. This dispersion of effort forced upon the Luftwaffe meant that even though German aircraft output increased from 15,000 in 1942 to 25,000 in 1943 hardly any additional forces could be diverted to the eastern front and the Red Air Force was finally able to gain air supremacy over wide areas in the east.

In addition to strategic assistance, which was bound to take time to materialize and which the Soviet leaders regarded as of little consequence, the Western Allies were prepared to give Russia supplies as well. Even though British resources were considerably stretched in 1941 and 1942 it was agreed that more efficient use could be made of fighter aircraft in Russia until such time that the Luftwaffe would be in a position to return the attack on England. Hence supplies of modern fighters, mainly Hurricanes, were sent from 1941 onwards, soon to be joined by a much larger stream of American Lend-Lease aid. By 1945 over 14,000 American aircraft had been dispatched to Russia, together with large stocks of aluminium and machinery to build more.[49] Despite protests that the material for Lend-Lease would be better employed at home, the Allies' purpose was as much a political one as a military one. It was a sign of good faith on the part of Britain and the United States that they were willing to continue the war, and also an affirmation of the strategic necessity of keeping Russia fighting. It was perhaps because a belligerent Russia was such a transparent necessity to

Anglo-American strategy that much of the technical and material aid was received by the Soviet Union with such ill grace.

However, Russian aircraft production was itself providing large quantities of material by the time Allied aid became available, and although both direct and indirect aid was useful, Russia's own success in the air was real enough. In fact the major bombing offensive and Mediterranean campaign promised by the Allies did not begin until the spring and summer of 1943 and by then the Red Air Force had achieved a high degree of control in the air over the battlefronts on its own. The Luftwaffe was still able to gain control for a short period of time over a limited area, particularly when air forces were concentrated as they were for the assault on Kursk. But this tended to be in the nature of the tactical use of air power. The choice of place and timing for any air offensive gave a good chance for any air force to achieve a temporary mastery. What the Luftwaffe now lacked was the capability either to destroy Russian air strength in its rear areas or to prevent the Red Army's massive use of aircraft in ground support operations over the eastern front as a whole. By returning to a policy of concentration large areas of the front were more or less abandoned for air purposes. Moreover such a switch now suited the Red Air Force since its massive numerical superiority now gave it the opportunity to overwhelm the enemy in large-scale pitched air battles. Throughout 1943 the Luftwaffe was overwhelmed by the sheer size of the Red Air Force as well as by its growing competence. For the summer offensives Russia was able to mobilize 10,000 front-line aircraft over the whole front against a total Luftwaffe combat strength in the west and east of only 3,551 serviceable aircraft. By January 1944 this had risen to 13,500 combat aircraft, by January 1945 to 15,500. The major drive on the Baltic front was supported by 7,000 Russian aircraft; that in the northern Ukraine by 2,800; and the final assault on Berlin and central Germany by a massive air army of 8,000 aircraft.[50]

Against these forces the Luftwaffe was able to offer only token resistance with dwindling resources. The reforms in organization and supply initiated by Milch in 1941 had come too late to affect the battles of 1943. What new production there was was needed for the defence of the Reich. Such defence had now become a major priority in order to keep the army fighting at all and out of sheer necessity the east was starved of the most modern equipment or the necessary replacements. Even the new tank destroyer aircraft, the Hs 129, equipped with the new armour-piercing cannon had to be sacrificed to efforts to keep the bombers at bay. Only 400 of them were produced in 1943 and 200 in 1944 even though its value had already been proved in the Kursk battles.[51] In order not to disturb production programmes any further, older types like the Ju 87 'Stuka' were kept in production. The medium-bomber programme which had been designed initially to give a powerful striking force on the eastern front against Russian troop concentrations had to be run down in favour of fighters. Because the strategic initiative in the air now lay with the attacker it made it difficult for the Luftwaffe to produce the kind of aircraft needed for Germany herself to carry out offensives, thus further disrupting chances of gaining a balanced aircraft production plan—a situation not unlike that facing Britain in the summer of 1940 when Beaverbrook's rapid expansion of fighter output seriously delayed the programmes for other aircraft types.

On top of all this the Luftwaffe was faced with political problems too.

Goering's use of the Stalingrad airlift as an attempt to bolster his sagging political fortunes at home finally convinced both the air staff and Hitler that there was a need for radical change. In the atmosphere of recrimination after February 1943 Goering was forced to give over more of the running of the Luftwaffe to Milch and in the political efforts to produce a total war effort in 1943 Goebbels and Speer felt obliged to finally by-pass Goering who, according to Speer, 'had relapsed into his lethargy, and for good'.[52] The conspicuous lack of top-level direction for the Luftwaffe in 1943 coupled as it was with the failure in Russia and the first wave of city bombings thus reduced still further the ability of the air forces to overcome the problems inherited from the early stages of the war and the production crisis. Hitler's now more frequent interventions in air affairs betrayed a personal ignorance of air fighting and air technology and a growing personal disillusionment with the air forces. It was Milch who had to bear the brunt of the political battles with hostile ministers and services for economic and labour resources. In early 1944 he bitterly complained that 'Air force armament has just not been given the proper treatment and support' and in the end capitulated to the pressures from the Speer ministry by placing aircraft production under its jurisdiction and abandoning everything in favour of the mass production of defence fighters to soften the impending blows from the combined bombing offensive in 1944.[53] By this time some units on the eastern front were compelled to fight with biplanes.

The campaign in the east was dominated throughout by the use of aircraft in combined operations. Major army offensives were usually preceded on both sides by a pre-emptive strike and by fierce air-to-air combat. In the Russian case the basic purpose of air activity at the front was to be 'a constant support for the infantry in the form of massed effective fire from . . . the air during the entire course of the offensive'.[54] The almost complete absence of long-range bomber operations was in sharp contrast to the war in the west and the Mediterranean. The Soviet Air Force devoted a mere 5 per cent of sorties to long-range operations and many that were carried out, such as the attacks on Berlin in 1941, were done so for propaganda purposes. Most Russian bombers were used for close support and attacks at the immediate rear of the battle zone. The initial designs for heavy bombers associated with the disgraced designer Tupolev, were dropped, and the Red Air Force lacked a satisfactory substitute until after the war. The long-range units were equipped with the Il-4 which had a very small bomb-load over long distances. A few four-engined Pe-8s were produced but production was restricted in favour of smaller aircraft because of the need to save resources.[55] Had Stalin personally been committed to heavy bombing, the necessary machines might have been available earlier. There was, however, fairly widespread scepticism among Russian leaders that bombing could be decisive or was worth the diversion of effort from the main strategic aim. In addition the shortage of suitable machines, the lack of technical aids for bombing, the problem of raw materials all contributed to an acceptance that for the likely duration of hostilities Russia would gain little by strategic bombing. Moreover the distances involved were usually prohibitive. The long range air arm (ADD) set up in March 1942 was used mainly to bomb front-line troop and tank concentrations and also carried out vital supply and transport work as well as supplying guerrillas behind German lines. Given its limited resources and prospects these aspects of bomber use made considerable military sense.[56]

For the Luftwaffe the situation was different. Experience in 1939 and 1940 had shown how important it was to have a strategic bomber capability and to attack targets (airfields, aircraft factories etc.) well in the enemy rear. Yet such activity was expressly forbidden by Hitler in the early stages of the campaign, betraying a failure to see how closely integrated 'strategic' and 'tactical' air operations actually were. Hitler was no doubt influenced in this decision by his personal disappointment at the failure of the Blitz. 'The munitions industry', he complained, 'cannot be interfered with effectively by air raids. We learned that lesson during our raids on English armament centres in the autumn of 1940. Usually the prescribed targets are not hit.'[57] He was also convinced that there would not be any necessity for strategic air operations because of the speed of the campaign. It was hoped that Russian air bases, stocks and factories would fall into German hands before they could be effectively destroyed from the air. Goering even created a special *Beutekommando* (booty command) for the purpose of seizing industrial resources and sending them back to Luftwaffe factories in the Reich.[58] When it had finally become clear that Russian aircraft supply was well-organized and revitalized many miles behind the front and that the Red Air Force did not disintegrate with the first strikes against it, German strategy returned rather haltingly to the policies of the autumn of 1940. During the winter of 1941–42 the shortages of aircraft and the supply crisis at the front reduced the effectiveness of operations like the bombing of Moscow but in 1942 Hitler resurrected the ambitions of the early Luftwaffe for bombing the Urals and beyond. The Luftwaffe chief of staff had already proposed using heavy bombers for 'far-ranging tasks of destruction'. Hitler demanded bombers that could attack 'in horizontal flight, by night, against long distance targets which lie so far from our front that they could not be reached with other aircraft types'.[59]

The decision to begin long-range bombing again was frustrated by many factors. The long distances and inadequate bomb-loads, combined with the shortages of supply and the unhappy history of the Heinkel He 177 four-engined bomber undermined every attempt to fulfil the new ambition. Yet its urgency was clear. The enormous numerical superiority enjoyed by the Soviet air force in 1943 prompted the attempts to re-introduce a long-range air strategy. On 23 June 1943 Speer set up a special committee of industrialists to study possible key targets in the Russian economic system. He pointed out that a campaign against the concentrated electricity plants in central Russia could have a possibly decisive effect on the Russian war effort.[60] Hitler ignored this suggestion—which certainly involved a degree of precision bombing and intelligence work to which the Luftwaffe was barely equal in 1943—and instead agreed to the formation of a new long-range force for attacking military industries in the east. The Luftwaffe study 'Battle against Russian Armament Industry' was published in November 1943 and the conversion of IV Air Corps under a new *Wiederauffrischungsstab Ost* completed in the middle of the winter. The plan was abandoned with none of the promised long-range bombers available. The operational preparation was still slight and few resources could be devoted on the scale necessary to have any decisive influence on Russian production.[61] It was argued, nevertheless, that Russian industry was highly concentrated in large plants and strategic air action against them might slow down the Russian advance. Not even the evidence of how quickly Soviet industry was reconstructed after the initial attack in 1941 reduced enthusiasm for bombing which was seen as the last chance in the east to prevent the inevitable. But the Luftwaffe was frustrated in its efforts by the earlier decision to concentrate on a limited role for air forces and not to prepare for a more general strategy when that might be required.

In the absence of any strategic novelties in aircraft use on the eastern front, the air war became much more a question of supply and deployment. More supply might, of course, have given the Luftwaffe more strategic flexibility. For the Russians more supply would have meant yet greater concentrations of ground attack and fighter forces at the front. For the German forces, problems with aircraft production, and in particular the crisis of 1941-42, were exacerbated by the fact that air forces had to be widely dispersed against other better armed air enemies. Soviet claims concerning the number of aircraft destroyed on the eastern front were exaggerated, although in the crucial stages before America entered the war fully, the Luftwaffe threw the main weight of its attacks eastwards where it suffered heavy losses. Technical difficulties and strategic miscalculation coupled with dispersion of effort meant that there were not enough resources on any front to gain decisive air supremacy. The situation might have been corrected by policies on supply and top-level organization but even these changes would either have taken years to come into operation or could not be carried out for political reasons. The Luftwaffe without Goering at its head, said Hitler, 'just did not bear thinking about'.[62] In Russia, on the other hand, supply of adequate, simply built and maintained aircraft was given the highest strategic priority. So, too, was a proper integration of aircraft command with that of the army and the civilian authorities. Soviet concentration on these two ambitions gave the air forces sufficient strategic and logistical superiority to force the Luftwaffe on to the defensive and to make it harder than ever to seize the initiative. It should always be remembered, however, that air power was only an auxiliary on the eastern front. The air war moved forward and backward with the front. It was the Red Army, drawing on air power for artillery cover of greater accuracy and decisiveness than was possible from the ground, that drove the German armies across central Europe. A large number of aircraft was an important bonus, but not necessarily more than that. Air power might have been more decisive only if the Luftwaffe had continued to use the strategies of 1940 with the same energy and resources, and had not imposed upon itself doctrines of such limited scope.

(ii) The United States and the War in Europe

The fact that Hitler moved east in 1941 and had planned to do so since 1940, had important implications for the British war effort. Though still powerless to prevent German initiatives from being successful in Greece and Crete, the British government was given a long period during which to prepare adequate defences in the mainland against the expected day when Hitler would turn west again.[63] Although it was true that Germany would have the luxury after a defeat of the Soviet Union to concentrate solely on defeating Britain, and Hitler gave specific directives for such a contingency, it was also true that Britain was much stronger than in 1940. In actual fact very little active planning was carried out in Germany for the renewed fight against Britain, and the crucial diversion of resources in the economy for the air effort was not carried out. Even victory against Russia therefore would not necessarily have led to the destruction of British resistance for a considerable time.

Britain now had another advantage; close ties with the United States in 1940 had been turned into firm commitments to provide assistance in 1941. In September 1940 the Army-Navy-British Purchasing Commission Joint Committee was set up to discuss and arrange sales of aircraft to Britain and to try to achieve some standardization of production. The United States undertook to expand its own aircraft industry enormously and to provide the bulk of the new aircraft to the British, an offer whose generosity was tempered by the fact, argued by General Marshall, that if Britain were defeated the aircraft would be needed anyway to defend the western hemisphere. Throughout 1941 the aid continued to expand.[64] Roosevelt himself preferred his policy of remaining the 'arsenal of democracy'. By late 1941 some 68 per cent of all aircraft production was sent to the active anti-Axis powers and of this figure some 75 per cent went to Britain, considerably strengthening Britain's position in the Middle East and providing an important reservoir of reserves for the air battles of 1942 in addition to what the British economy was itself capable of producing. Despite the drawbacks of the system of target planning in British aircraft production—a system in which unrealistic totals were proposed to act as a spur to industry—the aim of achieving total production of more than 2,000 a month was reached by the end of 1941 and sustained thereafter. The more optimistic ambition to achieve an output of 2,500 a month in 1941—that is at about three times the current rate of German production—had to be shelved because of the great industrial effort involved in producing heavy bombers and had to be made up by imports from the United States.[65] That the aircraft production effort should have exceeded that of the Axis powers so substantially reflected different strategic circumstances. In the course of 1941 and 1942 British survival depended both upon maintaining an adequate aerial home defence and an offensive air capability to undermine the German air effort at its sources within Germany. If this was sometimes at the expense of other services, it was only because the ability to defend Britain successfully had a necessary priority over the ability to attack.

Such a view was well understood in the United States. So much so that there developed growing pressure on the President to move from a policy of economic aid and moral encouragement to a policy of active war in defence of Britain. The Navy and Army were in general agreement that the time would soon come when it would be necessary to defend the western hemisphere, and that it would be more satisfactory from a military point of view if it could be defended using Britain as an advanced base, though there was disagreement over whether it should be a base for bombing or not.[66] Since both Roosevelt and Secretary for War Stimson were enthusiastic about the use of aircraft in any future war, it became doubly important to ensure that bases from which the Axis powers could be attacked from the air, both in Britain and the Mediterranean, should not be lost permanently for the Americans.[67] The first major discussions of strategy between Britain and America, the ABC 1 negotiations in March 1941, reached the conclusion that in the event of American entry into the war a sustained air offensive against Germany and Axis-controlled areas would be an essential part of overall strategy contributing to an eventual land offensive in Europe. The Joint Army-Navy Board approved the subsequent war plan, Rainbow 5, and it was on the strength of these recommendations that Roosevelt called in 9 July 1941 for an estimate of 'overall production requirements required to defeat our potential enemies'.[68]

A plan was quickly submitted by the War Department summarizing the economic and military effort that America would need to make in a state of active war with Germany and Japan. To this plan was attached an annexe hastily drawn up by the newly formed Air War Plans Division discussing the role of air strategy in the event of American participation in war. The annex which became known as AWPD-1 was more than simply a list of required supplies but was a clear expression of what strategic tasks the supplies would be needed for. In carrying out this task the air war planners in fact dictated from an early date the nature of American air strategy within the overall committment already made that the European Axis should be defeated first and should be defeated through an eventual massive invasion of the continent. From the start the air force favoured a general air strategy. AWPD-1 recommended that the first task was 'To conduct a sustained and unremitting air offensive against Germany and Italy to destroy their will and capability to continue the war', a view very much in accord with the ideas developed between the wars at the Air Corps Tactical School. Where the air planners differed from the War Department was in the hope that such an air offensive might 'make an invasion unnecessary'. To this were added other major tasks. The most important was 'To provide for the close and direct air support of the surface forces in the invasion of the Continent and for major land campaigns thereafter'. The defence of the western hemisphere and a strategic defence against Japan were the remaining tasks. For all these objectives the Air Staff demanded a total air force of 61,799 aircraft, including 37,000 trainer aircraft and 11,800 combat aircraft, the latter to include a complement of 5,000 heavy and very heavy bombers and to be covered by a reserve of 109 per cent.[69]

The overall plan was approved of by Marshall and finally by the President and formed the basis of American air strategy when war was declared in December 1941. In August 1942 the plan was replaced by AWPD-42 which took account of the mounting tasks of the air forces and raised the total front-line requirements to 19,520 aircraft with a total aircraft production requirement in 1943 of 146,000 aircraft.[70] Even when this was later reduced to a total of 127,000 the figure still exceeded total German aircraft production for the whole war. Like the British planners in 1941–42, the American leaders placed great emphasis on the need to achieve and maintain 'complete air ascendancy over the enemy' as a prelude to carrying out combined tasks and together with the British there grew the expectation that the bombing offensive at the centre of the air plans might bring about defeat of Germany by destroying the vital economic centres. At the very least it was expected that the air forces would so undermine German economic and military expansion that even in the event of the Anglo-American forces being outnumbered by Axis troops due to the German defeat of Russia, an invasion would still be possible.[71]

The American air forces had achieved a position of some influence in strategic and war preparation only comparatively recently. There existed a persistent difficulty before 1941 in granting equal status to the air forces within the overall Army structure. Although such subordination need not of itself have been a disadvantage, it was felt to be so by those in command of air forces, and the resolution of the disagreement not only had considerable implications for the way in which air planning became integrated into overall war planning, but also improved morale. The fact that Roosevelt was attracted to air warfare helped to smooth the path toward granting greater autonomy to the Army Air Forces. In March 1939 the Air Corps was given control over the General Headquarters Air Force to give it some say in operational work but in November 1940 this control was once again removed and the GHQ Air Force was given a separate status under the commander of the Army Field Forces. The Air Corps was opposed to the division of command which gave too much responsibility to army personnel in planning and directing air affairs. Stimson decided early in 1941 to place the air forces under a single commander. Following the appointment of an Assistant Secretary of War for Air a general reorganization resulted in the creation in June 1941 of the Army Air Forces, commanded by General Arnold, and directly responsible only to Army Chief of Staff. The AAF controlled both the combat and service commands although the relationship between the two sides and the relationship with the War Department was ill-defined. This lack of definition led eventually to a structuring of all air forces in Circular 59 of 9 March 1942 which altered the whole war command structure. The AAF were made co-equal under the Army Chief of Staff with the ground forces and service forces. General Arnold was allowed to act as Chief of Staff for the Air Forces—although legally only a deputy chief—and was thus able to control not only the building up of air forces but also how they would be used in operations. Sufficient autonomy had been granted to avoid a repetition under war conditions of the political struggles of the previous decade, and to make possible the execution of an independent and general air strategy.[72]

The establishment of an acceptable command structure for the AAF coincided with the efforts to establish a satisfactory framework for active co-operation between Britain and the United States. This was necessary not only to establish common strategic aims but also to integrate economic preparations and to devise a means for the mutually favourable conduct of operations. Both sides recognized from early in 1941 the wisdom of this course. At the ABC-1 staff conversations it had been decided that permanent military missions be established and this successful precedent was elaborated after the Washington conference between Roosevelt and Churchill into a system of permanent military and strategic collaboration through the Combined Chiefs of Staff. The establishment of this machinery had the effect of confirming Arnold's position as an effective chief of staff despite his subordinate constitutional position. His close involvement in all staff discussions both on the Combined Staffs and on the American Joint Staffs was a direct result of the autonomy enjoyed by the RAF within the British structure. Although there were often substantial disagreements between the Allies during the course of the war, the combined staff system ensured that such disagreements could be discussed and resolved through collaboration.[73]

The attack on Pearl Harbor, while turning the United States involuntarily into a combatant power, did not substantially alter the strategic plans and priorities established in all the combined discussions throughout 1941. Such discussions had begun in early 1941 and had produced by March a document agreed by American and British staff which gave priority to defeating the European Axis powers first and containing Japanese aggression in the east. While preparations were made to mount a land invasion of Europe, it was also intended both to protect British naval and economic interests in the Atlantic and Mediterranean, and to develop an economic offensive against Germany mounted primarily from the air.[74] The strategic outlines of the ABC-1 discussions remained remarkably secure over the following months of planning. For the British a massive invasion of the Continent was barely possible without American assistance; hence the importance of the policies of peripheral containment and blockade. But once America had entered the war such a possibility was secured. Since both Allies were agreed on the need to attack Germany first, and the Americans with uneven enthusiasm were prepared to support the British initiatives in the Mediterranean, the outlines of the next years of war, already to a certain extent shaped by the size and nature of the 'Victory' production programme, could be firmly established. Up until the Washington conference in January 1942 British strategy had had to count on the possibility, however remote in operational terms, that strategic bombing might bring an end to the war without a land invasion, because of the weakness of British land forces.[75] The entry of the United States with its vast army contributed to a reassessment of the future shape and requirements of an air war.

Air strategy assumed a particular importance for the Americans first of all because the air offensive was one of the few ways in which America could participate fully and quickly in the war against Germany. The Arnold-Slessor agreement later in 1942, which directed that only Americans should fly American aircraft, ensured that the vast supply programme from America would not be used in such a way that America bore the expense and the RAF took the glory.[76] Secondly, Stimson had already indicated his belief that the ascendancy enjoyed by the German forces in 1939–41 was due to the advantage of large tactical air forces, and one of the requirements that emerged from the early staff planning was for a very large tactical air force to support the final invasion of Europe. Finally, the adoption of an agreed policy on bombing promised the fulfilment of the Air Corps Tactical School belief that a strategic bombing offensive would so wear down the enemy economy and war-willingness that the final land attack would be carried out with relative ease and a minimum of casualties. Arnold shared with his British counterparts the hope that a land attack might not be necessary at all, but did not allow that view to divert resources from the grand strategic aim and the development of a comprehensive air strategy.

(iii) Air power in the Mediterranean and Atlantic

The circumstances of war would have compelled the Allies to develop a general air strategy, even had one not already existed. Serious reverses in the Far East, the failure to eliminate the threat to the Suez Canal and the growing problem in the Atlantic forced the diversion of resources to a wide range of theatres and purposes. Since the security of the Atlantic sea lanes and the eastern Mediterranean were essential prerequisites for the final assault on Europe itself the strategy for 1942 had gradually to move away from the concentration of air and ground forces for the final defeat of Germany to the strategy preferred by Churchill of blockade and encirclement. This move was undertaken at a time when it was still feared that Hitler would be victorious in Russia and could hence turn south in late 1942 and a separate, American, fear based largely on poor intelligence, that the German air force was much larger than it actually was.[77] The move demonstrated, too, that Allied strategy, particularly air strategy, was in some disarray. The failure in the Atlantic was to a large extent due to the failure to get air forces committed early enough and in large enough numbers to have a decisive influence. The collapse in the Mediterranean theatre, though not due to a shortage of aircraft, had demonstrated that air superiority there was not being exploited as successfully as it might be. Moreover there were additional problems caused through the lack of American combat experience and the lack of experience in inter-service and inter-allied co-operation.

For all these reasons the combined bomber offensive had to be postponed and was only slowly built up after the agreed Joint Directive in August 1942, while the build-up of AAF in Britain was delayed long enough to make it unlikely that an assault on Europe could have been attempted before 1944 even had the shipping space been available.[78] Since the combined offensive was seen as the crucial way of weakening the German Air Force before invasion any delays in its execution, however necessary, made the gaining of air supremacy in the near future seem unlikely, even though much of the evidence suggested that the Luftwaffe was extremely weak in the west. The beginning of the night-bombing campaign and the start of the so-called 'circuses' in March 1942 were both designed to reduce Luftwaffe effectiveness by attacking the aircraft industry on the one hand and enticing German fighter forces into unequal combat on the other.[79] But both these aims, already clearly expressed at the Arcadia conference, had to be defended against demands for air forces by the navies, and the demand for a prepared tactical force by both armies. The old arguments for combined operations in favour of 'independent' operations reasserted themselves as the insistent demands for action in the Atlantic battle and the Middle East made themselves felt in Allied strategy.

During these two campaigns the British seized the opportunity to develop practical ways of achieving air supremacy through the exercise of air power in a multiplicity of roles. These developments were to prove essential to the planning and execution of the later cross-Channel invasion. It marked the point at which those powers that favoured a more general air strategy became more easily distinguishable from those compelled by circumstance or inclination to adopt a more limited version. Seeing the success of the British example the AAF was persuaded under combat conditions to follow suit. But the rewards of such a strategy were not immediate. In the very nature of air warfare the winning of air superiority was a long-term process. For one thing the RAF had been slow in establishing the principles of co-operation with the army or in understanding the inter-relatedness of independent and tactical air operations. During 1942 and 1943 great efforts were devoted in the RAF and AAF to establishing large tactical air forces as well as forces for defence and bombing. Nor did the winning of air supremacy speed up the defeat of the Axis power in North Africa or the Atlantic as much as had been hoped. Had the Allies not had large numbers of aircraft and trained crews in 1942 the situation might have been considerably worse. Even faced with this substantial Allied advantage the German submarines and Rommel's Afrika Korps achieved much more than either Hitler had expected or the supply position warranted. In Rommel's case this was achieved with a rapidly shrinking Luftwaffe in the south and an almost non-existent Regia Aeronautica. In the Atlantic it was achieved without any effective German long-range bomber or a single aircraft carrier.

There was conflicting evidence as to whether Hitler ever took the southern theatre of operations very seriously, even had he been able to divert resources southwards. 'I'm glad', he remarked, 'that this call to the East has taken our attention off the Mediterranean'.[80] As the situation in Russia became more complicated Hitler continued to remain in two minds about what balance to keep between the demands of the two strategies. For a long time the area was considered to be in the Italian sphere of influence and the Italian commanders tended to treat the German forces as guests.[81] Hitler had at first believed that the British could achieve nothing decisive in the Mediterranean theatre in the time it would take him to defeat Russia and that the opportunity for defeating Britain would again present itself whether North Africa had been lost or not. Russia did not collapse in 1941, however, and the renewed attack on Britain had to be postponed. Nevertheless Hitler felt confident enough of victory in Russia to send Fliegerkorps II southwards to help his embattled Axis ally on the grounds that it was 'no longer required in the East'.[82]

The effect of dispatching more aircraft southwards was to weaken the Russian front without providing enough to have a decisive impact in the Mediterranean. Moreover those aircraft that did move southwards were faced with a mounting number of objectives as Hitler's Mediterranean strategy became more uncertain and the strategic tasks multiplied. The Luftwaffe was asked to achieve air mastery over the supply corridor to North Africa and to 'paralyse enemy traffic through the Mediterranean' and in the end was also to be asked to support the final offensive into Egypt.[83] The result was the same as on the Russian front; a growing dispersal of air effort and a rapid attrition of available air forces. Neither Raeder nor Kesselring, who both understood why the Allies paid so much attention to the Mediterranean, were able to persuade Hitler to concentrate on one or two crucial tasks there. He preferred to let the Luftwaffe cope with a wide range of tasks for which it patently did not have the resources. Fliegerkorps II arrived in Sicily with only 325 aircraft of which only 229 were serviceable while the British were able to fly into Malta some 700 fighter aircraft over the first half of 1942, more fighters than had been available at the beginning of the Battle of Britain.[84] In the end Hitler was not prepared to divert sufficient resources from what he saw as the main battle. Concluding that 'Egypt belongs more properly to the Italian sphere of influence' he was prepared to leave the bulk of the southern front to Italian efforts and in the end to abandon North Africa altogether.[85] For the Italians this had much more serious implications. Unable as they had been to contain British offensives without some German assistance they not surpisingly proved unable to prevent Britain gaining the initiative at sea and in the air when the balance of forces swung even more in favour of the Allies. If the expulsion of Rommel from Africa represented an acceptable strategic blow to Hitler, it spelt the end of Italian ambitions.

The Allies were thus presented in 1942 with the prospect of being able to impose grand strategic priorities on precisely that area which for the Germans represented a subsidiary strategy. German strategy was essentially defensive, Allied strategy offensive, however heavy-handed it appeared. The eventual success of the Allied air forces, though not always co-inciding with that of the other services—rested on two major developments. The first was the development of a sound doctrine of how to win and hold air superiority. The second was in developing a satisfactory system of co-operation both between the Allies and between services. It is tempting to say that Italian-German failures in the southern theatre owed not a little to the failure to appreciate or imitate such developments. Certainly in the field of co-operation and in the development of ideas concerning air superiority the gap between the two sides widened, although Axis problems stemmed as much from poor supply and strategic confusion as from tactical incompetence.

British air superiority in the desert war was based on a balance between the use of bomber and fighter forces and an emphasis on mobility and communications. Fighter aircraft were used for offensive sweeps against enemy fighters and forward airfields. Bombers were sent on night operations against supplies and air bases in the enemy rear, operations designed to be of direct assistance to the ground forces. In addition bombers were required to carry out long-range attacks against indirect targets which would contribute to an overall weakening of the enemy's ability to wage war. Of these targets the most important were communications, trade and military supplies. The division of tasks reflected a growing realization among British forces of the complementarity of bombing and of the interdependence of the different kinds of air activity. The emphasis throughout was on finding a policy for aircraft use to replace the traditional doctrine that aircraft must be closely linked with the battle area and with ground armies, while at the same time providing the most efficient air support for the surface strategy. Although British aircraft appeared in only small numbers, if at all, over the actual fighting, this was because the battle for air superiority was being fought elsewhere under conditions more favourable to the unique characteristics of the air weapon.

The British doctrine of air power also relied heavily on a number of important tactical innovations. Immediate ground support was dropped in favour of a more flexible combat policy and the various air forces were directed from a central air headquarters which, while working closely with the army on the ground, was not subordinate to its demands.[86] This flexibility required first of all an elaborate system of communications combined with considerable mobility. The need for the latter was greater the greater the distance involved. In the desert the rapid movement forward always brought the danger that air forces might be left behind, as Rommel was to find on several occasions. The problem was solved by creating Air Support Controls based on lorry transport containing radio and radar equipment that moved with the air units helping to direct the aircraft to where they were most needed.[87] Finally a permanent armed reconnaissance was established to produce as comprehensive a picture of enemy activities as possible while denying such opportunities to the enemy. Like the Russian air force, the RAF in North Africa gained considerably by concentrating on building up reserves and through the rapid and flexible deployment of bombers from one task to another as the need dictated. But unlike any other air force the RAF was able to achieve air superiority through the use of communications and radar and the prompt and flexible dissemination of intelligence. Above all the RAF emphasized an important tactical principle; that air warfare was a continuous pursuit. Given that air superiority could never be absolute as long as the enemy was capable of flying aircraft operationally, air activity would have to be continuous in order to maintain superiority. RAF command of the air in the desert was never lost over the whole of the first half of 1942 despite reverses on the ground and when the final battles came in November only 148 Axis aircraft were destroyed in the first twenty days of fighting because Axis air power had been eroded through continuous attrition throughout the summer.[88] The complementary use of bombers and fighters and good intelligence was put to good purpose in the final invasion of Europe later in the war, although the difficulties experienced in land fighting from November 1941 to July 1942 were a reminder that air power might not necessarily tip the balance unless surface forces enjoyed other substantial advantages as well.

The second development, towards better inter-service and inter-allied co-operation, was a natural extension of the first. In fact early problems in the implementation of the new air tactics stemmed directly from the failure to work out a satisfactory relationship between the services. Churchill himself had called for 'drastic reform' in the summer of 1941 and accused the Air Ministry of being 'most hard and unhelpful both to the army and to the navy . . .'[89] The problem was the same as the one faced earlier by Germany and Russia as to the nature of the relationship between the ground and air forces. The RAF suspected that the army would prefer to run the tactical air force from the ground, a fact which Brooke's demand for an integral air component did nothing to dispel. A satisfactory compromise was arrived at by creating a centralized air command with direct access to the theatre commander working side by side with the army as co-equals in combat. The various air headquarters were set up beside the army headquarters and a permanent liaison staff established. The ground forces could request assistance but could not require it and the close relationship of the two headquarters meant that the centrally directed air forces could sift through the various demands for help without the interference of superior army officers.[90] What was so surprising was that the system took so long to evolve, and having been developed failed to be imitated not only by the AAF but even by the RAF in other battles. When Coningham arrived to take over air command in the western desert he discovered that the lessons learnt so shortly before in Egypt had been forgotten and set about re-establishing close co-operation together with central direction of fighters and radar. Similarly the lessons on supply and maintenance from 1940-41 and on communications and mobility had to be relearned. Large numerical advantage was being frittered away by poor repair facilities and poor control of operations. The establishment of the Northwest African Air Service Command solved the first problem and the second was repaired by the extension of Tedder's tactical doctrines from the eastern desert.[91]

With the AAF there were two rather separate problems. The first was how to get the air forces of the two powers to work side by side. This was much more difficult in a combined offensive operation than in, for example, the bombing offensive where the British and American air forces agreed satisfactorily to differ, one to bomb at night and the other by day. The second problem was the fact that the AAF had its own political battles to fight with the other American services and could not simply adopt British tactical experience as its own. Very early on in the Torch campaign it became obvious that some kind of inter-allied central air command was necessary. AAF units were flying operations only within the narrow confines of their own army divisional sectors and in response to the immediate requirements of the ground forces. The appointment of Tedder as chief of the Mediterranean Air Command and of Coningham as chief of the Northwest Africa Air Forces restored central command and subordinated both AAF and RAF units to one commander.[92]

The problem of inter-service relationships on the American side was more complicated. By April 1942 the AAF had finally won the battle with the ground forces over a command doctrine in which the air commanders had some independent control over air forces instead of the structure favoured by the army of attaching small air units to each divisional and sub-divisional unit completely subordinate to the ground. Yet in practice the regulations in Field Manual 31-35 (Aviation in Support of Ground Forces) still kept the air forces tied to the needs of the army by insisting that 'the most important target at a particular time will usually be that target which constitutes the most serious threat to operations of the supported ground force. The final decision as to priority of targets rests with the commander of the supported unit'.[93] The lack of clarity in this relationship was encouraged by the fact that there was only one air liaison officer with each large ground unit with his own system of communication to airfields, and virtually no communication between air and ground. The adoption of the RAF form of organization worked only slowly. It was barely considered for the directive on air warfare published for Torch in October 1942. The rewriting of the Field Manual which the obvious failure in Tunisia had shown to be necessary only occurred in July 1943, and then only after the army had been able to win control over its own force of communications and artillery-spotting aircraft. Nevertheless the July changes incorporated in Field Manual 100-20 finally stated that 'land power and air power are co-equal and inter-independent forces; neither is an auxiliary of the other' and incorporated Tedder's tactical theory in a new series of priority targets for air forces.[94] Only when the command and tactical relationship was firmly established along the lines of greater co-operation and understanding of the exercise of air power were the Allies able to use their dominant numerical position to advantage, not only in Tunisia but in Italy and western Europe.

Some of these experiences were shared by the Axis powers as well. The difficulties in exercising joint commands in the southern theatre were made worse by the political interests of the two allied powers. Hitler saw the area as one of Italian influence; the German commanders were reluctant to take orders from anyone except the German leadership. At the highest level good co-operation depended on personality as much as good organization and even though Kesselring and Cavallero were able to work together, Rommel and Bastico in North Africa could not. In some cases Axis forces did co-operate successfully but the German forces continually expressed what Kesselring described as 'exasperation at our ally's inefficiency', refusing to accept Italian orders despite Hitler's own directive to the effect that the German Commander-in-Chief was directly subordinate to Mussolini and would receive instructions from the Comando Supremo.[95] The mutual distrust that evolved helped to explain the additional failure to establish a satisfactory basis for the winning of air supremacy. This failure was caused partly by the difficulties imposed by a shortage of proper air bases and trained servicing personnel as on the eastern front; and partly by the continued inability of the Axis leadership to see that air supremacy could only be won by the co-ordinated work of fighter and bomber aircraft, the use of good communications and radar and the careful planning of priorities and resources in such a way as to minimize losses and maximize military effectiveness. Thus it proved possible for the Axis powers to achieve temporary air mastery over Malta and the supply route to North Africa by concentrating every effort on one specific target, but only at the cost of weakening Axis air forces everywhere else, while eliminating Malta as an air base for only a handful of weeks.[96] Hitler encouraged these difficulties by his own failure to execute the invasion of Malta and later his insistence that valuable transport aircraft be frittered away on the relief of Tunis, by which time the Luftwaffe in the south was so short of aircraft, parts and trained crews that transport aircraft had to fly without fighter escort into the path of the increasingly numerous Allied air forces.[97]

The attrition suffered by Axis forces in the Mediterranean was a direct result of such strategic decisions. Yet even had the military position of the Axis air forces been improved by better use it is still doubtful whether they could have achieved much more, given that the Allies were committed to the strategic aim of achieving air supremacy by massive production programmes against an enemy whose strategy not only did not include such instructions but specifically created strategic confusion, dispersion of effort and an economy biased towards the ground forces. German aircraft production in 1942 of only 15,000 compared very unfavourably with a total Allied production of 71,000. The Italian contribution of only 7,000 aircraft over the whole period since 1940 was even more meagre. Moreover its quality had been so low that attrition was very high. When Italy surrendered there were only 447 operational aircraft available while 5,272 had been lost in combat or through accident.[98] What is so surprising is that it took so long during 1942 for Allied superiority to make itself felt. Once such a situation had been reached, however, it was only a question of time before the Luftwaffe in the south was eliminated as a threat and only a question of time before the Allied air offensive in the Mediterranean, particularly against shipping brought about more significant gains for the Allies. The attack on Axis supplies confirmed more than anything else that air supremacy had become an Allied prerogative. Between July 1942 and May 1943 some 897,000 tons of Axis merchant shipping was sunk in the Mediterranean of which 417,000 tons was sunk by aircraft.[99] Allied air power was now able not only to defeat the enemy air force but to significantly aid the defeat of enemy ground forces by taking independent strategic action.

If the Allies took time to establish air superiority in the Mediterranean theatre, even heavier weather was made of the Battle of the Atlantic. The ocean war was the second branch of the strategy finally decided upon for 1942, and was of crucial importance in the decision for the final invasion of Europe. The failure to secure Allied lines of communication not only threatened military efforts to relieve Russia but put Britain under the permanent threat of siege and the loss of crucial imports. By 1942 the Allies enjoyed certain advantages. The German effort in the Atlantic was now confined to U-boats. Any air effort in the area had been nullified by the increasing activity of the RAF in 1941 and the lack of strategic priority given to German air-naval operations. The same was largely true of surface vessels. The only attempt to get a large battleship out into the Atlantic ended with the confirmation, if such were needed, that ships like the *Bismarck* were always going to be vulnerable to air attack.[100] Nevertheless the shipping losses of 1942 and the first half of 1943 were so severe that the Atlantic Battle assumed a significance much greater than the Allies had initially expected, or for that matter Hitler himself.

For the Allies the Battle showed once again the difficulties in co-operation and command experienced in the Mediterranean. This time the problem was to some extent reversed; instead of ground forces grudgingly conceding the independence of the air, air forces only grudgingly conceded the importance of diverting effort to the naval war and accepting the temporary subordination to naval command. In the United States Admiral King was forced in 1942 to call on the AAF to supply bombers, particularly the long range Liberators, for anti-submarine work. The Army replied by forming the AAF Anti-Submarine Command but resisted naval demands to control 'tactics and allocations of force down to operational level'.[101] Only Marshall's personal insistence gave the navy control over 187 heavy bombers for the anti-submarine war in June 1942 and in return for a commitment that the AAF would have undivided control over the build-up of bomber forces for the combined offensive.[102] In Britain the crisis took an almost identical form. Bomber Command insisted that the threat from U-boats could only be met by attacking the sources of production rather than the end-product at sea. Harris deplored 'the purely defensive use of airpower' and tried to force a policy of concentrating on the bombing of Germany as a first priority.[103] Such resistance was in the face of naval demands for aircraft for a wide number of roles. In March 1942 Admiral Pound had drafted 'The Needs of the Navy' in which he insisted that the solution to the Atlantic Battle lay in 'largely increasing the strength of our land-based air forces working over the sea', including operational control over these aircraft and the right to train their crews.[104] The situation was not resolved until Churchill's establishment of the Anti-U-boat Warfare Committee in August 1942 which, while defending the need to continue the night bombing offensive, insisted that resources be diverted to the anti-submarine war, mainly in the form of long-range aircraft for Coastal Command which already came under the operational control of the Admiralty for Atlantic operations. From the winter of 1942-43 onwards the problem of rivalry between the services was overcome at the highest political level.[105]

Such rivalry proved to be only part of the problem. The basic difficulties were more technical. More aircraft and better co-operation went some way towards containing the threat from submarines but victory would only be possible by improving the means of detection. To achieve this the Allies developed a large carrier force working together with long range bombers to protect the convoys and to hunt for U-boats over a wider area, and advanced radar to accurately detect their presence.

By the beginning of 1942 the Royal Navy had only four modern carriers, the United States the same. Although large numbers of carriers were laid down in 1942 itself, this decision came far too late to prevent the massive attrition of Allied shipping in 1942 and 1943. Yet the evidence showed conclusively that convoys accompanied by escort carriers were considerably safer than those without. Moreover escort carriers proved to be difficult targets for submarines. Only one American escort carrier was sunk in the Atlantic throughout the war, while carrier-borne aircraft sank 33 submarines between April 1943 and September 1944 in addition to providing guidance for surface vessels and long-range aircraft in making attacks on submarine targets.[106]

Before carriers could become fully effective the other necessary technical breakthroughs had been made. The first was the development of suitable very long-range aircraft to patrol the 'Greenland Gap', that section of the Atlantic beyond the range of ordinary sea-going aircraft. These converted bomber aircraft became available in quantity only in 1943; by July the RAF had 37 such aircraft, the US navy 209.[107] The most important change was the introduction of 10-centimetre radar which could not be detected by submarines and gave Allied air forces a breathing space during which it became possible for submarines to be attacked on the surface without prior detection of the aircraft. This technical innovation coincided with a change in tactics introduced by Dönitz which increased the effectiveness of Allied aircraft even more. Where previously submarines had dived at the first indication of hostile aircraft, the difficulty in detecting radar and the successful destruction of an aircraft by submarine anti-aircraft fire persuaded the Germans to adopt a policy of fighting aircraft on the surface with improved anti-aircraft defences and by sailing in large groups to provide mutual defence.[108] But far from giving immunity such tactics made it even easier for approaching aircraft, using the new radar, to detect the submarines and to destroy them.

These changing circumstances rekindled the German navy's concern to co-operate more fully with the Luftwaffe. Only through air power could the threat to the German naval war be overcome. But lacking any aircraft carriers or a suitable long-range bomber, Dönitz's entreaties fell on deaf ears. Hitler refused to sanction a carrier programme because it would divert resources from army production. What heavy bombers there were were diverted during 1942 to the eastern front and to the renewed bombing operations against Britain, leaving only a skeleton force on the Atlantic coast for long-range reconnaissance.[109] Finally when Dönitz remonstrated with Hitler in September 1942 about 'the need for aircraft to support the U-boats to a much greater extent than has been the case up to the present time' he once again ran up against the hostility of Goering.[110] Neither Goering nor Hitler were persuaded that the navy's demand was as serious or as urgent as its leaders made out. Both were able to point to the growing success of the U-boat campaign even at a time of tactical crisis. It was not unreasonable to suppose that the Allies would not be able to find a satisfactory defence against the submarine. All the evidence suggested that a complete defence did not exist. Allied submarines in the Mediterranean had reaped a rich harvest as did German submarines in the Atlantic. The efforts of Bomber Command against the submarine pens proved quite fruitless. Of the 9,100 tons dropped on the U-boat bases on the Bay of Biscay not a single bomb penetrated to the submarine pens.[111]

In the end, however, the tactical changes that had so worried Raeder and Dönitz did provide a means of defeating the submarine. The additional effort devoted by the Allied air forces in terms of the area patrolled and the accuracy of detection exacted an attrition rate from the U-boat fleets that could not be supported. Unable to find an effective jamming device against centimetric radar the submarines became particularly vulnerable in the narrow approaches to their Biscay bases. Here Coastal Command, with 150 long-range aircraft, was able to contain the submarine threat during the course of 1943, more than justifying the diversion of resources and scientific effort to the waging of air war at sea.[112] Although there were complaints that too much effort had been diverted the Allies had been compelled to work on the assumption that Germany would increase its strategic commitment in the Atlantic, particularly by diverting air forces in large numbers to the naval war. The fact that such diversion did not occur did not make Allied preparations unreasonable, but served instead to demonstrate the gap that was growing between German and Allied appreciation of what air power was capable of doing. In both the Atlantic and the Mediterranean the Allies made use of the German priorities in the east to establish overwhelming air superiority and to use such superiority to the benefit of the surface forces in both a direct and indirect way. For Germany the strategic circumstances of 1942 and 1943 made it difficult to devote sufficient emphasis to either battle, and in particular to the diversion of the Luftwaffe to tasks other than army support on the Russian front. Even despite these circumstances, however, there was little evidence that Hitler or Goering thought such a diversion worth the effort. The Allied victory was thus a product not simply of different circumstances but of different views on the use of airpower and its relationship to the strategies of the other services.

(iv) From Casablanca to Victory

By the time the Allies met at Casablanca in January 1943 a favourable outcome to the battle at sea or in Africa had yet to be achieved. Victory in these two areas was shortly expected but poor preparation and co-operation had postponed it beyond initial expectations. There was still argument between the Allies as to the strategy most appropriate to the defeat of the Axis powers. Such indecisiveness reflected a fear that Russian defeat, apparently so nearly achieved at Stalingrad, would postpone the completion of the European war and make it far from a foregone conclusion. Nevertheless certain strategic facts were obvious. The Axis powers had lost the initiative in both the west and the Far East. Italy was close to defeat and the ring around Germany was drawing tighter month by month. For the air war this had certain implications. The first was that the bombing offensive was unlikely to be mounted on a sufficient scale in time for independent efforts to bring the war to an end through use of air power. The second was the fact that the other two services were determined that they should share in the final defeat of Germany. Air-power was an essential auxiliary in this objective but the conquest of Europe by land armies remained at the centre of Allied calculations.

The Casablanca conference provided an opportunity to discuss these issues within the context of grand strategy as a whole. One strategic principle emerged as central to the Allied view of the use of air power. It was considered essential to achieve air supremacy over Germany as a prelude to successful invasion of continental Europe. This was not only because a seaborne invasion against well-defended coasts gave many advantages to the defending forces but because, in the event of Russian defeat, air action would have to make up for the numerical advantage enjoyed by Germany by reducing its economic ability to wage war.[113] Harris reiterated this principle when resisting the diversion of bombing effort to submarine targets when he stated that 'the decided policy of the war is to bomb the enemy soft until a comparatively small land force . . . can overcome his remaining resistance'.[114] Because of the central place of air power in the strategy for eventual victory there was growing concern by late 1942 that insufficient aircraft were being produced by the Allies to achieve this aim. The problem was not, however, an insufficiency of aircraft but the danger of dispersion of effort. If some Allied airmen were unhappy about the movement of forces to the Mediterranean, there was even greater resistance to Admiral King's efforts to divert aircraft to the Pacific. Even though aircraft were diverted to the battle at Guadalcanal the insistence of the AAF on the need for a continued priority for bombing was confirmed at the Casablanca conference. Logistical arrangements were established in favour of a primary European commitment in 1943.[115]

The detailed Casablanca plans for the exercise of air power for the remainder of the European war were based on the need to achieve complete air mastery over the enemy. The lessons of the Mediterranean theatre were adapted to this central task. The first need was for continuous aerial warfare, what Arnold called the 'continuous application of massed air power against critical objectives'.[116] It was essential to disperse the effort of the Luftwaffe and to keep up a constant war of attrition, particularly by regular fighter intrusion by day, in order to wear down enemy resistance in the air. This policy was pursued during 1943 and early 1944 with increasing success, although it awaited the long-range fighter, which became available only late in the campaign. The second need was for a large tactical air force to achieve mastery over the invasion battlefield, to attack enemy concentrations in the rear and to provide good air intelligence of the front. On the need for such forces there was little disagreement. Nor was there any difficulty in insisting that a unified command structure should be adopted. The desert practice of close co-operation and flexible response from the air forces was introduced with good effect for the final invasion. The final need was for a bombing offensive to carry out on a grand scale a policy complementary to other strategic ambitions, through attacks against the sources of Luftwaffe production and by weakening the economic potential and war-willingness of the Third Reich. In the 'Directive for the Bomber Offensive' produced at Casablanca the air forces were instructed to 'take every opportunity to attack Germany by day, to destroy objectives that are unsuitable for night attack, to sustain continuous pressure on the German morale, to impose heavy losses on the German day fighter force and to contain German fighter strength away from the Russian and Mediterranean theatres of war'.[117] There was little indication that a decision in Europe was expected through air power alone and the American leaders in particular regarded the bombing offensive as simply a prelude to the final invasion.

There was, however, widespread debate on how such a combined bombing offensive should be carried out. Not only was there a question of target selection, but also the problem of command; and both these issues revolved around the question of whether the bombing served the invasion directly, or did so in an indirect way by reducing German economic performance and morale. The RAF had adopted night bombing because of the early success of German day defences and this of itself encouraged the belief that the indirect approach was the most successful. Pinpoint bombing of selected strategic targets for a pre-invasion campaign could not be carried out at night. The AAF insisted that daylight bombing was not only possible but was the only way to effectively destroy the main target systems and hence provide the necessary help to the planned invasion. The target system consisted of six main sectors containing 76 major targets. At Casablanca priority was given to bombing submarine construction yards first before all the other targets. By May 1943, when the failure of this attack had become recognized, the priority was finally given to attacks on the aircraft industry as an essential contribution to the reduction of fighter strength which threatened by mid-1943 to prevent any bombing at all.[118] On the need to attack the enemy fighter production there was general agreement. There was less agreement on some of the other targets but the directive to launch the Combined Bomber Offensive (CBO) in June 1943 finally produced a list of six priority areas: submarine construction, aircraft industry, ball bearings, oil, synthetic rubber and military transport vehicles. RAF bombing at night was regarded as complementary to the precision attacks on vital targets, if rather generously so. Any final decision on how direct the help for invasion should be was postponed and efforts concentrated on the build-up of bomber forces and tactical development.[119]

The bombing offensive depended too on how rapidly and in what quantity aircraft could be made available, and on the response of the Luftwaffe to bomber attack. Fear that there would not be enough heavy bombers had prompted the AAF to secure a high priority from Roosevelt for aircraft production in late 1942. By the middle of 1943 manpower problems had become increasingly acute, particularly for British production, and although the necessary air forces were provided they came later than originally intended and not in full force until March 1944. During 1943 bomber aircraft were diverted to the Mediterranean—though Portal believed this would be an advantage by varying the direction of attacks—and to the battle against the submarines.[120] In addition to this diversion of effort the German fighters were able to inflict sufficiently high loss rates to bring a temporary halt to the CBO in the autumn of 1943. It could not be undertaken again until long-range fighter escorts were provided. This delay proved to be only temporary, however. Experiments with long-range fighters using additional fuel tanks had been carried out through 1943 in anticipation of just such a need, and neared completion at the crucial period before the invasion of the Continent. Once the long-range fighters were available in large enough numbers the bombing offensive could once again be vigorously pursued.

The delay, however, had finally brought to an end the strategy of using the bomber offensive as an indirect weapon for easing invasion. Instead the bombers were diverted to tasks directly related to the invasion itself. Throughout 1943 preparations were made for launching 'Overlord' and at the Quadrant Conference in Quebec the CCS Final Report gave the Pointblank operation against the Luftwaffe and the air industry the highest priority as a 'pre-requisite to "Overlord" '.[121] From that point on the arguments hardened once again around how command over the bomber forces should be exercised and what targets would be most profitably attacked as a prelude to invasion. Despite the efforts of both Arnold and Harris to retain the original conception of the bombing offensive, the Chiefs of Staff decided that bombing should concentrate on defeating the Luftwaffe and disrupting enemy communications by a long-term transportation plan. In the final directive for 'Overlord' the strategic air forces were given the task 'to deplete the German air force and particularly the German fighter forces and to destroy and disorganize the facilities supporting them' and secondly to 'destroy and disrupt the enemy's rail communications, particularly those affecting the enemy's movement towards the Overlord lodgement area. . .'[122] Moreover the hard won independence of the two bomber forces was compromised by the changes in the command structure. Initially it had been proposed that a single air commander should control all tactical and bombing forces for the invasion. Since the command of the Allied Expeditionary Air Forces had been given to Leigh-Mallory neither bomber force was willing to accept direction by an airman with only fighter command experience. Moreover it was feared that such subordination would force the strategic bomber forces into no more than a tactical role in helping on the battlefield and in the immediate rear. The problem was finally surmounted by giving 'direction' of the strategic air forces to the Supreme Allied Commander who also had the responsibility for co-ordinating the efforts of the bomber forces with those of the invasion air forces. In effect direction was given to Eisenhower's deputy, Tedder, who had already had experience in strategic air command in the Mediterranean and who was consequently trusted by both Portal and Arnold.[123] The fierce inter-service arguments demonstrated yet again that co-operation as well as sound strategy were essential components in the use of air power.

The Overlord plan finally resolved the ambiguities and indecisiveness of bombing strategy. Given limited targets with high strategic priority instead of the earlier and more general instruction to undertake 'the progressive destruction and dislocation of the German military, industrial and economic systems' the bomber forces were highly successful. The attack code-named 'Big Week' in February 1944 finally undermined an already demoralized and weakened Luftwaffe, and the long-term interdiction policy caused the expected disruption of German lines of communication to great effect.[124] The invasion itself was achieved at a time when air mastery had clearly passed to the Allies. In fact had intelligence on the Luftwaffe been better it would have been obvious that the battles of 1942 had already so eroded the German air force that it was never able to regain the initiative. The tactical use of air forces conformed to the operational experience of the earlier campaigns and together with the use of bombers on strategic tasks ensured a permanent air supremacy.

The Allies also continued to enjoy a large numerical advantage. For the final invasion the Allied air forces were allowed a generous margin of reserves, a necessity predicted by the air planners on past experience. In addition the logistical preparations were so thorough and well executed that a high level of maintenance was established as well as remarkable mobility in the final advances towards the German frontiers. The IX Engineer Command was responsible for the building and rehabilitation of some 241 airfields during the operations and considerable economic and organizational effort went into the provision of satisfactory rear services.[125] Local shortages of suitable bomb types and of aviation fuel developed, but neither shortage was ever critical. Repair facilities for aircraft were also well established. Serviceability for fighter aircraft in the AAF always exceeded 80 per cent except for July 1944, and for bombers exceeded 80 per cent except in February and March 1945.[126] Such figures confirmed the fact that the Luftwaffe was no longer a serious threat. The long programme of attrition coupled with the bombing of aircraft production had reduced the Luftwaffe to a small and increasingly ineffective defence force by the summer of 1944. Unlike the Soviet air forces the Allies in the west had the opportunity to exercise air power without any significant opposition. What opposition there was was considerably exaggerated. The Allied invasion of Europe was in no way comparable to the German planned invasion of England in 1940. Not only did the German air force have the problem of stemming the Russian advance against

Soviet forces with a vast numerical air superiority, it was forced to face the powerful Allied threat in the west with barely more defence aircraft than the RAF had had in 1940. Despite the constant warnings that German air power was reviving in the summer and autumn of 1943, there was never any question, given the failure in German aircraft supply, but that air supremacy would be won by the Western Allies in a comparatively short period of time. Both in terms of production and in terms of combat aircraft available at the front the disparity was unbridgeable, as the following table shows:

Table 5: Production, Strength* and Losses of Britain, United States and Germany 1942-44 [127]

(i) Production and Strength (P, S)

	1942		1943		1944	
	P	S	P	S	P	S
U.S.A.	47,836	(a)6,610	85,898	(a)20,185	96,318	(a)32,957
		(b)12,800		(b)32,075		(b)46,244
U.K.	23,672	7,400	26,263	6,026	26,461	8,395
Germany	15,409	4,207	24,807	5,536	39,807	6,297
as % of Allies	21.5	(a)30	22.1	(a)21.1	32.4	(a)15.2
		(b)20.8		(b)14.5		(b)11.5

(ii) Losses 1939-45

	U.S.A.	U.K.	Germany
Bombers	9,949	11,965	21,807
Fighters	8,420	10,045	38,977
Night-fighters	–	–	9,827

* Strength is operational strength of front-line combat aircraft on all fronts. The American figure is for strength abroad (a) and strength including combat aircraft in America (b). The latter figure does not include naval combat strength at home but both figures include naval combat strength overseas. The dates for the strength figures are as follows:

U.S.A.   December 1942, December 1943, December 1944
U.K.   December 1942, 1 March 1943, 1 January 1945
Germany 30 December 1942, 30 December 1943, 31 December 1944

'Overlord' was not therefore a repeat of 'Sealion' as far as the air forces were concerned. It represented the fulfilment of the Allied belief first expressed in 1941 that vast numerical superiority was a necessary precondition for all strategic tasks in the air. It was in the nature of air warfare that Germany would still be able to mount air attacks until virtually the end of the war, but this could not obscure the fact that the Allied victory was won through overwhelming odds, as the German victory over Poland had been in 1939. On D-Day the Allies employed 12,837 aircraft, including 5,400 fighters, against a total strength in Luftflotte 3 of 300 aircraft. These aircraft, and the German reinforcements, were shot out of the skies in ten hours. For the Ardennes offensive in December the Luftwaffe massed a mere 900 aircraft for the final effort and these, too, were destroyed in a matter of days.[128] This was not simply a result of deficiencies of supply on the German side but was a fact of economic life. Britain and the United States had much larger resources to draw upon. The only way in which such numerical disparity could be overcome was through qualitative advantages; and in terms of technology, too, the Allied powers had a measurable lead in most, though not all, areas of advanced research.[129]

Having gained such air supremacy, however, it was quite another matter to relate such supremacy to the central strategic objectives. Almost a full year elapsed between the winning of air superiority and the end of the war. During that period a relentless bombing campaign was continued and the Allied ground forces benefited from almost complete air immunity. Yet although this supremacy certainly eased the progress of Allied troops into Europe and reduced German economic potential, the war could not be ended except by the occupation of territory. Against a well-armed and experienced enemy ground army such occupation was bound to be a slow process. Air power such as the Allies possessed after the spring of 1944 was indeed overwhelming; yet no way was found to exercise that air power decisively except in carrying out on a larger scale the kind of combined operations that had characterized all the earlier campaigns in Europe and the Mediterranean. All the great expectations of air power as a distinct war-winning weapon that had been kept alive, despite the failure in 1940, by the single-mindedness of the bomber school were confounded by the fact that even the winning of the war in the air could not measurably reduce the time that it took to defeat the German armies in Europe.

(v) The Collapse of the Luftwaffe

To confound Allied theories of air power even more, the German air force itself contributed substantially to its own weakness and eventual downfall. It took some time before Hitler would acknowledge that the initiative in the air war had been lost. Since he saw the air weapon as an essentially offensive force he refused to allow large resources to be diverted to defence at home, and instead increased efforts to produce a German bomber force to rival that of the Allies. Not only on the Russian front but in the attack against England Hitler insisted that a large-scale bombing capability should be retained. The irony was that the Luftwaffe had been unable to sustain such a capability with any serious military effect during the winter of 1940–41 when there was little opposition, and when the air forces contained a satisfactory balance between fighter and bomber forces. By 1943 when the Allies began to bomb Germany in strength not only was British defence very much better, but the balance within the Luftwaffe had moved in favour of fighters on the insistence of the Luftwaffe and air ministry staff.[130]

The lack of a German bombing offensive and the failures in Russia finally persuaded Hitler to take over more of the direction of the Luftwaffe himself. This fact only helped to exaggerate the many problems already faced by the air force. Hitler had his own views on air warfare, a very limited knowledge of how to use aircraft and very little understanding of air force logistics. He insisted that for defence purposes anti-aircraft guns would be sufficient, and therefore refused to sanction the diversion of resources to a defence in depth like that practised by the RAF in 1940. Secondly, he failed to understand how the system of air reserves operated, and insisted that reserves should be used for concentrated operations with the largest numbers that could be mobilized at any one time, thus risking the denuding of large parts of the Luftwaffe's future strength.[131] In his directive for opposing the D-Day landings on 16 June 1944 he required that 'half of all fighter units in Germany must be kept in readiness to support the army with low-level attacks; and in an emergency all units'.[132] This not only betrayed his view of the air force as primarily for close support of ground units but also his inability to grasp that air superiority could not be won with sudden attacks and heroic gestures, but only with a strategy of patient, routine and mundane operations, keeping a balance where possible between present emergency and a capability for the future. Later in the war Hitler accused the Luftwaffe of hoarding resources, mistaking the policy of reserve-building and long-term logistical planning for cowardice. As a result he continually resented the diversion of economic resources to aircraft production and preferred to place the main economic weight on the army as a potential war-winning service. To some extent his view was vindicated by the fact that air supremacy did not have quite the value that its fiercest proponents had hoped, but it did mean that Germany had virtually no way of preventing heavy bombing and thus protecting army as well as air force industry, and also less and less satisfactory intelligence about Allied forces, both of which facts reduced the effectiveness of ground forces in the slow retreat.[133]

Although the German military and political leadership opposed the idea of large-scale air defence German air commanders built up a defence force regardless, in the hope that neither Hitler nor Goering would object when faced with a *fait accompli*. On the basis of an initial air defence shield, the so-called Kammhuber Line, a series of defence areas were set up over the Reich with a complement of day and night fighters whose movements were co-ordinated by central combat stations set up at five main points opposing the Allied lines of intrusion. But there were many difficulties to overcome. The development of German air intelligence had been much slower than elsewhere. Much of the observation had been carried out by eye only, without the aid of radar, and a cumbersome system of communications had been set up whose effectiveness declined rapidly under the increased air activity of 1942. A unified, radar-based system did not emerge until the end of 1943. In fact the development of a satisfactory command and tactical relationship between night and day fighters was only developed by the autumn of 1942, long after the threat from British bombing had been presented.[134] Inter-service rivalry also produced difficulties. The army and navy, for example, ran separate air intelligence services of their own in the front-line areas. In overall weapons output the low production priority accorded the night fighters meant that the 3rd Luftwaffe fleet in France had no night fighters at all at one time, despite its crucial geographical position and the valuable French industrial targets offered to Allied bombers.[135] Under such circumstances it was perhaps surprising that the Luftwaffe achieved such success against bombers in 1943 that both the RAF and AAF suspended attacks for some months. The suspension was related to the preparations for 'Overlord' which were already in progress by late 1943, but it was also clear that even a modest air defence, such as the Luftwaffe was forced to fight with in 1943, was capable of success against a well-armed air enemy provided that a sufficiently high loss-rate could be inflicted. Given such success it was even more remarkable that Hitler failed to divert more effort to expanding air defences during the period when the CBO was in abeyance in late 1943. But instead resources continued to be sucked into army support in Russia and Italy leaving the Luftwaffe frustrated in its efforts to construct a more general air strategy around the defence of the Reich. When the Allies introduced the long-range day and night fighters, a move which the Luftwaffe had already anticipated, the balance swung back firmly in favour of the Allied air forces since so little had been done in the interval in the way of strengthening German defences.[136] Combined with a policy of large-scale production and a lead in radar technology air superiority passed to the Allies even over Germany itself. While Galland and Milch insisted on the need for a three- or fourfold numerical advantage of defending over attacking aircraft, the Luftwaffe command was forced to accept Goering's verdict that the long-range Allied fighters were simply short-range fighters that had drifted with the westerly wind.[137] As a result Goering continued to insist that the primary task of the fighters was still to break up the bomber formations and to ignore the escort fighters. This was, of course, a quite correct view in a situation where the Allies possessed no long-range fighter and the Germans large numbers of fighters; but since neither was in fact the case the delusions of the Luftwaffe commander-in-chief postponed for even longer the establishment of a satisfactory defence strategy to cope with Allied attacks. German resources were, on the contrary, very limited. The consequence was that as Allied fighters penetrated further into the Reich, the German fighters were never able to get close enough to the bombers in enough strength to inflict a high loss rate, let alone to break the formations up. The weakness of the Luftwaffe in the west was thus compounded of a lack of strategic priority and direction on the one hand, and tactical uncertainty on the other.[138]

While Hitler himself predicted in September 1943 that the mastery of the air would be regained for Germany in 'two to three months',[139] the Luftwaffe generals saw that the air war had a quite different character. Even the pause in the Allied air offensive, and the reasons for it, were not fully appreciated on the German side. For the Luftwaffe there were permanent difficulties to be overcome. The crucial years in the build-up of Luftwaffe strength had been in 1940–42. The multiplication of tasks and the insufficiency of resources from these years had inflicted weanesses that could not be overcome later in the war. The loss of initiative had produced an unbalanced air force as the bomber programme had to be cut back progressively in favour of fighters.[140] This tendency had been present even before 1939 as those favouring tactical air forces came to dominate the staff, and had been continued into the war after the failure of strategic bombing in 1940, and as the demands for fighter and ground attack aircraft from the eastern front had multiplied. The Luftwaffe was never able to build up a large enough offensive air force to be able to go back to the initiative and the production of a balanced air force designed to achieve air supremacy. The large new production of fighters in 1943 and 1944 made little difference to the situation, first of all because the loss rate had become too high by 1943, secondly because of the rapid deterioration in the training and number of crews available.

The first fact was inescapable. In 1943 the increase in strength failed to match the increases produced by Germany's enemies. By 1944 the so-called 'Production Miracle' of the Fighter Staff evaporated because of the ease with which Allied fighters and bombers were able to destroy aircraft on the ground or at the factories. During 1944 losses of fighter aircraft rose to 73 per cent of strength per month.[141] The higher the initial loss rates, the longer it took to build up sufficient stocks for future operations. Hitler's own attitude towards reserves made the task of conserving strength even harder. The effects of the increase in production, although a cause of anxiety and some surprise for Allied intelligence, were quickly dissipated because of the vast numerical superiority enjoyed by the Allies and the failure of either Hitler or Goering to create a workable air strategy. The shortage of aircraft was also accompanied by a growing shortage of crews. Test-pilots and training instructors had been drafted to the front for emergency operations in 1941. By 1944 the time devoted to training German pilots had fallen to less than half the time at the beginning of the war and a third of the time devoted to training an RAF pilot.[142] The loss rate among German pilots, particularly heavy on the eastern front, rose from an average of 615 per month before June 1941, to 1,167 per month between June 1941 and December 1943, and 1,755 in 1944.[143] Allied loss rates were high too, but the Allies benefited from being able to draw on the resources of all the United Nations.

One consequence of the long period of fighting with inadequate resources against well-armed air enemies was the deterioration in German morale. Air officers lacked confidence in their superior commanders; so much so that many tactical novelties were introduced at the front without being referred back to the authorities in Berlin. Morale was sapped, too, by the growing disillusionment of Hitler and the Nazi Party with the Luftwaffe's performance. The effects of bombing on the civilian population brought constant recriminations on the Luftwaffe from the local party administrators, and Hitler's own attacks on the air force leaders was a mixture of fear at the political consequences of continued bombing raids and desperation at the inability to offer adequate air protection to the armies that he was painfully withdrawing across Europe.[144] His disillusionment went so far that he finally ordered that the Luftwaffe should be disbanded and replaced by a vast anti-aircraft defence force. Although Goering was able to save his air force by appeals to past loyalty, Hitler refused to allow the Chief of Air Staff to enter the Supreme Headquarters for two months and kept up a personal vendetta against the Luftwaffe officers who were accused of cowardice, showmanship and corruption.[145] The only hope that Hitler held out was that some secret weapon would emerge in the air war which would give the initiative back to Germany. The V1 and V2 were thus given great priority in the belief that as a result of rocket attacks on London there would be 'such a storm of protest and war-weariness that the Government will be overthrown'.[146] When General Dornberger, responsible for the development of rockets, revealed to Hitler that the military value of the V2 was very limited Hitler angrily replied: 'But what I want is annihilation!'[147] Hitler had always treated air power as a terror weapon. In the final desperate months of war all serious development work was sacrificed in the effort to find the final war-winning secret weapon without which, as Hitler now realized, the war was lost. By this stage, however, the Luftwaffe had long ceased to be able to function properly. The air war lacked any firm direction either strategically or operationally. Resources had fallen to a mere fraction of what was necessary. Lacking material and purpose German airmen were volunteering for active service at the front with ground armies which, despite the lack of effective air support had succeeded in holding up the Allied armies in almost two years of retreating.[148]

(vi) Air Power and the War in Europe

The successful exercise of air power was slow to mature in the heat of actual conflict after 1941. For one thing it was by no means certain what 'successful' meant. German air power in 1940 had certainly been successful in the land campaigns, even though the Luftwaffe was defeated later through its failure to do more than support the German army. Allied air power had finally achieved air supremacy by the end of the war, but there was considerable confusion at the time as to why it had been so successful and even less agreement about the contribution of air power to the overall victory. The controversy surrounding air power stemmed to some extent from the question of the time-scale involved. Air supremacy took a long time to achieve. It involved the attrition of enemy air power rather than its complete defeat in a single major battle. It was as a result much harder to see exactly when air superiority had been won, or to recognize the critical moments when the initiative in air warfare passed from one side to the other. Another problem with air power was its experimental nature. For most of the early years of war the fighting powers were still at the stage of evolving air doctrines and battle tactics appropriate to the strategic demands made of aircraft. Amidst many mistakes and miscalculations a means appropriate to the end gradually emerged.

The clearest point to appear was the fundamental difference between British and American air power on the one hand, and that of the European forces on the other. Throughout the war the western powers had rigidly maintained that the exercise of air power should incorporate all the ways in which aircraft could be used in war. These different roles were pursued simultaneously, with carefully defined strategies for each purpose. German and Italian intentions were equally wide-ranging at the outset of war, but strategic uncertainty and the circumstances of war compelled the Axis powers to concentrate air power on the land battles and to abandon a broad concept of air power. The Soviet Union was also pressed hard by the circumstances of war, but had already determined some time before the German invasion that close army support made the best operational sense, given Russia's geographical position and the prevailing Stalinist military theory.

There were important differences in the situation facing both sides which helped to explain the different emphasis on air power. Most important of all were the contrasts in strategic circumstances. First of all the Western powers were excluded from Europe through the German victory. This meant that air power was one of the few ways of carrying the war on at all. Air power was crucial as a defence against German or Italian attempts to break further out of Europe and it was essential for carrying the offensive into Europe through bombing, blockade and the wearing down of Axis fighter strength. The second factor was the German invasion of Russia. Not only did this commit the bulk of German forces to a land war, and hence encourage the Luftwaffe in its more limited role, but it gave the western allies a long breathing-space in the west to build up large air forces and deploy them more or less at will. From this perspective the Russian armed forces gave greater help in the execution of western strategy than the west gave in return.

The difference in strategic circumstances also encouraged other differences as a direct result. Having more time to plan and prepare air warfare, the Allies were in a position to experiment with particular strategies and tactics and arrive at the best use of air power by a process of elimination. Germany once committed to the war in Russia, never had the same degree of time to think air power out properly, nor could sufficient intellectual or practical effort be diverted from the Eastern Front to pursue other air doctrines with any hope of success. That was made clear by the constant failure to mount a renewed bombing offensive of any value at all after the failure of the Blitz. The German high command was by no means unaware of alternatives. In fact the navy and air force staffs constantly demanded more air activity of an independent and offensive character. There were too many problems to overcome, however, to lift the Luftwaffe at short notice from a close-support force to the multi-purpose force wielded by the Allies. Where the Allies from the outset laid great store by the massive production of aircraft and resources for air warfare, the Luftwaffe was always in second place behind the army even had it used its industrial resources more productively. Where the Allies allowed the air force considerable latitude in finding the right strategy, and gave considerable freedom of command, the Axis forces were the prey of poor leadership which progressively abandoned authority over the air forces to the army, and to a limited role. Finally, the emphasis on science and technology that a general air strategy required, and which the western powers obligingly supplied, was insufficient in the Axis powers except for the more limited exercise of air power. This was true also for Russia, where aircraft production and research was concentrated almost exclusively on the requirements of the battlefront.

Above all there developed a clear difference in strategic emphasis. The Western Allies happily embraced air power as one of the most important instruments for achieving victory. The air force, particularly in Britain, had as much status and prestige as the army, and air strategy was widely discussed and examined at the highest level. In Germany the army enjoyed enormous prestige and Hitler, involved in the day-to-day running of the army machine, paid relatively little attention to the Luftwaffe. After he witnessed the failure of the air force in 1940 he was little persuaded of the vital importance of general air power, and alternative air strategies featured little in strategic discussions. Under such circumstances it was perhaps not surprising that when the war situation made it possible the Allies opted for the general use of air power in bombing, blockade, land support and the naval war; and the Axis for land support alone. The difference in emphasis then became in itself an important explanation as to why the Allies won the war in the air and not the fascist powers.

The second question, of how important air power was in explaining the Allied victory as a whole, was much harder to decide. The fact that it was important was not in doubt. General air strategy was not the same as an independent strategy, and throughout the war the Allies emphasized the complementarity and interdependence of air power with the army and the navy. The achievement of air supremacy on its own was no guarantee of victory, but combined with the efforts of the other services its contribution was substantial. This was particularly true of bombing. If there was doubt about the ability of bombers to carry out an autonomous strategy to any effect, there was no doubt that bombing made a major contribution to the winning of the key campaigns at sea and on land. To the end Eisenhower insisted that the bombers had an 'overriding priority of

The Air War in the Far East

Japan's war against the western powers possessed a strong sense of military unreality. It was clear that the United States would be able to use its vast material superiority to defeat Japan, though how long this would take depended on the course of the war in Europe. Both the Japanese offensive and the Allied response were more dependent on the use of air power than was the case in Europe with its traditional and influential land armies. For the Japanese, air power made up for naval inferiority and provided a flexible and versatile weapon with which to defend the projected 'southern region' of conquest. For the Allies aircraft formed a vital first line of defence in a weakly defended area, and when that line had been breached provided both the means to return to the offensive, a defence for major lines of communication and a means of communication in its own right. In the Pacific air power was linked closely with seapower and the emphasis that both the Japanese and American navies had placed on the aircraft carrier and marine aviation in the 1930s was fully justified by the events of the war. In China and south-east Asia land-based aircraft were also of great importance in keeping open lines of supply and in giving tactical support to land armies. In India the British depended on strategic air defence, as in 1940 over England, before forces could be built up for a combined attack on the Japanese positions in Burma and southern China. Because of this concentration on the strategic use of aircraft the winning of air supremacy was regarded as an essential prelude to the fulfilment of more general strategic ambitions. The Japanese inability to maintain the supremacy temporarily wrested from the Allies in early 1942, and the Allied determination to build up massive and diversified air power before resources for invasion could be diverted from the European theatre, led to the final defeat of Japan through blockade and destruction from the air. Technical inferiority, manpower shortages, comparative industrial backwardness and economic blockade continually undermined the effectiveness of the Japanese air forces; but defeat came through the fact that from the outset Japanese strategy had been a gamble for which resources were demonstrably inadequate.[1]

(i) The Victory of Japanese Air Power

The Japanese decision for war resulted from a number of strategic factors coinciding at once. One of the most important was the achievement of a non-aggression pact with Russia without which the risk of a southward invasion was too great. Throughout the late 1930s Japan had kept large air forces in the north against the Russian threat. A precondition of further imperialism was the neutralization of this threat.[2] When a pact was finally achieved in April 1941 it freed part of the Japanese army in Manchuria and allowed the movement south of aircraft for operations in South East Asia.[3] The second factor was the rapid shift in the course of the European war. By mid-1941 Japan was entitled to expect that Germany would defeat Britain and Russia within a short period of time, leaving the United States isolated. The European war had denuded the Far East of western forces and it became increasingly obvious that only in 1941 would the balance of forces so favour Japan that a decisive military blow could be struck that might persuade America to accept Japanese imperialism. The temporarily favourable strategic situation masked more pressing long-term arguments for war. The army and navy, although with very different strategic perspectives, nevertheless recognized the need to preserve the Japanese empire in China for reasons both political and economic. Both recognized, too, that the economic blockade to which Japan was exposed, because of the Chinese war, was undermining at an accelerating rate the ability to maintain the armed forces and hence any imperialism at all. In this the question of oil was crucial. In August 1941 General Suzuki was ordered to investigate the success of the plans for synthetic oil production inaugurated in the 1937 Synthetic Oil Industry Law. He reported that large new investments were necessary which would not produce the necessary oil until 1943-44.[4] Even before this report the Japanese navy had already reached the conclusion that the deteriorating economic situation justified war, however reluctantly such a decision might be taken. For the navy the ideal time to strike was in late 1941 before American forces were built up in the Pacific and before the oil situation became critical, though Yamamoto was sceptical of his ability to defeat America in the long term.[5] For the army war only became unavoidable when it became clear at the end of November 1941 that America would not reach a negotiated settlement unless Japan voluntarily abandoned her conquests in China. In both cases it had been hoped that war could be avoided; from the army's point of view because a favourable conclusion to the war with China first would have meant the release of forces to guard the north and to support a later anti-western offensive. The navy's insistence on war in late 1941 resulted not from a favourable relationship between the state of the Chinese war and the projected southern war but because of the nature of the military planning. Late 1941 was reluctantly accepted as the best time to strike.[6]

From the mid-1930s the Japanese navy had experimented with the idea of a combined aerial-naval strike against naval enemies in the Pacific. The close attention paid to aircraft carriers coupled with Commander Genda's championship of the mass carrier strike provided an ideal weapon with which to conduct trans-oceanic strategy stretched over a wide area of the Pacific. Once won, such an area could be defended by a fast carrier force combined with a land-based bomber air-force around the perimeter, and it was precisely this combination of aerial striking-power and naval mobility that Imperial General Headquarters adopted.[7] Studies for the execution of an attack were carried out in the wake of the successful British attack at Taranto, and war exercises in April and May 1941 confirmed its feasibility. By June 1941 Yamamoto ordered the preparation for mobilization and by the autumn Japan had 6 fleet carriers, 4 large fleet carriers and a total naval front-line strength of 1,400 aircraft which were to be deployed in an eastward strike against the United States base at Hawaii, and a southward movement to capture British and Dutch possessions in the south Pacific.[8] The army's preparations were less extensive because of the need to maintain some forces in Manchuria in case of Russian aggression; to continue the fight against the Chinese forces; and to defend mainland Japan. In consequence only 11 army divisions and two air divisions of some 700 aircraft could be diverted southwards for the capture of Burma, Malaya and the Dutch East Indies.[9]

The war with China had given much experience to both the army and navy in establishing air tactics and in organizing air forces to achieve maximum effect and satisfactory co-operation with the parent service. The army had originally organized aircraft in regiments of mixed types (*hiko rentai*) but these were replaced during the Chinese war by Groups (*sentai*) which were smaller, more flexible and more specialized. The navy organized aircraft in naval air corps (*kokutai*) usually of one aircraft type and attached either to a fleet or an area as the tactical situation required.[10] Use of bombers and dive-bombers on both sea and land targets had been perfected over China and in the China Sea and incorporated into naval planning through the recommendations of the Battle Lessons Committee set up during the Sino-Japanese conflict.[11] Considerable stress was laid on the acquisition of good aerial intelligence and this, combined with an insistence on the need for surprise, was put to good use in the attack on Pearl Harbor and the Philippines. So, too, was the insistence on a very high level of training for naval pilots, though this was partly to make up for the difficulty of supplying large numbers of aircraft and adequate reserves. Actual losses of aircraft, particularly through accident, were consequently low during the early stages of the war. Although the navy knew that it enjoyed numerical superiority in both carriers and aircraft in late 1941, the numbers available were much too small to sustain a long offensive or to fight an air war with America were it not preoccupied elsewhere. In 1940 only 4,768 aircraft were produced divided between the two services; in 1941 this total had risen to only 5,088.[12] Although this represented an increase of over 300 per cent against production in the first year of the Chinese war, the new war plans envisaged stretching the resources over three wide fronts against potentially powerful air enemies. Moreover the army aircraft did not compare well with the advanced aircraft of the Allies, and while those of the navy were more than adequate for the task in 1941 of defeating ageing and obsolete Allied aircraft they, too, could not match in speed or firepower the new generation of American and British models. Since much of this disparity was known in Japan, and since some of it was related to a lack of raw materials, the swift creation of a defensible southern region rich in resources, achieved largely through air-power exercised by ships, was calculated to be the best use to which Japan's limited forces could be put.

Japanese intelligence on Allied strength in the Far East was largely correct. Britain could not afford to keep large forces in the area particularly as preparations were in hand for a fresh offensive against Rommel and a future invasion of Europe. America, although beginning to rearm in sufficient measure to provide better defence in the Pacific, was obliged to send most of the modern equipment to Britain and Russia and had already subscribed to the British decision that victory in Europe must be secured first at the expense of anything more decisive in the Far East should Japan take the offensive. The relative weakness of the two powers was to a certain extent offset by the continued involvement of China in the war. Just as the western powers benefited from the German-Russian conflict so the Sino-Japanese war was thought to tie down sufficient Japanese forces to make any further imperialism unlikely.[13] American intelligence was in this respect misled. Arguing that Japan could not move both east and south at the same time stress was put on reinforcing the meagre forces in the Philippines as the most likely area for any future Japanese attack. Yet so unprepared for the actual outbreak of war were American forces that aircraft were huddled together in large groups on the airfields in the belief that sabotage was a greater threat than air attack.[14] The element of surprise in the Japanese attack was as complete as that of the German forces in Russia in June 1941. This kind of error reflected on the part of the United States, not an unwillingness to defend the Pacific area seriously, but a rational strategic calculation that the risk of actual war in the Pacific was more remote than the risk of war with Germany. The plan to reinforce and reorganize forces in the Pacific in late 1941 was intended to act as a deterrent by showing American intention to defend her position at some future date should the need arise. The reinforcement relied to a great extent on air power, and the heavy bomber in particular which could reach Japanese positions in Indo-China and Formosa from where it was not thought Japanese aircraft could effectively retaliate. The lack of systematic air reconnaissance, which after some disagreement between the army and navy only began to operate in December 1941, left further large gaps in knowledge about Japanese intentions and strengths, and like other preparations suffered from the demands being made on American resources elsewhere.[15]

One of the most insistent of these demands was the creation of a satisfactory hemisphere defence. The obvious weakness of American peacetime forces, created at a time when the United States enjoyed geographical immunity, had to be corrected first before commitments elsewhere could be fully honoured. In the air—from which most attacks on America were expected—large forces were built up for internal defence and grouped in four main defence areas.[16] The crucial areas outside mainland America, to which greater urgency was given, were Alaska, the Caribbean and the Panama Canal. The American navy had demonstrated years before the vulnerability of the canal to a carrier attack, yet adequate defences remained almost non-existent. The greatest difficulty was the almost complete lack of radar for early warning of air attack. Even when it was finally installed at the Canal Zone in 1941 it was of low technical standard, operated by poorly trained observers and for some time uncoordinated into the overall air defence scheme. In Alaska and the northern Pacific only two radar sets were available by late 1941, again on an experimental basis. In fact the whole radar programme was only inaugurated in May 1940 after inspection of the British system, and although widely introduced after the Japanese attacks, it was still unavailable on more than a rudimentary basis to give intelligence of surprise attacks in December 1941.[17]

Once hemisphere defence was organized, greater attention was given to defending Hawaii and the Philippines in the hope that any future war could be contained away from the mainland. In November 1940 a Hawaiian Air Force was created designed to be built around a complement of heavy bombers, the first of which arrived in May 1941. In July 1941 a study produced on 'The Air Situation in Hawaii' called for permanent heavy-bomber patrols with a strength of 72 aircraft and a functioning radar screen to provide adequate protection against a carrier strike. Neither the screen nor the bombers were available fully by the time of the attack on Pearl Harbor.[18] One reason for this was that reinforcements were directed south to the Philippines where an aggressive defence was to be established, again grouped around a force of heavy bombers. Although 272 were allocated to the region only 30 were available by December 1941. The remaining aircraft were obsolescent.[19] The position of the British and Dutch air forces was as bad. In the Far East the British Air Ministry had calculated in 1940 that some 336 modern aircraft were required for defence, a figure subsequently revised to 582. In fact by December only 158, again largely obsolete, aircraft were available.[20] Although Britain recognized that air power properly used was a crucial ingredient of imperial defence the resources could not be released from more pressing purposes. Instead a temporary policy of appeasement was substituted for the lack of an adequate air deterrent. In September 1941 the Chiefs of Staff instructed the British commander that 'Avoidance of war with Japan is the basis of Far East policy and provocation must be rigidly avoided'.[21] This instruction was made fully in the knowledge that air defences in the Far East were completely inadequate. There were few airfields, a small maintenance unit on Singapore, few spare parts and supplies, few trained pilots and so little intelligence on the Japanese that the RAF did not know of the existence of the Mitsubishi Zero fighter even though it had flown and been observed in action in China in the spring of 1940.[22] It was impossible to get early warning of attack and there were too few aircraft either to fulfil a reconnaissance role or to attack enemy shipping once located.

Under these circumstances it was not surprising that the Japanese attack was completely successful in all its respects. The outer perimeter was secured with few losses and at great speed and the major naval threat from the United States was temporarily eliminated at Hawaii. In global terms Japan was weaker than either of the two major western powers but in terms of the area chosen for attack the balance was very much in favour of the aggressor. This was true in terms of numbers and in terms of quality. In the Far East the western powers had only left a skeleton force supported with equipment that was obsolete or becoming so. It was inevitable that Japanese aggression would overcome this opposition. Success was not, however, entirely due to the relative strengths of the two sides. Japan secured victory because of good intelligence, careful planning and tactical superiority. The use of aircraft was vital in the overall plan, though it was the smooth working relationship established between navy, air force and ground forces that provided the key explanation for victory. The air forces provided the necessary preliminary air strikes, protection for fleet and transport movements, air cover over the battlefield and fighter protection for bomber aircraft. This last was particularly important as the bomber force was designed to destroy air installations and aircraft on the ground and had to be protected from enemy fighter interception in order to carry out its primary function. Unknown to American intelligence the Japanese 11th Air Fleet based on Formosa had carried out experiments to extend the range of the Zero fighter from a maximum of six hours flying to up to twelve hours in order to fly fighter cover direct from Formosa to the Philippines and back. The result was the complete elimination of all American air forces in the northern Philippines.[23] The scattered disposition of Allied air strength also gave a tactical advantage to Japanese forces which were able to concentrate air forces at each stage of the advance against dispersed Allied air strength.

Such concentration was made possible by the use of fast aircraft carriers. The carrier fleet under Nagumo that destroyed the American fleet in Hawaii continued to be used throughout the campaign to give protection to fleet movements and to speed up the advance in the south. Only where it was difficult to mount large concentrations of aircraft, particularly naval aircraft, was air superiority harder to achieve. Thus in the army attack on Burma the modern aircraft available to the RAF were much more successful in denying command of the air to the army air forces. The success of the Japanese army ground assault on Burma demonstrated, however, that British reliance on air power for imperial defence was of little use if it could not be combined with the ability of armies to hold and occupy land. Burma in fact represented the fullest extension of Japanese ambitions. Yamamoto argued for attacks on Ceylon, Australia and the supply route from America to the south Pacific. The army argued that it did not have the resources for anything more ambitious. The strategy decided upon was the protection of the perimeter, the exploitation of available raw materials to the full and the protection of all internal sea lanes while the war in China was brought to an end.[24] In fact so swift had been the initial victories that Japanese strategy was left in some confusion. Little thought had been given to the longer-term implications of the original plan. If for the Japanese it represented a *fait accompli* to flourish at the Allies in the hope of fresh negotiations, to the Allies it meant a fresh challenge to even greater military efforts to achieve uncompromising victory over the totalitarian powers.[25]

(ii) The Allied 'Defensive-Offensive'

British strategy in the face of the Japanese victory was straightforward: to safeguard India and the Indian Ocean by a limited defence and to prepare at a future date, to be determined by victory in the Middle East and Europe, for the eventual re-occupation of captured areas. The frontier with Burma was consequently strengthened and a large complement of modern aircraft made available. Madagascar was occupied and Ceylon and the outlying islands reinforced.[26] The major part of the Far Eastern plans was to be decided by the Americans within the wider framework of the Allied grand strategy. At the Arcadia conference early in 1942 it was agreed that in the Far East priority should be given to a vigorous defence in depth against further Japanese incursions; to encouraging Chinese resistance by direct military and economic aid; and to keeping open the vital lines of communication across the Pacific.[27] For the period when the offensive would again be taken plans were made for the acquisition of suitable bases without which the attacks would lack adequate air protection. In addition it was agreed that a large fast carrier force should be created for the Pacific to reproduce the tactical successes of the Japanese in concentration and mobility of air forces. The choice of Admiral King as supreme commander in the Pacific was from this point of view an important choice. He had commanded the carrier *Lexington* in 1930 and in 1933 became Chief of the

Naval Bureau of Aeronautics. Throughout the war he emphasized the importance of air power and the interdependence between ships and aircraft. To the Secretary of the Navy he later reported 'There has been no dispute as to "carriers versus battleships". Aircraft can do some things which ships cannot do. Ships can do some things which aircraft cannot do'. Although disagreements arose between the army and navy, often about control over aircraft, the naval high command was firmly committed to a strategy in which air power had an integral part to play.[28]

The immediate task was to reinforce the Far East and to keep open present lines of communication. At the Washington Conference it was agreed that for the emergency the essential route was the south-eastern supply line from Florida, through the Caribbean, Brazil and West Africa which fed aircraft and supplies to the Middle East, India, China and until February 1942, the Far East. Without this route material could not easily be brought to either Russia or China, whose continued belligerency was essential for longer-term Allied strategy.[29] A new supply route across the Pacific was also necessary to maintain a significant military presence in the Far East. The route had been begun before December 1941 with hurried attempts to construct airfields on an island chain from Hawaii and from the American west coast. The importance of air bases along the route was that adequate cover could be given to the movement of ships through the area, but it was also intended that aircraft should be flown direct across the Pacific to save shipping space and time. Moreover air transport aircraft could ferry supplies to key areas considerably faster than transport shipping. After some dispute as to jurisdiction over the activities of air transport both the army and navy agreed to the establishment in July 1942 of an Air Transport Command (equivalent in status to the other major AAF commands) charged with ferrying aircraft, personnel and supplies.[30] The establishment of secure supply routes was a crucial precondition for any move to the offensive against Japan or indeed for the maintenance of a satisfactory defence. In fact the decision to seize islands in the Solomons in late 1942 was taken in the hope of forestalling Japanese attacks on the supply route.

Supply was just as important for the China theatre, for the loss of Burma gave responsibility for maintaining supplies to the air force. The India-China route provided the only way of reinforcing the Chinese forces and the Americans fighting with them. To carry out the reinforcement the AAF created the Tenth Air Force operating with headquarters at New Delhi. Among its tasks were the defence of India, the protection of the India-China route and the command of a China Air Task Force for actual operations in China itself.[31] The main problems facing such a supply route lay in the lack of experienced personnel and sufficient transport aircraft or satisfactory air bases. In the face of such difficulties supply was only maintained for the political purpose of keeping Chiang Kai-shek in the war at all. Only Stilwell and Chennault, the American commanders in the China-India theatre, remained convinced that China provided the best avenue for the future attack on Japan and that air forces deployed there could both wear down Japanese resistance and help to bomb distant economic targets. It was certainly true that the activities of the China Air Task Force helped to contain Japanese army air power in central and eastern China; but the major problem remained that insufficient resources could be flown in to mount any more elaborate air offensive, and that if the Japanese decided, as they did in 1944, to begin an offensive to eliminate the American threat, it was unlikely that Chinese and American forces could contain it and at the same time provide a secure base for bombing before the war had been brought to an end via the Pacific. Despite arguments for a more positive commitment to the China theatre, air activities remained largely diversionary rather than central to overall Allied strategy. The major attempt later in the war to use a series of bases in China for bombing Japan with B-29 'Superfortresses', codenamed 'Matterhorn', broke down not only because of difficulties in supply and in airfield construction but because more suitable bases were secured more rapidly in the Pacific.[32]

American military strategy, like that of Japan, depended on the building up of large carrier and air forces in the central and south-western Pacific which would enable the Allies to move over from the defensive to what King called the 'defensive-offensive' stage of operations. The carriers had not been destroyed at Pearl Harbor and very rapidly the balance of carrier forces swung in favour of the United States through the swift expansion of a carrier and aircraft programme laid down in 1941, when the War Department had demanded industrial policies to utilize the 'great economic and industrial advantage over our potential enemies . . .'.[33] The number of aircraft planned for production for the American navy in 1942 exceeded total Japanese production for all purposes in 1942. Within only a few months of the attack at Pearl Harbor American forces were sufficient to prevent further Japanese expansion. The victories in the Coral Sea and at Midway, with better American intelligence and an imitation of Japanese carrier tactics destroyed any significant threat that Japan could pose in 1942 and early 1943 by eliminating the Japanese carrier force and the large part of its aircraft and trained crews.[34] Within a further six months the offensive had been mounted in the Pacific islands with a growing disparity of forces in America's favour. By January 1943 American front-line air-strength in the Far East already exceeded that of Japan and by January 1944 reached 11,442 against a Japanese strength of only 4,050.[35] Moreover the successful Japanese strategy based on a combination of naval land-based bombers operating with well-protected carrier fleets was lost sight of in the course of 1943 while defending important land bases at Guadalcanal, and Rabaul. Yamamoto instructed carrier aircraft to work from land to assist ground forces at Guadalcanal and in subsequent American advances, thus denuding the surface fleets of sufficient air cover and exposing the fleet units to regular American air attack. His successor Admiral Koga insisted on sending carrier aircraft to the defence of Rabaul and over two-thirds of the fleet air forces were lost in performing functions for which they had not been designed.

Japanese defence of the perimeter depended on being able to maintain sufficient resources to prevent American incursions. The shortages of aircraft, resulting from economic conditions as much as from poor planning, meant that Japan very quickly found her own strategy reversed. Dispersed forces, the difficulty of concentrating forces in all areas under attack, declining intelligence on Allied plans and dispositions, and a very limited strategic view based narrowly on the instruction to defend every outer area to the limit, accelerated the attrition and destruction of the Japanese air forces.[36] This situation had become obvious with the final destruction of the re-formed carrier fleets and air forces in the Battle of the Philippine Sea and the Battle of Leyte Gulf. In both cases the Japanese forces were considerably outnumbered. In the latter case insufficient knowledge of American intentions together with the insistence of the army that the Philippines should be defended at Luzon left too few aircraft for the decisive naval battle. The later army decision to defend at Leyte instead of Luzon played into the hands of the American carrier forces and speeded up the final reoccupation of the whole area.[37] In the whole battle for the south Pacific and south-west Pacific area all fifteen Japanese carriers brought into service since 1941 were sunk or damaged too severely for action, while of all the 27 fleet carriers added to the American navy only one was sunk.[38] With such obvious material disparity, encouraged by King's view that 'our guiding policy is to achieve not mere adequacy, but overwhelming superiority of material',[39] and the build up of massive air forces for the final defeat of Japan it became only a question of time before fanatical human resistance would be worn down by material power.

The almost immediate reversal of Japanese fortunes in 1942 against an enemy only able to divert some 15 per cent of all war resources to the Pacific theatre confirmed Japanese fears that a straightforward battle of resources could not possibly be won. Imperial General Headquarters finally announced a state of defence in February 1943 beginning the slow retreat at almost exactly the same time as German forces in Europe.[40] Any hope that contact could be established between German and Japanese troops following a defeat of Allied forces in the Middle East or Russian forces in the Caucasus had disappeared only months after Japanese entry into the war.[41] The only way in which the southern region could be defended was through a large increase in material and trained men, and despite great efforts the Japanese economy could not provide what was necessary even before the beginning of the American bombing offensive. The Japanese high command was aware of the need for large increases in production. Air plans laid down for the period from January 1944 to August 1945 called for a total output of 97,000 aircraft. Economic restrictions reduced the plan to 66,000 and in the end only 40,000 could be produced, most of the aircraft being light fighters. The major bottleneck proved to be engine production. Over the same period only 56,000 engines were produced instead of the planned 105,000 and the ratio of engines to airframes produced fell from 2.3:1 in 1941 to 1:1 in 1945.[42] The effect of this was to give a very short life to most aircraft for no satisfactory reserve of replacement engines could be built up. Despite the large increase in actual numbers produced the structure weight of the aircraft was small. The 5,000 aircraft produced in 1941 represented 26 per cent of the weight of American aircraft produced; the 28,000 in 1944 only 8 per cent.[43] This shift reflected the fact that after 1942 the balance between bombers and fighters in the air force swung sharply in favour of fighters. In 1941 fighters totalled 21 per cent of all production, bombers 29 per cent. In 1943 the proportions were 43 per cent and 25 per cent: in 1945 49 per cent and 17 per cent.[44] As with the Luftwaffe the swing was indicative of a loss of initiative in the air and made the task of restoring a balance and regaining a bomber striking capability much harder, particularly as the numbers of fighters produced was simply not adequate for the task of regaining air superiority.

That the number of aircraft produced was insufficient was demonstrated by the wide difference in strength between the Japanese and American air forces in the later stages of the war (see Table 6). Moreover the greater the disparity, the easier it became for the American air forces to eliminate those of the enemy, however substantial the increase in output. By 1944 the Japanese loss rate was so high that new production barely covered losses and there was no question of keeping reserves, as the following table demonstrates.

Table 6: American and Japanese Strength and Losses in the Pacific War [45]

	Japanese front-line strength	American front-line strength
January 1943	3,200	3,537
January 1944	4,050	11,442
January 1945	4,600	17,976
July 1945	4,100	21,908

	Japanese combat losses	American combat losses
December 1941–August 1945	army 17,760 navy 20,345	8,700

The situation was made worse for the Japanese forces because of the relative decline in performance. Against the new Allied aircraft even the Zero fighter was considerably inferior and other Japanese aircraft completely outmoded. Because few long-term plans had been made for replacements for existing aircraft models, the war saw both a hurried effort to find new types and a long series of modifications to existing models. The former effort failed largely because of the lack of design and engineering experience and the poor raw material position. The latter effort, although providing pilots with more weapons and armour protection, which earlier Japanese aircraft had lacked, made aircraft heavier and less manoeuvrable and resulted in many cases in an actual loss of performance over the war period. Competition between army and navy also complicated the introduction of new types by encouraging the development of too many new designs and spreading engineering resources far too thinly. The navy developed some 53 basic models with 112 variations, the army 37 basic and 52 variations. The jealous guardianship of a separate economic base for army and navy production led to much duplication and dispersion of effort. Both services developed machine-guns with different cartridges and electrical systems with different voltages.[46]

Nevertheless there were problems of supply and production about which little could be done. Throughout 1944 and 1945 an ever-increasing number of fighter aircraft had to be kept in homeland Japan for defence purposes. In June 1944 the number of home-defence fighters was 260, by July 1945 it had risen to 500.[47] Large numbers of aircraft had to be diverted as well to the Chinese theatre, to protect aircraft and raw material production and defend against bomber attacks. The most serious supply problems arose over raw materials and labour. Of these the most crucial were the shortages of aluminium and fuel oil. Even though great economies were made in the use of aluminium there was simply too little available to produce more than 40 per cent of the total aircraft planned. Shortages of fuel oil became so acute that all flight testing had to be abandoned and only one in ten aero-engines were tested before delivery.[48] Other material shortages, particularly of crucial alloy steels for engine output reduced the serviceability of naval aircraft from 80 per cent at the beginning of the war to as little as 20 per cent by the end, and partly accounted for why so many

Japanese aircraft were destroyed on the ground.[49] From the second quarter of 1942 Japanese fuel consumption exceeded total production and imports, and the gap was made up through the use of large stocks built up before 1942. More fuel would have been available had the American blockade not been aimed at fuel supplies in particular. As it was there was too little fuel to keep naval and air forces in operation or to fuel those increases in production necessary to defend oil imports and break the blockade.[50]

American strategy was designed to take advantage of the weak economic position of Japan, first of all by overwhelming resistance through sheer numbers, secondly by a long-term programme of blockade and attrition. In both enterprises the gaining of air superiority was vital. Aircraft, either from land bases or carriers, were the main instruments for carrying out the attrition of Japanese naval and air forces, the blockade on trade and, later in the war, the bombing of the mainland economy. The attrition of the Japanese air force, like that of the Luftwaffe, was a central concept in Allied plans for gaining command of the air, and emphasized once again the fact that air warfare was a continuous operation rather than a series of decisive battles. Although a concentrated Japanese air attack could still gain local and temporary supremacy, as over Guadalcanal in the early stages of the campaign, Japanese forces found themselves continually outnumbered from the middle of 1942 onwards, and by aircraft that were better powered and more heavily armed. In the final attempt to relieve New Guinea in June 1943 a force of 120 fighters and medium bombers was met by a force of over 100 superior American fighters. 107 Japanese aircraft were destroyed for the loss of six American. In the Battle of the Philippine Sea over 300 Japanese aircraft were destroyed for the loss of 23 American.[51] The unequal battles were made worse for the Japanese forces because of the problem of training crews. In the early stages of the war great reliance had been placed 'not in massed physical power, but in the perfection of expertness' and the navy in particular had based its training on the 'premise of the invincibility of a refined technique'.[52] Hence the emphasis in design on a highly manoeuvrable carrier fighter. But the loss of the skilled cadres in the Battle of Midway and in the Solomons in 1942 left the Japanese air forces short of skilled training staff and reliant on pilots who could not be given the careful and lengthy training of the original crews because of the shortages at the front. Not only were Japanese aircraft heavily outnumbered but the quality of personnel declined sharply as well. By 1944 the operational loss rate of pilots in the Japanese navy had reached 50 per cent.[53]

Additional difficulties were created for Japanese forces by the American attrition of shipping which left front-line forces short of fuel, supplies and adequate maintenance facilities, all of which the American forces possessed in growing abundance, flown or shipped in along the Pacific supply routes. Shipping losses consisted of both naval and merchant ships, although the air forces inflicted much greater losses on the former. Table 7 shows the total loss of Japanese warship and merchant tonnage and the cause.

Aircraft accounted for 50 per cent of all warship losses and 32 per cent of merchant losses, as well as assuming much of the responsibility in spotting ships to which naval units could then be directed. Blockade was also supported by army air forces operating from bases when they became available against more distant Japanese targets, particularly in the East Indies, Malaya and Indo-

Table 7: Japanese Warship and Merchant Losses and Cause 1941-45[54]

Warships		Merchant ships	
Cause	Tonnage	Cause	Tonnage
Naval aircraft	745,000	Navy submarines	4,774,000
Naval aircraft and other		Naval aircraft	1,543,000
agents	167,000		
Navy submarines	540,000	Navy & other agents	192,000
Navy surface vessels	278,000	AAF aircraft	668,000
AAF aircraft & mines	73,000	AAF mines	551,000
all other	157,000	Combinations of above	840,000

China where the oil, bauxite and other raw materials were located. In addition army bombers undertook part of the attack against Japanese air power by attacking bases and supply depots in the Japanese rear along the lines of tactical air attacks in the European theatre.[55]

As the perimeter was successfully penetrated under a large air umbrella and with the use of fast carrier task forces for capturing key islands and bases the possiblility for the Americans of using bombing for more than tactical support finally arrived. It was as this point approached that growing differences began to emerge between the American army strategy and that of the navy. The navy had been largely responsible for the successful offensive in the central and south Pacific and in giving considerable support to MacArthur in the army attacks in the south-west Pacific. The navy wished to continue the Pacific offensive as originally planned, capture Iwo Jima and Okinawa as advanced bases for the final assault on southern Japan. AAF heavy bombers operating from other Pacific bases would have the task of preparing the ground for a large-scale amphibious attack like that in Europe, codenamed 'Olympic'. In fact after the capture of Okinawa the American Third Fleet bombarded the coastline of Japan and destroyed remaining Japanese air power in a series of preparatory battles and had deployed some 26 aircraft carriers, 64 escort aircraft carriers and 14,000 combat aircraft for the final attack on Japan.[56] Against this strategy there developed several army views. The first stage of the army strategy was the re-occupation of the Philippines and Formosa, which, though not essential to the navy plan, was considered to be expedient on political grounds. It also gave the army units a more definite goal. The second prospect was the defeat of Japan through the China-Burma-India theatre. This view had been held as a possibility earlier in the war. The plan consisted essentially of two features. Attacks by American and British ground forces against Burma, Malaya, and in China itself, combined with a programme of heavy-bombing to destroy the Japanese economy and will-to-resist without a full-scale invasion of the Japanese homeland. The two strategic views were not in all respects mutually exclusive and in the end the army initiative in both Burma and the Philippines was carried out successfully.[57] The main debate was about the nature and purpose of a bombing offensive, and raised again the issue never resolved in the European campaign as to whether bombing was simply a prelude to combined operations or an operation in its own right.

(iii) Bombing and the Collapse of Japan

Early bombing operations in Burma and south China were largely tactical, aiming at Japanese air strength, supplies and communications near the front, or giving support to ground operations in northern Burma and south China. Yet from the start Stilwell and Chennault had hoped that air operations in China, which constituted almost the only active military aid to Chiang Kai-shek, would be a prelude to more aggressive air strategy launched from a series of bases for attacking Japan and Manchuria with heavy bombers. The bases promised would, it was argued, be at risk but could be adequately defended by the Chinese air forces in preparation and being trained by Chennault, and by the American task force.[58] The only major problem was supply over the 'Hump', the airlift route to south China, from which Chennault demanded at least 10,000 tons of supplies a month, and a minimum of 3,000 tons for his own 14th Air Force. The failure to match these demands was due largely to the difficulties in building air fields, particularly in Assam and Bengal. In both India and China the problem was getting sufficient native labour. Nevertheless enough supplies were maintained to allow Chennault to expand the 14th Air Force towards the 500 aircraft he had originally suggested and to maintain a Chinese/American military presence in eastern China from which to attack Japanese ports and shipping, and to drive a wedge between the Japanese positions in northern Indo-China and around Hankow.[59] On the continued success of this enterprise depended the future prospect of a defeat of Japanese army forces in China and the carrying out of a successful China-based bombing offensive.

It was under these circumstances that discussion opened in Washington over the future of strategic bombing in the east. In the Pacific and China areas one factor governing all bombing enterprises was range. Until bases could be captured close to Japan the only prospect of bombing was to produce an aircraft that could fly further. The B-29 'Superfortress' was presented by Arnold as the weapon most suitable for Far Eastern bombing attacks, and although developed too late for wide use in Europe, it was available for the end of the Pacific war. In fact when it was originally conceived in 1939 one of its primary war tasks was expected to be the high-level bombing of Japanese industry.[60] In May 1943 the decision was reached at the Trident conference to concentrate on a China initiative and to plan for the capture of Hong Kong and occupation of eastern China to provide a base to cut Japanese communications and bomb mainland Japan.[61] At Quebec in August the AAF had proposed in addition that huge new supplies be flown in via the India-China route to support a concentration of all the heavy bombers released from Europe in the event of an early German surrender. The proposal called for the construction of a chain of airfields on a 400 mile axis south and north of Changsa capable of handling the bombers, and in particular the ten groups of B-29 bombers scheduled for completion by October 1944. Arnold, calculating that the B-29 bases in the Marianas and Carolines would not be ready for over a year, endorsed the China plan and preparations were carried out for sending the supplies and bombers fc. carrying out 'Matterhorn'.[62] Arnold, too, had been responsible for calling in early 1943 for a plan from the Committee of Operations Analysts for the best target systems in Japan suitable for a strategy of eliminating Japan from the war. The Committee's emphasis on coke-ovens and hence steel as a top-priority target encouraged the China strategists since the coke ovens in Manchuria and Korea were well within the range of bombers stationed in western China.[63]

However the accelerated and successful pattern of offensive operations in the Pacific, approved in early 1944, completely altered the emphasis put on the China theatre. The projected capture of Saipan and other island bases meant that within two or three months after invasion major B-29 bases would be completed within easy striking distance of Tokyo and easily supplied from the Pacific. As a result the XX Bomber Command was withdrawn from China after only a handful of strategic bombing operations for continued campaigning from the Marianas bases. In fact the strategic picture had altered further with the Japanese attack on the main communications lines in central China and any thought of using Chinese forces for defeating Japan or of being able to safeguard heavy bomber bases disappeared.[64] The surviving base at Chengtu was unsuitable as a centre for conducting long-range operations as it was too far from mainland Japan. 'Matterhorn' was cancelled and the army air effort was moved to the Pacific theatre where, although it remained under AAF headquarters direct control, it was expected to play only a complementary role in the navy's overall plan for defeating Japan. This was not altogether satisfactory for the AAF. Even in China where the bombers' major strategic objective was to attack Inner Region Japan, most operations had been merely tactical in urgent support of operations in Burma or the Philippines or against Japanese-held ports and shipping. Arnold feared that this same dispersion of bombing effort to tactical purposes that had emerged in 1943 in Europe and in China in 1944, would be repeated in the Pacific and his personal command of the bombing forces reflected his desire to keep the bombers for a purely strategic purpose in attacking the mainland economy.[65]

The bombing attack was finally launched in November 1944 when the Japanese economy was already in decline, the merchant marine available a fraction of what was necessary and military resources and morale already low. The plan originally drawn up by the Committee of Operations Analysts was modified. It recommended three main target areas to achieve a victory through blockade and bombing alone; shipping, the aircraft industry, and six major urban-industrial complexes. If invasion were necessary it was recommended that shipping, aircraft resources and urban areas be attacked together with other more obviously tactical targets. In the end the Joint Chiefs of Staff insisted that the latter priorities be followed, in the belief that invasion of mainland Japan was unavoidable.[66] As a result the AAF found itself faced with the same problem of choosing between precise and indiscriminate targets that had confronted the Allied forces in Europe. Arnold had favoured precision bombing of aircraft industry targets at the opening of the campaign but tactical problems reduced their effectiveness and accelerated the move to area bombing from which the AAF had refrained as a primary target until late in the European war. In March 1945 the XXI Bomber Command commmander, LeMay, demanded and secured permission for urban area attacks with fire-bombing techniques.[67] He justified such a demand by pointing to the level of heavy-bomber losses in precision attacks due to Japanese fighter defence. This was largely an excuse. The defence was scanty compared with the defence available in Germany in the early months of the Combined Bomber Offensive. Only 500 aircraft with low serviceability were available, including only two groups of night-fighters with poor radar.[68] Because of the system of army command over air units, each fighter defence group was assigned to a specific territory and could not be used for operations in support of neighbouring areas. Ground-to-air communication was too poor for centralized control of fighters even in these smaller defence areas.[69] The Japanese defenders had the one advantage that the extreme concentration of Japanese industry allowed a high concentration of anti-aircraft fire around the threatened areas. But even this could not compensate for the sustained attrition of air forces or the deteriorating economic situation. Throughout 1945 there was little effective opposition.

It was under such circumstances that the Kamikaze tactics were introduced. Such tactics combined the Japanese military ethic with the pragmatic argument that suicide attacks constituted the most efficient use to which Japan's shrinking stock of aircraft could be put.[70] The fact that large numbers of training aircraft were also converted to suicide purposes reflected the finality of the Japanese decision, for no future air force could be reconstructed after the wastage of the Kamikaze campaign. Nor did the campaign itself show any appreciable results. Like the German rocket campaign its effect on morale at home was more important than its military effect, although in both cases the Allies gave the effort more attention than it merited. Although some 402 ships were hit only a quarter were sunk or severely damaged out of a fleet of thousands, while in the Okinawa campaign over 3,000 Japanese aircraft were destroyed.[71] Kamikaze sorties declined rapidly as the necessary aircraft and crews were destroyed. The figures for total sorties were as follows:

Table 8: Sorties by Suicide Pilots, October 1944 to August 1945[72]

October 1944	55	April 1945	1,162
November 1944	143	May 1945	596
December 1944	232	June 1945	210
January 1945	230	July 1945	20
February 1945	196	August 1945	59
March 1945	37		

The result of the attacks on the targets selected could not be assessed and pilot training was so poor by the last year of war that there was no guarantee that the targets would even be reached. The Allied use of 'decoy' ships on sentry duty for the main fleets diverted a great deal of the suicide effort from the main targets. The great majority of suicide aircraft were shot down by Allied fighters and anti-aircraft fire. The suicide campaign did nothing to halt the amphibious attacks or to prevent heavy bombing.

The urban bombing campaign was carried out from January 1945. At first on precise economic targets, which involved a certain amount of indiscriminate destruction, but gradually moving to a general urban bombing offensive to demoralize the urban population and to take advantage of the extreme vulnerability of the Japanese cities to fire-bombing techniques. Arnold himself, under pressure from the American government to make use of the Iwo Jima assault to bring the war to the Japanese homeland and to speed up the war in the east, abandoned precision bombing of all except aero-engine factories and allowed LeMay to develop tactics that would bring the largest bomb-load most accurately over the major industrial centres. By May 1945 incendiaries comprised 75 per cent of the bombload. Out of a total American tonnage of 153,000 tons dropped on Japan some 98,000 were fire-bombs.[73] The results of the first series of operations, although disappointing from an American point of view because of the slight damage done to aircraft factories, were sufficiently effective militarily to encourage LeMay and a number of Washington planners to call for a target programme designed to end the war by bombing alone instead of using the bombing as a prelude to invasion. In a private letter in April 1945 LeMay wrote 'I consider that for the first time strategic air bombardment faces a situation in which its strength is proportionate to the magnitude of its task. I feel that the destruction of Japan's ability to wage war lies within the capability of this command. . . .'[74]

Although the heavy bombers were diverted to help with the attack on Okinawa and to continue precision attacks on military targets, the bombing generals were given the opportunity to prove their point. The destruction of 58 cities by fire-bombing between May and August 1945 was to force the Japanese surrender through the collapse of morale and economic strength.[75] That this was not the navy's strategy underlined the fact that the AAF were anxious to redress the balance of prestige between the services by completing a strategic programme that had eluded them in Europe. By August the anxiety to prove the value of bombing led the XXI Bomber Command to undertake attacks by day as well as by night, while it was only with reluctance that the Command agreed to carry out mining operations for which naval aircraft were unsuitable.[76] In the end a combination of B-29 bombardment and the two atomic bomb attacks forced surrender. Moreover the damage at Hiroshima and Nagasaki could have been rendered by two conventional bombing attacks. By mid-August the conventional bomber force had destroyed an area thirty times greater than that destroyed by the new bombs and had already so undermined morale and the working of the civilian and military structures that surrender was only a matter of time. The atomic bombs and the Russian invasion of Manchuria simply accelerated a decision towards which many Japanese leaders had been moving since the early part of 1945. The effects of bomb devastation combined with those of blockade and the attrition of air forces had produced a situation in which Japan could not continue the war.[77]

Air power was more effective in the Far East than in the European theatre for several reasons. America had from the start placed great emphasis on a general air strategy in the Pacific and Asia as the fastest and surest way of containing Japan until forces could be released from the European area. Secondly the geography of the region placed a premium on air power combined with powerful naval support in the form of floating aerodromes. This was appreciated as much by the Japanese as by the Americans. Thirdly, the Americans in particular were able to draw on the lessons of battles in Europe and to deploy forces with greater economy and effect in the Pacific. American air power succeeded more conspicuously in the east because of the relative strength of the two main combatants. Japan's air force was outnumbered; its economy was weakened by American blockade strategy; its industrial homeland was poorly defended and provided an ideal target for fire-bombing which the Americans practised with greater ruthlessness and efficiency in the east than against the better-defended and less flammable targets in Europe.

Japan, too, placed great emphasis on air power and devoted the largest sector of its war economy to aircraft production and output of aircraft carriers. The Japanese forces knew that the seizure of the 'southern region' could only be effected by using the imbalance of air forces in the Pacific to paralyse American naval power and overwhelm weak resistance in the colonial areas. The failure to defend the area later was due partly to a reversal of the balance of forces but also to the failure to see beyond the initial programme and to plan military strategy accordingly. In this the Japanese assault resembled that of Germany against the Soviet Union. In both cases there were insufficient preparations for alternative contingencies and too little attention to the longer-term economic and military requirements should the immediate strategic object not be achieved. In both cases air power was developed in a limited role. In Japan's case it was primarily exercised in support of the navy. Admittedly, for Japan to be able to hold the outer perimeter successfully depended upon German success in Europe and the Middle East. Ironically Hitler hoped at the same time that Japan would keep America occupied in the Pacific leaving him with a freer hand in Europe.[78] In the event, America was able to develop very large forces very rapidly to cope with developments in both theatres. Moreover air power in a variety of roles had a full part to play in all the Allied endeavours in the Far East, reflecting as in Europe the advantages to be won from the general exercise of air power. Founded on a decisive technical and industrial superiority, Allied air forces were used in support of army and marine assaults, in general support for the navy, in defending the threatened frontiers with the Japanese empire and in a variety of tactical and strategic bombing roles. Perhaps most important of all, the Allies developed a strategy for the decisive exploitation of the advantage in the air without which the combat with Japan would have been far longer and less predictable.

5

The Strategic Bombing Offensives

In no other respect was the gap more obvious between those powers that exercised a general air strategy and those who preferred a more limited course than in the execution of a bombing offensive. All the powers had to make up their minds about bombing if only because it had featured so prominently in the doctrinal discussions of the 1930s. Most of them rejected bombing because the industrial and military effort involved was too great in terms of the reward, some because the resources simply did not exist whatever the arguments in favour of it. The effort involved in establishing a bombing offensive of adequate proportions was indeed a huge one. One reason for the failure of successive German attempts to mount one was a misunderstanding of the scale involved. Only Britain and the United States intended from the outset to pursue a bombing strategy and to devote large resources to it in the face of all the arguments for diverting such resources to other purposes. But even the carrying out of a bombing offensive did not settle the argument about whether it was worth the effort or not. This was the result of the difficulty in separating one circumstance from another in explaining the Axis collapse. But it was also the result of the nature of a bombing offensive itself. For many airmen it only made sense if it could ultimately achieve decisive results on its own and except for the rather special case of the atomic bombs this was not achieved beyond question. But for the Allied forces as a whole the bombing offensive made much more sense as an important instrument complementary to the ambitions and objectives of the armed forces as a whole. In this respect bombing was successful or not successful depending from which perspective it was viewed. Since it was the complementary nature of a bombing offensive, contributing to the winning of air supremacy and the winning of land and sea battles at the same time, that attracted Allied leadership to it in the first place, it would do more justice in assessing bombing to view it from this perspective. Within these narrower terms bombing did what was expected of it.

(i) Preparation and Purpose

The first power to mount a bombing offensive, though a comparatively ineffective one, was Germany. Even those powers more attracted by inclination or experience to army co-operation as a first priority were well aware by 1939 that they could not afford to ignore bombing altogether. Indeed until the failure of the Blitz the Luftwaffe, like the RAF, believed that bombing was an essential instrument when other forms of warfare had reached a stalemate. Nevertheless, a popular belief developed after the war that Germany did not plan to mount a bombing offensive, even though the very opposite was in fact the case. After the death in 1935 of Wever, the Luftwaffe Chief of Staff who favoured strategic bombing, other prominent staff officers kept alive the idea. Goering himself sanctioned the search for a suitable heavy bomber in 1937, shortly after cancelling contracts for earlier heavy bombers doomed to relative obsolescence from the start. Goering and his technical staff recognized that the bombing plan was a long-term one governed by the lack of the available raw materials for an early build-up of bomber forces.[1] Hitler, too, was attracted to bombing, particularly by its terroristic and deterrent character. But Hitler's view of bombing was coloured by a number of misconceptions born partly of his personal isolation from air affairs, with which he was administratively quite out of touch, and partly of his ignorance of air strategy and aircraft planning.

The first misconception lay in his belief that the medium-bomber fleet could be used for strategic tasks without the need for heavy bombers. In Britain and America on the other hand, it was assumed from the outset that it was necessary to build special-purpose weapons for strategic air warfare. Hitler was persuaded of this because of the Luftwaffe's tactical emphasis on dive-bombing, which was thought to be a much more efficient way of covering a target than by horizontal bombing, and because of the long range claimed for the new Luftwaffe medium bomber, the Junkers Ju 88.[2] Another problem with mounting any bombing offensive that went beyond mere tactical support for ground operations lay in the fact that Hitler failed to give his forces sufficient indication of the direction in which his foreign policy was moving thus encouraging the misconception that its aims were far more modest. Not until 1939 was the Luftwaffe instructed to prepare papers on the possibility of air attack against Britain. It was only in the same year that Hitler told the heads of the Wehrmacht that 'The ruthless employment of the Luftwaffe against the heart of the British will-to-resist can and will follow at the given moment'.[3] Not only did the air staff not realize that England or Russia would be possible targets for long-range bombing in the immediate future, believing that any war would not come before 1942, but Hitler gave no clear-cut strategic direction to the air forces to prepare for a bombing campaign; lacking such a directive the air force rested on the complacent assumption that when the time came operational plans and the neccessary material would be forthcoming. Hitler, while personally favouring the use of air forces in close co-operation with ground forces, fed this complacency by threatening to use his bombing forces in the diplomatic arena and creating the illusion that the Luftwaffe was more prepared for strategic air operations than was actually the case. The failure of the Blitz demonstrated not a lack of intention to bomb but a lack of preparation and time. If war had come in 1942 instead of 1939 Goering had planned to create a force of 2,400 medium and 800 heavy bombers.[4]

The situation in the west was different. In both Britain and America it was from within the air staffs themselves, indeed from within the tradition of the air services, that the view was developed that strategic bombing would play a crucial part in any later war. Nevertheless the important factor, demonstrated in the political influence on air planning in Germany, was the degree to which political leaders were attracted to the development, and later use, of bombing campaigns. Indeed in some cases the acceptance of bombing was an arbitrary fact, not necessarily reflecting an air force's ability or willingness to bomb. Stalin's rejection of long-range bombing was just such a case.[5] In Britain, on the other hand, the RAF was fortunate that it was Churchill rather than Chamberlain who assumed responsibility for strategy in 1940. Churchill had been the political champion of bombing in the 1930s. Chamberlain had been responsible for some of the moves towards an international ban on bomber use in 1938 and 1939. It was unlikely that any British Prime Minister would have completely reversed the RAF emphasis on bombing, but it was much more likely that Churchill would deliberately encourage it.[6] From the start Churchill gave bombing a high priority. Like Hitler he recognized its value as a political weapon as much as a military one. In 1940, for example, he promised as a political gesture 'continuous and relentless air offensive' and insisted that 'on no account should the limited bomber force be diverted from accurate bombing of military objectives reaching far into Germany' as a time when the crucial military role for bombing was limited to the attack on the forward areas for preparation of operation 'Sealion'.[7] Although his personal attitude towards bombing wavered with the actual course of bombing operations, he remained as he reminded Trenchard 'a champion of Bomber Command'.[8]

In America bombing was met by a more cautious reaction. The air staffs had built up a body of doctrine around Mitchell's theory of strategic air power which was unattractive to the other services, not least because it gave the air forces some claim to organizational independence, which was resisted until 1947. The air force officers who favoured bombing found allies, as well as enemies, in American politics. The President, for one, and Stimson, the Secretary for War, both supported bombing for political reasons, the most important of which was the hope that American isolationism would be easier to break down if intervention with a bombing campaign promised low casualties and expenditure for great military effect.[9] Roosevelt was also infected by Churchill's enthusiasm, even though much of this was pure rhetoric and properly regarded as such by the American war planners. When Churchill cabled to Roosevelt in July 1941 his opinion that 'the war would be won by bombing' the President was encouraged to support the proposed changes in the strategic planning which laid greater emphasis on bombing than in the ABC-1 plans. Roosevelt's attempt to reduce proposed army size in September 1941 was interpreted by those who resisted the proposal as evidence that he was the prisoner of British views on air strategy.[10] Though Roosevelt later accepted the principle rigidly adhered to by the Chief of Staff that no war could be fought which did not involve a confrontation of land armies, he remained as great a defender of the activities of the AAF bombing forces as Churchill of Bomber Command.

Both the American and British governments accepted a strategy that included bombing because there were important political and military arguments in favour of it. Although the emphasis on particular arguments altered with changes in the course of the war the arguments themselves changed very little. In the British case a major argument was the effect on public and international opinion. Indeed, one of the important considerations in the initial preparation of a bombing capability in the 1930s was the effect the absence of such a move would have on the electorate, whatever the military reasons for it. In 1940 the effect on the home population of promising and then initiating bombing attacks on Germany and Italy was argued as a justification in itself.[11] In 1940 and 1941 bombing clearly was the main instrument for offensive action against the Axis powers. Churchill wrote to Beaverbrook in July: 'when I look round to see how we can win the war I see that there is only one sure path. We have no Continental army which can defeat the German military power . . . there is one thing that will bring . . . [Hitler] down, and that is an absolutely devastating, exterminating attack by very heavy bombers from this country upon the Nazi homeland. We must be able to overwhelm them by this means, without which I do not see a way through.'[12] The effect of bombing on international opinion was equally important. Not only did bombing demonstrate that British war capability was undiminished, it was also argued that it acted as a deterrent, though from a military point of view a not particularly important deterrent, on further Axis operations against the west. The impact of the bombing on American opinion was clear. Hopkins wrote to Churchill from Washington: 'You have no idea of the thrill and encouragement which the Royal Air Force bombing has given to all of us here',[13] and Roosevelt's interest in air strategy stemmed from the period in 1940 and early 1941 when he witnessed the successive efforts of the British forces to defeat the Luftwaffe and to seize the initiative in the air offensive.

Bombing assumed a fresh international political significance when Germany invaded the Soviet Union. In answer to Stalin's importunity Churchill offered the prospect of 'a terrible winter of bombing' for Germany and continued throughout 1941 and 1942 to offer strategic bombing as the most decisive aid short of invasion that the west could provide.[14] It was hoped that the bombing would encourage Russian resistance. As long as Russia kept in the war, the British policy of blockade and attrition with bombing as a central feature was possible. In practical terms the strategy was designed to divert German resources from the Russian front and to reduce the German economy and hence keep Russia in the war, though its impact was not likely to be great at first. The same argument was used by the Americans in the Far East. The moral and political effect of launching a bombing offensive against Japan from Chinese bases was used as an argument for carrying such an offensive out even though preparation was poor and the targets still too far distant. Chiang Kai-shek, while not actively seeking a separate peace, was encouraged in his resistance to Japan by Roosevelt's haste, urged on by Hopkins, to expand air power in China and his final agreement that the first B-29s be operated from Chinese bases.[15] In the case of Russia in 1942 and China in 1943 it was important for Allied plans that both powers remain belligerent, and the promise of bombing was the least expensive way of encouraging them to be so.

The military arguments were both more detailed and more enduring. As a function of diplomatic calculation bombing remained only as important as the diplomatic situation at the time warranted. Hence the occasional fluctuation in the degree of support that Churchill was prepared to give to bombing. But as a military calculation bombing had a central if sometimes ill-defined role to play in both Britain and America. The arguments in Britain for using a bombing offensive rested first of all on the rather negative basis that the RAF had become committed to the bomber in the 1930s and that the programmes of development and training associated with bombing could not be ignored at the risk of huge wastage of military effort. Moreover since it was believed that Germany, too, was preparing to launch such an offensive it was argued that it was necessary to be able to mount a counter-offensive of greater sustained power than that of the enemy. This view remained intact even though British air defence had been set up to prove just the opposite, that bombers could not carry out an offensive in the face of heavy air opposition, a fact apparently confirmed by the failure of the Blitz. The positive purpose of a bombing offensive was essentially complementary to the general strategic aim of defeating the enemy power. This differed from the view held by the more extreme enthusiasts of the bombing strategy, but it was nevertheless the prevailing view. Bombing was a component part of a wider strategy, complementary to land invasion and to the exercise of tactical air power.[16] In both America and Britain the principle of complementarity not only conformed to the wishes of the other services which refused to accept that any one service was capable of ending the war on its own, but conformed too to the air view that a successful air offensive was necessary before any surface invasion could be undertaken. There was never any widespread acceptance that armies had been rendered redundant by air forces, and the objectives sought by bombers were those best designed to contribute to the success of the other services' operations.[17]

Such bombing objectives were obvious and few, although the emphasis placed on particular targets varied widely from service to service and from time to time as circumstances dictated. Trenchard had always stressed that morale was a key target for bombing. In 1940 Bomber Command began the first of a series of attacks against civilian morale because with the available resources the bombing of urban, civilian populations was all that was operationally possible. What 'morale' was or what effect its undermining might have were guesses. Churchill among others hoped that together with subversion in the conquered territories, the threat of bombing would encourage anti-Nazis to overthrow the government and come to terms, but such a policy was hard to justify at the expense of more tangible means of destroying enemy power. Nevertheless the argument about morale, and in particular of the inability of the German factory workers to withstand bombing, was maintained. In order to justify such attacks the Air Staff presented industrial workers as a factor of production which had to be rendered ineffective like transport or fuel. Thus the attack on morale merged into the attack on the economy.[18] The civilian attacks were justified further in 1941 by Portal's argument that 'the most vulnerable point in the German nation at war is the morale of her civilian population under air attack, and that until this morale has been broken it will not be possible to launch an army on the mainland of Europe with any prospect of success'.[19] Morale, too, was presented as a complementary target, without whose reduction the cornerstone of Allied policy, the invasion of Europe, could not be achieved. The Amercian planners argued differently. German civilian morale was not included as a primary target in two main air plans drawn up in 1941 and 1942.[20] American air intelligence believed that attacks against key economic systems, such as transport and electric power, would so demoralize the population that the same effects could be achieved without resorting to indiscriminate civilian bombing. Even against Japan, where urban bombing was much less discriminating, the arguments for urban bombing were based on the belief that Japanese industry was so dispersed among the small workshops and home industries of the cities that it was impossible to separate civilian from industrial targets. Moreover after the Imperial edict requiring all Japanese to fight for the defence of the homeland, American commanders treated all Japanese as military targets, thus eliminating any moral or strategic scruples that remained.[21]

The central target of the bombing offensives was not, however, morale but the economy. By a policy of blockade and the destruction of key economic and military installations it was argued that the ability of the Axis powers, and Germany in particular, to wage war would be undermined to such an extent that invasion and occupation would become relatively easy operations. The choice of which particular economic targets were the most vulnerable was left to the air staff planners to guess at. In Britain sharp differences of opinion developed before 1939 as to which were the most vulnerable targets. Oil, transportation, and the aircraft industry were regarded as crucial targets, but in what order they should be attacked depended upon operational experience which tended to confirm for the RAF that indiscriminate bombing of industrial targets was the best that could be hoped for.[22] The American planning was more elaborate. Beginning from the premise that the German economy was already by 1941 stretched taut by the campaign in Russia, air intelligence suggested that certain targets were particularly susceptible to disruption. The major targets were the electric power system, transport—in particular the railway system —and oil and petrol industries and supplies. In 1942, in Air War Plan-42, aluminium and synthetic rubber were added, the latter because of the mistaken belief that a large proportion of the German army was motorized. Submarine bases and production were added in 1942 and 1943 in response to the threat to the Atlantic sea-lanes.[23] One major difference between the British and American plans was the emphasis placed on defeat of the enemy air force. In the AWPD-1 American air intelligence described neutralization of the German air force as an 'intermediate objective, whose accomplishment may be essential to the accomplishment of the principal objectives'.[24] Based on the experience of German attacks on Britain in 1940, and British attacks in 1941, the American air force planned to destroy or neutralize German air bases and aircraft production as a prelude to carrying out the bombing offensive at all. In Britain, although the German aircraft industry always maintained a high priority, the strategic bombing doctrine did not involve a preliminary requirement to neutralize or destroy the enemy air forces. Such neutralization would follow as a consequence of the general disruption to the economy after bombing attack.[25] The switch to night bombing reflected this view, for continued day bombing required that the RAF achieve a degree of air superiority for which it was neither satisfactorily equipped nor sufficiently persuaded of the need.

Differences of emphasis, and even wider differences in intelligence estimates of the prospect of bomb attack, were a consequence of the large degree of strategic and operational ignorance surrounding a bombing offensive. Many of the effects expected from bombing were guesses and required a very much greater degree of faith in the results than was the case in making military or naval calculations. Because of such uncertainties there existed the temptation to look for much more strategic significance in bombing than the facts suggested. Hence, too, the rapid fluctuations between disillusionment and euphoria amongst those who supported bombing. Hitler, encouraged by Goering's hope that Britain could be forced to surrender through the winter bombing campaign for which preparations were clearly inadequate, expressed his frustration that 'the munitions industry . . . cannot be interfered with effectively by bombing', even though he directed the air force to prepare for renewed bombing operations against Britain once the war in Russia was ended.[26] In Britain the champions of bombing held out the prospect that bombing alone might end the war without the need for invasion or armies, a prospect sufficiently attractive and stated with sufficient force to give it wide political currency.[27] When Arnold visited London in 1941 Churchill's enthusiasm persuaded him that it was possible that 'air power alone . . . might bring Germany so completely to her knees that it might be unnecessary for the ground forces to make a landing'.[28] Thus encouraged the air planners in Washington included in the first air plan the strategic observation that 'If the air offensive is successful, a land offensive may not be necessary', a view reiterated forcefully in the Pacific theatre.[29]

Nevertheless in practice real limits were set to the speculative and ambitious views of the bomber school. The ambiguous and unpredictable nature of air power was recognized by those who planned overall military strategy. Charged with the more pressing task of producing a military and economic plan that might realistically defeat the fascist powers, the Chiefs of Staff and later the Combined Chiefs gave bombing only a component, and in some respects a minor role to play in these plans. Given the opposition to strategic bombing among the military and naval establishment, the very survival of the policy depended on political protection and vigorous dogmatism on the part of the air forces. At Casablanca faith in the bombing offensive, which had not as originally conceived yet taken place, was fought for against the rival claims of the armies faced at last with the prospect of land war in the near future. Bombing emerged as one of five forms of offensive action with the main emphasis on invasion by surface forces.[30] Later developments in 1943 confirmed that bombing was a complementary policy, primarily to help in the final land assault in Europe, performing 'strategic' air operations for the purpose of tactical support. Despite the opposition of those who argued for an independent bombing policy, the arguments in favour of bombing had from the start insisted that bombing was one part of the general plan, not an alternative to it.

(ii) Problems of Execution: Technology and Intelligence

Actual operational experience with bombing altered the emphasis on particular targets and introduced tactical debates, particularly over the usefulness of precision as opposed to area bombing, which became superimposed on the wider debate over strategy. The most important change, since it affected the ability to mount any offensive at all, was in the importance attached to defeating the opposing air force. The Blitz had already demonstrated that well-organized passive defences combined with good fighter interception could defeat daylight bombing and effectively disrupt bombing by night. There was little evidence to suggest that Germany was any less well defended than Britain had been in 1940. The complete failure of early RAF bombing raids by day confirmed such a view. The only solution was to so overwhelm or undermine the opposition that bombing could continue without interruption. Overwhelming the defences was largely out of the question, and was successfully achieved in the early stages of the offensive in the attack against Cologne only because of the defence's complete lack of preparation for so heavy a blow. The alternative of undermining the air force by direct attacks and attacks on the aircraft industry could only be undertaken when sufficient fighter cover could be provided into Germany and when attacks of sufficient precision could be made to destroy individual industries. As the American planners had realized the only way to achieve a strategic result by bombing was to use the bomber itself as an instrument for securing air supremacy. Operation 'Pointblank' was established for precisely this purpose, and although there was some resistance to the operation on the grounds that it was using bombers for preparing the way for land invasion and hence diverting the bombing effort from its principal objective, the judgement that 'the successful prosecution of the air offensive against the principal objectives is dependent upon a prior (or simultaneous) offensive against the German fighter strength' was generally accepted.[31]

The second question raised by the experience of operations was the more difficult one of whether daylight precision bombing or night bombing was the more effective. The debate about precision bombing was more bitter because it did not divide services, but allies. The British and German experience in the winter of 1940–41 confirmed that under prevailing technical conditions daylight bombing was too costly, and that night bombing was too inaccurate for the attack on precise targets. The RAF had the choice of awaiting a technical solution to the problem of daylight precision bombing or adopting the bombing of urban areas; the inclination of its doctrine and the political pressure for retaliation on Germany hastened the adoption of the latter course. Once adopted, and with elaborate target plans laid for area bombing, it became all the more difficult to change to alternative tactics and alternative targets. Even when Portal presented Harris with the means to adopt more economical precision bombing later in the war, the commitment of Bomber Command and its commander to the original decision was almost impossible to reverse.[32] Moreover the RAF sought to impose its tactical view on the American air forces in the belief that daylight precision bombing would be a waste of effort. Churchill in particular, disturbed, like Hitler, at the poor results of attacks on individual targets, pressed the AAF to conform to the British tactics at almost exactly the time that Portal began to express the view that precision attacks were now technically feasible and strategically desirable.[33] The RAF by concurring in American plans was able to leave the task of achieving air supremacy largely to the 8th Air Force by day, while leaving Bomber Command free to continue the search for war-winning bomber attacks at night. There were other reasons. The division of labour satisfied any anxieties caused by the renewed arguments over bombing tactics, for this had once again encouraged those opposed to bombing in Washington to call for the redeployment of the European heavy bombers. The additional argument that round-the-clock bombing would stretch German defence resources even more was true only to a limited extent since a large daylight defence had to be kept on a permanent footing in Germany anyway, against the time when day attacks might begin again. Large air defence forces had been similarly tied down in Britain since 1940 against the day when Hitler would renew his attempt at conquest from the air.

The tactical debates, however, were overshadowed throughout the bombing campaigns by two factors that decisively conditioned the nature and success of bombing: the collection and use made of intelligence and the state of bombing technology. Intelligence was a crucial part of the bombing campaigns. It was necessary not only to predict the most suitable targets and priorities, but for the equally important task of surveying bomb damage and overall results. No air force had begun to gather and assess the necessary intelligence required for launching a strategic offensive before war broke out. The RAF had established the Air Targets Sub-Committee in June 1936 to co-ordinate intelligence from various departments on the German economy and possible targets within it, but the amount of actual effort devoted to such intelligence was small and fell far short of what was required for the projected bombing.[34] Photo-reconnaissance was only carried out on a systematic basis from 1938 and then with only the smallest of staffs.[35] In Germany air intelligence was limited to acquiring good topographical material on Britain and France together with information on the current structure of the economy. The choice of targets in the Blitz was largely confined to aircraft industrial targets in order to prepare for the temporary air supremacy required for invasion. Very little high level appreciation of the weak and vital sectors of the British economy took place.[36] On the outbreak of war Bomber Command was able to draw more heavily on economic intelligence from the Ministry of Economic Warfare and from the expanded air intelligence sections. On this basis target systems based around oil and communications were chosen as those most exposed to attack and most vital to the German economy.[37] Full details were rapidly assembled on a wide variety of targets and the information disseminated throughout Bomber Command.

It was at this point that intelligence emerged not only as an instrument of bombing policy, but as its severest critic. Throughout 1940 and 1941 Bomber Command, on the basis of detailed target intelligence, encouraged the belief that bombing was accurate and the targets selected crucial for the German war economy. It was the development of post-operational intelligence that exposed the claims as grossly exaggerated. Bomber Command was protected in 1940 by the fact that only one bomber in four carried a camera, and in many cases the cameras carried failed to record the actual bomb hits and hence the likely damage. When the photographic intelligence increased in 1941 Lindemann called for an inquiry into the effectiveness of bombing in terms of the precise targets selected. The Butt report showed that only 30 per cent of the bombers arrived within five miles of the targets and in the Ruhr only 10 per cent.[38] Its implications were considerable. Although Bomber Command criticized the highly selective nature of the intelligence evidence used it was clear that with the technical means to hand area bombing was not only desirable, but was the only method available. Accepting this solution, Bomber Command moved to the opposite extreme in the use made of intelligence. While post-operational intelligence continually improved, the use made of target intelligence declined. The growing evidence that bombing was too inaccurate for precise bombing of selected targets pushed the RAF towards area bombing for which a minimum of intelligence was required. For area bombing Harris simply needed a long list of German cities and the industries located in them. Bomber Command remained more impervious to intelligence suggestions than other commands for the rest of the war, arguing that it had already been proved that area bombing at night was the only effective bombing policy. In addition Bomber Command vigorously represented to the American air forces the view that elaborate target systems were redundant.[39]

The American response was an equally vigorous defence of precise targets. American air intelligence had been non-existent before 1940. Arnold insisted on its creation because the War Department intelligence agencies reports were not circulated to the Air Corps as it was not directly represented on the General Staff.[40] Immediately work was begun on military-economic intelligence in order to offer firm support for the air force doctrines on bombing and the attacks on 'vital centres'. The recruitment of expert help in compiling such intelligence dictated to a certain extent the targets finally chosen. Electric power was selected because of the easy availability of details on electric power stations in the records of the large American banks that had loaned the money for their construction in the 1920s. The recruitment of an oil expert who had worked in Germany and Romania also gave added emphasis to oil as a target for which by 1941 target folders, aiming points and necessary bomb loads had been planned.[41] Much intelligence came from the RAF, particularly on transportation and the aircraft industry, and was handed over to American air intelligence at almost exactly the time that the RAF was moving towards an area bombing policy.[42] So extensive and detailed was the American target information that the War Plans Division planned on the precise basis of 66,045 sorties needed to destroy the nine major German target systems, and 51,480 sorties for the selected Japanese targets.[43] Decisions based on intelligence were, as in Britain, subjected to a hostile and critical review during the actual course of operations. Not only was daylight bombing criticized because of its poor accuracy—a fact again based on post-operational intelligence—but the economic intelligence on which the whole bombing campaign was based was questioned by the Joint Intelligence Committee. To try and give more weight to the original, and hurried, estimates of German economic targets Arnold established a Committee of Operations Analysts to assess the probable impact of bombing on the ability of the Axis to continue fighting or to make an attack on Europe likely of success. The committee produced a list of 19 priority target systems but laid emphasis on the target systems already selected, and confirmed the air forces in the reliability of the initial strategic intention to use precision bombing.[44] Only when post-operational intelligence was organized on the ground after the capture of North Africa and southern Italy, and the Bombing Survey (USSBS) was set up in the wake of the armies invading France, was it possible to test how effective economic target bombing had been. The reviews produced ambiguous results, although it was unambiguously shown that the optimistic 'scientific' planning for the destruction of economic targets had been considerably exaggerated, as had been the claims of the RAF in 1941.[45]

The criticisms from American air intelligence were sustained enough to encourage the deployment of heavy bombers in other roles and to confirm that strategic bombardment was from the view of the Joint Chiefs of Staff a preliminary to the actual surface invasion of Europe. Despite air force claims that the Combined Offensive would weaken or possibly destroy the German ability to wage war the conflicting intelligence, that the German war economy had considerably expanded in response to the bombing, encouraged the shift to selected targets for 'Overlord' just as it confirmed Harris in the wisdom of area bombing and the attack on morale. The advantage of both these targets lay in the fact that Harris did not have to produce quantifiable evidence—since morale in particular could not be quantified—in order to defend his bombing policy against the criticisms of scientific intelligence. Although intelligence gradually became available that morale was not cracking and that area attacks were less successful than had at first been supposed, Harris refused to accept the evidence, much of which was poorly corroborated. The claims of Bomber Command became as exaggerated during 1943 as they had been in 1941 now that they were once again free of the constraints of critical intelligence. In November he told Churchill that nineteen German cities had been completely destroyed and nineteen seriously damaged, that the Ruhr was 'largely out' and that he felt 'certain that Germany must collapse'.[46] In the face of large increases in war production discovered by the Ministry of Economic Warfare the claims of Bomber Command were clearly false. That such discrepancy should exist was a product of the difficult circumstances under which intelligence had to be assessed. Much operational analysis was conducted in order to criticize bombing: much preparatory intelligence was designed to persuade the critics otherwise. The more technical and specific the intelligence appeared the more persuasive its impact was thought to be, and the greater its defence of bombing strategy as a whole. Under these circumstances it was not always possible to use the best intelligence, and very easy to ignore much intelligence that did not confirm what the air forces wanted.[47]

Disagreements between intelligence agencies and with the services were fuelled by the second factor, the state of bombing technology. In fact the whole argument between those who favoured strategic bombing and those who favoured the dispersion of bombing among the other combined strategic objectives rested on the fact that the available technology placed severe limits on what bombing could and could not do. The major technical questions were concerned with range, bombload and accuracy of bombing. With the technical means available in 1940-42 the bombing strategy could not be carried out for the bombers lacked sufficient radius of action, carried too few bombs and those that were carried could not be guaranteed to land within miles of the chosen target. For the Luftwaffe this fact became readily apparent in the Blitz. The medium-bombers on which such emphasis had been laid were unequal to the strategic task. Not only was the range of the aircraft poorer than anticipated, the actual weight of bombs carried was far below what was necessary to inflict wide damage. The decision to use the medium-bomber, stemming from the arguments over the shortage of raw materials, absorbed resources that were only fractionally less than the heavy bombers of the Allies. The Ju 88-A4 weighed 21,000 lb, the B-17 27,000 lb, while the latter could carry up to five times the bomb-load of the medium bomber.[48] In terms of military efficiency the heavy bomber was clearly more satisfactory. It was for this reason that the Luftwaffe, in common with the Allies, searched for a satisfactory substitute for the medium bomber.

Only the heavy bomber could give sufficient range and carrying capacity to inflict large-scale damage to the vital targets. In Germany the search concentrated on the Heinkel He 177 but because of the slow pace of all research in Germany due to numerous stoppages in the development programmes and the deficiency of German aero-engine design, the aircraft failed to materialize in any quantity.[49] Those that did were technically unsatisfactory and the search for an alternative late in the war was carried out in a hurried and uncritical way so that any hope of overcoming the technical restrictions evaporated under the attacks of those very long-range bombers that Germany had sought to imitate. For the first years of the war Britain suffered from the same problem. The aircraft with which the bombing offensive was undertaken until the middle of 1942, and including the 1,000 bomber raid on Cologne, were essentially similar to those employed by the Luftwaffe and suffered from the same disabilities. The difference between the two sides arose from the fact that from the mid-1930s both the RAF and the American air forces, in accordance with the emphasis placed upon strategic bombing, had planned for a range of heavy bombers to replace the medium machines in the early 1940s.[50] In both countries it took time to overcome the technical difficulties both in developing and producing in quantity a large aircraft, but the technical limitations imposed on bombing were largely removed with the development of the Lancaster B-17, B-24 and B-29 (see Table 9 for a comparison of bomber aircraft performance). In the case of the B-29 it had

Table 9: Comparative Bomber Performance, United States, Britain and Germany

	Max. Bombload (lb)	Max Speed (m.p.h.)	Unloaded Wght (lb)	Max. Range (miles)
United States				
B-17E	20,800 (a)	317	32,250	2,000
B-24M	8,000 (b)	300	36,000	2,100
B-29B	20,000	364	69,000	4,200
B-36B	86,000	381	140,640	8,175
Britain				
Lancaster I	22,000	287	36,900	1,660 (c)
Mosquito XVI	4,000	415	14,600	1,795 (c)
Stirling Mk IV	14,000	270	43,200	2,010
Halifax Mk VI	13,000	312	39,000	2,400
Germany				
Ju 88 A-4	4,420	292	21,737	1,696
He 111 H-16	5,512	239	19,136	1,280
He 177 A-5	13,230 (d)	303	37,038	3,417 (d)
Do 17Z-2	2,205	255	11,484	720
He 274	8,820	360	46,958	2,640

(a) usual bombload was 17,600. 20,800 was the maximum for special missions
(b) in service with the RAF the B-24 had a maximum bombload of 12,800 over 990 miles and a maximum range of 2,290 miles.
(c) range with an average bombload. Range with maximum bombload was 1,040 for the Lancaster and 1,370 for the Mosquito.
(d) including mines or missiles carried externally. Range with a full bombload was substantially reduced. On the He 177 A-1 it was only 745 miles.

Source: for Britain: O. Thetford *Aircraft of the Royal Air Force 1918–1957* (London, 1957) pp. 66, 196, 301, 451
for the United States: F. Swanborough & P. M. Bowers *United States Military Aircraft since 1919* (London, 1963) pp. 92–6, 159–60, 162–65
for Germany: W. Green *Warplanes of the Third Reich* (London, 1970) pp. 122, 302–3, 344, 359, 455.

for long been predicted that any war with Japan would require a long-range bomber because of the likelihood of having to mount an offensive against Japan from distant United States bases. The relationship between technique and strategy was in this case a highly dependent one.[51]

The strategic implication of the heavy bomber policy was that the heavy aircraft with higher flying ceilings and better armament could not be so easily diverted from their targets as the medium bombers had been over England and Germany before 1942. But the problem of range was not only related to bombers but also to fighters. The ability of German fighters to fly higher and longer increased the rate of bomber loss. The increase in range and bombload had to be protected by long-range fighter aircraft. The tactical necessity for this had been predicted from early in the war and had been circumvented by the arguments that fighters with sufficient range were not technologically possible by 1943, and that the B-17 and B-24 were fast enough and well-armed enough to protect themselves.[52] Neither argument was sustained by events. The heavy bombers could not protect themselves sufficiently in daylight raids. By the end of 1943 the search for a long-range fighter was completed and the final technical barrier to carrying on an offensive was removed. The escort fighters were designed both to protect the bomb cargoes before reaching the target and to engage and destroy the enemy fighter forces. Until such a point was reached the balance of defensive against offensive technology favoured the former sufficiently to postpone the bombing as it had done in the Blitz in the winter of 1940–41.[53]

The technical restrictions placed on bombing through aircraft development were repeated in the question of bombs and the accuracy of their delivery. For one thing it took the RAF time to learn that incendiary bombs were more likely to damage targets than the high-explosive bombs available in the early stages of the war. In Germany the search for better bombs, particularly incendiary bombs, kept alive Goering's hope of retaliation with a much smaller bomber force than that of the Allies, for both Goering and Hitler had from an early date recognized the importance of fire-bombing.[54] In Britain bomb research concentrated on large or special-purpose bombs for specific targets, such as the U-boat pens in the attacks in 1943 and 1944. It was only the growing evidence of how effective fire-bombs were, which came about with the switch to area bombing, that encouraged the RAF to place greater emphasis on them. The large high-explosive bombs were better suited for precision attacks, particularly for the interdiction of communications. For the attacks on cities new incendiary techniques were developed, including the use of high explosive bombs to seal off a section of a city into which the fire-bombs were to be aimed, and such techniques enormously increased the destructive power of the conventional bomb attack. The firestorms in Germany and Japan had the same impact on life and property as the atomic attacks in 1945.[55]

Even with new bombs, the bombers had to find the targets. Any decision about the type of bomb to be used was governed by the degree of concentration of bombs that could be achieved on a given target. It was the belief that bombing was highly inaccurate that discouraged precision bombing plans in Germany in favour of indiscriminate bombing over larger and more easily identifiable targets. The same belief encouraged LeMay to move to area bombing of Japan because of the special difficulties in bomb-aiming through difficult weather conditions from a great height. The bombing of area targets was the main tactic used from the Luftwaffe attacks on London to the final attacks on Honshu. Yet precision bombing, and the technical means to achieve it, was finally developed during the war to such a degree that it was possible to carry out remarkable operations in the interdiction of crucial communications in the preparations and support for 'Overlord'.[56] Navigational aids were not new. The German aids available before the war were ignored by the RAF, preferring to rely on more traditional methods of navigation. The initial conquest and disruption of the German bomber 'beams' used in 1940 did not encourage the search for alternatives, for these were thought just as susceptible to intelligence in Germany and hence unreliable operationally. A similar conclusion was arrived at in Germany and the poor bombing accuracy of later attacks in the 'Little Blitz' resulted to some extent from the pilots' refusal to rely on radio aids even when available. The later British development of 'Gee', 'Oboe' and 'H$_2$S' did, however, improve the accuracy of British and American bombing even though Harris was sceptical of the real degree of accuracy obtained, and refused to divert Bomber Command from area targets when encouraged to do so by the Air Staff.[57] What the new aids did do was to perfect the area-bombing technique itself and to allow more blind-bombing on nights when traditional navigation could not be used, thus increasing the bomb tonnage that could be dropped in any one period, and guaranteeing that most of the tonnage would reach the large targets designated rather than dropping into open countryside or on the wrong city. The new aids also made possible a more vigorous defence of the technical and strategic possibilities of air power and silenced the critics who claimed that bombing without accuracy was not worth having.

(iii) The Strategic Argument

The restrictions imposed on bombing for most of the war through technical immaturity and inadequate intelligence led in turn to further problems. The criticisms of bombing from politicians and soldiers became more widespread as the gulf between the exaggerated claims of the air forces and the reality of bomber operations became more obvious. In Britain the political climate that had been so favourable to bombing in 1940 became more cautious. Churchill himself on learning of the conclusions of the Butt report wrote; 'the most we can say is that [bombing] will be a heavy and I trust seriously increasing annoyance'.[58] To Portal and Cherwell's highly technical defence of the bombing strategy, for which Churchill himself had largely been responsible, Churchill replied 'Everything is being done to create the bombing force desired on the largest possible scale, and there is no intention of changing this policy. I deprecate however placing unbounded confidence in this means of attack. .'.[59] To Cherwell, whose scientific advice had encouraged Churchill to advocate bombing in the first place, he wrote: 'It is very disputable whether bombing by itself will be a decisive factor in the present war'.[60] From 1941 onwards, although the War Cabinet never abandoned the bombing strategy, its proponents were compelled to defend the policy at every turn as well as divert the arguments of the other services that their need for bombers was more urgent.

Other politicians were prepared to go further than Churchill and to attack the principle of bombing itself rather than its poor performance. Such criticisms were neither widespread nor concerted enough to overturn bombing completely but they did reduce its public credibility. Beaverbrook, for one, attacked the whole strategic campaign. In the middle of the crisis over the Ministry of Production he wrote that 'The policy of bombing Germany. . . should no longer be regarded as of primary importance. Bomber squadrons should be flown forthwith to the Middle and Far East. .'. Eden agreed with him.[61] In the House of Commons Aneurin Bevan based his criticisms of Churchill's handling of the war on the argument that the British forces were fighting with the wrong weapons, and in particular that divebombers should have received production priority over heavy bombers.[62] In both these cases the argument against bombing was linked closely with the argument for a second front, though for rather different reasons. For those, particularly on the British left, who favoured the maximum assistance to Stalin in 1942 and 1943, the bombing policy was regarded, as it was by the Russians, as a poor alternative. Moral objections to bombing on the other hand, though ever-present, had much less political impact than objections on military or political grounds.[63]

Within the military sphere criticism of bombing was more active and imposed on the bombing offensives certain limitations. This was particularly the case in the United States where, although the political support for bombing changed little, the Chief of Staff and the Joint Chiefs remained emphatic that the central strategy of the war was the future conquest by armies of mainland Europe and the Japanese islands. The main criticism of bombing was that it diverted resources from these other purposes and for little strategic advantage.

In Britain in particular, whose economic resources were stretched much more than those of the United States, the decision to devote a significant share of manpower and material to the bombing offensive aroused the hostility of those commanders starved of sufficient air forces for other operations. Brooke fought a long battle with the Air Ministry over the allocation of aircraft to army co-operation and arrived at the conclusion that 'the Air Ministry outlook is so far divorced from the requirements of the Army that I see no solution to the problem except an Army Air Arm. .'.[64] Although sympathetic to the army position, the Combined Chiefs of Staff were no longer in a position by 1942 to reverse the bombing policy and could not have done so without an even more severe dislocation of the aircraft industry and loss of production. The problem over co-operation between the other services and the air forces lay in the fact that the initial strategic decision to bomb had been taken at a time when the expectations from bombing were high. The organizational and production effort already devoted to bombing was too considerable by the middle of the war to be lightly undone. Instead of abandoning bombing the other services had to be satisfied with the diversion of bombing effort from the primary objectives in Germany and Japan to tactical purposes in other battles.

Even the diversion of bombing to other tasks was not entirely a result of failure on the part of the bombing operations, but arose simply out of the pressing urgency of other strategies. The defeat of the submarine and the V-weapons, the campaign in the Mediterranean and the offensives in the Pacific all depended on the diverted bombers, though such diversion was resisted by the bomber commanders themselves.[65] Harris regarded the Atlantic battle as a defensive one for which bombers were not well-equipped and argued that bombers should be used to attack industry in Germany whence the submarines came. The frequent calls for heavy bombers in the Middle East and India were as frequently ignored.[66] All the discussions about the effectiveness of bombing had stressed that the objectives could only be achieved if such dispersion were avoided. The American AWPD-1 plan emphasized the need for 'tenaciously *concentrating all bombing* toward the destruction of [the chosen] objectives'.[67] The fact that concentration was not achieved, combined with the technical restrictions, imposed severe limits on what the bombing offensives could achieve at the time of their probation.

The main arguments surrounding bombing came to be concentrated in the end around the whole question of the best strategy for defeating Hitler. It was perhaps unfortunate for the bombing forces that the decision to prepare for invasion coincided with the beginning of the Combined Bombing Offensive itself. The armies had arrived in 1943 at the point where it was now possible to invade continental Europe, only to discover that the bombing offensive promised from three years before had not even seriously begun. Bombing had been chosen as a strategy in the first place to fill the obvious gap between the end of the campaign in western Europe and the time when Britain and her allies should re-enter. What it might achieve had been guessed at by optimistic politicians and airmen in the early years of war. What it had actually achieved was relatively little in terms either of tactical preparation for future invasion of in terms of an independent war-winning strategy. The gap had not been filled precisely because the operational and material preparation for bombing was a long-term undertaking, and could not be provided at short notice as a military stop-gap. In 1943 both the armies and the air forces had arrived independently at the stage where they could launch their own strategic operations, and although both were committed to the defeat of Germany there was disagreement as to which strategy should receive most emphasis. Harris and other airmen hoped for a combination of a Mediterranean initiative to secure southern bombing bases which, combined with bombardment from Britain, would bring Germany to surrender without invasion.[68] The American Joint Chiefs not only rejected any question of an independent bombing attack but even questioned the whole idea of a Mediterranean programme at all. The compromise that was reached gave the task of destroying the Axis powers to the armies in both the Mediterranean and across the English Channel while to the bomber forces it gave the subsidiary task of preparing the way by long-range tactical bombing for the subsequent invasion.

The strategy of complementary bombing was not such a radical step as Harris, Spaatz and Eaker thought. Bombing had always been planned for the purpose of lending support to ground operations. Its advocates had simply gone beyond what had initially been expected of the bomber forces. The 'Overlord' and 'Pointblank' operations took bombing back to its original state and insisted that its activities contribute to the general strategy. In the Pacific theatre bombing was given a more prominent position because the circumstances were different. The Joint Chiefs of Staff had always intended that the bombing of Japan should be carried out when suitable bases had been secured, because the chances of success were much greater and the risks involved in actual surface invasion too severe to reproduce the European strategy.[69] But even in the Pacific preparations were made for an eventual invasion for which bombing had prepared the way in case bombing did not prove as successful as expected. After the experience of heavy bombing in Europe it was the latter course that the American planners finally accepted, until it became clearer that bombing had indeed been more successful in the more vulnerable and less well-defended Japanese theatre. In Europe on the other hand, the army expressed doubts about the bombers' ability to mount even tactical bombing of sufficient strength to defeat the Luftwaffe and make invasion possible, and as a result issued directives through the Combined Chiefs to the bomber forces to concentrate on German fighter strength and transportation at the expense of all the other primary objectives.[70] Eisenhower had clearly intended that American bombers be prepared for this role from the start. He told Churchill in 1943 that precision daylight bombing was to be retained so as 'to have available the great force that would be needed to carry out the preparatory work in the areas selected for invasion'.[71] The Combined Chiefs echoed this intention by directing that 'all possible support must be afforded to the Allied Armies by our Air Forces to assist them in establishing themselves in the lodgement area. .'.[72] Although more opportunity arose after D-Day for taking up the attack against the primary objectives again it was clear that any end to the war would be a consequence of army operations assisted by the bombers rather than the other way around.

Despite the controversy surrounding the claims of the bombing strategists and the purposes of bombing the offensive was successful within the terms of the overall strategy agreed between the Allies. Those terms had always confined bombing to a primarily tactical role pursued by what others described as 'strategic' methods. More could not be achieved because more was not necessary to the fulfilment of the main objective. Nor was more asked for. The Luftwaffe was fatally weakened; German transportation was successfully interdicted; the submarine and V-weapons successfully combated from the air; the German economy increasingly eroded in the year-long conquest of mainland Europe. The heavy bombers of 1944 were the dive-bombers and medium bombers of the Blitzkrieg on a different scale. Those who favoured a maximum strategy for bombing were confounded through technical shortcomings, operational difficulties and the demands of the services as a whole. It was the rhetorical threat of bombing that created the illusion in the early years of war that bombing promised more than it could fulfil.

The ineffective flourishing of the bombing weapon both in the Blitz and in the early RAF bombing offensive demonstrated that all major combatants had prepared for an offensive which could only begin to take effect after 1942 or 1943. Any attempt to accelerate the preparation was bound to founder on the technical and organizational difficulties involved. Russia and Japan made little or no attempt to mount long-range bombing, since both recognized from the outset the futility of building such forces with poor resources and a complete lack of previous planning. Germany never abandoned the search but could not divert sufficient resources from the army effort to carry out sustained bombing. Britain used the bombing campaign for a particular political purpose but like Germany was never in a position to mount a serious offensive until 1943. Hence the growing criticism of the bombing campaign before 1943. Because so many influential people said that bombing was important, the belief grew in political and military circles that it must be so. Yet the period during which bombing was under such close and critical scrutiny was precisely the period when bombing was least likely to be effective. The belief that it had been ineffective in the later part of the war stemmed largely from this initial disappointment, and not from the actual fact of failure. From the point of view of general strategic intention bombing achieved all that was expected of it. Only those who expected bombing to win the war on its own were frustrated by events.

(iv) The Impact of Bombing

The bombing offensives did not take place in a vacuum, even if some of the planning, starved of appropriate intelligence, was forced to do so. The response of those powers against whom the offensives were directed both affected, and was affected by, the course of the bombing. Much of the response depended on the way in which bombing was perceived. In Japan there were few illusions about the impact bombing might have or the American intention in using it. Hence the stress on building a defence perimeter sufficiently far from the Japanese mainland to prevent bombing.[73] In Germany bombing was regarded differently. The perception was based partly on the experiences of the Blitz whose disappointing results, when combined with the heavy losses inflicted on Bomber Command's first sorties, allayed German fears that a sustained bombing campaign could be carried out. Hitler, too, believed that Germany had a certain geographical protection having conquered western Europe, arguing that the range to be covered by British aircraft was so great that the effort of bombing could not be sustained. So firm was the belief that when the first long-range fighters were shot down over Germany both and Hitler and Goering refused to believe it, preferring the suggestion that they were short-range fighters drifting with the prevailing winds.[74] The most costly miscalculation was the belief that the Allies were carrying out only a morale-breaking exercise, mistaking the economic warfare for terror-bombing. To a certain extent the mistake was not altogether surprising since most of the early bomb attacks failed to hit an obvious military target even when intended. The randomness of inaccurate area bombing certainly suggested attacks directed at morale rather than the economy. Yet because of the perception of bombing as a terror weapon, Hitler failed to provide adequate preparations for air defence of the economy when the full attack was launched. Arguing, just as the British had done in 1940, that German morale could not crack because of the nature of the German racial personality, he concluded that 'the devastation actually works in our favour, because it is creating a body of people with nothing to lose—people who will therefore fight on with utter fanaticism'.[75] The only concern over morale was the effect on the prestige of the Nazi regime as it became apparent that no effective protection against bombing had been prepared. Thinking back to the 1930s when bombing had been used as a diplomatic terror weapon, Hitler determined to mount a counter-offensive against British bombing to try to produce a situation of stalemate in which neither side would lightly risk more terror-bombing for fear of retaliation.

The renewed German strategic bombing offensive was hastily planned and prepared in the early stages of the attack on Russia in the east, and as such suffered from the persistent inability to transfer sufficient resources from that attack to the bomb attack on Britain. The response to the British threat was nevertheless real enough. An air command was activated with orders to attack British cities, and although starved of resources, carried out a series of raids in

1942 and the winter of 1943–44. The first raids were relatively ineffective largely due to Hitler's insistence on attacking small cultural centres in so-called 'Baedeker raids' as retaliation for attacks on Lübeck and Rostock.[76] Little or no preparation went into attacks on the economy or vital military targets. The second period of bombing suffered from the fact that neither Hitler nor Goering understood the need for large numbers and bombloads, a fact that the poor early efforts of Bomber Command should have confirmed. Goering talked optimistically of the effects to be expected from attacks on London in 1943 with 150 aircraft, forgetting that the largest attack against London has been made in 1941 with over 600 medium bombers.[77] In the end no significant attack could be mounted through a shortage of trained pilots and the necessary aircraft and the considerable improvement of the British night defences. The attempt to persuade Hitler to mount an economic offensive like that carried out in the Blitz ended in failure. Raeder told Hitler in February 1941 that 'the Air Force must attempt to hit Great Britain where it hurts most, by attacking her imports' and although Hitler did not disagree with the naval view he did not give the attacks high priority or compel the Luftwaffe to divert resources to helping the war at sea.[78] In 1943 Speer tried once again to demonstrate to Hitler that bombing of economic targets was the best strategy, establishing one committee to examine the Russian economy and another to recommend vital industrial targets in Britain. The suggested targets gave top priority to the electricity systems which Speer endeavoured to persuade Hitler to attack, but without success.

The main reason why German plans came to little lay with the difficulty of producing sufficient aircraft after the production crisis of 1941. When production began to be increased priority went to fighter and fighter-bomber aircraft for the Russian front. The proportion of bombers produced fell, and as the initiative slipped away from the Luftwaffe so the imbalance between bomber and other aircraft produced increased, just at the time that Allied bomber production was multiplying, as the following table shows:

Table 10: Bomber Production and Bomb Tonnages Delivered [79] *1940–45*

	Germany		Britain and America (b)	
		Bomb Tonnage (a)		Bomb Tonnage on
	Bombers	on U.K.	Bombers	Europe
1940	2,852	36,844	3,529	14,631
1941	3,373	21,858	4,668	35,509
1942	4,502	3,260	18,880	53,755
1943	4,789	2,298	37,083	226,513
1944	1,982	9,151	42,906	1,188,577
1945	–	761	23,554	477,051
	17,498	**74,172**	**130,620**	**1,996,036**

(a) including V-weapons   (b) American figures included only for 1942–45

Hitler himself never abandoned the search for a suitable bomber and resisted the plans to increase fighter production in 1944 at the expense of bombers, though in the end he was forced to concede that no production at all would be possible unless fighter defences were strengthened. As late as January 1945 he instructed Speer to produce 'a high-speed heavy bomber with wide range and large bombload' and insisted on retaining the Arado 234C jet bomber in production plans though only a few were produced for combat.[80] The final counter-offensive was launched in 1944 with the V-weapons which Hitler deluded himself into believing could devastate London and bring 'such a storm of protest and war-weariness that the Government will be overthrown'.[81] Yet in 1944 not a quarter of the tonnage dropped in 1940 could be delivered. Hitler's strategic intention—the search for a terror bombing weapon—ran far ahead of the ability of the German economy to supply the right weapons in the right numbers.

As the enemy bombing offensive increased in scale so Hitler was forced to rely more on static and passive defences instead of a bombing counter-offensive. Both Hitler and Goering believed anti-aircraft fire to be a more effective defence than aircraft. Combined with satisfactory passive defence preparation Hitler insisted on using anti-aircraft fire in preference to diverting large numbers of aircraft from the Russian front or to increasing aircraft production. In this he was influenced by his own prejudices. The 88mm anti-aircraft gun was one which Hitler personally favoured for its versatility and performance. It was consistently given a high production priority as was the research associated with gun radar. When Hitler reached the final point of disillusionment with the air force in 1944 he instructed Speer to disband the Luftwaffe and produce a vast anti-aircraft army to protect German industry.[82]

As a consequence of this it was difficult to persuade Hitler to accept active defence. The attempts from early in the war to divert aircraft to home defence resulted in protracted political struggles between Hitler and the air and economics ministries. To the end of the war he regarded the aircraft as an essentially offensive weapon. Although he finally conceded the need for aircraft defence each step towards its achievement was grudgingly made. The Luftwaffe staff supported Hitler's view in the early years of the war. Jeschonnek, the Chief of Staff, refused to expand fighter production to meet the expected bombing, arguing that the easy successes against British bombing in 1940 and 1941 would be repeated against the heavy bombers. In July 1942 he commented at a lecture: 'Every four-engined bomber the Western Allies build makes me happy, for we will bring these four-engined bombers down just like we brought down the two-engined ones . . .'.[83] Relations between the General Staff and State Secretary Milch were too poor to allow Milch's emphasis on a priority for home defence to carry much strategic weight. It was only in the face of bombing attacks on oil targets in 1944 which threatened not simply air power, but the armies in Russia as well, that Hitler and Goering agreed to Milch and Speer's proposals for fighter defence.[84] A Reich air fleet was established in May and June out of the large increases in fighter production, but before it could be used for defensive purposes Hitler ordered its use in repelling the Allied invasion. In July Speer wrote insistently to Hitler to 'reserve a significantly larger part of the fighter plane production for the home front'.[85] Again faced with an economic crisis, in this case the threat of a total loss of fuel production, Hitler agreed to divert a force of 2,000 fighter aircraft to protect vital fuel installations and industries, but during September and October the strength of the daylight fighter forces in Germany fell to only 200 and the promised new Reich air fleet was diverted to other tasks.[86]

The consequences of the failure to develop satisfactory air defences were profound. Allied bombing of economic targets was much more successful than the earlier experiences of bombing against good defences had suggested. The political consequences, although never approaching the collapse of war-willing-ness that Allied air commanders sought, nevertheless contributed to the self-inflicted elements in the decline of the Luftwaffe. Bombing finally destroyed Hitler's confidence in his air forces, encouraging him to assume more of the operational control himself and to turn the Luftwaffe even more towards a tactical support role in the east. Goering failed to recover political favour even though Hitler hesitated to expose publicly Goering's responsibility for the failure of the air defences.[87] The effect of the bombing on public opinion encouraged Goebbels and the *Gauleiter* to work against Goering, yet further undermining the authority and credibility of the air force commander and damaging morale amongst the air staffs.[88] By 1944 the difficulty in getting a large air strength established for fresh strategic tasks was exaggerated by the hostility with which the other services and the Nazi party regarded the air force. From a *corps d'élite* in 1939 the Luftwaffe had become the scapegoat for military failures on all fronts, incapable of regaining the initiative in the air or of protecting the Reich from attack.

Of much greater significance was the effect of bombing on the German economy. The actual amount of physical destruction was far less than the Allies expected, until the middle of 1944 when the increased weight of bombs dropped and the increasing precision of attacks made destruction more likely. Factory plant was effectively repaired quickly or dispersed among smaller producers and the attack on morale, although reducing labour efficiency, did not seriously weaken industrial performance because of the regular recruitment of foreign labour and the capital-intensive nature of much German industry.[89] The success of the attack on oil was due to the fact that for the first time a large amount of physical destruction was concentrated on a highly capital-intensive industry with few opportunities for effective dispersal.[90] The same was true of attacks on steel production. The indiscriminate attacks of Bomber Command, although inter-rupting the smooth operation of the economy over a period of time, failed to effect enough destruction of capital stock that was difficult to replace. Attacks against the aircraft industry, on the other hand, which were begun by both Allied forces in early 1944 were effective in part because of the damage done to special machine tools of which there was a permanent shortage in specialized large-scale aircraft manufacture.[91] In addition to physical destruction, the German economy suffered a physical dislocation in the effort devoted to coping with the bombing. A greater diversion of German resources arose through defence against bomb attack itself. By 1944 some two million soldiers and civilians were engaged in ground anti-aircraft defence. This was more than the total employed in the whole of the aircraft industry. A large quantity of war material was produced specifically for defence against bombing. Speer estimated that 30 per cent of total gun output and 20 per cent of heavy ammunition in 1944 was intended for anti-aircraft defences. Some 50 per cent of electro-technical production and 33 per cent of the optical industry was devoted to radar and signals equipment for anti-aircraft installations, starving the front of essential communications resources. In addition material had to be diverted from new capital investment to satisfy the demands for repairs to damaged factories and communications.[92] Similar resources were tied down in Britain and Russia as well, but as the threat from German bombing rapidly receded so did the size of the defence forces against air attack as a proportion of the total war effort. In Germany the reverse happened.

To Allied intelligence the German economy appeared in a different light. The evidence, which was confirmed by the Strategic Bombing Surveys conducted at the end of the war, suggested that the German economy far from declining from an earlier peak due to the increased bombing effort was in fact expanding at a faster rate than before.[93] The strategic decisions for such expansion did not stem from the fact of bombing itself, but from the struggles on the eastern front. The plans to expand aircraft production stemmed from the middle of 1941 when it had already been shown how inadequate production was for current needs.[94] As the war in Russia widened so the demands for new material escalated well beyond what Hitler had initially expected. It was not bombing that spurred on the German economy to greater efforts, for those efforts were already at the planning stage well before bombing became an economic threat or was perceived as such.

But bombing was much more effective than the Allies believed. The important consequence of the bombing was not that it failed to stem the increase in arms production, but that it prevented the increase from being very considerably greater then it was. Bombing placed a ceiling on German war production which was well below what Germany, with skilful and more urgent management of its resources, was capable of producing after 1943. After that date Hitler and the economic administration were determined to expand output to the limit. In aircraft production, for example, plans were laid in 1944 for an annual rate of production of 80,000 aircraft a year in 1945.[95] Vast new factories were under construction for the mass-production of aero-engines and aircraft.[96] In fact in 1944 Germany's aircraft production reached a peak of only 36,000; Japan, with a much smaller and less advanced industrial base had been able to produce 28,000 aircraft in the same year. The impact of even this increase was heavily reduced by the destruction of assembled aircraft at the factories, and the loss of fuel and spare parts for those aircraft that eventually reached the front-line units. The large new factories were bombed and in most cases abandoned.[97] Substantial though increases in German output appeared, they might have been greater still but for bombing. There were, to be sure, other constraints on production, particularly power and certain raw materials.[98] Indeed Hitler's own strategy of a low level of economic mobilization in the early years of war contributed much to the later difficulties in increasing production. But even had these restrictions not been overcome, the absence of bombing would have freed resources held down in anti-aircraft and repair work; would have eliminated wastage caused by bombing; and would have allowed the industrial planners the same freedom as that enjoyed in the United States to plan, build and operate the war economy without interruption and as near to the economic optimum as possible.

It was this freedom to plan war production without interruption and hence to achieve a smooth flow of war supplies that was destroyed by bombing. Instead, bombing increasingly dictated to the German authorities how the economy was to be organized. Once bombing began German industry was forced to adopt a more improvised and flexible approach to production planning. To some extent improvisation was successful in preventing a greater toll of current production being exacted by the bombers, but in the nature of improvisation severe limitations were placed on the long-term development of the war economy. The decision to move factories into disused mines and caves or to hide them in forest clearings, while allowing some production to continue right until the end of the war was not the basis for any large-scale increase in mass-produced war material.[99]

The very fact of dispersal itself produced a number of constraints. Design bureaux found themselves located miles away from the factories with which they were associated. Factory size was severely restricted by the need to break up large and easily visible buildings into smaller units Yet in the aircraft and tank industries the tendency before bombing began was to operate larger and larger units in order to win all the necessary production economies. These economies were lost in many cases with dispersal forced by bombing.[100] So, too, were the gains made by the rationalization of war industry undertaken in the middle of the war by Speer and the Industrial Councils. Many more machine tools had to be distributed to the smaller dispersed plants, and because each unit was smaller than the large factory complex that had been disperesed, work with special machine tools for mass-production had to be abandoned in favour of using general purpose tools again, which often required a considerable amount of hand-work.[101] The dispersal also put a heavier demand on skilled labour which could be diluted in the larger units, in which semi-skilled workers operated the new machinery under supervision, but which was needed again when factories were dispersed because of the renewed emphasis on skilled workmanship rather than machine-production.[102] Moreover dispersal made it more likely that casual interruption to the flow of parts and materials due to the bombing of communications would be increased. Many factories were left with finished aircraft or engines that were missing a few crucial parts, either held up in transit or bombed in the area attacks. The more elaborate the dispersal became, the more acute the problems of supply.

This was even more the case when during the course of 1943 the Air Ministry agreed to the dispersal of production into occupied Europe, The European aircraft industry had until then been relatively little used by the Germans. Factories had been dismantled in Yugoslavia, Poland and Russia and the machinery sent back to the Reich. In France and Czechoslovakia some limited production of parts and inessential aircraft had been undertaken since the occupation began. Goering's decision to reverse the original policy of not utilizing foreign industry was an answer not only to the failure of aircraft production within Germany, but to the threat of more bombing.[103] However the new dispersal outside the Reich brought many of the same problems. The German aircraft industry had used the French facilities for carrying on research which was proscribed in Germany itself because it was not immediately related to war needs. The new instructions forced the firms to turn these facilities over to full aircraft production. The lack of tools and skilled labour, much of which had been taken off into the Reich, meant that resources had to be sent out of Germany to meet the new requirements. Moreover the Allies had already begun to bomb French factories as well.[104] The resulting confusion reduced the Luftwaffe's production in France to a total of only 2,500, mostly trainer aircraft, for the whole war period. The same situation prevailed in central Europe. Resources had to be taken out of the Reich and distributed among a large number of Czech and Hungarian enterprises while the Air Ministry made great efforts to complete the construction of large factories to replace the dispersed workshops in comparatively bomb-safe areas.[105] The aircraft production capacity of the conquered areas was approximately 14,000 aircraft per year before occupation. Had the German administration been able to utilize this capacity fully during 1943 and 1944 the production of armaments would have been significantly greater. But at just the point when Germany was poised to plan and produce large increases in output over and above those already planned, bombing reduced the possibility and left instead a desperate improvisation. Such increases would still have been subject to raw material limitations, but the amount of war material that Germany might have been able to produce for the crucial battles of 1944 and 1945 without bombing would have meant a longer and far more costly battle for the final defeat of fascism, and might have made necessary the use of atomic weapons in Europe as well.[106]

In Japan bombing was far more successful in terms of direct destruction. Not only were Japanese defences weak and poorly organized, no attempt was made to meet the American threat with a counter-offensive. The standard bombers lacked range or carrying capacity and the proposed trans-oceanic bomber, the *Fugako*, was judged to be too demanding on limited production resources and suffered the same fate as the bombers proposed in Germany for attacking the United States.[107] The fire-bombing campaign that began in March 1945 despite Stimson's moral qualms and Roosevelt's delusion that the air forces were 'blowing to bits carefully selected targets',[108] reduced Japan's already shrinking war capability dramatically. By July 1945 Japanese production was 35 per cent of its wartime peak, where in the case of Germany it was conservatively calculated that only 10 per cent of planned current production was lost through bombing in 1944.[109] The effect on morale, while not sufficient to lead to the overthrow of the regime, reduced the ability or willingness to work. The evacuation into the countryside served only to confuse still further the running of the economy, which relied increasingly on production in home workshops and in those few towns not yet bombed because of the instructions to the American commanders to leave suitable targets for the use of the atomic bomb.[110] The scale of the attacks in March and April were sufficient to force the Japanese authorities to begin to search seriously for peace, and the failure to find a satisfactory settlement did not reflect an indifference to the suffering inflicted on the civilian population but the entrenched position of the army in Japanese political life, and the fear of reprisal for defeatism. Conventional bombing had so seriously undermined the prestige of the army that surrender was openly discussed well before the use of atomic weapons. When the final decision was made by the Emperor for surrender it was in the knowledge that the peace party in the Cabinet had predicted an end to the war through bombing in September, a month earlier than the date given by LeMay to Arnold.[111] Indeed the difference between the atomic bomb and a conventional B-29 attack was largely academic in the case of Japan where the cities were ideally suited to area fire-bombing, which produced largely the same effects. The use of the atomic bomb, whatever the wider diplomatic and strategic purposes in using it, represented the culmination of a bombing policy begun by Britain and Germany five years before.[112]

The object of bombing was in the end to bring as large an amount of destruction as cheaply as possible to the enemy homeland, indiscriminately

6

Leadership, Organization and Training

The record of the air forces during the Second World War was governed to a considerable extent by questions of leadership, organization and training. Although a great many similarities existed in the way in which forces were organized and trained in different countries, there remained differences of military tradition, differences in the availability of resources and fundamental differences in the nature of the political and administrative structure in which air strategy was shaped. These contrasts were often of kind rather than quality. There was no international standard of comparison for judging the less tangible aspects of warfare since they reflected national circumstances and the impact of war. Indeed no country was immune from incompetence and misjudgement in the air war, all the more so since air power was a new and untested weapon.[1] From its nature, however, air power made certain demands on all the powers. It required an ability to link together military and engineering traditions, an ability that differed widely with national conditions. It required a satisfactory ratio between pilots and aircraft within overall strategy, as pilot training was a long and complex affair and losses high. Replacing pilot losses was quite unlike the more familiar task of replenishing infantry divisions. Any failure to provide sufficient engineers, pilots and technical ground staff, without which no air force could operate, placed severe limitations on the future combat performance of those air forces in which the failure developed. In the end all such questions depended on the intentions of those who led the air forces and decided air strategy. How the air force was integrated into this wider political and military context was often crucial in explaining its material and moral performance. Failures in strategic direction or in the way in which strategy was translated, via the air officer corps, into action could not be undone however numerous or well-equipped the air squadrons were. It is thus with leadership in this wider sense that any discussion of organization and morale must begin.

(i) Leadership in the Air War

In almost all cases air forces were administered by government departments and operated by air staffs. In Britain and France the air ministries were in turn responsible to parliaments. In America the air force was not an independent service and was represented at higher levels of government by the War Department of which its administration formed a part. In Russia, Germany and Italy the highest authority for deciding questions on air affairs was the individual state leader, although in Russia the decisions were usually collective decisions based on initiatives theoretically inspired by Stalin.[2] Immediately below the government departments were the air staffs. Although the status of the staffs differed according to the degree of independence enjoyed by the air force within the military structure, the function of the senior air officers was largely the same. These functions included the operation of the air force, its day-to-day military administration and the discussion and recommendation of strategy and tactics. In some cases this included the technical and industrial planning unless a separate office existed for questions of supply.

Air policy and air strategy were developed through co-operation between the staffs and the civilian authorities; sometimes, as in Japan and Russia, through the agency of the armed forces supreme command, sometimes as in Britain and Germany through direct ministerial channels. Policy-making at the highest level was the result of close co-operation between the professional airmen and the civilian leadership. In almost all cases such co-operation, though fraught with problems of personality and inter-service rivalry, was essential in order to place air affairs in the wider context of the war, and in order for those with the technical and military expertise to pursue arguments and define priorities for which they could claim competence. Although civilian leadership possessed final authority such authority could not be properly exercised unless there existed a high degree of consultation and discussion for which the staff and ministerial committee system proved the most satisfactory under the circumstances of war.

The committee system was central to the task of running the air war. The technical complexity of air forces and the novelty of their use and organization made such co-operation essential. It had other advantages too. It prevented any one figure or group of figures, either from the military or the government, being able to dominate decision-making and to prevent professional consultation. Such a system fitted in more easily with democratic traditions of government and worked more effectively for the western Allies than for the other powers. During the war the western Allies were compelled to develop joint machinery for co-operation and discussion in strategic and technical affairs. This machinery simplified the policy-making process and encouraged more direct contact in the committee-room between the air staffs and the central civilian administration. The western powers enjoyed in general a more developed tradition of consultation and exhibited less antipathy between the civilian and military establishments. Although criticism was levelled against committee leadership on the grounds that judgements were slow to be arrived at, and were over-cautious, this had little effect in reducing executive work by committee. The value of wide-ranging consultation and co-operation, the widely differing worlds of economic, scientific and military life and the complex and detailed nature of wartime administration, led the Allied powers in particular towards more, rather than less, committee work.[3]

To the democracies it appeared that a greater danger than the constraints imposed by committee work was the prospect of the arbitrary and dictatorial intervention of powerful political personalities in air affairs capable of rendering committee work ineffective or superfluous. Even democracies demonstrated such a tendency, though it was habitually mitigated by pressures from the forces and the parliaments against the abuse of power. Churchill, though prepared at times to go against his service chiefs in the pursuit of ill-favoured arguments and plans, found it was politically inexpedient to continue the pursuit at the expense of co-operation and action.[4] Churchill's central reliance on strategic bombing, for example, at the start of the war was modified as more information and experience compelled the service chiefs and senior ministers to argue successfully against his over-optimistic view. The danger of arriving at the wrong conclusion in a system of representative government was thus reduced by the political dangers to which those who made decisions were exposed. Despite Stimson's complaint of Roosevelt's efforts 'to keep all the threads in his own hands',[5] the fact that re-election was probable during the course of the war coupled with traditions of consultation and constitutionality kept democratic leadership within strict limits. Leadership at the top became a genuinely shared experience.

This was less true for the European Axis powers; not that dictatorship *per se* encouraged inefficiency or misjudgment—as the Soviet Union demonstrated—but because of the particular structure of authority under fascism. With its fusion of military and political office, its intense compartmentalization, its corruption and inefficiency and most of all because of the concentration of power in the hands of one man, fascism brought a wide range of handicaps to the exercise of sound administrative and military judgment. Mussolini, as Minister of Aviation as well as head of the government, was unable to devote a fraction of the time necessary to air affairs because of other commitments. He was, too, untrained for the kind of technical and administrative tasks required in a modern air service. Although the result was to leave much of the day-to-day work in the air force to its responsible and professional leaders, final decisions rested with Mussolini whose ideas on air warfare were shaped as much by arbitrary and unpredictable factors as by the careful assessment of information and ideas. It was Mussolini's fascination with Douhetism that inspired him to place supreme and uncritical faith in heavy bombers, ignoring the need for anti-aircraft defences, modern fighters or even air-raid shelters.[6]

This situation was in some ways even more serious in Germany, for Hitler considered himself an expert on military technology and was dismissive of his general staff officers whom he regarded as conservative and convention-bound.[7] The result was that since Hitler was the final source of all authority in a thorough, almost literal, sense any question with regard to the use of the air forces had to be decided by Hitler. By the end of war this had reached the level where Hitler himself personally ordered the day-to-day operations of air units on the eastern front, by-passing the commander-in-chief, the air staff and the front commanders.[8] But this had not always been the case. In the early years of the build-up of the Luftwaffe and in the early years of war, Hitler relied heavily on Goering, whose main claim to authority derived not from a military career but from his political role in the party and the state. Being a political creature, Goering used his position in the Luftwaffe as a means to increase political influence at the expense of other leaders, and being in Hitler's confidence he was able to insist on the autonomy of his air force. Such autonomy cut off the Luftwaffe from regular top-level co-operation with the other services, or with the supreme command, and during the war cut off the Luftwaffe from the rest of the war economy. The 'leadership principle' thus encouraged a lack of liaison between rival hierarchies, and led instead to duplication of effort and bureaucratization as Goering attempted to establish an independent administrative and economic base. The isolationism of the air force produced a growing communictions gap between Hitler and the air force. There were no regular meetings with the air commander-in-chief, and those that there were became less frequent as the war progressed. The supreme headquarters had Luftwaffe liaison officers of low rank and little authority.[9] Hitler's personal preference for the informal gathering of information from frontline pilots and favoured members of his entourage distorted yet further the kind of information that passed from the air force to the political leadership.[10] Such distortion was compounded by the way in which Goering deliberately misrepresented the strength or ability of the air force in order to retain Hitler's indulgence and boost his own political fortunes. Even when the exaggerated claims of the Luftwaffe commander had been exposed in the declining air effectiveness of 1941 and 1942 Hitler retained a naive faith in the ability of the air force to redress the strategic balance, a faith based on ignorance of air force affairs coupled with respect for Goering's political position.[11]

Had Goering been a successful air leader the lack of communication with the rest of the military and political leadership might have been offset. However, like Hitler, Goering lacked any real professional claim to high military office. Preferring to surround himself with subordinates who were rewarded for party loyalty and past favours, Goering attempted to reproduce in the air force the kind of authority structure practised by Hitler in the state. This was at the expense of both the air staff, whose chief was treated by Goering as a mere adjutant, and of more able administrators such as Milch in the air ministry, who were penalized because of Goering's fear that his own amateurish leadership would contrast with others' professional competence.[12] In the end Goering preferred to surround himself with unqualified advisers and loyal, uncritical comrades. By 1944 the air staff was itself being bypassed by Goering's 'Kindergarten' of younger officers who formed an inner clique in pursuit of Goering's favour.[13] By this time, however, Goering had abandoned all attempt to command the air force or to pay serious attention to the technical and economic aspects of aircraft production, even though power itself was not relinquished and Hitler hesitated to take it from him.

It was at this stage that Hitler came to take over more direct responsibility, although ultimate responsibility had always been his. Bringing a personal ignorance of air affairs and a limited technical knowledge, Hitler's interventions assumed an arbitrary and often damaging character. Hitler insisted that the air force produce a final devastating weapon with which to confound the Allies, finding the air force attractive precisely because it held out the promise from the 1930s of achieving decisive results at a stroke, heroically and overwhelmingly. Of the V2 rocket he commented 'If we had these rockets in 1939 we should never have had this war'.[14] Whether rockets or jet-bombers, Hitler's military appreciation of their capability betrayed a romantic and uncritical approach to air affairs that he demonstrated much less often with the army. When, however, the air force, even under Hitler's more careful supervision failed to produce even a tactical support force in 1944, and no devastating weapon, he insisted on the disbanding of the air units and their replacement with a large anti-aircraft army.[15] Only with great difficulty was Goering able to salvage the Luftwaffe, but the damage had been done. In between bouts of uncontrollable abuse at the air forces, culminating in an excited telephone call to the chief-of-staff that 'the entire Luftwaffe command should be hanged immediately', Hitler ignored the air force, preferring to complete the struggle with the army.[16] To Hitler's constant complaints about the air force Goebbels responded in his diary that 'it is no good the Führer saying today that he had wanted the right thing but had not insisted on it.'[17] Relying too heavily on political allies as military commanders, ill-informed about air affairs and yet anxious to retain ultimate control over the strategy that contained them, dismissive of the professional airman in favour of occasional and unorthodox insights, fascist leadership contrasted sharply with the administration and leadership against which it was fighting. The lack of proper strategic direction distorted the effect of deficiencies elsewhere in training and preparation, which under different circumstances might well have been mastered, as were many of the deficiencies of the enemy. The failure at the top of the Axis air forces was not just one of a number of explanations for poor strategic performance but was the primary cause.

(ii) Organization in the Armed Forces

The degree and extent to which air forces were integrated into political and administrative life was closely linked with a second question: integration into the armed forces. The central issue for an air force was its constitutional position. In the eyes of the other services this amounted to the degree of independence an air force should be given, and the extent to which allowances should be made for the air forces' special needs in operations and supply.

The relationship between the air force and the other services revolved around the question of independence. Where the air force was a component part of one of the older services considerable efforts were made to maintain the status quo and deny autonomy. Where air forces had already won independence there existed a high degree of rivalry between the services over questions of co-operation and command, although until 1935 the only independent air force of any significance was the RAF. The question of an independent air force arose out of different ways of interpreting the role of air forces. While armies emphasized the need for unity of command, not only at the front but at the highest level as well, the air forces stressed that the whole purpose of having an air force was to allow it the opportunity to carry out the maximum of which an force was capable and hence to give it its freedom. In fact the RAF had won its autonomy largely because of the victory of the bomber school in its insistence that in any future conflict an independently mounted strategic bombing offensive would be the main role performed by air forces. Those who favoured a tactical air force, linked closely to ground forces, with allies in the naval demand for a separate naval air arm, argued that the main purpose of air forces was an auxiliary one, and should not be jeopardized by giving the air forces autonomy. Throughout the 1930s an often acrimonious division existed between the RAF and the rest of the military estabishment over the closely related arguments about air doctrine and independence.[18]

The demand for independence was pursued no less vigorously in other major air forces, either because the bombing strategy was paramount, as in the United

States, or because there were political reasons, as in Germany. In America the air forces were subsidiary until 1941. The pressure to reverse the constitutional position of the services came from the public on the one hand, increasingly anxious about air defence, and from Roosevelt and Stimson who were persuaded both of the importance of air power as demonstrated in the German victories and the British defence in 1940 and of the need for greater autonomy for air forces.[19] The American politicians and military leaders were influenced in this decision by the success of the RAF organization. Time was spent studying it during early 1941, and the re-organization of hemisphere defence relied on the lessons drawn from these studies.[20] Marshall was less convinced, arguing until the end of 1941 that German success had come through 'subordination of air power to the supreme command of the armed forces' and that a different situation would compromise the principle of unity of command.[21] In private he ascribed air force demands for independence less charitably to the fact that the older but low-ranking air officers were looking for opportunities for promotion by giving the air force a separate status.[22] Marshall was persuaded to accept change, however, because of the obvious inefficiency of the prevailing system. Arnold provided the impetus for change by recommending a new structure of command and organization for air forces, but the final approval came from Marshall and Roosevelt in the wake of the public outcry at the disaster at Pearl Harbor.[23] Even with the creation of the Army Air Forces outlined in War Dept. Circular 59 in March 1942 the air force failed to achieve the degree of independence enjoyed by the RAF. This was not achieved until 1947 when it had become clear beyond all doubt that the strategic tasks of the air force differed in kind from those of the army. What the limited autonomy did bring was a unity of command over air forces, regular consultation with the air force commander in the highest political and military circles, and the creation of a separate air staff. Relations between army ground and air units in the field were not finally resolved until 1943, when the ground army unwillingly conceded that it was co-equal with the air forces and had to work with the air officers in co-operation, rather than by giving orders.[24]

In Russia and Germany, where the armed forces preferred to emphasize the tactical use of air power, there was a curious divergence in the way in which the air forces were organized as the war developed. At the outbreak of war the Soviet air forces had been an integral part of the army, subordinate to the front commanders. Although the air force remained nominally part of the army throughout the war, one of the first reforms to be carried through in the wake of the German attack was to give the air force virtual operational and constitutional autonomy in order to make it more flexible. At the highest command level the air forces won separate representation, partly because the service was so specialized in its function, partly because of the large increase in the size and importance of the Soviet General Headquarters strategic air forces, which were so organized as to be independent of the front-line armies.[25] The German air force, on the other hand, had had considerable constitutional independence from the start. The separation had been largely the result of Goering's insistence that the Luftwaffe should be as free as possible from the intervention of the traditional army whose staff Hitler derided as an 'exclusive clique of particularly arrogant dunces and national pests'.[26] The German army had indeed objected to the creation of a separate force, and had in 1933 attempted to forestall Hitler by establishing an army-controlled air bureau.[27] But in fact the independence of the Luftwaffe was a political rather than a doctrinal one. As far as the function of the air force was concerned it remained closely tied to the needs of the army, and was subject to the directives of the army-dominated supreme headquarters. After the failure of air force operations over England in 1940 the integration of the air force with the army became closer, reaffirming the preference for limited air power of both Hitler and the army staff. Goering's lack of firm control over the air force, and his growing isolation and indolence, allowed the army to assume considerable operational control as well. The effect was to stifle later Luftwaffe efforts to embark on strategic tasks of its own, and to confirm Hitler's own preference for air forces that played a narrowly defined role at the battlefront.

Japan alone of all the major air powers pursued a different line. The army and navy had established bureaux for air affairs in 1919 and 1916 respectively, and from those dates onwards retained control over their own individual air forces. Because of the tradition of the Japanese navy and the geographic need for a large naval force, the navy's air arm was the larger and more important of the two. Both army and navy air forces were represented at Army and Navy Headquarters by commanding officers of the Army Air and Navy Air HQ, but at the Imperial General Headquarters the interests of the air were served by the army and navy chiefs of staff. The army air corps was given an equal status with the other army branches, but in the navy the air forces were assigned subordinately to the individual fleets, or to the carrier fleet.[28] This structure was little questioned. It produced, however, instead of a struggle for influence over air forces between the air force and the army, a rivalry between the two air forces themselves. The rivalry took the form of a vigorous competition for resources, a technical exclusiveness, and a failure on many occasions to satisfactorily co-ordinate the operations of army and navy air forces together. In mainland Japan the defence system broke down on the fact that every attempt to centralize the system came up against the entrenched rivalry of the two air services. The meagre radar network was further weakened by the fact that in 19 of the 30 radar sites the navy and army air forces had their own separate stations side by side, duplicating information. Other air forces were not immune from internal rivalry, but only in Japan did such rivalry seriously affect the performance in the air war.[29]

There were other sources of conflict, too. Rivalry between the air forces and the other services took a variety of forms. At root much of the rivalry was fanned by the fear than an independent air force hoped to supplant the older services by the use of strategies that rendered armies and navies redundant. For example, although there were sound strategic arguments for an invasion of continental Europe in 1943, the plans were defended with such force because they promised a major role to armies and navies and a subordinate role to the air forces. The air force alternative of a war of attrition from the air was attacked, not just on technical grounds, but because it deliberately challenged the army view of war. The more forcefully the armies insisted on ground operations, the easier it became for armies to insist on the creation of air forces that were primarily tactical in composition and operation. For Russia and Germany on the eastern front these questions did not arise for both sides were committed throughout to the primacy of tactical support. In the west the insistence after 1943 on the creation of large tactical air forces, although of great value in the final invasion, was seen by some air force leaders as an attempt to sabotage their efforts to achieve a decision through bombing alone and to confound those critics who revealed how exaggerated the initial claims for the impact of air warfare had been.[30] The fact that such claims had been made in the first place encouraged rivalry over other questions. The air forces took the largest slice of financial and economic resources even in countries committed to a large land army. In many cases they took the best recruits. The loss of these resources to the other services gave scope to those who claimed that money could be better spent on something else. In Germany in 1939 the other services were able to get the air force budget substantially reduced, thus imposing an additional restriction on the pre-war period of expansion.[31] In Britain the programme of heavy bombers was restricted as the war progressed, because the original plans would have diverted even greater resources from urgent economic priorities for other services.[32] When to this use of large resources was added the failure to use them as effectively as had been promised, the temptation was to curtail the air force in favour of other services, or, in the case of Germany, to try to abolish the air force altogether. On balance such rivalry was confined to occasional open conflict or personal hostility, puncturing relations between the services that were otherwise sensible and cordial, but air forces were always in a position of having to justify their existence and their doctrines to a much greater extent than armies and navies.

The importance of such rivalry, and of the constitutional question in general, was the way in which this influenced the final use of air forces. The fact that Britain and the United States mounted large-scale bombing offensives, and that other powers did not, was a reflection of the degree of independence enjoyed by the air forces. Where the relationship was primarily a subsidiary one the tactical use of aircraft predominated. In Britain and America the air staffs were correspondingly more powerful and more fully integrated into the policy-making process. Air officers held high rank in the General Staffs, and in the command of large-scale operations, not just because of their position in the air force but because they had more general command qualities. In Germany the senior air commanders were seldom in a position to command ground troops directly, or to trespass on the staff work at the supreme headquarters, and those like Kesselring who did were army officers who had temporarily adopted an air uniform. Army traditions were too strong to allow the air force a greater say in the overall running of the war, while Goering had instilled the Luftwaffe with a feeling of isolationism which discouraged it from claiming a more important role. The same was true in Japan and Russia, where air commanders, because of the specialization of their role, were confined largely to air operations and not brought more fully into the supreme military establishment. Such a distinction explained in part the greater emphasis placed upon air warfare in the west, and the failure in Germany and Japan to anticipate the decline in air power and take steps at the highest level to reverse it.

(iii) The Air Force Officer Corps

The different status enjoyed by the air forces during the war was reflected in patterns of recruitment and the available numbers of senior air officers, particularly those of staff quality. Differences in the nature and establishment of the senior officer corps had considerable repercussions on the performance of air forces throughout the war. For most of the combatant powers air force staffs were created only shortly before the actual outbreak of war, or were expanded from a small base during the period of rearmament. Only in Britain and France did there exist large established air forces with a strong staff tradition, and only in Britain was that allied to an independent, professional air force.

Of all the major air powers Britain alone enjoyed the benefits of a continuous stream of trained staff and command officers throughout the inter-war period whose background and technical knowledge were exclusively concerned with air forces. The danger of conservatism that such a situation might have produced, was avoided to a great extent by the fact that the air force had to fight to maintain its independence and its strategic ambitions against those who doubted the usefulness of both. Under those circumstances it was the other service staffs who found themselves in a conservative position; the air forces who held the promise of major change in warfare in the future.[33] The value of a long staff tradition lay in the fact that the exercise of air power required a high level of technical knowledge and competence, as well as a thorough familiarity with all aspects of tactics and organization. This took time to acquire. Its usefulness was qualified only by a lack of combat experience. Under conditions of war the air staff was able to make a significant contribution to war planning on the basis of past training and the lessons of recent combat. The RAF never lacked a supply of commanders and air staff officers of high professional standard, although the staff was helped considerably by working closely with the Air Ministry and the Air Council. This drew competent civilians together with the regular airmen in a continual review of priorities and plans, and eased the path of administration between the two sides while bringing argument therapeutically into the open.[34]

Although a staff tradition was important for the success of British air power, the absence of such a tradition was not in itself a handicap to performance in war. The important factor was the way in which such a deficiency was approached. In America, lacking even a separate air staff until 1941 and with a total of only 1,600 Air Corps officers in 1938, there was no recourse but to recruit from outside the air service for senior officer material. Lovett was himself recruited by Stimson from a bank career to become Assistant Secretary for War for the air forces, and the link with the business and professional world was maintained in the recruitment of air staff officers, particularly for special administrative and service roles.[35] In November 1941 the AAF brought in the Wallace Clark Company of management consultants to advise on the establishment of the air force administration, reflecting Arnold's desire to apply the methods of American business to the task of running a major air force. A Directorate of Management Control was established to help administer the force, and the Organisational Planning and Statistical Control units developed by the Directorate became the core of the future Operational and intelligence organizations set up in 1942 and 1943 for the rational assessment of war experience.[36] Many of the staff for these tasks were recruited from civilian life and were given ranks appropriate to the function. Combat commands were given to airmen with military experience, but because of the small size of the officer corps promotion was rapid and younger men were given responsibilities which in the ground army were undertaken by more senior soldiers. Some of the experience that the younger air force officers lacked was compensated for by the sharing of experiences with the RAF. The Combined Chiefs of Staff organization, in which the RAF played a major role, gave an opportunity to the AAF to play an important part in the overall conduct of the war that its lack of senior staff officers might have prevented. On one thing the British and American experience was united, on the importance of involving officers and civilians with technical and engineering experience in the air forces. The engineering officers were of equal status with those in combat and administrative positions. In most cases career air officers already possessed a considerable amount of technical training. Where gaps existed during the war civilians were brought in to organize technical and engineering functions, and in the AAF in particular considerable emphasis was laid on the engineering staffs, on whose contribution the combat staffs were largely dependent.[37] The use of civilians also made it easier, particularly for the RAF, to co-operate with the economic and administrative departments responsible for supply, research and maintenance, all of which proved to be vital functions for the survival of a modern air force.

Germany and Russia, like America, had to build up an air officer corps during the 1930s and lacked any effective continuity with the air forces of the First World War. From the period of the First Five-Year Plan the Russian air force expanded rapidly. Enjoying the status under the Chief of Staff enjoyed by the artillery and cavalry and subject to command from the ground, the Russian air force did not require a large number of senior officers for staff work. The air force was required to provide close support for ground troops which could be organized satisfactorily by officers with an army background, as it was in Japan.[38] Even at the level of the supreme command army and civilian personnel assumed considerable direct control over air forces. Because of the limited use to which Soviet air forces were put at the front greater emphasis was laid on the technical side of air force administration. The officers responsible for maintenance, supply and production were given high status and were closely involved in economic and technical questions, and such a position was reflected in the success of Soviet aircraft production in contrast with the lack of initiative demonstrated at the front, although to some extent this was the result of Stalin's personal intervention. His conservatism discouraged strategic experiment in air warfare.[39] In this respect the purges had less effect on the air force than might have been the case if a large corps of competent air staff officers had already been in existence. For the air force the purges were in some ways a positive advantage. Those removed from office during the late 1930s were among the older generation of army officers working in the air force, or those who had risen to high office for earlier political services. By the early 1940s younger officers were rapidly promoted whose training and experience was more professional from the point of view of air force needs, and many of whom were promoted for military competence rather than political loyalty.[40] During the period between 1937 and 1942 the turnover of senior air officers was not unlike the changes taking place in many air forces which were intent upon eradicating conservatism and incompetence (the RAF, for example, experienced some 17 major changes in senior command positions between 1938 and 1943).[41] Most of those promoted during the war in Russia achieved their positions through military success rather than political manoeuvre. In fact officers in the air force were offered the prospect of membership of the Communist Party only after they had distinguished themselves in combat. The number of air officers who were Communists rose from 58,000 in 1941 to 123,000 in 1943.[42] In Germany by contrast political loyalty was an avenue to advancement without previous proof of military competence. If there also existed evidence of political life interfering with recruitment and promotion in the Russian air forces it was much less than Russia's allies and enemies supposed.

In Germany politics intruded much more openly. In the ministerial offices, many of which carried a military title as well, those known for Nazi sympathies and those favoured by Goering as old acquaintances or new allies were given positions. Younger officers were promoted on the basis of political reliability and devotion to the air leader. This led to the recruitment of those quite clearly unsuitable for office, such as Udet who was promoted to head the Technical Office. Nor did many of the political appointments bring experience from the outside world as the civilians recruited in America did. Udet had been a stunt artist, film star and was a noted *bon viveur*; another of Goering's comrades was a cigar salesman; yet another had shared Goering's experience of confinement during the 1920s for morphine addiction.[43] Even Goering himself lacked any professional experience as a senior military figure, on account of which he preferred to surround himself with those whom he regarded as his intellectual as well as political inferiors.

For those who were recruited into the Luftwaffe after 1935 from a military background there was a further problem. The Prussian staff tradition placed great demands on the new Luftwaffe staff for the high standards it maintained. The new Luftwaffe staff was required to keep up standards of entry and activity which under the additional strain of poor leadership, and the short time in which to establish a staff, simply could not be maintained. Some of the new Luftwaffe staff and command came from this Prussian tradition. When the air force was activated officers with some flying experience were seconded to work for the Luftwaffe. The shortage of officers then led to the transfer of army officers with no air experience but who had served with the Reichswehr through the 1920s, including a number of cavalry officers who were less essential to the army needs in the 1930s.[44] This fusion of officer personnel contributed to the army-mindedness of the air force, and encouraged the pursuit of a tactical air force closely co-operating with the army units. But it also had the unfortunate consequence of dividing the air officer corps into those who regarded themselves as heirs of the Prussian tradition, and those who came from an unorthodox, particularly technical, background. Part of the hostility felt between regular soldiers and the *parvenus* arose from the fact that newcomers were given high military office without having followed the normal army channels. Milch was recruited as a civilian and was given the rank of colonel in 1933, rising to field marshal in 1940, at the expense of others who had risen to high rank by the traditional route.[45] Jeschonnek as chief of the air staff, and a regular army officer before 1933, led the conflict between the two sides. Firmly committed to the Prussian tradition he was, according to Milch, 'contemptuous of other walks of life'.[46] Such contempt took the unfortunate form of a deep distrust of the engineering officers, who were grouped into a separate engineers' officer corps, and deliberately kept apart from the regular air staff by Goering. Since both branches were in theory co-equal under the commander-in-chief their mutual hostility and constitutional distinctness discouraged proper contacts between those who provided the aircraft and those who used them, a fact made explicit by orders prohibiting engineering personnel from visiting front units.[47]

137

Unlike all the other major air powers the German air force did not bring in civilians as advisers, or recruit extensively from other spheres during the war, to compensate for shortages in the service, insisting that the work of the Luftwaffe was more properly conducted by soldiers. This exclusiveness had the effect of diluting what staff officer material was available and left the Luftwaffe short of the necessary numbers to carry out the traditional and wide-ranging staff tasks. This was caused to some extent too by the policy of insisting that staff officers should have combat experience. Not only did this lead to a situation where almost a quarter of the staff officers during the war were killed, but it meant that little continuity could be maintained at staff level, while those units entrusted to staff officers on a tour of duty often had to devote valuable time to instructing the staff officers in carrying out combat duties.[48] In 1942 Hitler turned the policy on its head with even more disastrous consequences. He ordered that the Luftwaffe general staff vacancies should be filled only by those who had distinguished themselves in combat at the front. Not only did this then denude the front of the best commanders, it gave no guarantee that such officers, with no staff training, would be capable of the more challenging work behind the lines.[49] The subsequent demoralization of the Luftwaffe in its efforts to maintain Prussian standards of military organization with insufficient numbers, poorly trained, together with the failure to integrate the engineering and combat traditions, complemented the failure in leadership at the top.

Those air forces that developed a flexible, professional air leadership combined effectively with help from civilian sources, particularly those involved in business and technical occupations, were operated more effectively than those where military tradition and contempt for business discouraged open contact. In both Germany and Japan such contempt was, for historical reasons, widespread among the military leadership. In America and Russia there was no alternative but to bring in personnel from other spheres of life to compensate for shortages within the military sphere. Although there was little difference between the training and aptitudes of individual officers, differences in tradition, organization and recruitment led to substantial contrasts in the performance of the officer corps as a whole.

(iv) Recruitment and Training

The same range of contrasts was shown in recruitment and training in general. Again there were many similarities in the way in which air force personnel was selected and trained and in the overall organization of air forces. Yet national circumstances, combined with the problems created by war, brought major differences as well. Recruitment into the service differed from that of the navy and army in a number of ways. In the first place air forces were much smaller and more selective than the army and navy (see Table 11). Air forces were compelled to be much more selective because of the nature of air-force service. Pilots and skilled aircrew required extensive training for operations that made greater demands on the individual than those in surface warfare. The work was also much more technical. All air forces insisted that aircrew should be taught aeronautics as well as air combat. Finally all air forces contained a much higher ratio of officers to men than the other services, almost all pilots achieving officer status.[51]

Table 11: Air Force and Army Maximum Size during World War II[50]

	Air Force (a)	Army
Germany (b)	990,000	4,647,000
United States	2,372,292	8,200,000
Great Britain	1,002,000	2,920,000
U.S.S.R.	1,250,000	5,550,000

(a) Not including anti-aircraft forces

(b) Figures for November 1943, not including 393,000 Luftwaffe ground troops on the eastern front.

Selection for air force service was based on high educational and physical standards, not only because of the nature of the work involved, but because many of those recruited would become officers and were expected to fulfil the qualities required of officer material. In the AAF men were recruited on the basis of special examination or of two years of college education, taking 40 per cent of those recruits classified in the top two classes of the Army General Classification.[52] This was reflected, too, in the low rate of non-white entry. Although the armed forces had agreed that a proportion of 10.6 per cent of the total service personnel should be black, the air force took only 6.1 per cent at the peak and only 0.3 per cent of the officers were non-white.[53] In Japan preference was given to those with higher or advanced secondary education, who would be commissioned as officers after training, while those with lower qualifications recruited from the ranks of the army were not.[54] The same was true of European recruitment which reflected to a great extent the class structure of European societies. Those from higher social and educational backgrounds were recruited for training as pilots, those from working class backgrounds for training as non-flying personnel, ground crew and maintenance workers. The distinction was not always a rigid one, and it was less so in Germany, but it reflected the sense that flying recruits were a special elite and they were procured accordingly. So clearly was this the case that in Russia ideology dictated that this elitism should be eliminated by giving the trained pilots only NCO status, and confining them to a rigorous barracks existence for the first four years after qualifying. But even in Russia the pressure for creating an elite was hard to resist, and pilots passed out as fully commissioned officers with special privileges after the outbreak of war.[55]

Pilots, however, constituted only a fraction of total air force personnel. Those recruited for non-flying purposes came from a wide variety of backgrounds and made up the bulk of the air forces. Many were recruited from among those already serving in the army among the enlisted ranks. In most air forces which were based on conscription there was a certain degree of choice for those conscripts who volunteered for one service in preference to another. Almost all air forces depended to some extent in recruiting personnel from the unofficial and semi-official air organizations that existed before the war broke out, for these tapped sources of enthusiasm and interest in air affairs from the civilian population. In Germany the Nazi Party Air Corps (NSFK) trained sports and glider pilots and mechanics, and encouraged an interest in sports clubs and air activity in general.[56] In Russia the *Osoaviakhim* organization, which served the same purpose as the NSFK, had an estimated 13 million members in 1936, ran 150 air sports clubs and had presented 8,000 pilot and 20,000 glider certificates.

By 1940 it had trained 24,000 pilots and 3,000 mechanics, and the three year *Osoaviakhim* certificate enabled the holder to enter the Red Air Force as a volunteer without the preliminary selection and training.[57] Similar pre-service experience was provided through cadet schemes in Britain and Japan, although in Britain the volunteer air reservists proved a more important source, as the cadet scheme did not fully materialize until 1938 as the Air Defence Cadet Corps.[58] The existence of an informal procurement area for air service both simplified the selection process and provided a large reserve of men with an active interest in, and experience of, air activity. This fact was perhaps more important from the point of view of acquiring suitable ground personnel than pilots, since pilots required long periods of intensive training for which non-professional preparation was less satisfactory.

During the war the supply of large numbers of skilled ground crew and engineers was an essential factor in keeping an air force in being. No air force was unaware of this necessity, but there were limits imposed on the amount of maintenance and engineering personnel available. Part of the problem lay in the fact that much of this skilled labour was required more urgently in the aircraft factories, and the air forces and economic ministries fought over how it should be divided. There were limits imposed as well by the general level of preparedness for air warfare, and the extent to which sufficient engineering resources were available in the economy. In America the shortage of engineering personnel had been the result of a law, approved in 1926, restricting the number of non-flying officers in the air force to 10 per cent.[59] In Europe, too, little attention had been paid to the need to expand ground services rapidly and extensively in wartime, although there existed a pool of skilled engineer officers and mechanics who were used both to train the wartime recruits and to run the major service commands and air bases. One way in which the shortages were satisfied was the close involvement of the aircraft industry itself in the programme of salvage, repair and maintenance, so that the necessary skilled labour was not lost irretrievably to the industry.[60] In Germany the manufacturers were compelled to provide the Luftwaffe with small trained staffs, to be sent on a tour of air bases to instruct in repair and maintenance, and to carry out mechanical work themselves.

In Russia and Britain separate maintenance and service commands were set up after levels of serviceability at the front had been found to be far from satisfactory under combat conditions. In the Russian case the failure of maintenance in 1941 prompted the creation of a central service command using special mobile airfield units carrying six to seven days' fighting equipment which could be moved forward with the army to give rapid and flexible repair facilities. In 1943 the units worked on an average of 540 aircraft a day; by 1945 on 4,000 a day. In Britain the shortage of engineering and ground personnel prompted the central organization of maintenance which, under the impact of scientific Operational Research recommendations, developed 'Planned Flying and Maintenance' procedures designed to achieve 'the last ounce of operational effort per maintenance man-hour out of the aircraft available'. In Germany and Japan no separate command for services was created, and although in the German case maintenance was efficiently operated at a local level, lack of overall supervision, lack of mobility and finally a lack of resources under the impact of bombing, led to deteriorating rates of serviceability.[61] Where the Allied forces enjoyed rates of serviceability in excess of 80 per cent in the invasion of Europe, German serviceability during the same period averaged only 65 per cent and during the war in the east in 1942 sank as low as 53 per cent. Japanese serviceability in the Pacific battles of 1944 and 1945 was between 50 and 60 per cent, although Allied estimates put the level at well below 50 per cent.[62]

Differences in serviceability also reflected different levels of success in coping with labour shortages. In America and Britain some of the shortages in ground personnel were met by mobilizing women for air base work, and in America women were supplemented by recruiting civilian unskilled and disabled labour for work at air depots, a total of 137,000 between January 1942 and December 1944.[63] In Russia, too, much of the work was undertaken by women. Only in Germany and Japan were women not extensively mobilized for this kind of war work. As the war progressed the failure to mobilize sufficient personnel for air services, coupled with the lack of emphasis placed on the service sector by creating large and co-equal service commands, reduced the efficiency of the Axis air forces. In Germany this was not a fundamental weakness, and the mobilization of skilled engineering recruits continued to the end of the war, even if under increasingly difficult conditions. Shortages of adequately qualified pilots proved much more damaging. In Japan, on the other hand, there existed severe shortages of technically trained forces for the air services. In the final Pacific battles the army lost some 56 per cent of its maintenance personnel; in the loss of the Philippines and in the battles for the Solomons and the central Pacific the navy lost 40,000 skilled ground workers. In the spring of 1945 some 50,000 trainees were removed from flying training and forced to take up ground service work for which they were not well-prepared.[64] Industry was also compelled to provide more skilled men. While this recruitment had little effect on raising levels of maintenance and serviceability it starved the industry of vital labour in an economy with a relatively underdeveloped engineering sector. In the case of Japan the problem of a shortage of ground personnel was a major factor in the rapid weakening of Japanese air power. The air war could not be fought with air-craft and pilots alone, but relied on the mobilizing of sufficient skilled technical and administrative resources to keep the air forces in as permanent a state of opera-tional readiness as possible. It was as much an engineer's war as a soldier's war.

The key problem in recruitment was the procurement and training of pilots. Training presented two rather separate problems. The first was how training should be carried out, and how much training there should be. The second was how many pilots should be trained. The amount of training fluctuated with the conditions of war, as did estimates of needs and the number of men actually trained. Until the war itself raised questions about training standards and manpower shortages patterns of training were similar in all air forces. Pilots were trained in a general elementary way until specializing in fighter or bomber or ground attack training. The number of hours flown before posting to combat units varied between 150 and 250 hours when pilots did further operational training.[65] The introduction of advanced training was not universal before the war, but under war conditions all air forces found it necessary to provide an intermediate stage between the completion of specialized training and actual combat. The transfer direct to the battlefront led to high wastage, as well as diverting the energies of front commanders, who were forced to cope with unprepared new pilots.

Standards of training were higher in Germany and Japan both in the length of the training period, the range of training covered, and the emphasis placed upon excellence in combat which grew out of the peculiar military traditions of the two countries. Since the Luftwaffe pilots were an elite corps, within an elite service, they were trained to perform in battle more efficiently and destructively than a normal trainee. Constant references to the pilots as 'knights' created in the military establishment a mythology around air fighting in which the pilots promised to restore the individual and heroic in place of the mass.[66] In Japan such attitudes were even more explicit. The fighter pilots compared themselves to the traditional *kendo* of Japan and demanded aircraft that would display their skills to best advantage. They insisted that fighters should be light and extremely manoeuvrable, even to the point of refusing all armour protection in the expectation that the highest soldierly training would substitute for deficiencies in design. In the Japanese forces it was possible for those who were to use the weapons, even of low rank, to make demands which the producers were forced to accept.[67] Japanese pilots were brought to believe that a 'spiritual con-viction in victory would balance any scientific advantage'.[68] The strictest individual discipline was maintained over the air trainees. Not only were they forced on entry to the service to learn in three days the 27,000 sacred words of the Emperor laying down the duties of a soldier, but punishment consisted of physical beating. Training and aeronautical manuals also had to be learned by rote.[69]

Japanese pilots trained for the elite Combined Fleet carrier force all had over 800 hours' flying experience, some three to four times the amount of flying time in other air forces.[70] Both the German and Japanese air forces benefited in the early stages of the war from the high standard of training. In the Japanese case the capture of the entire southern region brought only the lightest casualties in the air, which confirmed the air leaders in the wisdom of relying on quality rather than quantity. The danger of such reliance lay in the fact that it was very much harder to replace an over-trained pilot. Against greater numbers and better aircraft excellent training remained a limited form of defence and depen-dence on the 'invincibility of a refined technique' blinded the air force to the need for large numbers of aircraft, and competent rather than outstanding pilots.

The second question all air forces had to answer concerned numbers. There was no doubt that training had to be expanded on the outbreak of war, and all the major powers except Japan rapidly increased the number of training schools and the levels of pilot recruitment.[71] As pilots took anything up to three years for thorough training in peacetime, it was important to make the right guesses as to the possible course of the war and the requirements for pilots in the future. A number of factors governed how such guesses were made. The first was the availability of aircraft. Where aircraft plans were modest either through strategic intention, as in Germany, or through economic limitation, as in Japan, the number of trained pilots required was correspondingly lower. In Britain and America, where the initial estimates of aircraft needs were high and were based on a long war hypothesis, the number of pilots planned was very much greater. In Germany and Japan lower estimates of pilot needs were based to some extent on combat experience, for losses in the early months of the European and Far Eastern wars were comparatively light. The Polish campaign, for example, cost the Luftwaffe 400 aircrew of whom about half were pilots.[72] As a result of an underestimation of pilot losses the German, and later the Japanese air forces undertook a major expansion of numbers only under the full impact of war, at considerable cost in training standards. A related problem lay in the kind of war that was expected. Hoping for short wars the Axis powers lacked urgency in training personnel for the prospect of a long-term conflict, hoping that the higher levels achieved before the war would provide a satisfactory reserve.

Britain, by contrast, lacking trained flying personnel in 1939, and anxious about the effect this would have on air force performance, geared the expansion schemes to the prospect of a long and escalating conflict. With current resources the RAF planned in 1939 to train 5,800 pilots a year, rising to 11,000 pilots a year by 1942.[73] This was soon shown to be insufficient. A political initiative undertaken by the government created conditions for considerably expanding training facilities by using the empire. The Empire Air Training Scheme set up in 1939 utilized both the manpower and the facilities for flying school expansion available in Canada, where there were 360 training schools by the end of the war, Australia, New Zealand and in southern Africa. By the end of the war over 200,000 aircrew had been trained in empire countries, in addition to the 88,000 trained in Britain. Of this total about 40 per cent were pilots.[74] Although there were local or temporary pilot shortages, particularly in the early stages of the war, the luxury of training airmen in the war free empire areas actually allowed the period of training and the amount of flying time per trainee to increase after 1942.[75] Other factors helped to improve standards of training. Operational aircraft were diverted to the training schools, despite complaints from the front, in order to give all crews advanced training on the aircraft they would later be flying in combat. This made good a particular deficiency in British training at the outbreak of war. So too did the development of a corps of instructors, who were constantly replenished from those with some combat experience, and whose retention in a training capacity was again defended at the highest political level as a fact essential to the future waging of successful air warfare.[76]

America, too, constantly revised training programmes in the expectation of a long and large-scale war. In 1939 plans were laid for training 1,200 pilots a year by 1941. In 1940 the plan was raised to 7,000 per year, in 1941 to 30,000. The AWPD Plan 1 argued for an annual output of 85,000 pilots to cope with the maximum contingency of a war with Germany and Japan lasting a number of years. From training 11,000 pilots in 1941 American flying schools trained 82,700 in 1943 in addition to 240,000 ground crew, some fifteen times the number being trained in Japan at the same time.[77] American numbers expanded at a rate faster than necessary, partly because losses were much lower than anticipated, and partly because Arnold, alarmed at the prospect that conscription would reduce the numbers volunteering for air pilot training, embarked on a campaign during 1943 to recruit cadets under 18 years of age and to encourage pre-draft air force enlistment. By the end of 1943 the manpower shortage had become a surplus. Air recruitment was cut back substantially to a rate of 60,000 a year, and in April 1944 to 40,000. In order to cope with the demand for air training the educational and physical qualifications were raised at the end of 1943 in contrast to almost all other air powers, where they were lowered.[78] In Russia by the same stage of the war the educational requirement for pilot training had been reduced from seven years' full schooling to five, not because of a shortage of candidates for training, but because of a shortage of those with the necessary qualifications. Soviet air training had run at a high level even before the outbreak of war, and continued to expand throughout the war from an estimated 18 flying schools in 1938 to 130 in 1945, at a rate of more than 60,000 crewmen per year. Training time had to be cut back substantially in 1941 and 1942 to cope with the high loss rate of the early battles in the east. Time spent on advanced training fell from a year to 8 months, and most fighter pilots in 1942 had less than 100 hours' flying experience instead of the 150–200 enjoyed at the beginning of the war. In 1943 due to the insistence of the supreme command training standards were restored, and once air superiority had been gained in the east were futher expanded and extended.[79] Because of the limited role of aircraft in the Russian war the more advanced training in night and blind-flying techniques were less necessary. Had air strategy been different the shortage of specialist training would have limited the use of Soviet aircraft on strategic tasks.

For the Axis powers the expansion of training for pilots, particularly after the early emphasis on skill to achieve rapid victory which created an under-estimate of future needs, proved to be a major problem as the initiative in the war moved in favour of the Allies. Apart from the obvious limit of population resources, which inevitably gave an advantage in sheer numbers to the Allies, the course of the war created further obstacles in providing sufficient personnel. In Japan the flying training programme began far too late to be effective for the combat expected in 1943 and 1944. Having begun the war with some 3,500 army and 2,500 navy pilots, existing facilities provided only 5,000 pilots in 1942 and 5,400 in 1943. With the destruction of the best pilots in the battles from Midway to Rabaul—over 10,000 were killed in 1942 and 1943—there developed a desperate shortage. New plans for a massive expansion were laid in 1943 to produce 30,000 pilots a year by 1945, but the figure was unrealistic.[80] The new recruits had to be sent into battle with only 60 or 70 hours of flying time, against American pilots in better aircraft and with five times the flying experience, which in turn increased the attrition rate, and encouraged the use of recruits with even less training. The spiral of growing attrition finally led to suicide tactics, since 'special attack group' training only required some 60 hours' flying time and the barest of preliminary preparation.[81] Another factor in the declining ability of the Japanese air force to provide flying personnel lay with the failure to circulate combat crews from front activity to rest centres and flying schools. The result was that those pilots whose skills could have been used in forming cadres for training future pilots were instead frittered away in combat. The argument for not resting crews rested on the assumption that warriors should prove their heroism through experiencing hardship, yet further evidence of the way in which an inflexible military tradition failed to take account of the more mundane but nevertheless vital questions of supply.[82]

In the German case it was not tradition that affected training as much as the problems of war. The Luftwaffe was given no priority in gaining qualified recruits, and the demands of the army for manpower in the battles on the eastern front reduced the potential pool of recruits from which the air force could draw. In the winter of 1943–44 some 200,000 men were transferred on Hitler's orders from the Luftwaffe to the army, and when in 1944 the air force requested that all other forces release suitably qualified men to help to make up the shortage of pilots none was forthcoming.[83] The pressure of a manpower shortage coincided with a rapid increase in the loss rate. From the beginning of war until the outbreak of war with Russia monthly losses of aircrew had averaged 615. Between June 1941 and December 1943 the figure rose to 1,167 and in 1944 reached an average of 1,754 per month.[84] The problem of mounting losses escalated as it did in Japan, because the earlier failure to increase Luftwaffe size gave so great an advantage to the Allies. Allied aircraft were able to exact an increasing rate of loss, and place even greater pressures on a training scheme that was already stretched to the limit. The situation was made worse by Hitler's and Goering's insistence that flying instructors and training aircraft should be used in combat. As early as the winter of 1941, when experienced pilots were needed to fly in supplies to the Demyansk pocket, the training schools were required to release skilled personnel. Convinced of early victory Hitler again insisted that present emergencies should have priority over future contingencies by drafting instructors for service in the Mediterranean and the east throughout 1942. When the war did not take the course Hitler had predicted, the training programmes became confused and improvisatory.[85] In addition the shortage of German aircraft, again a result of earlier misjudgement, forced the schools progressively to abandon training on operational types all of which were now sent directly to the front. This was the one stage of the training programme to which both Britain and America gave more, rather than less, emphasis during the later stages of the war. Its decline in Germany left many operational units themselves with the task of giving advanced training to newly posted pilots in the midst of combat.

This situation, itself reminiscent of the pressure under which the RAF had operated in 1940, was not necessarily a disadvantage. But when it was combined with both the relative and comparative decline of training standards it became more significant. In 1943, under pressure from the Director of Training, Goering closed down the 'C' schools which gave advanced training, particularly in blind flying and navigation. Elementary training was given on gliders instead of powered aircraft from 1943, partly due to the shortage of fuel which confined flying training in 1944 to 150 hours or less, and in 1945 to 100 hours, and partly due to the accelerating rate of pilot loss that forced the Luftwaffe to cut back training time to less than half that enjoyed by the Allied pilots.[86] Bomber pilots were retrained to fly fighters with little success; with mounting losses in all commands, morale declined. The irony was that in both Germany and Japan the output of aircraft actually reached a peak in 1944 at the time when pilot efficiency was in decline, the reverse of the position at the beginning of the war, and a reflection of the fact that it took considerably longer to train a pilot than to build an aeroplane. By that stage the initiative had passed to the Allies to such an extent that the new aircraft were destroyed on the ground and in the factories before they could be used. At the end of the war the Japanese air force had 8,000 more crewmen than aircraft. But the weakening of combat efficiency was so widespread that even had more aircraft been available for actual combat at the end of the war it could not have led to a regaining of initiative in the air by the Axis forces.

(v) Morale and the Military Tradition

The effect of the problems of war on morale, whether of the staff or of the troops, depended to some extent on the simple fact of victory. Allied airmen in the west, supplied with adequate weapons and training, and with confidence in the adopted strategy, were little affected by moral considerations. Even acceptable loss rates were placed at low levels, particularly in the bombing operations, in order to avoid any decline in combat morale.[87] Among the Axis powers the fact of retreat and defeats, or in Russia the prospect of defeat before 1943, while raising the threshold of military effort and individual war willingness gave moral questions a greater prominence. This was true in two important respects: in the attempt to raise political consciousness among the forces to stiffen resistance, and in the increasing emphasis on the virtues of the traditional military ethic.

In the Soviet Union the degree of political activity in the air forces increased after June 1941 with the compulsory re-introduction of political commissars, who although not actually charged with military command were in a position to pass judgements on the commander's actions and report them when necessary to higher political authority.[88] The purpose of the political commissars was to raise the awareness of the troops of the ideological nature of the struggle with fascism. It was also in the spirit of the directive issued through Stalin for the 'Restructuring of Political and Party Work' which called for the introduction of a 'militant, aggressive attitude' and 'increase in the authority of the comman-der-leader'.[89] This political work stressed not only questions of ideology but was intended to raise and sustain war-willingness. Given the level of demoralization and confusion into which Soviet forces were thrown after the initial defeats in 1941 it must be counted as one factor among a number which revived the air forces for the successful defence in 1942. To what extent remains a matter of speculation.

In Germany the political perspective was more complicated. The Nazi party attempted throughout the war to educate the air force in particular in the ways of the Nazi movement in order to raise morale and fighting spirit. For this reason the Luftwaffe was popularly regarded as a Nazi service. Such an image was consistent with the wider political ambitions of Goering who used the Luftwaffe as part of his power-base in the party. Yet political indoctrination was no more noticeable or successful than in the army.[90] Indeed the lack of proper Nazi zeal contributed to Himmler's bid to found an SS air force in 1944, recruiting from among the SS ranks and suitable Luftwaffe candidates.[91] There was, however, a large number of Nazi party members in the upper echelons of the Luftwaffe, and not a few owed their position in the service to past Nazi loyalty, including Jeschonnek whose blind faith in the Führer led him to store up five years of criticism of his leaders which he allowed to be revealed only after his suicide in 1943.[92] Where it had been expected that enthusiasm for National Socialism would invigorate the air force and lift morale, party mem-bership itself encouraged careerism and stifled criticism. In the Russian forces criticism—though not always constructive criticism—was one of the main tasks of the commissars, and promotion for officers depended on military success.

The Luftwaffe also presented Hitler with a political problem of his own. The failure to stem the bombing brought fears of popular agitation against the government, just as it brought popular and widespread recrimination on the Luftwaffe leaders themselves. The result was a growing hostility between the party, particularly the local *Gauleiter* who bore the brunt of the political backlash against bombing, and the air force that took the form by 1944 of a continuous stream of criticism and abuse over the poor level of air force performance. This in turn fed Hitler's belief that the Luftwaffe had betrayed him, and to widespread demoralization among the air forces at the inadequacy and corruption of its leadership was added the final knowledge that the Führer too, was convinced of its demoralization and cowardice.[93] That individual morale remained much the same as that in the other services until the end of the war could not overcome the moral crisis at the centre of the air force for its failure to match up to the Party's military or political expectations.

In Japan faith in victory remained secure until near the end of the war. The armed forces closely controlled the dissemination of information to such an extent that many Japanese soldiers claimed after the war that any knowledge of defeat only became available after the conquest of Okinawa.[94] Obedience to the Emperor and a strict military discipline prevented criticism. When the head of the Aeronautical Research Institute publicly rebuked the forces for using unserviceable aircraft, which would increase the likelihood of the crew's death, he was physically attacked by a special army unit created to strike out defeatism.[95] Under these circumstances fighting morale remained high in the face of impossible military conditions, even to the extent of self-sacrifice. In Germany too the air force was constantly reminded that 'the supreme calling of each German soldier is to die for his Führer'.[96] In Japan sacrifice was demanded for the sake of the Emperor, and for the sake of personal honour. This was reflected in the growth of the Kamikaze campaign. After some limited success with ramming aircraft and ships at the cost of both aircraft and crew the air forces stationed in the Philippines developed special attack units, the Tokubetsu-Kogekitai, which were organized for suicide missions 'as a temporary expedient' because of the impossibility of using aircraft in any other effective role.[97] The decision to enforce the military code to the point of self-sacrifice was not new in Japanese military life. Soldiers were trained to give their lives for the Emperor and the first suicide squadrons were composed of volunteers. Later all pilots were ordered to undertake suicide missions, and preparations were accordingly made to prepare all the remaining 10,000 aircraft, mainly trainer and obsolete models, for suicide attacks when the Allied forces invaded mainland Japan. Pilots who returned from suicide missions were imprisoned, and substantial moral pressure was put on the trained crews to make the sacrifice.[98] But far from evoking widespread resistance, the evidence of demoralization stemmed more from the relative failure of suicide attacks than from the fact of having to make such attacks in the first place. That such discipline could be maintained in the face of obvious defeat was a final confirmation of the power of the Japanese military tradition, just as that defeat itself stemmed in part from too great a reliance on a military ideal instead of military materialism upon which American strength was based.

The same ideal permeated the military establishment in Germany as well, and was vulgarized by European fascism in general. The air forces served to reinforce it because of the novelty of air power and the emphasis it placed on individual courage, discipline and endeavour. Such idealism helped to spread a mythology surrounding those who flew the aircraft. The romance of aircraft life was real enough in contrast to more mundane and routine tasks in other fields. Where the more militarized societies of Germany and Japan failed was in the marriage of the ideal with the material. In Britain and America material considerations prevailed. Numbers of aircraft and numbers of crewmen counted as much, if not more, than the soldierly virtues in building up the base of Allied supremacy. Where the contrast was most marked was in the expectations and illusions of those who commanded the armed forces. Hitler, Mussolini and Tojo deluded themselves into believing that the world belonged by rights to the warrior. Their launching of aggressive war was a sign of an inner military strength which would overcome all material obstacles and from which victory would flow. The Allies demonstrated that military virtue alone was no substitute for material power.

Above: The biplane fighter, a legacy from the First World War, was still in use during the Second. This Italian fighter, shot down over England during the Battle of Britain, showed the dangers of falling behind in the technical race.

Right: Some biplanes survived the whole war. The British 'Swordfish', seen here armed with modern rocket weaponry, gave sturdy service in the war at sea.

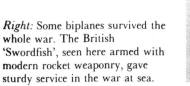

The Air War was fought on both sides with standard, dependable monoplane fighters and dive-bombers. The German 'Stuka' (*above*) saw frontline service throughout the war. The performance of aircraft was improved through modification. The Yak-9 fighter (*below*) appeared in this long-range version in 1944 to help the Soviet Air Force gain greater fighter penetration on the Eastern Front.

Aircraft played a vital role in the war at sea, particularly in the Pacific war. The American 'Hellcat' fighter-bomber (*above*) proved to be among the most versatile of the new range of naval aircraft. Naval aircraft were also used extensively in the Mediterranean. The Cant Z506 of the Italian air force saw service on both sides (*below*). Here they are serving with the Allies in the summer of 1944.

The He 177 heavy bomber (*above*) was the air weapon at the centre of the renewed efforts of the Luftwaffe to mount a strategic bombing offensive. Poor engine performance and a host of minor technical difficulties delayed its introduction.

Italy, too, attempted strategic bombing, but with little success. Here Cant Z1007 bombers are dropping bombs over Malta in the unsuccessful attempt to destroy Maltese resistance from the air.

Every air force depended on the ground crews. Large numbers of skilled engineers and mechanics were essential. So, too, were the unskilled workers, mainly women, drafted in to run the air bases. Here a woman worker is loading an 8,000 lb. bomb onto a Lancaster (*above*). Czech mechanics (*below*) are servicing a Spitfire during the Battle of Britain.

The Hero. Pilots everywhere were the heroes of the Air War. Their individual courage and daring contrasted sharply with more mundane tasks elsewhere, though production and invention were every bit as important in winning the war in the air.

The aircraft industry was a vital factor in the Air War. The efficient use of resources, particularly labour, helped the Allies establish a vast numerical superiority. The use of women in aircraft factories was widespread in Britain (as these three pictures show), the United States and Russia.

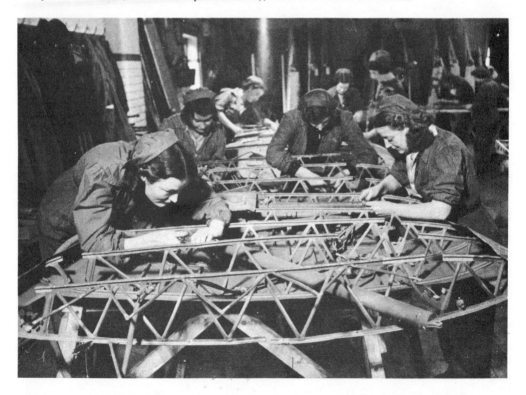

Science and intelligence came together in the radar war. German radar (*left*) was only marginally behind that of the Allies by the end of the war. Its use on the battlefield was also vital. British mobile radar and communications units (*below*) were one of the keys to the success of the RAF in North Africa.

The point at which industry and air intelligence coincided. The mass manufacture of 'Window', an effective jamming aid against German radar, expanded rapidly after its successful use over Hamburg.

From biplanes to rockets. The Second World War saw a rapid increase in the pace of technical change.
The German V-2 rocket heralded the missile age, though its impact was far less than Hitler had hoped.

Credit: Imperial War Museum

7

The Aircraft Economies

Throughout the war the supply of aircraft of high performance played a decisive part in the successful conduct of operations. The Allied powers enjoyed such an advantage in this respect that their air strategy was conducted with few material constraints. A major explanation for the failure of the Axis powers in air warfare was the failure to produce aircraft in numbers that even approached those produced by their enemies, or to produce aircraft so superior in quality that numbers did not matter. The record of production is set out in Table 12 below.[1] The difference in structure weight of aircraft produced, rather than in sheer numbers of aircraft, gave an even more marked superiority in economic performance to the Allies. The reasons for the wide disparity in production performance did not lie simply in the fact that the Allies together were a more powerful and larger economic force than the Axis powers, although that was certainly the case after the entry of Russia and America into the war. Germany, for example, while possessing a larger industrial base in 1939 than Britain, failed to produce as many aircraft as the British economy until 1944. Nevertheless, even if the Axis powers had given the maximum economic commitment to aircraft production it was a simple economic fact that the British Empire, Russia and the United States were capable of producing a much larger number and weight of aircraft than Germany, Italy and Japan. Some indication of the degree of economic advantage can be gained by a comparison of some basic economic statistics for the pre-war years. these figures are set out in Table 13 below.[2] It should be remembered that the figures before 1939 disguised a number of factors. Britain and America had large unused resources, particularly labour, while Germany had reached a condition of full employment. Secondly in the manufacture of finished goods the disparity between the two sides was wider still. Germany relied heavily on the production of industrial raw materials and capital goods whereas the Allies, and in particular Britain and the United States, had a higher proportion of end-manufacture. This made the task for Germany a different one from that of the Allies. Where Germany had to convert heavy industry to the task of mass production of the finished product, Britain and America had to increase the input of industrial raw materials and machinery to the finishing sector. Of the two tasks the former proved the more difficult under war conditions. All economies faced such questions in the mobilization

Table 12: Aircraft and Aero-engine Production of the Major Powers by Number and Weight 1939–45

A: Number of Aircraft

	1939	1940	1941	1942	1943	1944	1945*
U.S.A.	5,856	12,804	26,277	47,836	85,898	96,318	49,761
U.S.S.R.	10,382	10,565	15,735	25,436	34,900	40,300	20,900
Britain	7,940	15,049	20,094	23,672	26,263	26,461	12,070
Br. Commonwealth	250	1,100	2,600	4,575	4,700	4,575	2,075
Total	**24,178**	**39,518**	**64,706**	**101,519**	**151,761**	**167,654**	**84,806**
Germany	8,295	10,247	11,776	15,409	24,807	39,807	7,540
Japan	4,467	4,768	5,088	8,861	16,693	28,180	11,066
Italy	1,800	1,800	2,400	2,400	1,600	–	–
Total	**14,562**	**16,815**	**19,264**	**26,670**	**43,100**	**67,987**	**18,606**

B: Number of Aero-engines

	1939	1940	1941	1942	1943	1944	1945*
U.S.A.	–	15,513	58,181	138,089	227,116	256,912	106,350
U.S.S.R.	–	–	20,000	38,000	49,000	52,000	–
Britain	12,499	24,074	36,551	53,916	57,985	56,931	22,821
Total	**–**	**–**	**–**	**230,005**	**334,101**	**365,843**	**–**
Germany	3,865	15,510	22,400	37,000	50,700	54,600	–
Japan	–	–	12,151	16,999	28,541	46,526	12,380
Total	**–**	**–**	**34,551**	**53,999**	**79,241**	**101,126**	**–**

* Germany Jan.–April. Russia Jan.–June. Japan Jan.–Aug. GB Jan.–Aug. U.S.A. Jan.–Dec.

C: By Structure Weight (m. lb)

	1939	1940	1941	1942	1943	1944	1945*
U.S.A.	–	–	81.5	274.9	650.6	951.6	429.9*
Britain	29	59	87	134	185	208	95
Germany	–	–	88	114	163	199	–
Japan	–	–	21.2	36.5	65.5	111	70

* U.S.A. Jan.–June. Britain Jan.–Sept. Japan Jan.–Aug.

D: Axis Production as a Percentage of Allied Production

	1939	1940	1941	1942	1943	1944	1945
Aircraft, by number	60	43	30	26	28	40	22
Aircraft, by weight (excl. U.S.S.R.)	–	–	65	37	27	27	–

of resources, the allocation and supply of raw materials and labour, and in the administration of war production. Problems in any one of these areas were capable of reducing what on paper would have appeared a much better production capability than that actually achieved in practice during the war.

Table 13: Comparative Economic Statistics, Allied and Axis Powers in 1938

	Population	Total Labour Force	% of world manufacturing*
U.S.A.	141,940,000	52,800,000 (1940)	32.2
U.S.S.R.	170,400,000	70,000,000	18.5
U.K.	47,600,000	22,900,000 (1939)	9.2
Total	**359,940,000**	**145,700,000**	**59.9**
Germany	79,200,000(a)	36,200,000 (1939)	10.7
Italy	43,430,000	21,000,000 (1936)	2.7
Japan	72,750,000	34,100,000 (1940)	3.5
Total	**195,380,000**	**91,300,000**	**16.9**

Production	Steel (m. tons)	Coal (m. tons)	Electricity (mrd. kWh)	Motor Vehicles
U.S.A.	28.8	354.5	116.6	2,489,085
U.S.S.R.	18.0	132.9	39.4	200,000
U.K.	10.5	230.7	25.7	447,561
Total	**57.3**	**718.1**	**181.7**	**3,136,646**
Germany (a)	23.3	186.2	58.3	340,719
Italy	2.3	1.9	15.5	70,777
Japan	5.8(b)	53.0(b)	35 (1939)	32,744
Total	**31.4**	**241.1**	**108.8**	**444,240**

* Column three is for 1936–38 average
(a) Including Austria
(b) Figure for steel is 1937; that for coal is an estimate for 1938

(i) Production and Strategy

A more important explanation for the disparity in production, which was wider than the crude economic comparisons might suggest, lay in the area of strategic intention and in the level of economic efficiency. Britain and America from the outset of war intended to produce very large numbers of aircraft in preference to diverting resources to the other services. This required a very high level of industrial mobilization. Germany and Japan produced insufficient air resources for their purposes because the leadership did not intend to produce more until it was too late. By the time the economic insufficiency had been understood in the middle course of the war it was far too late to switch priorities satisfactorily. Moreover the demands made on the Axis economies by the army or navy made such a switch impossible without severely affecting the fighting ability of the surface forces. Hence Axis economies remained much more committed to army or navy production, and lacked the freedom of choice to produce many more aircraft without exciting tensions between the services, or substantially altering the agreed strategy. Instead great efforts had to be made to increase productivity by making existing resources stretch further. At root the problem lay with the over-optimistic assessment of future needs by the Axis leaders. In Hitler's case a relatively low level of aircraft production fitted in with the belief that the war would be a short one, and satisfied the demand for maintaining a high level of consumer goods production. It fitted in, too, with what Goering told him about the limits set by raw materials and factory capacity, an argument that both leaders accepted uncritically.[3] In Japan too little planning had gone into the stage beyond the initial victory, in the misguided expectation of a negotiated settlement with the United States after the end of the southern conquest. In both these cases strategic intention coupled to the existence of other economic priorities reduced the production capacity devoted to aircraft, thus further emphasizing an already existing economic imbalance.

To this was added the question of efficiency. All the major economies found the efficient production of large numbers of aircraft measured in terms of resource utilization difficult to achieve. Aircraft production brought with it several problems of its own. First of all it was the most expensive service, requiring more finance than either of the other two services. Every increase in aircraft production had to be debated with the army and navy. Both services resented the fact that the lion's share of scarce resources went to the air force, whose function they regarded as auxiliary. Secondly aircraft production was a major user of labour, in particular skilled labour, which was in short supply during the war. Finally aircraft industries had proved to be relatively inefficient users of resources in the 1930s. Usually dependent on a high level of government contracts and finance and hence less dependent on the market, there was insufficient pressure to economize and rationalize. Under conditions of war any country that found ways of increasing the efficiency of its aircraft industry would be able to widen the production gap still further between itself and less efficient enemies.[4] On the whole the Axis aircraft economies, including that of Nazi Germany, were less efficient users of resources than the Allies. The comparative backwardness of the Japanese and Italian economies was an important cause of this disparity, but not the whole cause. In the final full year of war the Japanese economy produced almost as many combat aircraft as the German from a considerably smaller economic base. Where German industry was able to produce aircraft of excellent quality in the kinder economic climate of peace it was unable to satisfactorily solve the question of quantity, even when the leadership finally changed economic strategy in favour of a production effort to match that of the Allies.

Planning and organization were the most important stages in aircraft production. How demands for aircraft were formulated determined the performance of the aircraft industry. Any hiatus in the organizational structure for carrying out the production plans was likely to have a considerable influence on the ability of an economy to produce what it was fully capable of producing. For aircraft production such questions were vital. The product itself was so large and complex and the resources—particularly aluminium, skilled labour and special machinery—in relatively short supply, that the successful planning and co-ordination of production was an essential prerequisite for the fulfilment of any plan.[5] Planning as such operated at a number of different levels, but the general economic strategy in which such planning took place was determined at the top of the political and military machine. The decision to mobilize the British, and later the Soviet and American economies to the full for war purposes created an environment for aircraft planning in which the demand for large numbers of high-quality aircraft did not seem utopian. The demands of the services for large numbers of aircraft in turn fuelled the determination of the political leadership to demand economic sacrifices in favour of war production.

In Britain the decision to aim high in aircraft production stemmed first and foremost from the central position of air strategy in overall military plans. It stemmed secondly from the fact that the British government expected a much higher level of aircraft output from the Axis powers than was actually achieved, and prepared accordingly. The decision to plan for 2,000 and then 2,500 and 3,000 aircraft a month was based on the assumption that German industry was capable of producing certainly the same number, and probably slightly more than the British industry.[6] In America the Air Corps itself had laid modest plans for the expansion in 1940–42 amounting to an initial objective for 5,500 aircraft per year.[7] This reflected the unwillingness of Congress to vote greater funds, but it also revealed the unwillingness of the air force leaders to think of anything more ambitious under conditions of peace. In May 1940 Roosevelt issued a demand for an aircraft programme of 50,000 aircraft by 1942. Faced with such an extraordinary increase in funds and material the air force hesitated to plan the necessary expansion. It was the political persistence of Roosevelt, coupled with the release of the largest single appropriation of federal funds for military purposes in the history of Congress that finally persuaded the air force to accept the new figures, and work on an assumption that from 30–50,000 aircraft a year were to be produced for the duration of the crisis.[8] Roosevelt's original figure was taken 'out of the air.' The rhetorical—and political—impact of the 50,000 programme, which became temporarily a major item of public discussion, was in itself an explanation for its origin. In the wake of Pearl Harbor Roosevelt, shocked by the apparent strength of the Japanese air forces, and anxious to satisfy public alarm at the attack, raised the demand for aircraft production to 125,000 a year, of which 100,000 were to be combat aircraft.[9] The figures bore no relation to what the industry was capable of producing, nor any relation to what the air forces were demanding. But they did set targets so vast that arguments about the feasibility of the earlier and more realistic air corps programmes disappeared in favour of arguments about the production of tens of thousands of aircraft. Such figures were clearly not beyond the scope of the American economy as a whole, and fitted in well with the American intention to create 'an overwhelming superiority of material'.[10] The war economic authorities, however, saw that to meet the demands of the surface forces, air production would have to be cut back. Although the original Presidential demand had not been an actual order, there was protracted political debate over the decision to reduce the 125,000 goal. Not until autumn 1942 was the programme abandoned in favour of a goal of 90–100,000 in 1943, and throughout the period Nelson as head of the War Production Board insisted that 'the aircraft programme as a whole be preferred over all other production'.[11] That neither the British goal of 36,000 aircraft a year nor the American goal of 125,000 a year were achieved was due not solely to the unrealistic and 'target' nature of the planning, but to changes in quality, particularly the transition to heavier four-engined aircraft without which these totals might have been surpassed in 1944. In terms of structure weight Roosevelt's initial demands were eventually met, and even exceeded. What was important about the programmes was the fact that neither industrial limitations, nor air force conservatism, were allowed to dull the economic imagination of those who were charged with the overall direction of economic and industrial policy. From the 1920s onwards the British and American planners had intended that in the event of war quite a different level of production was to be expected, in which the guesses at future requirements would depend on what sort of war was being fought, and only secondarily on whether the economy could bear the effort.[12]

For the Axis powers the situation was the exact reverse. This was not just a reflection of the lower priority accorded to aircraft production, since in Japan it enjoyed a priority similar to that enjoyed in the Allied economies. Nor was it only a reflection of smaller economic resources. Both Germany and Japan proved able by 1944 to produce four or five times as many aircraft as in the first year of war. In both Germany and Japan however, the leadership failed to impose economic demands that matched strategic demands. The reasons for the failure were complex. In Germany it was clear that Hitler imagined a much greater aircraft production to be in the pipeline than was actually the case. His demand in 1938 for a quintupling of the air force was largely side-stepped by the planners on the argument that industrial capacity and raw material supplies did not support any such programme.[13] From that date onwards until the crisis of aircraft production in the middle of 1941 Hitler paid virtually no attention to the question, satisfied that the performance of the Luftwaffe was not a question of numbers but of tactics. Between 1939 and 1942 the German aircraft industry, the air ministry and the air staff talked a language of production 'realism' in which huge future targets were discounted in favour of figures which it was known were realistically capable of fulfilment given the current state of the industry and degree of economic mobilization.[14] No-one was in a position to insist either on a higher degree of mobilization or on higher aircraft programmes and those who were, such as Goering or Hitler himself, lacked the necessary strategic imagination or remained in ignorance of the true state of affairs.[15] Thus German aircraft planning reached a level of 2,000 per month for 1944 only in September 1941, and did not reach a level of planning of 3,000 a month until a year later. Not until 1944 did the German air ministry begin to discuss plans on the same huge 'target' scale as those of the Allies, and by that time the economic effort involved would not have borne fruit in terms of more aircraft for several years.[16]

The contrast with the Allied response to planning was partly a result of differences in the political structure and the way decisions were arrived at. There was little open discussion and consultation on the Axis side. There were other problems too. An explanation for the low level of production lay partly in the demands of the air staff itself. When challenged by Milch in 1942 to accept a higher level of fighter production of 360 a month, which was modest by Allied standards, Jeschonnek replied that he 'would not know what to do with 360 fighters'.[17] But it also lay with the low level of economic mobilization in Germany, occasioned both by inefficiency and Hitler's hope for a short war. In order to keep a balance between consumer production, the demands of the army, which had the greatest influence on the war economic departments, and those of the air force, it was unlikely that large-scale plans could be laid. The fact that even the more modest plans were unfulfilled by, at times, a considerable margin, encouraged even the more optimistic authorities in the belief that Germany was producing all of which she was capable.[18]

In Japan the same confused situation surrounded planning. Actual production in the early years of war, like that of Germany, was not significantly above peace-time levels. This fact was questioned only when the early victories gave way to strategic disaster by the end of 1942. Neither the army nor the navy had any long-term plan for aircraft expansion, nor did there exist any central agency whose task it was to instruct the services in economic possibilities or to plan the mobilization of the civilian economy for war purposes. Only in 1943 with the creation of the Munitions Ministry and the programme of industrial conversion were large numbers at last mooted.[19] As in Germany, however, the large new programmes were unrealizeable within a time-scale that would be of any strategic importance to the war effort. The relatively low level of economic mobilization for war, and the inefficiency of the aircraft industry, again dictated the direction of planning. When Fujihara carried out an administrative inspection of the aircraft industry in the middle of 1943 he calculated that the available capacity if properly utilized could produce not the 8–10,000 currently produced, but 53,000 aircraft per year.[20] In both the German and Japanese case, however, it was the general character of the early strategy and the element of miscalculation as to risks and needs that kept planning levels low, reflecting once again a more fundamental division between those leaderships that thought in terms of economic power, and those that counted upon military prowess.

(ii) The Organization of Aircraft Production

Planning the number of aircraft to be produced had to be followed or accompanied by the creation of an organization for putting the planning into practice, and for carrying out further planning. The creation of such an administrative apparatus raised questions about the degree of centralization or de-centralization, about jurisdictional definition and about authority. The response to such organizational problems varied widely between the belligerent powers. Over the question of centralization there existed a paradoxical division between the fascist powers and the Allies. Where the British, American and Soviet governments favoured from the start the creation of an administrative machine that was highly centralized and highly co-ordinated, the Axis, for political reasons as well as for reasons of administrative tradition, followed a largely centrifugal path until persuaded by the inefficiencies of the system to do otherwise.

The British had originally given authority over aircraft production to the air force itself, but as it became obvious during the late 1930s that civilian ministries and departments would have a much more important role to play in the running of the future war economy, more of the control over aircraft resources passed to outside bodies. In 1940 the Ministry of Aircraft Production was established as a separate entity, on the grounds that aircraft were such a complex product that a special department was required to cope with them, and that if such a department remained an integral part of the Air Ministry the latter would be swamped by its supply side at the expense of the military.[21] The MAP worked closely with the Production Executive, which later became the Ministry of Production, and with the departments allocating labour and resources. Clear lines of responsibility were drawn from the War Cabinet with its economic sub-committees through the central production agencies to the MAP which in turn created an elaborate centralized structure for the main aircraft producers and the regional authorities. Thus administrative and political authority flowed from the same sources and a constant overview of the economic situation was possible in such a way that aircraft production and its resources could be balanced against the needs of other departments. It by no means worked perfectly, but it worked sufficiently well to avoid the debilitating effect on production of administrative chaos and misjudgment.[22]

The same situation prevailed in the United States. Lacking any administrative department capable of assuming responsibility for war production Roosevelt established the National Defense Advisory Council which was placed under the control of the industrialist Knudsen, and was turned during the mobilization period into the Office of Production Management and finally into the War Production Board charged with the general executive administration of the war economy.[23] The Aircraft Production Board was established within the economic organization and although enjoying the same degree of autonomy as MAP in practice, it remained within the central structure for running the war economy and allocating resources. In both the British and American cases considerable attention was paid to the definition of function and the many administrative quarrels—what Churchill praised as 'honest differences of opinion'—arose over the working out of jurisdictional competence. Such differences of opinion tended to strengthen rather than weaken the system by arriving, through discussion, at the best level of competent co-operative administration that circumstances would allow.[24] In both cases too, the running of the actual economic side of the air war was left in the hands of civilian authorities; much of the planning and technical detail was worked out together with the air forces, but in the end the job of producing what was required was left to those with more experience of the job of production. In the Soviet Union the same degree of administrative centralization prevailed. Here again the task of aircraft production was concentrated in the hands of a separate, central, organization, the Commissariat for Aviation Industry set up in 1939 under Kaganovich. From 1940 its deputy director was the energetic aircraft designer and producer, Yakovlev.[25] In all three Allied war economies the nature of authority was also carefully defined. The organization that was required to take the important day-to-day decisions concerned with aircraft production was given the executive authority to do so. Although these executive branches were responsible to the higher political authority, such delegation saved valuable time in decision-making and avoided any more damaging conflicts caused by an excess of offices and committees without authority.

In the Axis powers there did indeed exist a powerful central authority but in the task of aircraft production such authority was poorly exercised. The first reason lay in the nature of the source of political authority itself. Hitler as the Führer, Mussolini as the Duce and the Japanese Emperor, while the nominal sources of such authority, exercised it in a constitutional rather than administrative way. Between Hitler and the various ministerial departments there existed a huge administrative gulf. No cabinet meetings were held, much of the routine and a great deal of the major administrative decisions were taken at a lower level without reference to the leader and amidst great confusion over competence and jurisdiction. Delegated authority was little understood and counted for little in the face of internal party rivalries. In Italy Mussolini's personal incompetence and dislike for routine encouraged a great reliance on 'experts' who, lacking executive authority, were forced to operate in the wake of the Duce's spasmodic direction.[26] In Japan the Emperor's authority was nominal, real power lying with the armed forces and the ministries who were subject to so little general central direction that Tojo was forced to pass legislation so that he could compel ministers to do what the Prime Minister directed.[27] Under such circumstances it was unlikely that a fully centralized political or administrative machine could be created for the running of the war economy and of aircraft production within it. Moreover the lack of a strong centralist tradition gave added weight to the authority of the services themselves. Where in all the Allied countries production was taken out of the hands of the air forces, in all the Axis powers it remained there. The Luftwaffe retained complete control over all aircraft production directly under Goering who was clearly not competent for the task, not just through lack of experience but through lack of time. His main concern was the military side of the air force. Personal rivalry prevented the civilian side of the Ministry under Milch from achieving any real say in aircraft production until 1941, and then in only a partial way. The aircraft economy was run by soldiers to fulfil Goering's political ambition to keep all air matters firmly in his control, and the air staff belief that only air officers were competent to run aircraft production and procurement.[28] In Italy and Japan the same situation emerged. In Japan traditions of military autonomy and a general military distrust of the civilian establishment (and big business in particular) kept aircraft production firmly in the hands of the army and navy, whose own internal rivalry left aircraft production even more isolated and decentralized than might otherwise have been the case. The administrative isolationism in both Germany and Japan fitted in well with a tradition of ministerial and bureaucratic autonomy. Decision-making remained confined within the service procurement agencies and constricted by administrative protocol. Such decisions were in consequence often taken in a vacuum because the competent offices lacked sufficient executive authority, and because they were usually taken without reference to the outside agencies responsible for supplying goods or planning wider economic questions. What was a decision within the air force economic office became only one argument among many in the confused administrative establishment outside. Lacking a central reviewing body of sufficient authority the simplest of requests for machinery or raw materials assumed the proportions of a major political struggle for resources.

To be sure, the Allies found aircraft production a far from easy administrative task. Their answer lay in introducing a high degree of co-ordination and co-operation. Imposing as such production did on so many other economic areas it was clearly important to achieve as high a degree of co-operation and co-ordination as possible while resisting tendencies to fragment the running of aircraft production between too many smaller offices. In both the American and British economic administration special offices were created whose specific task was to co-ordinate. The Directorate of Planning, Programmes and Statistics was placed in such a position that it could see the progress made in the individual departments and ensure that they were as far as possible in balance. In addition information was passed on to all the departments involved of what was happening elsewhere.[29] The Aircraft Scheduling Unit and later the Aircraft Resources Control Office performed some of the same functions for the American system.[30] Equally important was the whole question of co-operation. Both vertical and horizontal liaison was vital for aircraft production because planning could not be carried out without some knowledge of what was happening in other services or offices, nor without reference to the broader strategic decisions taken at the top of the administrative tree. Here to some extent the Allies in the west benefited from the decisions taken early in the war to co-operate on questions of production. Although such co-operation never reached the same level as strategic co-operation, the Joint Purchasing Commission, and later the Joint Aircraft Board worked on the allocation of aircraft, standardization procedures and general questions to do with aircraft production planning. The system of co-operation between allies had the advantage that it held each other's war administration up to scrutiny, and allowed a pooling of administrative experience which led to the final refinements of the administrative process during the course of 1943.[31] In the Axis powers the initial inclination to isolationism made co-operation much harder to achieve. Moreover in Germany the hierarchical and formal nature of the bureaucratic structure made what co-operation there was often unmanageable. Udet's production committee meetings contained over 60 representatives and the proceedings involved so much protocol that agenda could not be completed and decisions had to be postponed for lack of agreement.[32] Co-operation for the purposes of co-ordinating plans and allocating resources failed to materialize.

Where the aircraft production agencies in the Allied powers were themselves established as co-ordinating and co-operative instruments the same was not true elsewhere, or at least not until the shortcomings of the fascist economic administration were finally exposed. In Japan a long struggle developed during 1943 to give more power to the civilian authorities in running the economy. The Cabinet Advisory Board was established to survey the necessary changes and in November 1943 a Munitions Ministry was established with a specific charge to take over aircraft production from the army and navy and unify it under civilian control. But by that stage the services were too committed to the aircraft programme to lightly give it up and the inter-service rivalry and lack of co-operation continued. They continued to submit demands for resources which by-passed the new agency and refused in many cases to be bound by ministerial directives. When Fujihara replaced Tojo as Munitions Minister in 1944 he found that the services simply ignored the new administrative structure and put pressure on the firms to supply what was wanted according to traditional practice.[33] In Germany the reform of the economic administration began during 1941 and was completed during 1942 by the creation of a Central Planning Board and a series of production associations under Speer. But even these reforms had only partial success. There was still a central machinery lacking to link the various civilian and military departments together and aircraft production, although subject to considerable internal reforms, remained independent. The struggle for resources continued and the confusion of administrative departments, particularly under the political fact of Goering's declining influence, became in some ways yet more pronounced. In the end Milch insisted, against Goering's hostility, on the fusion of aircraft production with the Ministry of War Production through the creation of the 'Fighter Staff'.[34] The 'Production Miracle' that resulted, although planned beforehand by Milch, was only possible because of the final centralization of all production. The persistent difficulties experienced with aircraft production in 1943 and early 1944 were a direct product of the fact that there was still too little administrative co-ordination and too rigid a system of administrative practice. Speer's control over fighter production brought a degree of flexibility and improvization into the aircraft economy which it had hitherto lacked. When centralization did come in Germany and Japan it came late, and under conditions of emergency, and although the record of aircraft production improved as a result it was not always possible to eradicate the political and administrative tendencies of the earlier years of war. Thus no sooner had such reforms been achieved in Japan than administration was dispersed to cope with the emergency of blockade and bombing, and power returned more to the army and navy. In Germany the success of the Fighter Staff was increasingly compromised by the dismissal of Milch, the political decline of Speer and the squabbling over administrative spoils that developed during 1944 between the *Gauleiter*, the SS and the more successful of the Nazi ministers.[35]

(iii) Industry, Bureaucracy and Administration

The final problem that organization posed beside centralization and co-ordination was the question of producing a corps of satisfactory administrators. Here politics intruded openly into the administration of aircraft production. In Italy and Germany the key administrators were party members. In the case of Italy Fascists were so closely involved in the administrative apparatus that it was difficult for Mussolini to reform even when finally aware of the need in 1943. The changes brought about in February removed some of the older Fascists from positions of authority but replaced them with younger Fascists loyal to Mussolini rather than with trained administrators or industrialists.[36] In Japan the difficulties in administration were not due entirely to the absence of able administrators but to the demands of the junior officers for a say in how the air forces were run and supplied. After the reforms of 1943 it was the political pressure of the officer groups that fuelled the hostility between civilian and service organizations and kept much of the running of aircraft production in military hands. In Germany the problem of Nazi penetration of the administrative apparatus was less acute because many of the officials had been administrators before they were Nazis. But in the crucial positions in the ministry and in aircraft production promotion depended less on merit and more on party loyalty. Goering himself was a poor administrator. Those he chose for high office were equally ill-equipped for the task. Even Milch whose energy was used to great effect in improving the performance of aircraft production after 1942 was compelled to play a political game at the same time as carrying out his other duties, to the detriment of sound administrative practice. In both Japan and Germany the additional problem of keeping control over production in the hands of the services narrowed down the area of recruitment for administrative work and created a division between civilian and military experience that only began to be breached as the war situation deteriorated.

By contrast the homogeneity of the British political, industrial and administrative establishment was a considerable advantage. Lacking a strict bureaucratic tradition and a large reserve of skilled administrators, officials were recruited from industry and politics as well as the Civil Service, to fill administrative posts. Such homogeneity, born largely of a common class experience and a shared environment in Whitehall that was both informal and co-operative, allowed for a greater degree of co-operation and flexibility than might otherwise have been the case. In Germany with a strong tradition of an established bureaucracy it was much harder to break down barriers between departments where, even if recruitment patterns were not markedly different (which was often the case), there were entrenched administrative prerogatives and forms to be maintained. The American system, too, had an *ad hoc* character, very much in the spirit of federal administrative practice. American administrators were also recruited from a wide spectrum of the managerial and professional elites where there was experience of administration but no bureaucratic tradition.[37]

The recruitment of administrators demonstrated a critical difference between the Allied and Axis powers in the degree to which industry was co-opted into the work of organizing aircraft production. One obvious advantage in wedding industrial experience to the running of the war economy was the degree of shared experience between the two situations. In the capitalist west this choice was an obvious one. A war in defence of an economic system represented by a political structure sympathetic to capitalism involved industrialists as closely as it did soldiers. Thus in America the senior administrators of the war economy were almost all drawn from large-scale industry; industry co-operated closely with the authorities and created its own administration in the National Aircraft War Production Council.[38] In Britain contact between industry and administration was very strong, the exchange of personnel regular, and the crucial positions in the MAP given to men, like Beaverbrook himself, with wide commercial experience. It was precisely because of such close ties that the British and American governments were able to impose financial regulations and to create large government-owned plants with the minimum of resistance from the *laissez-faire* industrial establishment. Nor was this process confined simply to the western capitalist powers. Soviet Russia created an administrative cadre for the war economy out of those with experience in industrial and planning management under the industrialization drive. In this particular case the Soviet experience of predictive planning was even more wide-ranging than that in the western industrial corporations. Since so much of the production of aircraft was a question of proper scheduling and prediction, the experience of the Five Year Plans in precisely those areas made the conversion to wartime administration relatively smooth. Moreover unlike the planning in Italy and Germany, Soviet planning was more directly concerned with the production and distribution of goods, and less with capital flows and trade into which most fascist energy was put. Under the difficult and improvised conditions of economic mobilization in Russia following the German attack, the experience of state economic planning was a positive advantage without which the Soviet economy might well have collapsed.[39]

In Germany and Japan the relationship between the wartime administration and industry was much more complicated. In Japan the Zaibatsu while retaining great influence and economic power were not brought into the running of the war in any way which could fully utilize the administrative and planning abilities of its leaders except with the grudging consent of the army and navy authorities. In aircraft production, in which the leading Zaibatsu played a prominent role, planning was largely denied them. With the creation of the control associations and later of the Ministry of Munitions the situation was reversed to a limited extent, but since both the armed forces and the Zaibatsu continued to maintain domination in their respective spheres it proved impossible to subordinate the interests of the one to the other, either by forcing the military to accept more help from business, or to make business entirely subordinate to the needs of war and the military. The remarkable increases in production brought about by the work of the large industrialists after 1943, although insufficient to alter the conclusion of the war, indicated the extent to which the more successful integration of Japanese capitalism into the war machinery at an earlier date might have improved the productive performance. But to do this would have required a greater commitment to war economy in the first place for which big business was not enthusiastic. For the capitalists a low level of economic mobilization meant more civilian production, with higher profit levels, and the opportunity to carry out economic imperialism into the newly conquered areas, a task that in itself diverted considerable administrative and economic effort from the problem of war production.[40]

In Germany, too, there were other problems facing the large cartels and trusts, not the least of which was the nature of capitalism itself under the impact of Nazi imperialism. They were involved at first very little in running the war economy. Much economic effort was diverted to keeping civilian production going as well as to the task of competing for resources abroad in the conquered territories. This diversion of industrial effort from the central task of mobilizing the economy for war complemented both the *Wehrmacht*'s own reluctance to introduce industrialists into the administration of war production and the Nazis' desire to control and exploit German industry for the war effort by placing severe limits on the activity of big businessmen in national politics. Anxious to preserve the basis of private capitalism, the big firms, while often critical of the Nazi war administration, allowed the bureaucrats and soldiers to arrange the war economy since that was their function.[41] In the case of both Germany and Japan the irony was that they contained the most concentrated industrial structures of all the belligerent powers, with industrialists whose experience of production, predictive planning and economic administration in general was much greater than that of the political and bureaucratic leadership whose orders they followed. This fact became apparent in Germany when first Udet, and then Milch, organized an advisory council of industrialists which had a considerable effect on improving productivity. Through Speer greater responsibility was given to German industry, with guarantees for the survival of private capitalism after the end of the war, and under these circumstances industry became much more closely involved in production. Nevertheless the relationship between government and industry never reached the same level as in the western powers because of the structure of the Nazi state. The centralized economy continued to be run by an uneasy alliance of fascist placemen, traditional bureaucrats and soldiers.[42]

Under different political circumstances the differences between the administration of the Allies and the Axis powers might not have been so great. The German civil service was relatively efficient, in fact in some ways too efficient for the often informal and improvisatory nature of war economics. Japanese industry, too, was aggressive and successful when confined to the task of trading penetration of the Far East but found it a quite different task to convert an economy with a cheap consumer-goods base to the mass output of advanced war material. Allied success reflected the existence of greater administrative experience, and of a broader spread of organizational resources. Moreover, the Allies' political structures, whether socialist or capitalist, exhibited a greater degree of unity between the industrial and non-industrial establishment. For aircraft production these factors proved vital because of the sheer scale of the administrative and economic effort required to keep large air fleets in being. For the

Axis powers it was not simply lack of intention but difficulties in turning intention readily into production reality that reduced the number of aircraft available. Had such self-imposed limitations not existed, Axis mobilization might have been considerably greater. The fact that they did demonstrated how important was the stage between planning a war and fighting a battle.

(iv) The Mobilization of Industry

The degree of industrial and financial mobilization for war thus depended to a large extent on decisions taken in a wider political and economic context. It also depended for its character on the nature of the particular economy. Large-scale industrial mobilization for war was a much more straightforward task in the United States than in Japan or Italy. For aircraft production in particular, which was a high user of resources due to the size, expense and complexity of each unit, there were two ways in which mobilization for war could be carried out. The first was through the expansion of productive facilities, either newly constructed or drawn from the wider industrial economy. The second was through rationalization of existing industry in order to extract a larger product from the same floorspace, machinery and labour. For all the powers rationalization followed rather than accompanied the expansion of plant facilities; first of all because the pressures on the war economy, making it necessary to find ways of saving on materials and labour, only developed some time after the outbreak of war; secondly, because the gains to be made in the usual way from increasing scale of production could not be realized until large aircraft programmes were under way, and the initial design problems worked out.

None of the belligerent powers failed during the war to expand aircraft production facilities considerably. But there were substantial differences in the form such expansion took and in its timing. Much of the initial expansion was pre-war, carried out to cope with the rearmament race. In Germany and Japan such expansion was concentrated in the main aircraft producers themselves. In the German case Goering's constant entreaties for production at full stretch, as if a condition of war already existed, made it difficult for manufacturers to keep any capacity in reserve and forced them to hurry investment programmes through without paying sufficient attention to longer-term needs. Thus on the outbreak of war the industry was already operating at what it claimed to be full capacity.[43] Lacking sufficient urgency, however, for a greater level of economic mobilization, the investment programmes both before and after 1939, were modest in scale. In fact over the first three years of war the construction of facilities actually declined from a peak in 1938–39 without any corresponding expansion into other industrial sectors. By contrast peak expenditure on construction in Britain came in 1940–42.[44] In Japan the problem was a little different. There a small aircraft industry in the mid-1930s had to be turned quickly into a large producer within the severe limits imposed by Japan's relatively weaker financial and industrial position. By 1941 the largest firms had already expanded aircraft capacity some 350 per cent in four years. From the very nature of such expansion the later investment programmes would take time to bear fruit and it was not until 1942–43 that the large Zaibatsu investments carried out in 1940 fulfilled capacity.

For Britain the same sort of problem had to be faced in the 1930s. A small aircraft industry, financially weak, had to be expanded at great speed after 1936.

The solution arrived at was to create a skeleton industry capable of being filled out with production flesh in the event of war. The additional capacity was provided either in the aircraft firms themselves, whose actual peace-time production was much lower than capacity under mobilization, or through the 'shadow' factory scheme through which non-aircraft firms, and in particular, the motor industry, undertook to run facilities financed by the government and constructed before the war for immediate utilization on the outbreak of hostilities. By 1939 the Air Ministry was able to announce that 'there was little need for more aircraft factories', although the 'shadow' schemes were continually expanded up to 1942 to cope with sub-contracts. The importance of the 'shadow' scheme was demonstrated during the war by the fact that some 70 per cent of all Spitfire production came from the factory built by the Nuffield Organization in the late 1930s, the largest in Europe. Facilities for the 2,000 aircraft a month planned for war already existed by the end of 1940 and needed only to be manned and managed by those industries whose civilian production was sharply curtailed on the outbreak of war.[45] In this case, as in Germany, the creation of a pre-war aircraft production capacity was related to expected needs, but whereas German capacity was close to full employment by 1940 with few plans for a second major expansion, British capacity was in the early stages of being utilized. The wide margin in production in 1941 between the two powers was a reflection of a different set of investment decisions taken in the pre-war period.

The expansion of production was different again for the two largest economies, Russia and the United States. The Russian industry was already the largest in 1939 in terms of current production. The third Five Year Plan gave even greater emphasis to the construction of aircraft facilities which were concentrated in a few giant plants in both eastern and western Russia. At the time of the German invasion plant expansion in Siberia was already taking place in case of such a contingency, and the factories moved eastwards in the evacuation were in many cases married up with facilities that simply needed the addition of men and machinery to begin operation. In the east, free from the threat of German bombing and invasion, and compelled to concentrate production because of the lack of an engineering infrastructure into which to disperse, enormous factories were established such as State Aircraft Factory 26 which produced 97,000 Klinov aero-engines in four years on a site of 6 square kilometers. By contrast the largest German manufacturer, Junkers, produced only 89,000 engines over six years at eight different sites.[46]

The same freedom from fear of enemy action allowed the United States to build up large industrial installations and to concentrate production as much as possible. Unlike Russia, America had only a small aircraft industry at the end of the 1930s geared largely to civilian needs. In fact the United States was so far behind the other prospective belligerent powers in terms of aircraft production that both the German and Japanese intelligence services underestimated considerably America's ability to convert quickly to aircraft production.[47] In contrast the American industry expanded very rapidly in line with the large plans laid down by the Roosevelt directives of 1940 and 1941. Some of the work of expansion had already begun on the basis of orders from Britain and France, but the bulk of the new expansion came from government financing of facilities either at the original aircraft plant or at a new location, chosen because of its proximity to labour and engineering sub-contractors. In all cases, as in Britain, the plants were managed and run by private companies whether they owned them or not. It was only on the basis of the promise of government aid that much of the expansion could take place. So urgent, however, did Congress consider the need for aircraft production that not only were large funds allocated for it during 1940 but the government was authorized to prepare the conversion of other industrial sectors to the programme.[48] The expansion of floorspace for aircraft output (including main components) was as follows:

Table 14: Floorspace for Aircraft and Main Components Manufacture in the United States 1939–44 (000 sq.ft.)[49]

Date	Airframe	Engines	Propellors	Total
1 Jan. 1939	7,479	1,726	250	9,455
1 Jan. 1940	9,606	3,018	492	13,116
1 Jan. 1941	17,943	6,463	1,050	25,456
June 1943	77,536	31,829	5,240	114,605
Dec. 1943	110,423	54,189	6,835	171,447
Dec. 1944	102,951	54,888	7,888	165,727

Beside such figures the efforts to expand plant elsewhere were dwarfed. In Britain productive floorspace at airframe factories expanded from 4.9 million square feet in August 1938 to 22.15 million square feet in October 1941, rising to a peak of 28.8 million square feet in March 1944. In Germany the renewed construction plans begun with the Goering-Programme in 1941 called for an expansion of only 6.6 million square feet for airframe and aero-engine capacity.[50]

One of the main reasons why American capacity was expanded so rapidly lay with the willingness of the government to utilize resources outside the aircraft industry. The main sub-contractor for aircraft production, particularly for the production of engines, was the motor industry. This was not because of any basic similarity of product, except for engines, but because the motor industry had very large production installations, skilled workers and a large supply of tools available for conversion to war purposes. In October 1940 Knudsen compelled the car industry to enter negotiations with the aircraft industry over mobilization and the result was the Automotive Committee for Air Defense. The committee arranged the conversion programmes and negotiated with the government over contracts and finance, insisting that new facilities should be provided and paid for by the state, like the shadow-factory scheme in Britain.[51] Much of the existing motor vehicle capacity was used for trucks, tanks and cars during the war. The contribution of the motor industry was in running and building new plants side by side with their own, or as in the case of the giant Ford plant at Willow Run, building a new plant completely from scratch at a new site.[52] The contribution in terms of management and machinery—some 66 per cent of automobile industry tools in 1942 going into the new aircraft and engine factories—made possible the rapid increase in aircraft output. The motor industry produced over 50 per cent of all aero-engines, and 66 per cent of all combat engines as well as 40 per cent of all airframe production by weight. At its peak the Ford plant for B-24 bombers produced in weight the equivalent of 50 per cent of the peak of German aircraft production on its own.[53] Without the conversion of the motor industry the aircraft producers themselves would have been unable to cope with the scale of contracts available from 1941 onwards, even though they, too, were rapidly expanded in size throughout the period. Other sectors of American industry, notably the domestic appliance and electrical industry were also drafted into the aircraft programme as sub-contractors, including the electrical giants General Electric and Westinghouse.

In Europe, conversion was much less important except in Britain where a similar relationship with the motor industry was established. The decision in Britain to use the motor industry was an old one which finally bore fruit in the establishment of a special group under Herbert Austin in 1936 charged with the task of finding new or spare capacity for aircraft and engine production.[54] By 1940 most of the major producers, even including Nuffield despite his reluctance to be directed in his efforts by the state, had plans for conversion to war production, although very few were to build whole aircraft. The MAP preferred to have the converted industry integrated more fully with the established armament firms and both Rolls-Royce and Vickers, the largest aero-engine and aircraft producers, were given charge over 'shadow' factories and major sub-contractors, including the large Nuffield plant at Castle Bromwich.[55] The conversion did not stop with the motor industry. The English Electric Company was drafted in for aircraft work, expanding its facilities from under 300,000 square feet to over 2 million square feet by 1942. In London, nine passenger transport depots were converted for the production of heavy bombers. Throughout the Midlands and the North smaller engineering firms were brought into the programme for sub-assemblies and assemblies, for final aircraft assembly at the large aircraft works. By the end of the war 45 per cent of the crucial heavy bombers had been produced by outside contractors and two-thirds of the standard light bombers. In terms of weight some 22 per cent of all aircraft production was undertaken outside the air firms themselves.[56] Although this was a smaller contribution than in the United States the programme of conversion planned for from the mid-1930s played an important role, particularly in the early stages of the war, when it was necessary to expand output as rapidly as possible.

By contrast Germany failed to mobilize the motor industry until well into the war, and then with only partial success. The motor industry as a whole ran at only 50 per cent of capacity at its peak for all armaments production. The major plants were only incorporated late into sub-contracting work for aircraft, and never produced completed aircraft. The huge Volkswagen complex remained greatly under-utilized despite Goering's insistence on bringing it onto the list of firms to be used for air orders. The long-drawn out negotiations with the Adam Opel Company resulted in a late and partial conversion to aircraft sub-contracting which was so badly planned that tooling had been completed for an obsolescent type shortly before the firm was directed to tool up for a newer model, with the result that the largest continental car firm failed to provide more than a fraction of what it was capable of producing, either for the army or the air force.[57] Otherwise the German air ministry depended on the expansion of the established aircraft firms and made little attempt to convert other industrial branches in deference to the demands to maintain consumer output, and in the belief that the current needs could be met for the time being from the existing capacity.

In Russia the problem while taking a similar form had a different origin. The engineering industry generally, and the car industry in particular, was too underdeveloped to allow widespread sub-contracting and conversion. In fact in the areas in eastern Russia where the evacuated firms were directed there were so few firms with which contracts could be made that a large proportion of the aircraft parts were made on the premises.[58] The state custom of designating all firms as State Aircraft Factories (GAZ) working on aircraft orders disguised any conversion that might have taken place. The industrial underdevelopment of Japan also made it difficult to convert other industries readily for war purposes. The large aircraft companies were already under the control of the major Zaibatsu so that conversion in this case simply meant substituting one product for another. The only other area open for conversion was into the light manufacturing sector, particularly in textiles, woodworking, and light metal working. This did not prove particularly suitable as the workforce and facilities were unused to the requirements of heavier engineering, and were usually too small as individual plants to cope with the scale of orders. The conversion was also largely unplanned and occurred only later in the war when the possibility of large increases in output resulting from new investment was much lower.[59]

The degree to which conversion was practiced should not be over-emphasized. That it occurred in the Allied economies came about as a result of the urgent determination of these governments to provide a large-scale air rearmament. Moreover both the British and American governments were prepared to provide the funds on a generous scale for the purpose. There was much more directly state-funded building in the British and American aircraft industries than in Germany or Japan. The German government gave insufficient funds both before the war and in the early stages of it to cover the needs of the aircraft industry. In 1939 the air budget was cut, and under mobilization aircraft factories found it increasingly difficult to get the necessary finance to cover new building. Fritz Todt, who was in charge of both construction and the munitions industries (except aircraft), starved the aircraft industry of funds. The air ministry demands up to 1941 ran 100 per cent higher than the quota planned by Todt, while the actual provision for building was in practice only a third of the original quota.[60] Too much money was still tied up, as in Japan, in consumer industries or in personal incomes. Not until the war was well under way did either of the two powers increase the levels of personal taxation necessary to cope with huge war contracts, and even then the level was below that in Britain and America.[61] This difference in urgency was reflected in the level of expansion of the aircraft industries. Here the crucial question was one of timing. The British effort to reach a capacity capable of meeting the maximum strategic demands was developed between 1936 and 1941. Thereafter capacity increased only slowly. In the United States the mobilization effort was concentrated in the years 1940-42. By the end of 1942 over 80 per cent of the sums allocated to aircraft production expansion had been spent, and the remaining 20 per cent was mainly for replacement of tools and equipment rather than for factory space.[62] As was to be expected the Axis timing differed in direct proportion to the shifts in Axis strategy. The first expansion period for the German aircraft industry was 1935-38. With the conclusion of the Milch scheme for reaching a balanced peace-time force with a low level of replacement, insufficient effort was devoted to the next stage of expansion, with the result that Germany entered and fought the war for the first two years with a capacity not much greater than the last year of peace, although the industry was so inefficient that a greater output could legitimately have been expected from it. In 1941 and 1942 a renewed effort was made to extend the manufacturing area for aircraft. Large new factories were planned and approved, and in one case actually completed. But under conditions of war, and subject to more adventurous bombing, it proved impossible to expand fast enough. Even under conditions of peace and early mobilization the American industry found that the average time between the start of an airframe plant and full operation was 31 months, and for aero-engines 23 months. In Germany the bulk of the new large-scale projects never materialized and the new plants for aero-engines in Austria, completed finally by Speer in 1942–43 took over five years from the original directive to the final output of an engine. They never began operating fully as a result of Allied bombing. In view of such difficulties the German air ministry insisted instead on a general dispersal, into both the German and European economies, in order to avoid bombing and to increase production.[63]

The dispersal late in the war differed from the conversion for war purposes carried out by the Allies. In the latter case the conversion was pre-planned. Moreover most of the expansion in Britain, America and Russia was in new facilities constructed for the purpose and operated by established aircraft firms or licensees. The German dispersal was into small firms widely scattered over the Reich and occupied Europe. In some cases such dispersal did not represent a net gain, but was cancelled out by facilities abandoned or destroyed in the Reich. Much of it was poorly planned and co-ordinated because carried out under increasingly improvised economic and administrative conditions.[64] Most of the new contracts went to firms with little experience of large-scale production of anything as complicated as an aircraft, or aero-engine. Most aircraft firms resisted dispersal until it became unavoidable. By 1943 it had become clear that larger factories rather than more smaller ones were what were needed to expand German output. Nevertheless, for want of an alternative due to the strategic miscalculations of the early years, dispersal did allow the German aircraft industry to survive longer into 1944 and 1945 then might otherwise have been the case. The same was true in Japan where decentralization had to be hurriedly introduced late in 1944 under the threat of heavy bombing. By March of the following year the major Mitsubishi and Nakajima plants had dispersed 60 per cent of their tools to small production units scattered in the countryside, or in less vulnerable urban areas.[65] Like their German counterparts the manufacturers resisted dispersal for as long as possible in order to meet the increased production demands for aircraft. In January they were finally compelled by imperial decree to disperse and to use underground facilities, as in Germany. Underground facilities provided a means for supplying a basic minimum of armament, but were difficult to maintain, and except for one or two cases were too small to cope with the efficient production of aircraft. As fast as underground factories were created plants on the surface were destroyed by bombing so that both German and Japanese aircraft production was carried on in the final months of war from a rapidly shrinking industrial foundation.[66] In the United States the effort devoted to aircraft production also shrank in the last year of war. But symbolically it was because too much capacity was available. Many plants had failed to run at full capacity since 1942 and the labour and tools were needed more urgently elsewhere. Labour in the industry declined 20 per cent over 1944, and floorspace in airframe production by eight million square feet.

(v) The Efficiency of Aircraft Production

Mobilization was not just a question of how big the aircraft industry was nor of how far it had spread into adjacent industrial sectors. It was also a question of how efficiently such capacity was utilized. That great gains in war production could be made by utilizing resources better was demonstrated everywhere. In aircraft production in particular the nature of the product encouraged production inefficiencies. So much of the final assembly was a question of organizing the supply and flow of numerous components. Bottlenecks in the supply of parts held up the output of finished aircraft even in the United States. Aircraft were also constantly undergoing modifications in design. If such changes were incorporated in a model currently in large-scale production further delays were the result. Some major model types underwent in excess of 50,000 minor design changes in the course of a production life. Aircraft production was hard to convert to methods of mass production, because not all parts of the process of building and assembly could be mechanized, and there always existed the danger that the supply of parts would be thrown out of balance because of the contrast between mechanized and partially mechanized suppliers. One of the greatest barriers to efficient production was ignorance. Managerial conservatism led to resistance to new methods and a general scepticism over the ability of rationalization to improve productivity in an industry with a specialized product and a history of poor productivity performance. Conservative managers were sometimes supported in such views by airmen, equally unfamiliar with industrial methods, who were anxious to preserve quality at the cost of quality by authorizing numerous design changes, or new models for production.

The result of such attitudes was widely differing levels of efficiency. Measured in terms of airframe weight produced per man-day the following table shows the contrast between American and Axis efficiency:

Table 15: Output of Aircraft in Pounds per Man-day in Japan, Germany and the U.S.A. 1941–45[68]

Year	U.S.A.	Japan	as % of U.S.A.	Germany	as % of U.S.A.
1941	1.42	0.63	44	1.15	81
1942	1.88	0.63	34	1.30	69
1943	1.88	0.71	38	1.50	80
1944	2.76	0.71	26	1.25	45
1945	2.36	0.42	18	–	–

Efforts to improve the operating efficiency of the aircraft industry were common to all the powers. Measured in crude terms the use of labour, floorspace and materials improved in efficiency over the course of the war. In Britain the Production Efficiency Board, set up by MAP in 1943, gave advice and recommendations on rationalization. In Germany a special rationalization drive was initiated in 1941 to help with the new production programmes. By 1943 regular surveys of the industry were carried out in order to assess the effect of schemes to improve productivity.[69] In Japan in 1943 the realization of how inefficiently production resources were being utilized led to considerable efforts to enforce efficiency. Nevertheless, substantial differences survived between the industries of the belligerent powers to suggest that efficiency was as important as capacity in determining aircraft output.

To a great extent gains in efficiency depended on changes in scale. The aircraft industry had been small in scale during the 1930s. Under conditions of war it became necessary to move to large-scale production. The larger the factory, the greater the opportunity for economies of scale and organization. In Russia and the United States aircraft and aero-engine factories were on average much larger than in Europe. Japan, too, operated a number of very large plants, if much less efficiently. The average size of American airframe factories was two million square feet. In Britain the figure was an average of 0.75 million sq. ft.,[70] although the production at the main British factories for combat aircraft was on a much larger scale than the average. Spitfires were produced at the rate of 320 per month in the peak quarter at Castle Bromwich.[71] By comparison the peak output of the largest Russian factory reached 1,500 per month, and in the American industry 500 per month.[72] In both Britain and Germany the average factory size tended to be smaller, with those in Germany the smallest of all. In Germany the largest producer, Junkers, had only two factories in 1944 with over 10,000 employees, one of 14,000 and another of 12,000. Britain by comparison had 12 factories of over 10,000 including two firms of 25,000 employees each, which in turn contrasted with American experience in which the majority of aircraft factories employed between 20,000 and 40,000.[73] Moreover, the contrast developed further in sub-contracting practice. In Germany and Britain small firms were drafted in for aircraft production work. At the peak MAP had contracts with 12,000 firms, the German air ministry with over 17,000, many of these in workshops employing only a handful of workers.[74] In America small businesses were starved of orders and even after legislation compelling the large munitions firms to place contracts with smaller firms, the situation continued. Aircraft manufacturers argued that small firms were too inefficient to cope with the scale of orders, and preferred to sub-contract to medium and large companies.[75]

The major advantage of larger scale was the greater opportunity it gave to the introduction of more modern factory methods. Aircraft production in the early 1930s did not lend itself easily to such methods. Production was usually carried out in workshop batches with workers moving from aircraft to aircraft, carrying out tasks in an unscheduled way on one or two aircraft at a time, using a large degree of handwork. Tools were usually of a general-purpose kind so that the largest number of operations could be performed by skilled men working in groups on each aircraft. During the course of the war the best practice at the largest American plants resembled that of the major car firms. Flow production methods were introduced, long and narrow factory halls built for moving aircraft from stage to stage of its assembly, while conveyor belts fed parts into the main line at appropriate points. Workers were scheduled carefully to perform particular tasks at particular sites along the assembly line, while general-purpose tools were replaced by special machinery designed for a higher level of automation. A high degree of standardization and interchangeability was introduced and handwork reduced to a minimum.[76]

Methods such as these were widely adopted throughout American aircraft and components factories. Aero-engine production was more automated than final airframe production, as was the output of sub-assemblies. There were limits to the extent to which aircraft could be handled by machinery on an assembly line. Nevertheless the Ford plant at Willow Run, despite opposition to the scheme from the air authorities, undertook to mass-produce the B-24 bomber, and by breaking production down into 20,000 separate operations it was finally achieved in 1944. The plant became the only one of its kind to integrate car manufacturing methods and experience completely with that of aircraft.[77] A high degree of automation and rationalization emerged in British aircraft firms as well, some of it based on American experience, and through the use of American advisers and special machinery (as in the Soviet Union).[78] The fact that the car industry was brought into aircraft production, even though less extensively than in the United States, gave British industry the opportunity to adopt the best known practices from commercial mass-production experience. British factory practice was still far below that of the most efficient American firms but not as far as many people feared. British developments in the mass consumer goods industry in the 1920s and 1930s had made it essential to adopt more modern factory methods to survive. The large firms who contributed personnel and capacity to the aircraft industry were able to adapt habits which were essential for commercial survival to the needs of wartime production.

In Germany and Japan such changes were less successful, although both countries might have come closer to the level of British performance had it not been for the economic dislocation of bombing and blockade.[79] In Germany the aircraft factories were slow to adopt new methods and were permeated by many built-in inefficiencies which it proved hard to overcome. One of the hardest was the degree of handwork involved in producing aircraft. Handworker methods survived through the legacy of the early industry in the 1930s and because of the high degree of skill acquired by the individual *Meister* (the master-craftsmen) through a long and rigorous apprenticeship. The workforce resisted attempts to undermine the skills or to dilute the workforce by using new methods and semi-skilled labour. Batch production gave way only slowly to line production, while time-and-motion studies on which American practice rested were either not introduced or where they were, proved unworkable because of the traditional methods of work payment and use of skills. Conveyor belt production and rational factory organization developed only slowly and many factories still had little evidence of modern methods even by 1945.[80] The use of capacity was so inefficient that when Milch compelled some degree of improvement in 1942 the industry was able to produce another 40 per cent more aircraft with virtually the same amount of labour and less aluminium than the year before.[81] Japanese factory methods were even more primitive. Lacking a sufficiently strong machine-tool industry, or sufficient trained men, and relying on small suppliers with very widely differing standards rationalization was difficult to effect. The problem was the consequence partly of competition between the army and navy who could not even agree on a common voltage for electrical components until late in the war.[82] But as in Germany a major barrier to greater efficiency was the problem of organizing and scheduling the flow of production.

Production scheduling was a widespread problem. In nearly all American, and an important number of British firms, some system of production control was introduced during the war to cope with the buying in of parts and their rational scheduling for use in the factory. Without such systems aircraft production was continually threatened by a shortage of vital components or materials. In Germany reliance on a large number of small contractors, which expanded after the dispersal forced by bombing, led to constant interruptions to the flow of parts for assembly. Britain, too, had found the same problem at the time of the Blitz, and had introduced a system whereby crucial parts were made in two or three establishments so that interruption by one firm could be compensated for by expanding production at another. But even in Britain the difficulties persisted long after the threat from bombing had disappeared.[83] Similar schemes introduced in Germany and Japan broke down because of the threat of bombing and the more random distribution of contracts that resulted. Throughout 1943 and 1944 German manufacturers, while improving productive performance at the main plants considerably, were often forced to slow down the rate of final assembly because of shortages of components.[84] One advantage enjoyed by the Russian factories was the shortage of small firms with whom contracts could be arranged. Instead most of the parts and components were made in the same establishment. Indeed many Russian aircraft firms had their own furnaces and foundries and an internal supply of electricity. Where the Allies enjoyed the opportunities of concentrating production processes, or of arranging careful scheduling, the Axis powers found the conditions of war leading to a growing attenuation of the production process through decentralization, as well as constant and frustrating interruption to the flow of resources.

(vi) Labour and Raw Materials

Differences in the way in which capital was utilized were reflected in the whole question of labour utilization. Labour was a crucial factor in aircraft production because of the numbers involved. Aircraft industries took the largest slice of the available civilian workforce. The mobilization of labour resources, like that of capital, involved a question of scale on the one hand—how many workers could the aircraft industry obtain; and of efficiency—how productive the workforce could be. All the combatant powers enormously expanded the available workforce over the war period as the following table shows:

Table 16: Labour in the Aircraft Industry at Selected Dates 1940-45[85]

		1940	1941	1942	1943	1944	1945
U.K.	A	973,000	1,259,400	1,526,000	1,678,200	1,440,300	1,107,200
U.S.A.	B	200,000	347,000	471,000	1,345,600	2,102,000	1,464,000
U.S.S.R.	B	350,000	500,000	–	–	750,000	–
Germany	A	1,000,000	1,850,000	1,800,000	–	–	–
	B	276,136	300,000	–	452,330	545,600	–
Japan	B	–	236,947	343,581	482,771	756,256	825,582

A All air orders   B Airframe and engine industry

Figures for United Kingdom are for 31 December each year: for the United States the figures are for the annual peak: for Germany the date for 1940 is 1 April, for 1941 the dates are 'autumn 1941' and June 1941, the date for 1942 is November, for 1943 1 January and for 1944, June: figures for Japan are average monthly employment figures.

Although there were large increases in the size of the workforce, all the powers experienced a problem of labour shortage. To some extent the shortages were an illusion created by the fierce struggle for labour resources between the services and the different branches of industry. Firms and services were encouraged to inflate demands as a tactical device in the hope that by setting unrealistically high demands there would be a greater chance of obtaining what was really needed. Moreover little attempt was made to assess how labour needs would change under conditions of large-scale semi-automated production. Initial estimates were often sharply reduced once labour-saving production planning was introduced with the more rational factory methods. In Britain and America the aircraft industry enjoyed the first priority for most of the war in the allocation of workers. In fact so much so that in 1943 MAP's priority was finally removed to ensure a fairer distribution of workers to other requirements, and in the United States an excess developed which forced a cutback in numbers of 20 per cent during the course of 1944.[86] The problem of recruitment in the western powers was solved by the mobilization of women and the movement of men from inessential production or unemployment to war work. By the end of the war over a third of the workforce in both countries was female. In America the adoption of new production methods also made it possible to recruit unskilled labour. Large new sources of such labour were tapped in the inner regions of the United States where the aircraft industry had only 6 per cent of its workforce in 1942. By the end of the war over 50 per cent of the workforce, much of it unskilled, was concentrated in the central industrial districts. In order to preserve the necessary skilled labour to work with the unskilled a system of reserved occupations and factories was operated, but dilution of skills was widespread. Conscription tended to take the younger, semi-skilled men who could be replaced either by older men or by using women and students.[87] The same labour catchment area was adopted through necessity in the Soviet Union. By 1945 over two-thirds of workers in the aircraft industry were women. Although there developed a serious shortage of skilled workers during the period 1941–42 of changeover to more routine and modern factory methods, there were reserves available. The training schemes carried out since the period of the first Five-Year Plan provided a crucial source. In addition the aircraft industry was already a large employer of skilled labour before the war, and was able to provide from its own resources sufficient engineering labour to cope with the kind of production initiated under war conditions.[88]

The level of labour mobilization in Germany was much lower until the large-scale recruitment of foreign forced labour in 1942 and 1943. The number of extra women drafted into war work was negligible, particularly in the aircraft industry.[89] In the struggle for labour resources the air ministry was at a considerable disadvantage politically, since labour recruitment and allocation was controlled by agencies directly linked to the army, and unsympathetic to the Luftwaffe demands. During 1942 the number of workers allocated rose hardly at all despite the large numbers drafted in from Europe.[90] Over the whole period the army continued to recruit skilled workers even in the protected factories. In all the aircraft factories an average of between 45 and 50 per cent of the workforce was composed of foreign labour by the end of the war. This workforce was largely unskilled as far as aircraft producers were concerned, and little effort was made to allocate workers with appropriate skills to the right job in the Reich.[91] One problem that a relatively low level of labour mobilization posed was the difficulty of operating on a shift system. Although the ministry had intended from the start of the war that a two- or three-shift system should become the norm many aircraft factories were still working one shift only even by 1944.[92] Where Russian and British factories worked round-the-clock to cope with the production made necessary by crisis in 1940 and 1941, the German industry lacked the urgency to move to shift working and fell back on the argument that too few workers could be found even for normal day work. The failure to adopt shift working also reflected a fear of the effect of unsocial hours on the workforce, a factor which led to a falling off in night-shift work in Britain, too, after the middle of the war.[93] Hitler's anxiety to placate the workforce, and his personal intervention to prevent female labour mobilization together contributed to a comparatively low level of both capital and labour utilization.

Japan had similar policies on labour mobilization, although gradually the proportion of women coming into the aircraft industry expanded under the urgent aircraft expansion programme of 1943–44. Not until the need for more aircraft production was made apparent did efforts begin to recruit students, Koreans and women in large numbers for war production. At the same time, however, large numbers of skilled workers were recruited for the services. The army refused to acknowledge the priority for naval work and continued up to 1945 to recruit skilled labour from naval aircraft firms as well as from its own factories to such an extent that an already small skilled engineering corps was diluted to the level of one skilled foreman for every 2,000 unskilled operatives. So poor was the quality of the largely untrained workforce that an estimated 30 per cent of all engine parts proved to be unusable because of poor workmanship.[94]

The whole question of efficient use of labour was related, as the Japanese case showed, to the nature of the labour recruited. There was obviously a problem if too little skilled labour was available. The dilution of the workforce to the extent that only 10 per cent of aircraft workers could be regarded as skilled, in what was already a technically backward industry by Allied standards, sharply reduced the ability of the Japanese to produce large numbers of technically sound aircraft.[95] Yet there was also a danger of relying too much on skilled labour. The fact that emerged most clearly from the experience of labour mobilization was that unskilled labour, provided it was adequately trained, and provided that more mechanized and routine production methods could be introduced, was more productive than labour in the pre-war aircraft industry with its high reliance on skilled workers. In the United States the dilution of the workforce was readily accepted because of the use made of new factory methods. Airframe weight per employee/month increased from 21 pounds in January 1941 to a peak of 96 pounds in May 1944.[96] Aircraft production itself was broken down into a long series of easily learnt processes which required the minimum of manual skill. In Britain and Germany, however, the habit of using highly skilled workers was hard to lose. In Britain the dilution of labour only began in earnest after 1941 when the trade unions finally agreed to accept it, but it gradually became a fact of life. Moreover by 1943–44, when MAP labour demands were cut dramatically, it was discovered that even a comparatively low level of improvement in factory methods led to substantial improvements in productivity.[97]

In Germany the task of dilution was more complicated. First of all the *Meister* resisted the reduction in training time and the changes in apprenticeship regulations necessitated by wartime conditions. Secondly the aircraft firms had always relied heavily for production on a high degree of skilled work, and the factory methods had been introduced in the expectation that such methods, and the high quality of finish required for aircraft, would be maintained under war conditions. In addition the use of small sub-contracted firms encouraged the retention of an unnecessarily high level of skilled labour since smallness of scale discouraged the production innovation necessary for the use of less skilled workers. The preoccupation with skilled labour then became an obsession with the ministry as well. For the first two or three years of war the skilled labour shortage was combated by every means possible in defence of the high standards of workmanship traditionally associated with German engineering. So much so that most aircraft firms habitually blamed labour shortages as the explanation for poor performance. Trapped to some extent in a situation of high skilled-labour input neither the industry nor the Luftwaffe appreciated early enough the advantages to be gained from using unskilled labour with different production methods. The shortage of engineers was thus exaggerated by the commitment to high standards of workmanship and a large skilled workforce. The lack of engineers was real enough and had been a habitual problem since the 1930s, finding its root cause in the rapid decline in enrolment at German technical engineering schools after 1933. But where elsewhere the lack was overcome by doing without skilled men, in Germany it remained a basic bottleneck until dilution was finally accepted late and hurriedly in 1944.[98] The price paid for a very high standard of finish was a smaller number of aircraft completed. When the dilution could no longer be ignored or resisted, firms began to introduce more rationalization and the productivity performance began to rise. It was an eloquent tribute to the effectiveness of unskilled labour that peak German and Japanese aircraft production was achieved at the period of peak labour dilution.

Labour productivity was also related to conditions, which depended in turn on the political as much as the economic environment. Conditions, for example, in the Soviet Union were considerably below those regarded as acceptable in the western industrial powers, Allied and Axis. Not only were workers conscripted and moved to the aircraft plants, pay and rations were both low. In the period of evacuation workers were compelled to operate machines in the open, and in factories with earth floors.[99] Yet although productivity remained relatively low—estimated at a third that of American aircraft industry—the Russian workforce faced special circumstances in defence aginst Germany, and shared hardships in the prospect of victory. In the Soviet Union resistance against conditions was politically unacceptable, as it was in Germany and Japan. In all three cases labour was compelled to accept conditions imposed from above, Unions had been abolished and the right to strike suspended. The response to the situation led in Germany to high levels of absenteeism, labour obstructionism and high labour turnover.[100] In Japan conscripted labour was compelled to go where the government directed and workers were frozen in factories and occupations to reduce labour turnover. To get round the problem of high labour cost more women were recruited whose rate of pay never rose beyond 50 per cent of that paid to men. Moreover, despite the wartime inflation wage rates rose only slowly because of controls over labour.[101] In Germany too, although labour was treated with some circumspection, wage rates did not keep pace with the rate of inflation and forced labour was poorly rewarded. The only thing that pushed wages up was competition between the firms in what became a black-market for labour operating side by side with the official government controls.[102]

In the west there was a different political climate. Both government and labour had an interest in establishing grounds for co-operation. Although widespread controls were introduced over the allocation of labour, and strikes were difficult to start, labour policies were pursued as far as possible in co-operation with the trade union organizations. As a result conditions of work were subject to negotiation, while the labour market worked in favour of workers due to scarcity. In Britain it was agreed that differences in wage levels for workers moved from high-wage to low-wage areas would be paid for by the state, while wage levels in war industry as a whole rose in step with inflation.[103] To get around the problem of high labour costs that this situation produced the new factory methods were essential. In the United States labour cost per pound of airframe weight fell by two-thirds between 1941 and 1944.[104] In countries like Germany and Japan, where production methods were not changed rapidly enough, labour costs were partly responsible for compelling those changes that finally did take place, although by the end of the war the degree of compulsory and slave labour in the fascist powers reduced the overall labour cost substantially at the expense of labour conditions. Such direct physical exploitation was a false economy, however, because forced labourers although contributing to the overall increase in productivity brought about by the use of unskilled labour and new methods were unwilling and apathetic workers. When subjected to the additional pressures of bombing the result was widespread demoralization and absenteeism.[105] Where direct political oppression was added to the fear of economic decline under conditions of wartime finance, the productive effort of the workforce was correspondingly, and unsurprisingly, lower.

Differences in capital and labour utilization were also accompanied by a number of resource problems which were not susceptible to organizational or technical rationalization. Resources problems were, however, often exaggerated. Shortages could be overcome either through improvisation or through better utilization. Lack of aluminium in Russia forced factories to use wood construction until the final months of war. Lack of aluminium in Germany was partly overcome by the elimination of waste caused through the technical miscalculation of aluminium needs per aircraft. Nor were governments unaware of resource deficiencies. Efforts were always directed towards those factors of production in short supply rather than those which were adequate or in abundance. Standards differed also from economy to economy. Where the use of wood for aircraft production in Russia was not a handicap in terms of gross output, the need to resort to it in Japan proved of little value because of the poor quality of work and lack of experience in plywood and resin technology.[106] Resource limitation was also a result of how successfully aircraft production could compete for resources with the other services. Since many resources were essentially finite there were clearly defined economic boundaries beyond which war production could not be taken. Yet as with labour utilization the development of more rational methods of production and greater vigilance exposed a high level of waste particularly in those economies most exposed to shortages.

The best example was the use of aluminium. Supplies of aluminium, as the most convenient metal for aircraft construction, had to be expanded rapidly during the war to meet rising demand. For the Allies this meant expanding supplies from North America from where most Russian and a large proportion of British aluminium was supplied. British home production of aluminium actually declined between 1939 and 1941 while imports increased by almost 250 per cent over the same period.[107] Although aluminium exports provided some difficulties for American industry in the early period of expansion the War Production Board argued that the problem was self-imposed through poor distribution and hoarding. By 1943 these problems had been eliminated through better scheduling of raw materials through the Controlled Materials Plan and the AAF scheduling unit.[108] Three large new aluminium plants were actually cancelled in 1943 for fear of excess production. Aluminium supplies in Germany, Japan and Italy were also considerably expanded. As the world's largest producer in 1939 Germany did not anticipate aluminium shortages. Nevertheless the Luftwaffe had to fight for its claim to aluminium just as it fought for labour and other resources. Where the Allied powers reserved aluminium almost completely for air force use, and even in the United States some 80 per cent of production was scheduled for the air forces, the Luftwaffe only obtained 45 per cent of supplies in 1939 and no more than 60 per cent in 1944 when every effort was made to expand aircraft output.[109] In defence of such allocation the other users accused the aircraft industry of hoarding and inefficient use. Both charges proved true. Wasteful shop methods combined with inter-firm rivalry had led to enormous wastage, but the greatest source of wastage had been in Udet's initial decision to allocate seven to eight tons of aluminium per aircraft, greatly in excess of needs. This miscalculation encouraged hoarding and led to high levels of scrapping. Milch discovered that over half a ton of aluminium was wasted in the production of each aero-engine.[110] In Japan aluminium allocation had also been at too high a level, dropping from eight tons per aircraft in early 1942 to two to three tons by the end of the war. Japanese firms were also found to be hoarding the metal and using it for inessential civilian production.[111] In Britain strict controls over civilian use and careful scheduling produced a much larger number of aircraft from a smaller aluminium base. Thus in 1941 Britain produced some 20,094 aircraft from 161,000 tons of aluminium produced and imported, whereas Germany produced 11,776 from total production and imports of 382,000 tons, of which 206,000 tons were allocated to the Luftwaffe.[112] Although Milch was able to improve the distribution of the material, the German war economy failed to give sufficient priority to air force needs with the result that many more aircraft could have been produced from an abundant material in which most other belligerents experienced real shortages.

From some limitations, however, there was no escape. Heavy machinery and special machine tools were in short supply for aircraft production everywhere, but the size and experience of the American and British special machinery industries more than compensated for Germany's larger supply of general purpose tools. Japan and Italy were generally short of most tools, specialized or otherwise and during the war only limited success was achieved in increasing engineering supplies.[113] Limitations imposed by energy supplies and transport were also widespread. The impact of the war through blockade and bombing on these particular sectors was in the end critical for both the German and Japanese industrial structures. Nevertheless even these limitations proved to be a spur to greater production efforts both through increasing the scale of planning and improving efficiency.

(vii) The Quality of Aircraft

There exists a danger in any explanation of wartime economic performance in exaggerating degrees of inefficiency. All the powers, with perhaps the exception of the United States, were plagued with resource and mobilization difficulties. It was in the nature of things that efforts would be made to overcome them, and what appeared to be a considerable gap in productive performance between two powers could be closed by wide differences in factor endowment. Thus had the Axis problems been simply those of resources and organization it was not unlikely that they would have been overcome through ingenuity and improvisation as in the First World War. The Soviet Union had far fewer industrial advantages than Germany after the economic dislocation of the invasion and occupation of most of industrialized Russia, yet nevertheless managed to produce more aircraft than Germany in every year of the war. Moreover the evidence suggests that great efforts were made in Germany and Japan as well to expand output to unprecedented levels. The reasons for their comparative failure in the field of aircraft output rests with one critical residual difference between the Axis and Allied powers in the way in which aircraft models were selected and design changes incorporated.

Well-organized product selection was vital in aircraft production. The design and production development of aircraft was a long and expensive path. Any mistake in choosing replacement aircraft could cost months of output because of the effort put into changing factory tooling, the scheduling of resources and the acquisition of labour for the projected new type. Too many aircraft in the programme diluted production effort, made standardization difficult and reduced sharply the gains to be made from long production runs. Too many design changes to aircraft already in production, unless properly organized, could equally cost months of output because of the difficulty in changing tools, jigs and installations to cope with the modifications, as well as producing constant interruptions to the flow of components and uncertainty in long-term production planning. One answer to the problem was to insist as Russian producers did on a rigorous policy of standardization and production continuity. Modifications were incorporated when necessary, particularly to improve engine performance, but models were frozen in production for relatively long periods giving the Soviet air forces large numbers at the cost of a marginally less effective product. The success of the Red Air Force demonstrated that the risk was in this case worth taking. The Soviet Air Force also relied for most of the war on a very small number of aircraft types: two fighters, one fighter bomber, one medium-bomber, two trainers. Such concentration reduced the risk of losing production through too rapid a turnover of aircraft models.[114]

The western Allies similarly attempted to concentrate production. But more important than this they concentrated considerable effort on the task of choosing aircraft types in such a way as to keep a balance between production and performance, between quantity and quality. This necessitated introducing as few new types as possible. Despite the constant complaints in both Britain and America over the length of time involved in developing a compeletely new aircraft type the situation turned out to be a blessing in disguise. Instead most of the aircraft with which the war was fought were modified versions of an original design. In some cases the modification produced effectively a different aircraft. Thus the Lancaster bomber and the Mustang fighter emerged as what appeared to be new aircraft though in fact they had an established pedigree. The essential thing about such modifications was that they should interrupt the production life of aircraft as little as possible.[115] In America a system was chosen in which modifications would be accumulated over a period of time introduced in a batch to prevent interruptions to large production runs. In some cases quality suffered. Many argued that the Ford plant's long delay in producing B-24s in mass-production at Willow Run had rendered the aircraft obsolescent; yet large quantities were produced in 1944 and 1945 to considerable operational effect. For those small modifications that needed to be introduced in the course of a production run special Modification Centres were established where skilled workers would introduce the necessary changes immediately before delivery to the air units.[116] In Britain the system was more wasteful in terms of quantity but maintained a higher average quality. Major modifications were introduced as and when the military situation justified or in response to technical changes in, for example, engine power. But the modifications were carefully screened by an MAP Aircraft Modifications Committee to ensure that only urgent changes should be incorporated, and to discuss with industry the best way of making such changes with the least interruption to output. Such a situation was much less wasteful of effort than the complete design and introduction of new aircraft types. Vickers Supermarine company spent 330,000 man-hours on the design of the Spitfire Mark I, but only 620,000 man-hours on all the subsequent fifteen Spitfire marks. For jigging and tooling-up for the Spitfire Mark I some 800,000 man-hours were expended. The average time for all subsequent marks was 69,000.[117] In both the British and American case civilians had as much say as the airmen in choosing new types or design changes, with considerable influence given to the industrialists themselves as the organizers most likely to suffer from too many alterations. By avoiding domination by air force demands, and through a permanent awareness of the production effect of design changes, the interruption to production was kept to an acceptable level. Although it remained the single most important explanation for shortfalls in production the quality of aircraft remained high and the quantity more than adequate.

In Italy and Japan there existed simply too many types introduced at too fast a rate to guarantee sufficient output. Italian designers continued to produce a wide range of designs throughout the war and those in charge of the air force and air ministry departments whose task it was to select air force weapons were unequal to the demands made of them. The result was an imbalance in favour of development at the expense of production.[118] In Japan the problem of model selection had its root in the division between the army and the navy and in the influence of the services on aircraft production. The first factor resulted in the army and navy producing their own aircraft to perform identical functions and insisting that all development work be kept separate. During the war the navy produced 53 basic models with 112 variations, the army 37 basic models with 52 variations. America, by contrast, concentrated on the production of 18 models for the army and navy together.[119] Even when compelled in 1944 to undertake more co-operative aircraft development the navy and army ignored the directives and continued to develop proscribed projects in secret.[120] In addition modifications were forced upon industry in a bewildering stream, largely because of the influence of the front-line airmen whose views were regarded as the most important factor in considering changes to aircraft in production. Shortages of engineering and technical staff were so severe that many firms concentrated efforts on the minor alterations and abandoned attempts at more major mark changes. The continuing control over the design and introduction of new models enjoyed by the military, which survived the attempt to control aircraft production through the Ministry of Munitions, led to a constant stream of ill-planned and uncertain directives to firms on model changes and priorities which the firms found impossible to cope with.[121] At the aircraft plants so many models were introduced, cancelled then reintroduced or modified that production runs were confined to small numbers only with a resulting poor use of capacity. The firms' tradition of taking the orders that the military gave them without question meant that Japan lacked the advantage enjoyed in the west of close co-operation between industrial, civilian and military authorities over technical production questions. Moreover the struggle waged between the army and navy over the production of better quality weapons led to a division of effort between research establishments and between individual firms, and to the secreting of information.[122] Not only did production suffer dramatically through poor control over design and modification, so also did quality.

In Germany the problem if less severe was still critical. It was the result of rather similar circumstances: poor technical and production appreciation, a high degree of inter-firm design rivalry and a disproportionate influence of the air force itself on design changes. The first problem was largely of Goering's own making. Udet was given organizationally wide powers over the whole area of technical selection and design. His advisers came mainly from an air force background or were promoted through the party and lacked sufficient technical training. Decisions taken from 1939–41 on new aircraft types to be introduced proved disastrous, not only because Udet and many others failed to realize how long the development of an aircraft took but because of Goering's damaging 'production stops' on development of weapons for the immediate future.[123] Moreover Udet was the victim of a high degree of inter-firm rivalry in design. Easily influenced and technically unversed, Udet was readily persuaded to accept aircraft projects without sufficient review and to take assurances as to future performance uncritically. Such rivalry was exacerbated by the fact that many of the firms' managers were originally designers. This meant in effect that design and development questions tended to take priority in the firms over production questions.[124] The entrepreneurs believed it to be more important to have a variety of new designs to offer to the ministry than to be able to produce a standard design as efficiently as possible. During the war the air force developed no fewer than 86 aircraft designs.[125] When Milch assumed control over the technical sector in 1941 he found all the major replacement projects in disarray. In fighter, heavy-bomber and medium-bomber development aircraft had been chosen and scheduled for production years ahead of their true development time. Firms were tooled-up to take on the production of the new types but because they were far from ready for serial production the plans had to be scrapped. The resulting loss of output at Messerschmitt, Junkers and Heinkel was considerably greater than the loss caused by bombing.[126] Instead of building the new models, the Luftwaffe was forced at short notice to begin a programme of modifying established types in order to make up for lost output. But because the decision on modification was taken by the military with little heed of production problems, such modification was a constant source of production delays. The air staff presented the industry in a disorganized way with a stream of minor alterations which they were compelled to incorporate at once and over which the military, including the front-line generals from whom many of the requests for changes came, kept a close scrutiny.[127] This combination of poor standardization, intensive preoccupation with design and unorganized modification led not only to a loss of quantity but eventually to a loss of quality as well. Only in 1944 with Speer's insistence on continuous uninterrupted production of a handful of aircraft models was the problem tackled for the first time and by then it was too late.[128]

In all the Axis powers the common denominator was the exclusive role of the military in choosing designs and ordering modifications without sufficient attention to the economics of aircraft production. Without a coherent production plan the firms responded by producing an unscheduled stream of designs. This satisfied the military demand for better and better weapons in theory only. In practice the military failed to distinguish the best weapons, and found itself confused by promises from the firms which could not be fulfilled technically. Insistence on the pursuit of quality at all costs led to short production runs and constant interruptions to the flow of production which demoralized the producers and frustrated the soldiers.

(viii) Finance, Capitalism and the War Effort

The problem of product selection, like so many in the production of aircraft, was closely related to the extent to which industry was brought into the running of the war economy. That British and American businessmen were integrated into the organization and planning of aircraft production was not simply a reflection of a particular closeness between the governmental and commercial elites but of an anxiety on the part of firms to be involved from the start in questions to do with contracts, production and particularly finance. As a factor of production, management had to be considered not only in terms of its efficient use but in terms of the pursuit of profit. The first consideration was of course important. Even in the United States management resources were stretched by the demands of war economics and the running of large establishments. In Britain and Germany many of the managers who were running large-scale aircraft plants had begun in small-scale industry with the result that it was not always easy for firms to introduce modern methods or reorganize production scale through lack of managerial experience.[129] This problem was particularly acute in Germany where so many of the leading managers were primarily designers whose experience of production management was limited. In a number of prominent cases loss in output was directly attributable to managerial error.[130] All governments, however, reserved to themselves the right to remove, by one means or another, inefficient managers. In Russia, in the absence of any commercial pressure, it was purely managerial efficiency that counted, thus giving more opportunity for promoting able managers. Where elsewhere accidents of ownership or influence affected managerial performance, the whole purpose of Russian management was to manage better. This did not necessarily mean that all the best managers rose to the top, but it did mean that poor managers remained there only briefly. State control over managerial personnel was not in this case a disadvantage since war economics demanded production rather than commercial efficiency.

180

For the capitalist powers, however, the key question was finance, not efficiency. The precise financial relationship between the firms and the state was of the greatest importance. Since governments were dealing with private firms run by entrepreneurs or on behalf of shareholders, it was impossible to ignore wider financial issues. Moreover, fear of wartime profiteering encouraged governments to formalize relations with industry as early as possible to avoid any problems for production caused by later friction.[131] The difficulty was to keep sufficient profit incentive to encourage firms to cut costs and boost production while keeping profits at a level acceptable to public opinion. In the end it was public fear of profiteering that had to be muzzled in order to encourage greater industrial efforts. In Britain the Stamp Survey in June 1940 found 'patriotism and peril curiously transient as complete substitutes for the old incentives', and the general criticism of the Excess Profits Tax led in January 1941 to its revision in favour of the firms.[132] The system of finance for war purposes was never satisfactorily worked out. The aircraft industry obtained nearly all its investment for expansion either through government loans or through the direct construction of government-owned installations operated by private firms. Operating costs were calculated periodically and contracts based on a fixed-price. Over the course of the war the fixed-price often proved unworkable because of the rapid inflation of labour and raw material costs coinciding in many cases with economies of scale. This encouraged the efficient firms to seek out economies where they could in order to widen the profit margins on fixed-price contracts. Investigation of such profit inflation was then left to the taxation authorities. This kind of profit-seeking was tolerated because it had the advantage that it encouraged improvements in productivity which the cost-plus contract did not. It was an avenue to higher profits that satisfied both sides.[133] On a firm's own capital a return of 8 per cent was allowed, which together with incentive allowances for higher turnover and the operation of government-owned assets, left some firms in a position to make almost 20 per cent on capital employed on the firm's own behalf.[134] Some, but by no means all of this, would be subject to Excess Profits Tax. Only those firms working entirely with government facilities received a low rate of return of 1 per cent on contracts, but since much of the early expansion of the aircraft industry had been though private capital there were few firms in this situation.[135] By 1944 the growing efficiency of the British firms had indeed led to a widening gap between estimated percentage profit on cost and actual profit. In 1941 the average had been 4.41 per cent estimate and 6.38 per cent actual. In 1944 the figures were 2.88 and 5.74.[136] Excess Profits Tax was used to cope with the anomaly but retrospective penalties were hard to calculate. The biggest advantage was not, however, to do with profits. Most firms emerged with vastly expanded assets at the end of the war, many in a position to buy out the government-owned facilities at generous prices. It also gave encouragement to the process of concentration and eliminated lesser competitors for future peace-time commercial contests; and all largely at government expense.[137]

The same uncertainty in relations between business and government prevailed in the United States. Firms were reluctant to undertake aircraft work until the conditions of finance were altered. Many outside firms, particularly in the car industry, refused to take up war orders in 1940 and 1941 unless the state provided all the funds for expansion, or unless all private firms in a particular

181

sector were compelled to take war contracts.[138] Such resistance was fed by the fact that the firms were experiencing a rising consumer boom for the first time since the Great Crash and were not willing to sacrifice the increase in profits. The question of contracts even in the aircraft industry was equally thorny. The Vinson-Trammell Act of 1934 had restricted profits to 10 per cent on contracts which, as in Britain, were negotiated at a fixed price. In 1939 the level was raised to 12 per cent. The efforts of Congress in 1940 to reduce it to 8 per cent were strongly resisted,[139] and were accepted only in return for certain concessions for big business. Depreciation for tax was allowed to be accelerated from 10–16 years to five years. An excess profits tax was substituted for fixed profits contracts in order to encourage greater efforts to efficiency. Anti-trust suits were indefinitely postponed. Finally firms were provided with almost all new expansion investment by the government and were allowed to calculate profit rates on the basis of facilities that they had not built and did not own.[140] This had the advantage of disguising profit levels. The Douglas company, for example, had net profits after tax of 51 per cent of net worth in 1941, yet the overall rate of profit for the industry in 1941 was only 7.4 per cent.[141] Contracts were negotiated over the period and regularly adjusted to take account of cost economies. Each plant contained a government cost inspector to ensure that excess profits were not going undetected, but although his powers were increased by the contract Renegotiation Act of 1942, it was not always desirable to enforce too low a profit level in case it discouraged improvements in productivity.[142] Turnover expanded so rapidly, however, that even though the average rate of post-tax profits fell to only 1 per cent by 1944, the aggregate profits expanded to record levels. In addition, as in Britain, the firms had the advantage of enormously expanded assets at relatively low cost in a sector which had traditionally found difficulty in raising capital.[143] In both Britain and America the commercial interests of capitalism were respected. In both cases a high degree of co-operation and integration was achieved. In both cases there existed substantial incentives to improving production through financial reward; and most important of all the risk was undertaken by the state while the operating profit was taken by private industry.

Capitalism was recruited in Japan and Germany much more slowly and with considerable political conflict. Over the mobilization period in Japan the military attempted to control Zaibatsu financial policies, particularly through profit and dividend control designed to keep more money in the firms for reinvestment in war industry. The problem here was not profit as such, for the large holding companies continued to make substantial profits until 1944 and profitable operations could be used to subsidize those such as aircraft production where the risks were greater. It was much more a question of the relationship between the military and the capitalist elite.[144] Until 1943 the integration of business into the war-economic organization was much less than in the west. Only in 1943 did the Zaibatsu, in the struggle to create the Munitions Ministry, insist on less interference from the military and more responsibility for industry. In the end the contest became one of priorities: the Japanese trusts were anxious to preserve private capitalism from military interference, to expand operations profitably and to continue the process of concentration of economic power in their own hands; the military were concerned to turn the Japanese economy into a satisfactory war-making machine. Efforts to get the government to run the aircraft factories were resisted by the Munitions Ministry, run by Zaibatsu executives, on the basis that it was best 'to encourage private management to increase production'.[145] As it turned out the industrialists were much better at achieving the militarists' aims once they had obtained a lower level of military intervention. The same was true of the German economy when Speer finally persuaded Hitler to accept a policy of 'self-responsibility' of industry in 1942–43 in order to get private capitalism more involved in the running of the war economy and less subject to bureaucratic or military interference. In the German aircraft industry, however, the situation was more complicated. Over half of aircraft production came from state-owned firms managed by managers appointed by the state and given a certain amount of preferential treatment as a result.[146] The private firms resisted the intervention of the state and feared the erosion of private capitalism. The ministry constantly accused the private firms of 'business egoism' and gave less generous treatment in the provision of funds. The firms in return accused the ministry of back-door nationalization.[147] Because over half the industry was state-run traditional financial incentives were harder to apply. Much of the profit that was enjoyed by private firms in the west went back into Reich funds in Germany, and all expansion during the war in large production facilities was concentrated in the state-run sector at Goering's request.[148] Even after the Speer reforms there still existed in the aircraft industry a distrust of the state, and of the air ministry leadership in particular, reflecting the more general divorce between military and civilian life that was common to the Axis services. Severe bomb damage, coupled with long negotiations over compensation, and Hitler's demand for the destruction of industrial installations, although unfulfilled, created yet further economic and political difficulties for private aircraft manufacturers. During the critical early years of war when a fusion of capitalist and political elites was completed in the west, the Axis powers paid the penalty for rapid economic and technical advance within a more traditionalist political structure.

Aircraft production was vital to the waging of air warfare. This fact was demonstrated throughout the conflict from 1939 to 1945. That the economic potential of those countries that became allies against the fascist powers was very considerably greater than those of their enemies was also clear. It is much more difficult to explain why the Axis powers failed to mobilize productive resources as efficiently or as fully as their economic resources would allow or to the same extent as the Allied powers. The Allies' industrial and organizational problems were often as great, and in the case of the Soviet Union even greater. The crucial difference was in economic strategy and the timing of mobilization. The Allies were poorly prepared before hostilities and responded by a massive and swift mobilization: the Axis was relatively well prepared and failed to perceive the urgency to expand economic resources from an early enough date. The future organizational confusion and inefficiency was caused in part by the difficulties of changing strategy in mid-stream in an area as complex as aircraft production. To the extent that aircraft production was an economic race the late starter was hit in two ways. Not only was it difficult to catch up numerically with enemy production, but any additional production was likely to be eaten up

8

Science, Research and Intelligence

Behind the administrative and economic effort to train, equip and operate large air forces lay the widespread mobilization of the nations' intellectual resources. The need for such mobilization had increased in direct proportion to the increasingly technical nature of warfare. In air warfare the necessity was greatest of all for it was the point at which most areas of advanced scientific and engineering research coincided. In questions of engine power and efficiency, radio and signals equipment, explosives and armament, air forces made the greatest demands. In the most advanced weapons, in radar, rocketry, jet propulsion and nuclear research, the air forces were the first to express serious military interest and through active research made possible their diffusion to the other services. To sustain a high level of technological competence and innovation in the air war required the systematic involvement of the science community. It also required the diversion of large research funds and scientific and technical facilities because of the complexity of the air weapon. The intellectual effort could not be left to the services' own small engineering staffs, as the First World War had shown. The more widely civilian and industrial scientists were recruited for war work the more likely that scientific problems would be solved. Small-scale scientific support might produce a necessary breakthrough in a particular field, but what was more important for the air war was movement forward on a broad front of research, making use of what was immediately useful but also preparing the new generation of weapons and anticipating those of the enemy. This could only be guaranteed by the massive cover for scientific contingencies produced by a close alliance of the scientific and military elites. Science also had a contribution to make to the services' own intellectual endeavours in intelligence. Air intelligence consisted of two distinct parts. The first was intelligence for the use of air forces in making strategic and operational decisions. This was helped during the war by the development of scientific intelligence sections in the complicated areas of navigation and signals. The second was air intelligence gathered for the use of the armed forces as a whole through aerial reconnaissance. During the course of the war accurate photographic intelligence provided one of the most important sources on the enemy's preparations, while the denying of such evidence to the enemy became in itself an essential part of air force operations.

(i) Science and the Air War

The onset of war by no means initiated the involvement of science in military aviation. Advanced aeronautical research had continued throughout the inter-war period; the links between air forces and aeronautical researchers, though more developed in some countries than in others, were forged everywhere.[1] In Germany and Britain in particular the pace of air research and the degree of co-operation between science and the air force had both increased substantially during the course of the 1930s. The Tizard Committee for Air Defence established in 1934 made considerable strides in linking together soldiers, government scientists, administrators and the university scientific staff for air research and development in the period before 1939.[2] In Germany large-scale air research for military purposes was established for the first time by the new Luftwaffe, which was thus compelled to make use of scientific resources in the firms and universities, although it retained greater military control over air research than in Britain.[3]

Despite the recognition well before 1939 of the major role science would play in any future war involving air power, the most important step was to procure as much scientific effort for war as possible once hostilities had actually begun, and in this endeavour there emerged obvious contrasts. Although the British scientific establishment was smaller and less well-funded than its German equivalent it was recruited much more energetically for war. By 1939 a list of 5,000 leading scientists and engineers had been prepared for mobilization for war work in particular fields. On the outbreak of war those with scientific training were given reserved occupational status to avoid conscription of young scientists. A special Scientific Advisory Committee of the cabinet was established under Lord Hankey to help organize and distribute the scientific personnel and to begin a programme of training an additional scientific work force. Eventually over 50,000 were trained and sent to the service research departments and industry.[4] The efforts of those involved with scientific mobilization were supported by the Government and by the armed forces themselves. Churchill, although largely ignorant himself about science, professed a profound respect for what he called 'the Wizard War'. Influenced by his contact with Lindemann as his personal scientific and economic adviser, Churchill remained committed over the war years to involving science as fully as possible, and to help it escape from 'the prejudice of any one particular uniformed profession'.[5] The RAF in particular respected and co-operated with scientists, while many of the senior commanders had had previous experience in the directorates for research and development and thus understood its significance.[6]

The attitude of the German leadership towards science was more ambivalent. Although Goering had great interest in research and granted large funds to research institutes, his understanding of the role science played in war was rudimentary. Moreover the organization of science in Germany was played out against a political background that militated against the rational exploitation of scientific resources for war. It proved impossible to place responsibility for organizing science under one ministry or committee. The SS, the Education Ministry, the Goering administrative empire, and the individual services all had claims to reconcile while Hitler, who disliked fundamental research in favour of gadgetry, paid very little attention to employing science for war. Partly due to his belief that any war would be so short that science could not provide anything new within the required time, and partly due to his isolation from the party squabbles over research and its control, Hitler failed to take any basic interest in recruiting science for war until the obvious failure in this respect forced him to do so in 1944.[7] Where Churchill chose as his principal confidant a scientific adviser, Hitler chose to surround himself with astrologers.

There was an additional problem in Germany. Resistance to National Socialism had led to an emigration of scientific personnel in large numbers and to an internal struggle over Nazi intrusion into appointments and projected research. The emigration had a double disadvantage for Germany, for not only were many prominent scientists no longer willing to work for the German scientific effort under Hitler, but they were actively working for Allied governments. The internal conflicts sapped the energy of scientists who became involved both in resisting demotions and political appointments and in defending scientific theory against the attacks of 'Aryan science'. The growing disillusionment with research in the universities and institutes encouraged many scientists to move into the shelter of industrial research where they were able by choice to isolate themselves from the unfavourable working environment in which their colleagues still laboured against Nazi interference.[8] The result of the defensive attitude taken by German science was the promotion of those who professed an active support for the Party. Those placed in high office in the research institutes and the services were often promoted for political loyalty rather than academic merit.[9] Where this might not have affected the overall standards of research too much—and standards in Germany remained high throughout the war—it did affect the way in which scientific effort was organized and co-ordinated for war purposes. So poor was such co-ordination that a large number of scientists and engineers were conscripted for the armed forces and returned in only a piecemeal fashion towards the end of the war.[10] Only in 1944, on the basis of widespread criticism, particularly from those working in aeronautical research, did Germany produce a central research agency under Osenberg to co-ordinate the diffuse labours of the various research authorities. But by that date reform came far too late and largely in response to Hitler's demands for miracle weapons, echoed by Goering. The *Reichsforschungsrat,* the leading research authority directly under Goering, had 800 projects on hand in 1944 of which 70 per cent were in agriculture and forestry and only 3 per cent in physics.[11] From such a small and politically dominated base it was impossible to fulfil the demand made forcefully at the Academy for Aeronautical Research in 1943 'to utilize the full potentialities of universities and engineering schools'.[12]

The United States had a scientific tradition that was much more German in the sense that considerable effort had been devoted before 1939 to promoting widespread and well-funded research directed towards industry and the interests of pure science. But the United States also paralleled British initiatives in organizing science on a national scale and adapting that organization to the requirements of the armed forces. The National Advisory Committee for Aeronautics, founded during the First World War, acted as a springboard for the recruitment of science from industry and the universities. Its chairman, Dr. Vannevar Bush, became director of the Office of Scientific Research and Development which emerged as the national agency for scientific mobilization, while Bush and Compton, the director of the Massachusetts Institute of Technology, became the spokesman of science at a political level.[13] Roosevelt, like Churchill, did not need to be persuaded of the significance of science in war. Nor did the armed forces. In fact the way in which the military and scientific establishments came together was crucial to the use made of research potential in all the belligerent powers.

In both Britain and America the control exercised over research was shared fully between the services and the civilian agencies. Final decisions about weapons research and procurement rested with the political executive. At all levels the co-operation between the two sides was complete. Service members were invited to serve on the scientific administrative boards and scientists were given full access to the military committees. At a lower level the research centres and laboratories not directly controlled by the services were staffed with service liaison officers who were able to report requirements to the scientists and report back successes directly to the commanders.[14] A reciprocal arrangement operated with the forces at the front. In the air force in particular scientists and engineers were invited to the front in large numbers to observe weapons under combat conditions and to discuss with officers with combat experience tactical innovations that relied on science. This led in Britain to the introduction of Operational Research (OR), in which the scientists came to be involved closely in actual strategic and tactical decision-making on the basis of applying scientific statistical and analytical methods to operations.[15] This proved to be particularly vital for air warfare. OR was concentrated in the bombing war, with its demands for predictive analysis of the cost of operations as well as scientific analysis of results; and in radar work, particularly in anti-aircraft tactics and the Battle of the Atlantic. But under the encouragement of the air force commanders every Command in the RAF developed its own OR section which had equal status with the military.[16] In the United States, where the habit of adapting scientific and managerial methods was more typical, Operations Analysis groups provided the same service for the army and navy air forces.[17] Such close contact, even in areas traditionally reserved for the military establishment, repeated the situation in economics and in administration in which the American and British air forces were compelled to work within a strategic framework decided by civilians and soldiers together.

The reluctance of the Axis air forces to be subjected to control by civilians, or to be forced to co-operate with them was repeated in relations between science and the military in Germany and Japan. In Japan the military control over research was extensive and was fuelled to a considerable extent by rivalry between the army and navy, both of which built up separate research establishments whose secrets were jealously guarded. The Japanese military authorities distrusted many of those scientists with a western education and recruited far less widely from the universities than in the west.[18] There was thus little co-ordination of effort. So exaggerated did the secretiveness and rivalry become that both navy and army produced separate radar aids to the identification of friendly aircraft and were unable to distinguish each other's aircraft from those of the enemy.[19] In Germany the military similarly controlled large areas of research. For the Luftwaffe facilities were provided on the most generous scale under the protection of Goering who gradually drew all research in Germany under his loose jurisdiction.[20] On military matters the scientists were largely excluded. Certainly no operational research on the scale practised by the Allies was developed, nor were scientists allowed to sit on staff committees and contribute to tactical and strategic decisions. Engineers and scientists were discouraged from visiting the front and were not usually allowed to witness the testing of weapons on which they had worked, nor to match tactical experience with personal research programmes. Moreover the military pre-occupation with protocol led to the conscription of scientists for war work without military rank which automatically excluded them from the military decision-making process and made them subordinate to full officers.[21] The alternative recourse for scientists of appealing to the political over the military authority was not available in the Luftwaffe since the two authorities were the same.

In the western democracies scientific and military elites were able to reach mutual decisions as co-equals. In Germany science was the servant of the armed forces. If the Luftwaffe willingly exploited science, it did so only to the extent that the Luftwaffe staff believed desirable, thus reducing the intellectual resources for sound technical judgement to the research sub-section of the Air Ministry Technical Office. The extreme compartmentalization of function that denied scientists access to the working of the war itself, explained the apparent paradox of a country rich in research resources but unable to exploit the advantages that such riches bestowed. Nor was the Luftwaffe able to make up for the deficiencies of scientific organization by using industrial research facilities to the full, although most of the important and pioneering work on aircraft was undertaken at the firm institutes.[22] Here the problem was an unregulated flood of research from firms, anxious to promote their own designs at the expense of those of their rivals, competing for the attention of military technicians in the air ministry who were unequal to the task of sorting the necessary from the unnecessary research. The response of the military authorities, whose scientific competence was far below that of the industrial researchers they controlled, was to fluctuate between widespread proscription of all research in favour of immediate development and production targets, and the indiscriminate support of all projects in the hope that one might turn out to be a war-winning weapon.[23]

The experience of research in Germany, where large resources were diverted to science, emphasized the importance of organization in the mobilization of scientific efforts. For science there were particular organizational problems. The utilization of science for the war effort required a high degree of co-operation since much of the necessary research was co-operative in nature. Secondly science required, paradoxically, great operational freedom and close project supervision at the same time.[24] The first point was made obvious through relations between science, the air forces and industry. In jet research for example too much service control in Britain and too much industrial freedom in Germany postponed the emergence of a satisfactory jet aircraft. Though years behind in jet research, the American co-operative effort between air force, academic and industrial research produced a jet aircraft in a considerably shorter time than the European pioneers. In the west a high level of co-operation was the result of a greater degree of homogeneity in professional life. Although there were numerous conflicts of scientific opinion, scientists, managers and soldiers co-operated freely as equals in reaching technical decisions. In Japan and Germany even where a willingness to co-operate existed professional or social exclusiveness often placed barriers in the way.

Co-operation in science itself, as distinct from organizational co-operation,

189

was even more important. In order to advance as rapidly as possible on a broad technological front it was necessary not only to have access to the work and results of other native scientists but to be able to tap sources of discovery abroad. Before the outbreak of war aeronautics was an international discipline. Speed, height and range records passed rapidly from country to country as the common stock of knowledge was refined or advanced through particular breakthroughs.[25] In aero-engine design in particular the achievements of British and American engineers were widely imitated. In high-speed aircraft design German and Italian designers remained in the forefront, until their ideas became common currency. Japan and Russia drew fully on American and German design experience; Germany and Russia collaborated on aircraft work during the 1920s; the 'secret' Luftwaffe acquired crucial supplies from Britain and the United States in the early years of concealed expansion.[26] Although the major industrial powers were all capable on their own of making substantial advances in air technology, the speed with which such technology changed in the 1930s was a reflection of a pooling of theory and experimentation.

On the outbreak of war international scientific co-operation broke down. Although it was possible to copy captured technology, the Axis powers were thrown back upon their own resources. For Japan, whose aircraft industry was based very largely on imitation, it made it very difficult to reduce what was in effect a considerable technical gap between native and western air technology.[27] Nor was there any effective co-operation between the fascist allies. Germany refused to pass over to the Japanese or Italians the advanced weapons technology that the latter lacked. Only in the face of imminent defeat did Germany dispatch blueprints on the best weapons, including jet research, to the Japanese who were unable in the short time demanded to make use of them.[28] Germany, too, was cut off from the scientific world abroad. Many of the research facilities of Europe were removed by scientists fleeing to Britain or America in the face of invasion. German technical espionage abroad was ineffective. In sharp contrast the degree of co-operation agreed between the Allies was very much greater. For Russia this was of particular significance. Since the Soviet aircraft industry was considerably behind the technical level achieved in Britain and America, the onset of Lend-Lease, which involved advanced war material as well as scientific and technical advice, drew Russia closer to the threshold of aircraft technology.[29] Despite the political difficulties involved a wealth of secret information was passed between Britain and the United States in every area of air technology. This meant in effect that the Allies were able to draw on the intellectual scientific resources of most of the non-fascist world, including the scientists who had fled from Europe.[30] Moreover resistance to German occupation, or to Nazism in Germany itself caused a considerable amount of scientific intelligence to pass into Allied hands. Such intelligence confirmed that the Allies had indeed established a broad technical lead through the widespread application of science to war.[31] Under such circumstances Germany was unable to compete. The technical lead enjoyed by the German air force before 1939 could not be maintained; not just because it was squandered, but because German scientists were forced to work from a much narrower research base than the Allies.

The second organizational requirement, for operational flexibility combined with close supervision of research and development, was a need necessary both to science itself and to the effective organization of science for war. Science relied on being given the maximum freedom in formulating the problems to be solved and producing the appropriate experimental and research conditions for solving them. Scientific advance could not be carried out to order, particularly military order, for where airmen tended to see weapons technology as fixed at any one time, it was the scientists' task to ensure that it was not.[32] In very few instances did airmen fail to grasp the importance of giving researchers the freedom to undertake pure research without military interference. But there also existed dangers in allowing scientists too much freedom. While fundamental theoretical research was very necessary, it was essential to maintain a balance between general research and the specific requirements of war. One danger was the duplication of effort. Only a central control over research could prevent a number of different centres from working separately on the same object. In Japan and Germany the general lack of co-ordinated central direction coupled with the failure to adequately break down barriers between the researchers and the services, led to a situation in which the same research was being carried out in air force establishments, universities and firms, in many cases unknown to each other.[33] Another danger lay in the encouragement of too much long-term research, in which many scientists were more interested, at the expense of the short-term military need. To avoid both these dangers the answer was to create a satisfactory selection procedure and adequate development facilities in order to extract as much as possible from the research effort in terms of current needs and future prospects.

(ii) Research, Development and the Quality of Weapons

The quality of weapons depended not only on the available technology but on the way in which weapons were developed, tested and chosen. The selection procedure was a crucial factor governing the use of science. There were a number of determinants. Strategy itself affected questions of quality. In Germany, for example, the belief in a short war in both 1940 and again in 1941 led to development stoppages in order to concentrate all efforts on the production and engineering problems of immediate usefulness.[34] On the Allied side a resolute acceptance of a large-scale bombing capability led to an emphasis on bombing technology and large aircraft development. A second determinant was knowledge of what the enemy was doing. In Britain and the United States it was assumed from the outset that German science would be equal to the achievements in the west and that there were few 'safe' areas of research in which it could be expected that neither side would concentrate its efforts. By contrast the German military leadership considered that in a number of important fields Germany had a measurable lead—including radar and nuclear research—and that the effort in those areas could be relaxed in favour of areas where there was less confidence of superiority.[35] Finally, quality was influenced by particular scientific and engineering traditions. Where there was a greater emphasis on pure research, as in the USSR and Germany, the onus was placed on the engineering staffs to turn the theory into workable weapons; where the tradition was more empirical, as in Britain and America, workable devices were produced even in advance of the theory. The cavity magnetron, which made possible the creation of centimetric radar, was constructed with a great deal of laboratory improvization but why it worked was not fully understood until later in the war.[36] In war this distinction between inventive and innovatory traditions, between pure and applied research, was very important. Where German scientists knew of the possibilities they lacked the facilities to experiment, or in many cases regarded experimentation as a less prestigious occupation fit to be left to the service engineers. Yet it was the ability to turn scientific discoveries, even in an unperfected form, quickly into devices for the front that counted in war.

All air forces were aware of the question of quality although reactions to it differed according to strategic priorities and research possibilities. In the USSR the need to maintain production continuity kept innovation to a minimum. Only under the more favourable production circumstances of the last years of war was it possible to introduce new types and to concentrate more energy on qualitative improvement.[37] To some extent the same decision was reached in Britain and America in the early stages of war. In 1940 current needs were emphasized by Beaverbrook at MAP at the expense of future developments. Efforts were concentrated on five 'preferred types' and development cut back to cover only the most urgent projects.[38] In the United States the call to expand aircraft output considerably in 1940 lead Arnold to insist that priority be given to aircraft to be delivered 'within the next 6 months, or a year' and to announce to Marshall that 'every effort was being made to . . . defer our present research and development'.[39] In both cases the deferment was a temporary response to the strategic situation. As soon as it became feasible both the RAF and the AAF returned to what was regarded as a proper balance between research and current needs, between quality and quantity. Lovett in the War Department insisted on 'all possible speed on advance research and experimentation' in overruling Arnold's earlier directives. By the spring of 1941 MAP restored suspended projects and re-established the usual priority for research and development projects.[40] The German development stoppages of 1940 and 1941 differed from those of the Allies. They were not in order to meet an urgent need, but precisely because such a need was lacking. Believing that the war would be won with the weapons in hand Hitler ordered a restriction on any development work that would not be of immediate use including radar and jet aircraft. The restrictions were also designed to restrain the aircraft firms from undertaking too much unscheduled research at the expense of production, although its effect was to encourage such work to continue in secret.[41] The problem in Germany was that there existed no satisfactory alternative once the development ban was lifted again.

The selection process in the Luftwaffe was weakened by a number of factors. The first was the complex problem of timetabling. The difficulty in gauging how long a new design took to develop was common to all air forces. In the Luftwaffe neither Udet nor Goering, who were responsible for such decisions, understood either the pace of technological change, or the importance of long-term technical planning. Udet persistently postponed taking what he regarded as difficult political and technical decisions on replacement technology and finally committed suicide in 1941 at the time when it had become obvious that in almost every field the planned replacement had not been properly developed.[42] Hitler and Goering had an equally optimistic view on the length of time involved in the development of air weapons. Moreover in his anxiety to retain Hitler's favour, Goering promised new weapons well in advance of their actual development time and then tried to speed up the timetable to the point of undermining the project altogether.[43] To some extent this was a result of Hitler's own search for secret or 'wonder' weapons and his way of dealing with those researchers whom he regarded as malingerers. This encouraged the random selection of projects that appealed to Hitler's weapons mentality. It discouraged other researchers from making known novel weapons research in case Hitler should take up their cause and berate them for subsequent delays or promises unfulfilled.[44] This was true for the German aircraft firms as well. In efforts to get contracts and find favour with Goering, performances were promised and schedules agreed that often bore little relation to reality while Goering lacked the technical competence or a satisfactory selection organization for seeing this in advance.[45] In the end it was an industrial engineer, Robert Lusser from Heinkel, who, in a widely publicized report in 1942 explained to the RLM that the development work on all aircraft types took at least five years and sometimes longer, and that efforts to speed the process up only led to greater difficulties at the production stage and in operations.[46] Only in 1942, under the guidance of Milch, did the Luftwaffe finally acknowledge that it was not possible to introduce any new aircraft types that would substantially improve current performance until 1945 or 1946. Another problem with the Luftwaffe selection process was the lack of effective supervision over research designed to bridge the gap between pure and applied traditions. There was too little emphasis on actual development and testing, and too small and unskilled a technical workforce in the ministry to decide on what research could be satisfactorily turned into end products and what could not. Had the selection process been more co-ordinated with civilian experts and brought to the highest administrative levels in a well-organized way Germany might well have possessed a range of jet-powered aircraft considerably superior in performance to Allied aircraft by 1942–43.

In America and Britain great emphasis was given to turning research into weapons quickly. This was often at the expense of pure or long-term research as the American experience with jet aircraft demonstrated. The establishment by the War Department of the New Developments Division in 1943 was intended to restore the balance between pure and applied weapons research.[47] The selection process in both Britain and America was closely supervised by a wide range of competent military and academic committees. In the British case development was carried on through the closest co-operation between researchers and airmen. At the Telecommunications Research Establishment almost all the projects were turned into operational products because those that would clearly produce no useful results were rejected before research time was wasted on them.[48] Under such circumstances some lines of research were sacrificed that had a future significance, but against such disadvantages could be laid the fact of the close co-ordination and supervision of research for application to anticipated air force needs. On the question of timetabling development MAP took a conservative position. On the assumption that small aircraft took over five years to develop, and large aircraft eight years it was seen from the outset that very few new aircraft could be developed for the war in hand.[49] Only the Mosquito bomber disproved the contention that new aircraft would take time to develop and that it was better under such circumstances to encourage the improvement of existing types.[50] The same decision was reached in the United States. Modification was preferred to invention as it promised faster results. That such a decision should be taken also reflected an important point about the particular technical threshold at which aeronautics had arrived.

By the end of the 1930s it was apparent that the piston-engined monoplane was nearing the end of its technical development. All the advanced economic and technical powers were approaching this end at rates that differed only by small margins. There only remained improvements to be made in engine capacity, metallurgy, radio equipment, navigation aids and armament. It was precisely in these areas that the policy of modification to improve quality was implemented, first by the Allies and then, with great haste, by Germany.[51] The only possibility of a radical departure in aircraft technology lay in the discovery of a new source of engine power and in bombs of a higher level of destructiveness. Both these possibilities were being explored for the first time in the years just before the outbreak of war, but neither was advanced enough in development to contribute to the kind of air warfare both sides expected to be waging in 1939. When war broke out the Luftwaffe enjoyed a marginal lead in air technology of a conventional kind. The difficulties of mobilizing scientific and research efforts sufficiently, the lack of urgency in the early years of war and the search for a new generation of conventional aircraft whose performance turned out to be no better than the aircraft already in use reduced that lead and finally in the course of 1942 and 1943 lost it altogether to the western Allies. The British and American air forces had concentrated research efforts at what were seen to be critical points: engine power, armament, radio and radar equipment.[52] This research produced by the middle of the war aircraft capable of a much further range, greater load capacity, better navigation and higher speeds. From 1942 the Luftwaffe too began to concentrate on the weapons already in use and to modify them in the same way as the Allies, with considerable success. But being forced back onto the defensive in 1943 the Luftwaffe was compelled to gear research and development much more to the initiatives of the Allies. Radar and radio aids for night-fighters, better armament for attacking the heavy bombers, fighters with a greater ceiling (to be able to reach the Mosquito bombers) were all defensive responses. Moreover they elicited in turn an offensive response from the Allies' own research stations. Even the jet aircraft which finally came into production in 1944 was ordered by Hitler to act as a fighter-bomber rather than a fighter in a vain attempt to halt the bombing by a renewed threat of German retaliation. Even if Germany was not far behind, the important point was that German technology was now following, not leading.

The other alternative facing the Luftwaffe was to develop new kinds of weapons altogether. Yet here again poor strategic planning from the top, coupled with the difficulties in mobilizing science led to long delays. Moreover the arbitrary way in which Hitler gave preference to some projects and not to others made it uncertain that the most strategically useful research would be promoted above the rest. The attitude of the German leadership to the prospect of atomic weapons was sceptical. Hitler doubted whether such a weapon would be completed during the war he planned and the scientific and military establishment were generally agreed that German research was so in advance of the Allies in this area that there was no danger of such weapons being produced by the enemy during the war either.[53] But with rocket and pilotless aircraft technology Hitler and Goering found a weapon of such apparent novelty and with great terroristic potential that it was given the highest priority once Hitler became aware of its value. Yet Hitler's enthusiasm showed his failure to evaluate projects within a wider strategic context. General Dornberger, who had led the research team working on rockets, told Hitler that the rockets were of a very limited use, that they were not accurate and, carrying only a ton of explosives, had a destructive power much less than that of a heavy bomber. He calculated that the rocket Hitler required, capable of carrying a ten-ton warhead, would take a further five years of research and a rocket fuel which had not yet been developed.[54] The same problem emerged with jet development in Germany. The RLM showed little enthusiasm for the project which was not expected to yield results within the span of the current war. Yet when Hitler discovered the potential of the project he assumed a personal responsibility for it to ensure that there would be no more delays. His policy of speeding up the development programme and of penalizing those who stood in the way of innovation had the opposite effect to the one he wanted, bringing into service aircraft that were insufficiently developed while demoralizing those whose research abilities were needed to complete development.[55]

There were similar misjudgements on the Allies' side. Yet the massing of research and development at the critical areas within a selection process that was responsible for sorting the strategically desirable from all that was theoretically possible, produced sufficient technological momentum to produce a balance between the development of current types and the production of novel weapons. British evaluation of the atomic bomb research in 1940 produced the conclusion that a satisfactory device could be produced before the end of the war.[56] American scientists and soldiers reached the same conclusion. Stimson later wrote that 'It was our common objective, throughout the war to be the first to produce an atomic weapon and use it. . . . The entire purpose was the production of a military weapon.'[57] Nor were the Allies far behind Germany in jet research. The jet engine had been promoted by the Air Ministry in Britain from the mid-1930s. It gained a priority in the middle of 1941 when it was realized that jet aircraft might be used towards the end of a war fought with otherwise conventional air weapons.[58] Although inferior to the German Me 262, the British Meteor jet fighter became operational against V1 weapons in the middle of 1944. Only the realization that German research was not as advanced as had been at first feared, slowed up the pace of development as research resources were diverted elsewhere. In January 1945 MAP finally gave jet aircraft overriding priority with a demand for 'as many high quality jet aircraft as quickly as is humanly possible'; but this was for the sake of defence in peacetime rather than war against Germany or Japan.[59]

Only in rocket technology was there a lag with German research. In this case it had been correctly judged that rockets would not have a sufficient strategic return for the research effort involved except in the case of aircraft mounted rocket armament.[60] The lead taken by German long-range rocket research was thus of little strategic value and leads which might have existed elsewhere were squandered through poor strategic appreciation. In Japan there was also evidence of poor project selection, although the problem for Japan was a general backwardness in research which it was difficult to make up during the war under conditions of isolation. The lack of a satisfactory evaluative machinery led for example to the diversion of considerable resources to the search for a 'death ray'; a search that western powers had abandoned in the 1930s. By the end of the war the Japanese 'ray' could kill a rabbit after five minutes at a distance of 1,000 yards.[61] Even without such self-inflicted waste of resources, there had been little chance that the Axis powers would be able to produce or use the secret weapons popularly feared in the west. Instead massive scientific mobilization, combined with a close alliance between military and scientific elites, gave the Allies the opportunity for eroding what technical gaps still existed between the sides in 1939 and of extending those technical leads already enjoyed.

(iii) Intelligence and the Air War

Science also had a major contribution to make to the whole area of air intelligence. This contribution increased in importance as the war progressed when air forces explored the war effort for resources to help in their own intelligence work. Air intelligence consisted of a number of very distinct areas. On the one hand the collection of information about enemy air forces; on the other intelligence efforts to improve air force operational efficiency through operational research and the application of scientific intelligence to navigation signals and radar. Aircraft were also used for intelligence work for the armed forces as a whole, particularly in photo-reconnaissance work.

The ordinary work of air intelligence required little elaborate organization until it became necessary to know more about the advanced weapons being produced on either side. It was even possible for the United States air force to have no intelligence department of its own at all until 1940 when Arnold's bid to give greater autonomy to the Air Corps uncovered the hitherto poor intelligence provided on air matters by the G2 office of the War Department.[62] The German air intelligence sector dated from the early 1920s and was taken over from the army when Goering assumed command of the Luftwaffe. Its main task was to evaluate foreign air forces and to prepare target folders for air attacks on potential enemy military and economic targets. Until 1939 the work was done satisfactorily, and throughout the war the section dealing with foreign air forces provided good and prompt reports of new aircraft in service with enemy air forces.[63] Air intelligence in Britain had a similar pedigree, though in the reorganization of intelligence services in the mid-1930s intelligence was given a more senior position than its German equivalent. In 1935 a Deputy Directorate of Intelligence was formed within the Directorate of Operations and Intelligence, and on the outbreak of war it achieved the status of a full directorate in its own right. In the second period of organizational change in the winter of 1941 air intelligence was again enlarged and its status increased when the Director of Intelligence became an Assistant Chief of Air Staff.[64] The expansion of the intelligence sector to include a scientific section was carried out at the same time. The main tasks of British air intelligence in collecting information on foreign air forces and operations improved considerably with the re-organization, while contacts with the operational commands ensured that any information of import-ance would be disseminated quickly to the air force units.[65] One problem that German intelligence suffered from was the difficulty of getting its results broadcast where they were needed. This was not just because it lacked sufficient authority within the air force structure but because of the attitude of Goering to the information he received. The final head of Luftwaffe intelligence reported that the Luftwaffe high command 'did not take the ... service seriously' and 'produced their own judgement of the enemy'.[66] Goering's excessive optimism and lack of critical understanding led him to question the reports of his intelligence branch, particularly when they gave information that he did not want to hear. Intelligence situation reports became christened 'lie reports' and their findings neglected.[67] The uncovering of the Rote Kapelle spy ring in 1942 with its contacts in Luftwaffe intelligence destroyed the leadership's confidence in its integrity.[68] This was a difficulty any air force in defeat was bound to face. Having to present the description of that defeat to Goering or Hitler encouraged over-optimism and a lack of realism in intelligence assessments, and made them far less useful to German air commands than they might have been.

The effects of such intelligence judgements on the war itself were often of considerable importance. Overall strategy was, for example, dependent on an assessment of what an enemy was producing and hence what an enemy air force would be operationally capable of. Before the outbreak of war the tendency was for German production and strength to be exaggerated by the western Allies. This spurred on efforts to greater rearmament than might otherwise have been undertaken. Actual figures of production during the 1930s were known with some accuracy, but the growing fear of Germany also fuelled less critical and exaggerated claims about German air strength.[69] Even air intelligence overestimated the number of aircraft Germany would produce under war conditions, and consequently exaggerated the degree of reserves available for the Luftwaffe.[70] On the other hand German air intelligence underestimated the potential strength of the western allies. Information on the French air force was accurate enough. The main miscalculation involved the strength and effectiveness of the RAF. The result was the poor intelligence available for the Battle of Britain. Not only was British aircraft production substantially miscalculated, but the degree of destruction wrought on the RAF was widely and wishfully exaggerated (as were British claims about the Luftwaffe). False intelligence claims contributed on several occasions during 1940 to the short-lived belief that the RAF had been defeated.[71]

This initial failure began the long process of undermining the credibility of German air intelligence with the German military and political leadership. The same happened with the attack on the USSR and the entry of the United States into the war. In the first case the general Luftwaffe view that the Russian air force was weak, poorly organized and composed largely of obsolete aircraft although correct in some respects was in its overall judgement of the Red Air Force misleading. Yet it was on the basis of such information that Hitler expected a short campaign and that Goering believed the Russian air forces to be defeated within the first three weeks of the German attack. The advice of the German air attaché in Moscow, Aschenbrenner, was overlooked because it contradicted the view maintained by Luftwaffe intelligence and supported uncritically by Goering.[72] The same mistake was made about the United States. Goering's public expression of contempt for the American economy was matched by intelligence reports from the Luftwaffe that America could only produce at the most 16,000 aircraft in the first year of war. In fact over 47,000 were produced, helping to lay the foundation of Allied superiority in the air over the Axis powers.[73] The same mistake was made by the Japanese in estimating American potential. The Axis decision to go to war with the United States, though made separately, was strongly influenced by a joint misconception about Allied potential strength. As the war progressed the obvious contrast between Axis assessment and military reality led to a reversal of judgement. German intelligence began to overestimate Allied strength in 1944, having very little information on which to base such assessments except for an espionage source in Stockholm, while Allied intelligence, impressed by the effects claimed by the Combined Bomber Offensive, began to underestimate German production throughout 1944.[74] By this stage the discussion was largely academic. Both sides knew that there existed a wide disparity of numbers while Allied intelligence knew that German production even under the 'Fighter Staff' was still numerically insufficient to materially affect the issue.

For Britain and the United States conventional intelligence was used in the conduct of the bombing offensive. Intelligence was used to assess the effect of attacks, to select targets and to estimate the degree of effort required on particular operations.[75] In all three areas scientific intelligence, which was much more developed and influential than its German counterpart, was used to reach a judgement. In some cases scientific solutions, such as the use of proper navigational aids, had a considerable effect on the success of operations. In other areas conventional counter-intelligence was used, with particularly good effect in the diversion of V-weapon attacks from London.[76] The gathering of satisfactory intelligence on bomb damage had a considerable impact on the course of the bombing campaign. In 1941 photo-reconnaissance evidence confirmed that accurate bombing was a myth. The shift to area bombing that followed called for rather different forms of intelligence on the impact on German morale. Evidence such as there was was conflicting. A comprehensive picture of the impact of bomb damage was begun in 1943 with Operational Research assessments of bombing campaigns in North Africa and the attack on Italy, and the subsequent diversion of bombing to targets for 'Overlord' followed by a precise target attack on oil and communications resulted from the conclusions of OR that morale was too diffuse and unsystematic a target.[77] To the end of the war in Europe, however, Bomber Command placed too much faith in an intuitive assessment of likely bomb effect and continued to area bomb at night. After the war the bombing surveys confirmed that the more conservative analysis of the effects of bombing by Allied intelligence had been justified. On the Axis side, however, fear of bombing was partly a product of ignorance of Allied intentions. Intelligence on the Combined Offensive, and on the later B-29 bombing of Japan, was slight and although it improved in Germany with the capture of airmen and the reclamation of damaged Allied bombers, intelligence information was never sufficient to predict major shifts in tactics or strategy, to prepare for technical innovations in advance, or even to fully prepare for attacks on the vulnerable points of the economy.[78]

The increasing difficulties facing German intelligence stemmed from the same isolation from which scientific research suffered. Good intelligence information could only be obtained by espionage and in this respect German efforts were persistently thwarted. German spies in Russia and America provided little and were uncovered with relative ease. The development of a good counter-intelligence network by the British provided a stream of misinformation on air affairs throughout the war.[79] Knowledge on Russia was particularly hard to obtain. Before the war Soviet isolation proved almost impossible for German sources to penetrate. Once the Nazi-Soviet pact had been concluded Hitler ordered that all espionage against the Soviet Union cease altogether including photo-reconnaissance, almost the only source of information. When the ban was lifted again a year later it was too late to begin the process of infiltration, and air intelligence remained largely in ignorance of the state of the Russian air force.[80] Russian successes in Germany and occupied Europe were by contrast impressive. Knowledge of German air force secrets was fed by the Rote Kapelle spy ring, whose key figure, Schulze-Boysen, was an intelligence officer on Goering's staff. Over 500 confidential reports were sent to Moscow from this source alone, including up-to-date technical information on Luftwaffe developments in aircraft and weapons.[81] British espionage also provided valuable information, particularly on radar and secret weapons development. It proved much easier to recruit committed anti-fascists in Europe for espionage work than for fascism to recruit its very limited band of supporters abroad.[82] Air intelligence in the Luftwaffe was not unaware of the shortcomings. In 1944 its chief complained about staffing problems. Not only were there too few officers for all the intelligence tasks required, many of them were retired soldiers brought back into service because they spoke a foreign language and not because they had experience of intelligence work. Moreover relations between Luftwaffe intelligence and the air branch of the Abwehr, whose responsibility it was to actually procure information abroad, were poor for much of the war.[83] Allied intelligence services were certainly not free of inter-departmental rivalry, but air intelligence as a whole was given greater prominence in the decision-making process and brought civilian and military intelligence resources together more fully than in Germany. This was particularly the case in the vital area of de-coding in which Allied successes against Luftwaffe cryptography added another important dimension to intelligence knowledge of enemy intentions. This was a source largely denied to the German forces except on the eastern front.[84]

Another problem confronting the Axis powers was the deteriorating returns from photo-reconnaissance intelligence. In the Far East such intelligence had been satisfactory enough for the preliminary stages of war preparation, but the rapid deterioration of Japanese air power and the failure to develop reconnaissance aircraft of sufficient speed or height made it difficult to acquire not only long-range strategic information but even tactical information about American intentions.[85] For Germany the acquisition of tactical photographic information was highly developed by the outbreak of war and remained so throughout the war. The need of the army for rapid and decentralized information on battlefield movements was the main task of German photographic intelligence.[86] Strategic intelligence from photographic reconnaissance was much less well developed, and over the course of the war seriously declined, particularly in the west. One reason lay with the nature of German strategy with its concentration on tactical air forces for immediate support of ground troops. The photographic intelligence units were decentralized in order to provide information readily for each small army unit. There was little experience of centralized investigation of photographic evidence, nor was a top-level organization for extracting and disseminating photographic intelligence built up. The personnel involved were low-ranking and were trained more as photo-readers than as interpreters.[87] Moreover the Luftwaffe insistence on the use of armed reconnaissance aircraft, capable of fighting for photographic intelligence, a legacy of battlefield experience, led to increasing difficulties as older, converted bomber types were forced to combat with advanced Allied fighter aircraft.

There were technical problems too. German cameras could not be loaded into small, fast aircraft, a fact which discouraged the Luftwaffe yet further from innovation in strategic reconnaissance. In the Mediterranean the attempt to achieve great height as a protection by pressurizing older Ju 86 civil aircraft failed at almost the first attempt because of new British developments in high altitude fighters.[88] Another technical problem facing German reconnaissance was the existence of good radar on the part of the Allies, a fact that also contributed to the decline of Japanese reconnaissance efforts. It was impossible to escape detection by enemy defences. Even low-flying sorties could be detected from the middle of the war with the new centimetric radar. The situation by 1942 had reached the point where Axis photographic information on strategic preparations in the Middle East was almost non-existent, and for the final invasion of Europe in 1944 it was confined only to those photographic sorties permitted by the RAF for deception purposes.[89] Only the introduction of a limited number of the new Arado 234 jet aircraft improved strategic reconnaissance, but far too late to overcome the element of surprise achieved by the Allies in most operations from late 1942.[90]

The Allied experience was almost exactly the reverse. In Britain photographic intelligence had been poorly prepared. The Blenheim aircraft designed for the purpose was intended to act as a combat reconnaissance aircraft for which it was clearly inadequate; camera equipment was, by German standards, technically backward; and there was no satisfactory organization for relaying tactical photographic intelligence to the army units under combat conditions.[91] Improvements came about because of strategic circumstances. After the fall of France photo-reconnaissance was the only way of getting information quickly on German intentions. It was also the only way of providing pre- and post-operational intelligence on bombing. It was in this enterprise that the strategic importance of photo-reconnaissance was recognized from an early date. The Battle of France also brought about tactical changes. During May 1940 the decision was made to abandon the fighting reconnaissance tactic and to adopt the practice already demonstrated by the ad hoc Photographic Development Unit of using high-altitude and speed as ways of evading German defence. Spitfires were modified for such work, long-range was added by using additional fuel tanks, and virtual immunity for strategic photographic reconnaissance achieved for the crucial war period from summer 1940 until the summer of 1944.[92] More important the intelligence thus acquired was interpreted and disseminated through higher echelon intelligence agencies which were in turn integrated into the wider intelligence system.[93] Tactical air reconnaissance similarly improved for the Allies through better communication and equipment, and more advanced camera technology due to the recruitment of the American optical industry.[94] The armed forces in general came to expect a high level of photographic intelligence for almost all operational preparation.

(iv) Scientific Intelligence

The greatest contrast between the intelligence efforts of the two sides lay, however, in the degree to which science was utilized for intelligence purposes. This was not universally the case. Russian radar remained below the standards of German radar, and low-level tactical radio intelligence was readily accessible on the eastern front to both sides.[95] But in the west and in the far eastern war great emphasis was placed on radar and radio both for intelligence and for successful air operations. To some extent the difference in emphasis was based on strategic needs. The critical area for scientific intelligence in Britain in the early years of preparation and war was satisfactory aerial defence, with a good early warning system for short-term intelligence purposes. Later, with the onset of the bombing offensives, it became necessary to use radar and radio aids as means of confusing the intelligence effort of the enemy as well as for improving navigation and bombing accuracy.

In 1940 the gap in research was not as wide as British intelligence at first believed. The difference lay in how radar was used. German strategy emphasized a flexible radar use for battlefield intelligence and the appropriate technology was produced for accurate prediction of range and speed, though not altitude, of attacking aircraft. There also existed a small chain of radar stations on the north German coast for warning against British attacks.[96] Had the situation been reversed in 1940 and the battle been fought over Germany instead of Britain, radar would have provided ample advance warning for the Luftwaffe as it did for the RAF. Nevertheless the main weight of German radar research was for use with the army at the battlefront and only secondarily for defence purposes. The lack of a sustained bombing offensive also reduced the urgency of radar research. There were other contrasts as well. Where in Germany the Luftwaffe signals section had the main task of undertaking research and scientific intelligence tasks in the Luftwaffe with little outside contact, the British and American radar and radio effort was one of the first to be brought into the civilian scientific war effort as fully as possible.[97] University, service and industrial resources were used to the full to solve particular problems as they arose and to anticipate the next steps to be attempted by the enemy in the radio war. The German effort lacked the same urgency, in fact Hitler proscribed further research in 1940, and the poor recruitment of science in areas regarded as less essential led to a particular shortage of radio scientists and engineers.[98] With the onset of the bombing offensive, though not before, it became apparent that German radar was caught in a position of permanent inferiority given the current state of radio technology. Every attempt to combat Allied radar and radio was in response to initiatives undertaken by the Allies who were all the time in the process of developing yet more sophisticated means of identification or deception. In fact the most successful period of German night-fighting came in the winter of 1943-44 when the Luftwaffe gave up producing its own radio novelties and used those of the enemy for accurate interception.[99] The late development of centimetric radar sets, which was abandoned early in the war as impossible to achieve practically within the likely duration of hostilities, did close the gap rapidly again between German and Allied radio technology, but they were developed only by late 1944 when the problem was an insufficiency of aircraft in which to mount them.[100] By that year air superiority had been largely achieved. In preparation for 'Overlord' even the radar network that the Germans possessed in France proved inoperable because the precision attacks on coastal stations by the RAF of such accuracy and comprehensiveness that the invasion remained concealed until the arrival at the Normandy beaches. Moreover the improvements made on the German side in centralized reception and dissemination of radio information that had been lacking at the beginning of the war were frequently overwhelmed by the sheer diversity of intelligence methods devised to black out defensive radar, jam radio communications and obscure the actual bombing target.[101] When the same methods were tried by the AAF against Japan, Japanese radar, which was technically much more underdeveloped, was unable to cope and anti-aircraft crews were forced to rely on chance searchlight interceptions in the absence of effective gun-laying radar.[102] The pace of the radio war had developed so rapidly during the war, and had required so great a concentration of effort, that the weapons available to the Allied bombers were as distant from the weapons of 1940, with which the Japanese were still armed, as those of 1940 had been from the First World War.

To some extent the intellectual effort of the air war, like the economic effort, was a question of resources. The complex and expensive new technology with which the air war was fought could no longer be produced in small workshops by enthusiastic aircraft engineers but required large government-sponsored teams of researchers with the most up-to-date scientific and engineering facilities. Some of the belligerent powers were therefore excluded *a priori* from competing effectively in the scientific race. Germany was by no means one of these. Generously endowed with scientific resources, both material and human, and with a lead in theoretical physics in a number of areas important to air warfare, the possibility appeared to exist that the lack of quantity of German aircraft could be adequately compensated for by a large marginal advantage in quality. That this failed to be the case was due partly to the circumstances of war—the isolation of the science community, the differences between offensive and defensive strategies for science; but it was due more to strategic miscalculation, military inflexibility and the widespread intervention of fascist politics, both grand and petty, which reduced the willingness of the scientific community to work for German victory or demoralized those in research or intelligence who were committted to doing so. In many areas to do with research it was not simply Nazi misjudgements that affected the overall degree of intellectual mobilization, but also the dominant place that the military enjoyed in the making of war. Such dominance required, for example, thorough direction over research, the integration of PR units with the army, and the recruitment for the front of skilled radio technicians needed by the intelligence services. Such inflexibility made it difficult to establish the same degree of contact and co-operation between academics, administrators and soldiers as was enjoyed in all the Allied powers. The peculiar organizational and political structure of Nazism, which discouraged centralization and reduced areas of useful co-operation was the final factor in explaining the low level of mobilization in Germany of the one other resource, besides the Prussian tradition, of which the Nazi leadership might have made use in planning and executing aggressive war. This is not to detract from the scientific achievements of the Allies which were in themselves considerable. The contrast presented by the close co-operation of military and civilian experts in operational research, scientific intelligence and technical development in Britain and the United States showed what could be achieved, even by the slow starter, provided intellectual resources were properly used; and provided the organization was flexible enough to allow scientists and engineers to give advice, without restraint, not only to the commanders in battle, but to the politicians who directed the war.

9

Conclusions

Aircraft did not replace navies and armies during the Second World War. Although the use to which aircraft were put expanded and matured during the war years, the fact remained that successful warfare still depended upon the movement of armies to occupy land, and the movement of ships to provide supplies and men. Aircraft made such endeavours more secure and more expeditious but they did not, as some feared, make them obsolete. Indeed the popular expectations of air warfare, shared to some extent by uncritical soldiers and politicians, were rapidly disillusioned. Britain still depended decisively on her maritime and trading strength, even if aircraft were needed to safeguard it. The great land armies of Europe were the instruments of victory for the Germans from 1939–41, for the Russians after 1942, using aircraft as one element in an extensive armoury. Nevertheless air power became in a number of theatres the component without which the military machine could not be made to work. In the war in the Far East aircraft decided sea battles, symbolized in the Battle of the Coral Sea in which not a naval gun was fired though great losses were sustained from air attack on both sides. In the western European theatre the bombing offensive, whether used for tactical purposes or against strategic targets in Germany, created the conditions necessary for the transition for the Allies from defensive to offensive strategy. At the same time it forced the German forces, as it was designed to do, to a defensive position in the west through which it became increasingly difficult to regain the initiative. Yet in all these enterprises the air force conformed to the general ambition of the forces as a whole. The central goal of defeating the enemy forces and destroying the will to resist could be achieved only by combined operations. An autonomous air strategy was only possible with the nuclear technology made available in the last days of the Pacific war.

There was, however, a distinction between the role of air power in support of the armed forces as a whole, and the role of air power in defeating the enemy air force. The winning of the war in the air in this narrower sense was carried on both alongside and in harness with the general war. Implicit in pre-war air doctrine had been the view that air power should be exercised in both ways, as a vital means of support for surface forces and as the means of destroying enemy air power. But during the war there developed an explicit dichotomy between those powers that practised a limited air strategy and those who developed a general air strategy. The limited use of air power was confined to one major role in support of the other services. In the case of Germany it was used in support of the army; in the case of Japan in local support of the navy. Certainly in the German case a general strategy had been attempted in 1940 but was repudiated precisely because of its ineffectiveness in the Battle of Britain and the Blitz. Indeed as long as Germany was fighting enemies, such as Russia, who also accepted a limited air strategy, the lack of a more general air strategy did not matter. In 1940 and early 1941 a limited air strategy had proved more than effective in all the campaigns from Norway to Greece. It is easy to understand why Germany settled at the time of the invasion of Russia for a limited strategy. Yet in the air Germany was forced to fight not just on two fronts, but two different kinds of air war altogether. On the eastern front a limited air war was fought; in the west a general air war. Germany's limited supply of aircraft and resources could not easily be spread between the two, and Hitler favoured the more limited strategy. He did so because it kept control over the air forces more in his hands, and because his whole strategy was geared to defeating Russia first before turning back to deal with the RAF.

Both Britain and the United States practised a general air strategy. A general air strategy involved the pursuit of all four of the major aspects of air doctrine simultaneously, while providing sufficient material resources to meet the demands of such a policy. Thus both powers placed equal emphasis, though not necessarily equal resources, on air defence, strategic bombing, aero-naval co-operation and air support for ground troops. In the British case this meant the resources were thinly spread in the early years of war and only air defence proved its strategic worth. But by 1941, in fact at the time that Germany was adopting a more limited air power, resources had expanded sufficiently to cope with the wide range of air force demands. The adoption of a general strategy showed sharp contrasts with the limited strategy of the Axis powers.

In the first place a general air strategy necessitated giving greater autonomy to air forces, making them co-equal with the other two services. Without such autonomy it was difficult for air forces to keep a major share in decision making or to construct strategies of their own. In the second place a general strategy required the diversion of massive economic resources to sustain it. Without such an industrial and scientific commitment a general air strategy could not be maintained because each major air force function consumed large material resources in its own right. Hence the importance attached by the western Allies to total economic mobilization. Finally a general strategy required what its name implied, the pursuit of all objectives at the same time and continuously. This was an important factor since they were all interdependent. Air and army co-operation, for example, relied on air power at sea to safeguard supplies and on independent bombing to undermine the enemy economy. It was possible to have one kind of air power without the others, but as the German limited air strategy showed, this was at the expense of strategic priorities elsewhere. In the German case a general air strategy involving a large-scale air defence at home, combined with a large commitment to naval aviation, would have made air force co-operation with the army on the Russian front more, rather than less, secure. It was the realization from early in the war that air power, to be effective, could not be divisible that distinguished the attitude of the Allies from that of the Axis powers.

The contrast between general and limited air power illustrated more general differences in strategic circumstances. From the start the British and American governments were committed to a massive exercise of air power and geared government policy to such an end. Roosevelt was inspired by a firm conviction of the importance of air power. In May 1941 he expressed the hope that 'command of the air by the democracies must be and can be achieved. Every month the democracies are gaining in the relative strength of the air forces. We must see to it that the process is hastened and that the democratic superiority in the air is made absolute'.[1] To this view he stuck throughout the war. 'The Nazis and fascists have asked for it', he told Congress, 'and they are going to get it . . . we and the British and the Russians will hit them from the air heavily and relentlessly . . .'.[2] From the outset German and Japanese air policy was more cautious. In the German case this was rooted in Hitler's openly expressed belief that 'a country cannot be brought to defeat by an Air Force',[3] a belief reflected in the growing emphasis on land power. In Japan air power was only possible in conjunction with sea power, since there was no enemy within bombing range. Moreover it was argued that the economy could ill afford to sustain a heavier commitment to air forces at the expense of the other services. There was also an element of miscalculation. Believing the air forces to be strong enough to achieve victory, neither country prepared adequately for failure. When forced to face powerful air enemies to whom air power was a central military tool, it was too late to regain the initiative. The effort required for creating large air forces was a huge one, quite misunderstood before the outbreak of war. Unless willing energies were harnessed from the start to the building of massive air strength, it was very difficult to build it up at short notice or to divert sufficient resources to the effort.

To distinguish thus between a general and limited air strategy helps to explain why the Allies won the air war in its direct sense, in the defeat of the enemy air force and the winning of command in the air. Resources could have been allocated differently between services, but it is still difficult to escape the conclusion that the adoption of a general air strategy was an important factor in explaining victory in the war as a whole as well. Even the Soviet war effort, with its doctrine of limited air power, was helped in the same way by the western Allies' pursuit of a general air policy. Air power provided two important and more general functions. First of all it protected and defended the Allies' own forces and territory against attack by enemy forces of all kinds. Secondly it was used to speed up and protect Allied offensive operations by surface forces. Had either function been neglected it would be fair to conclude that the Allied forces would have been faced with a far more formidable task in terms of time and in terms of cost. Conversely had the Axis powers developed a greater commitment to air strategy, then defeat would have been not only slower, but far less inexorable than it turned out to be.

The difficult question to answer is not whether air power was important, but how important it was. There can be no definite conclusion about how decisive air power was. There was too much inter-dependence between the services and between strategies to produce a list of components that were either more or less decisive. Just as an aircraft could not be flown without a propeller, nor a propeller fly without its aircraft, so was air power related to the war effort. The introduction of the jet engine, to continue the metaphor, produced as great a revolution in air power as, for example, nuclear weapons did in military strategy as a whole. But changes as decisive as these, though in evidence at the end of the war, were decisive for the future of war, not for the war fought between 1939 and 1945. The only conclusion that the evidence bears is the more negative conclusion that victory for either side could not have been gained without the exercise of air power.

At the time, however, this conclusion was never in doubt. The air war assumed a significance in the popular mind out of all proportion to the contribution of air forces to victory or to the technical capabilities of the air weapon. That this should have been so is not altogether surprising. Until war had actually broken out imagination was allowed full play with air power. Popular fears were fed by politicians anxious to gain support for rearmament or to press a particular foreign policy against conflicting counsels. During the war itself political calculation combined with the actual experience of bombing continued to give the air war more domestic impact than any other aspect of the conflict. Popular fears were understandable. For one thing the information available on air warfare was highly selective. During the 1930s great efforts were made to conceal the scope of air rearmament and air plans, with the result that what information did become available often gave rise to temporary panics among the communities that felt themselves to be at risk. The bombing of Guernica and Italian gas-bombing in the Abyssinian war were but two examples. Moreover the selective nature of air information played into the hands of those who pressed for more rearmament. Exaggerated reports of the possible effect of bomb damage, or the technical capacity of aircraft, were given wide currency either to alarm public opinion sufficiently to create pressure on government, or to exert direct pressure on the government itself to pay more attention to air affairs.

Part cause, part effect, of the popular view of air warfare was the growing importance of air power for propaganda purposes. Such propaganda was widespread, from Hitler's attempts to bluff other powers into believing German air strength to be greater than it actually was to the Soviet claim that: 'Aviation is the highest expression of our achievements. Our aviation is the child of Stalinist industrialization.'[4] It was used everywhere for avowedly political and strategic purposes. In the 1930s it was used extensively by the fascist powers to show how air power embodied the spirit of the new fascist soldiers. It was used just as widely in the Soviet Union as an open expression of the challenge of socialism against the west and as a mark of Stalin's personal responsibility for the creation of modern Russia. 'Observing comrade Stalin's daily work in the area of aviation', wrote Kaganovich in 1936, 'we can say without any trace of exaggeration that the founder and the creator of our Soviet aviation is our teacher and leader comrade Stalin.'[5] When Hitler caused the film of Luftwaffe experience in Poland, 'The Baptism of Fire', to be shown in the embassies of neutral countries in 1940 and 1941 the object was to complete the myth that German air power was invincible, and was in itself the cause of Axis victories.

When war broke out the Allies, too, made use of the powerful imagery and appeal of air power in their propaganda. The Battle of Britain was used as a symbol of democratic resistance to fascism and dominated the themes of British propaganda throughout the war. The air attack at Pearl Harbor became the great betrayal that justified the American people in their resolve to punish Japan. In both cases ample justification for the future bombing campaigns was created. Churchill's belief that his government should be seen to be hitting back at the Axis powers justified the early exaggeration of the efficacy of bombing and its support above all other operations in the winter and summer of 1941. Both Britain and the United States took advantage of the hostile propaganda surrounding Axis bombings to explain the devotion of huge resources to the Allied bombing even in the face of hostile criticism at home on moral and military grounds, or in the face of opinion-poll evidence which suggested that revenge was not in fact a strong motive force among those who had themselves been subjected to bombing.[6] Bombing, too, created a counter-propaganda. From 1942 onwards Goebbels put increasing emphasis on terror-bombing in the Nazi efforts to encourage resistance against the Allies.[7] Similarly in Japan the threat of bombing was used to increase mobilization and participation in the war, while the actual and demoralizing experience of bombing was used by the military authorities to justify policies of fanatical resistance. In a more general sense the air war provided all the belligerents with a powerful set of military myths with which to arouse enthusiasm for war. Airmen everywhere became the heroes of the war. Because of the highly individualist character of air combat the public was made much more aware of the contribution of the air forces to victory. Fighter aces had relatively little competition from submarine captains and tank drivers. The success and courage of individual airmen was used to inspire resistance to attack and commitment to war. The story of the Japanese airman who led his squadron back to base and filed a combat report while, it was later alleged, clinically dead gained wide currency precisely because it underpinned old military virtues of sacrifice and duty in one of the few remaining areas of combat where the individual soldier was still distinguishable from the mass.[8] In these ways air power was used to construct a popular image of the war, and the reasons for fighting it, of enduring quality.

The growth of such 'air-mindedness' resulted not only from propaganda and the air power culture that developed during the war, but also from the fact that for many non-combatants the war only bore upon them in a military sense through air attack. The very nature of the weapon determined from the outset that civilian communities would not remain immune from attack. If some effort was made in Europe to prevent this from happening indiscriminately as a direct act of military policy, no such effort was made in the war between China and Japan; and it was the latter example that prevailed everywhere once it became clear that military purposes were served directly by bomb attack on rear areas. Moreover the British decision to concentrate on German working-class housing as a specific target system in 1941, and the later American decision to treat Japanese cities as military targets of a general character, made it inevitable that civilian communities would be drawn into the military struggle. Even those countries not subject to air attack, or only to a limited extent, were compelled to adopt widespread measures of civil and passive defence so that the expectation of bombing as much as its reality linked civilians to the war in a regular and positive way.

In those communities actually exposed to bombing the periods of physical attack itself were brief and spasmodic, and the spread of destruction beyond the large industrial cities was slight. It was the more general social impact of bombing that made the bomber the weapon of total war. The widespread destruction of urban housing, the constant interruptions to normal civilian life, the movement of refugees and evacuees from bombing, all brought much larger sections of the community into direct contact with the results of the air war. Nor were the casualties themselves insignificant compared with casualties in battle. In Germany the air war killed more civilians than all British and American casualties together. In Japan more people were killed in six months of heavy aerial bombardment than in the whole United States war effort.[9] In China a large percentage of the dead from the war with Japan were the casualties of bombing. Such figures certainly affected morale. Comparatively lower casualties during the Blitz on Britain in 1940-41 led to conditions of demoralization in certain areas.[10] Yet not even in those countries exposed to heavy and continuous bomb attack did morale in any general sense give way. This was partly because governments could not easily be compelled to accept surrender on the basis of the suffering of the civilian community while the armies were still fighting; and partly because those communities suffering from demoralizing bomb attack retained insufficient political energy to demand that a government surrender rather than face further attacks. In Japan it was high political pressure rather than popular pressure from below that led to the efforts to secure an end to the war, a fact that demonstrated how fallacious had been the expectation that bombing would turn populations against governments and end the war through internal convulsions. Bombing was more successful in interrupting production and bringing the military machine to a halt than in carrying out those tasks of terror and intimidation so publicized in the pre-war period. Despite the horror of bombing and the way in which it imposed a widespread and direct involvement in the war, the ordeal remained subsidiary to the contest over economic and military power with which the air war was primarily concerned. In terms of the effect of bomb destruction on the course of the war, it was the destruction of industrial resources, including labour, that determined a country's ability to continue the war, not the dislocation of community life itself. In fact in Germany at precisely the time that bombing was reaching its peak in terms of the destruction of cities and disruption of civilian life, the German economy had achieved peak output. The political and military consequences of bombardment on civilian populations thus assumed a character quite different from that anticipated. Such destruction became, in Portal's unfortunate phrase, 'incidental'.[11]

The war in the air had a wider impact in other ways as well, for many of the contrasts between the ways in which nations prosecuted air warfare indicated more fundamental contrasts in the way in which the war was fought and organized. One theme dominating the history of the air war was the relative importance of the military establishment in organizing a nation for war. In the Axis powers militarism and military society were central and dominating features of the war effort. In part this was due to the ambitions of fascist leaders, as in Italy, eager to prove the martial spirit of the new Italian masters. But in Japan and Germany modern totalitarianism was fused with a military tradition of old standing in a self-conscious assertion of the values of the military world over those of the modern industrial and class world. There were military traditions among the Allied powers as well, but such tradition as there was remained subordinate to the modern administrative and industrial societies for whom the armed forces were now a specialized agency rather than an important social fact.

Certain advantages lay with the militarist powers. A higher degree of preparation, better training, better fighting qualities were demonstrated in the Axis victories from 1939 to 1942. The slow retreat back through Europe again demonstrated the strength of German military society when engaged upon military tasks, even against overwhelming odds. But it had many disadvantages. The air war, for example, was the one area of warfare that relied completely upon its contacts with the modern world, through scientific research, advanced technology, good civilian organization, rational industrial methods and the wide recruitment of non-military personnel. In all these areas military domination over the task of waging war had damaging consequences. Civilians and the military co-operated poorly, partly on the assumption that most of the waging of war was a military responsibility. Science was indifferently mobilized. The economy was not fully understood and was poorly recruited until it was too late to make up for past errors. Advanced technology was unsatisfactorily organized and integrated into the war effort because it needed experts in their own field rather than administrative and scientific soldiers to make the selection of weapons and organize production. Had it been otherwise German scientific and industrial strength would have weighed much more heavily in the conflict. At a more general level the claims of the traditional services were inevitably to be preferred to the claims of the air forces. Where air forces were given a prominent role in the war efforts of the Allied powers, which all had a detached interest in developing the best instruments to win the war, the Axis powers, while paying lip-service to the military modernism of air power, remained primarily concerned with the interests, both military and social, of the older services. If there existed resentments between the services of the Allied powers this was not allowed to deflect the political authorities from placing as much weight upon air power as their strategy warranted.

Another general contrast was the extent to which both sides stressed personal military endeavour. In Japan it was the pilot rather than the aircraft that counted. Good pilots were expected to be capable of overcoming even the most advanced technology pitted against them. In Germany, too, the fighting qualities of the airmen were stressed above everything else. To Hitler what counted was the will. If pilots and soldiers possessed sufficient faith in victory, and fought with sufficient tenacity and courage, no mere numerical or technical advantage could overcome them. Goering, on the strength of his experiences in the First World War, retained a naive belief that 'personal heroism must always count for more than technical novelties'.[12] However much the Axis powers attempted to halt defeat by a final economic effort, there still existed the romantic expectation that valour must triumph over mere material power.

If there was no shortage of valour on the Allied side, it was nevertheless the additional mobilization of non-military resources that won not only the air war but the wider war as well. Being less well prepared militarily and with a proportionately smaller military establishment, the Allied powers had no other recourse but to use the administrative and political elites for the task of planning and running the war. In Russia this situation was underlined by the desire of the party to utilize all the resources released through the modernization drive to stem fascism; and to leave control over such mobilization in the hands of the civilian Communist authorities. In Britain and the United States the political structure itself, coupled with the high degree of social modernization characteristic of such a structure, dictated that the war, while fought by soldiers, would be planned, supplied, researched for and profited from by civilians. Hence the stress in the western powers on economic effort, on massive production as a key to victory; hence the concentration on scientific mobilization; hence, too, the degree to which the war efforts of both countries relied from the start on the co-operation and participation of bureaucrats, managers and engineers or, for that matter, of women.

The differences in outlook of the Allied and Axis powers were nowhere more obvious than in the degree to which industry was mobilized for war purposes. In the west the war achieved the character of a war in defence of democratic capitalism, a character confirmed by Stimson's remark that 'If you are going to try to go to war, or to prepare for war, in a capitalist country you have got to let businesses make money out of the process . . .'.[13] On such a basis British and American industry co-operated to the full in the waging of war. In Germany and Japan the interests of business were not identical with the interests of the political and military leadership. Industry was compelled to take orders rather than to work in partnership, to be a servant to military ambition. There were certainly rewards for such service, but there was also extensive interference and control from the military side which stifled industrial initiative and weakened the economic effort through internal conflicts over the role of the state and the degree of military coercion. Economic mobilization remained much more firmly under military direction and suffered accordingly from the fact that soldiers were not businessmen and very few of them were engineers. It would be wrong to see this contrast as simply a clash between capitalism and fascism, for Soviet Russia was not capitalist though it shared the same pattern of economic mobilization as its western allies. The clash was one of industrialism against a militarism inexpertly binding industrialism to its purpose. Indeed Germany, Italy and Japan had large capitalist sectors. It was precisely the inability of fascist militarism to mobilize such industry as fully as possible, or to allow it the freedom to profit widely from war, or to integrate it fully into the complex process of planning the production and development of weapons that distinguished its efforts from those of its enemies. This was of critical importance in the air war because the industrial and research effort required was so much greater in terms of the military rewards than it was for armies and navies.

At another level the Axis failure to harness modernization to its imperialism reflected a failure to break down social barriers. The important social consequence of the war for the Allied powers was not breaking down social barriers between classes—in fact they were in most cases confirmed—but in breaking down barriers between elites. This meant ensuring that soldiers and engineers co-operated fully in scientific and technical fields and even in the field of battle itself; that managers and entrepreneurs and designers were given at least equal weight with the military in the general political framework within which the war was conducted. It was much harder to achieve such a crossing of social frontiers in the Axis powers. In Germany and Japan military distrust of, and disdain for, commercial life and the values of modern civilian institutions made it much harder to produce co-operation between the two sides; just as the exclusiveness and protectionism of the other elites, whether academic, commercial or bureaucratic obstructed the military in what efforts were made to penetrate and use them for the war effort. When the competing interests of the fascist party elites were introduced as well the result was political confusion and conflict rather than co-operation in the national interest. Such constraints, although overcome to some extent by the end of the war, were nevertheless sufficient to cancel out those advantages which the military tradition on its own supplied, The development of nuclear weapons subsequently allowed the military establishment of the major powers **to** retreat to a much more selective and soldierly environment again, though conscious of the debt owed to science and industry. But the Axis powers were caught at a stage where the nature of warfare and war technology made necessary the total commitment of social resources. In the air war the inability to carry out such mobilization effectively was an important determinant of victory once Axis sights were raised to that of a world struggle. The war of 1939–45 saw a unique and incongruous union of traditional and industrialized warfare. Nowhere were the contradictions that such a union produced more clearly expressed and more decisive than in the air war.

Notes

Chapter 1

1 N. Polmar, *Aircraft Carriers* (London, 1969), pp. 23-34; S. Roskill, *Naval Policy between the Wars* (2 vols., London, 1968-76), I, pp. 220-1; P. Kemp, *Fleet Air Arm* (London, 1954), pp. 50-89.

2 Polmar, p. 85; G. Till, 'Airpower and the Battleship in the 1920s' in B. Ranft (ed.), *Technical Change and British Naval Policy 1860-1939* (London, 1977), p. 115.

3 S. Roskill, *The War at Sea* (4 vols., HMSO, 1954-61), I, pp. 30-2; R. Jackson, *Strike from the Sea* (London, 1970), pp. 50-5; Till, pp. 109-14, 117-22; Roskill, *Naval Policy*, I, pp. 534-5; N. Gibbs, *Grand Strategy: Volume I* (HMSO, 1976), pp. 366-70 (hereafter cited as *GS*, I); J. Slessor, *The Central Blue* (London, 1956), pp. 188-9.

4 Polmar, pp. 47-50, 68; Roskill, *Naval Policy*, I, pp. 323-4, 530-1.

5 Polmar, pp. 131-2; S. E. Morison, *History of U.S. Naval Operations in World War II* (15 vols., Oxford 1948-62), III, pp. 22-4; J. Horikoshi, M. Okumiya, *The Zero Fighter* (London, 1958), pp. 27-8; D. Brown, *Carrier Operations in World War II* (2 vols., London, 1974), II, pp. 10-12.

6 Polmar, pp. 135-5; D. A. Thomas, *Japan's War at Sea* (London, 1978), pp. 21-2; J. D. Potter, *Admiral of the Pacific: the Life of Yamamoto* (London, 1960), pp. 55-7.

7 Polmar, p. 43; Morison, I, pp. xlv-xlix.

8 S. E. Morison, *The Two Ocean War*, pp. 13-14.

9 Roskill, *Naval Policy*, I, pp. 413-15; II, pp. 210-11; E. E. Wilson, *Air Power for Peace* (New York, 1945), pp. 91-4; Morison, *Two Ocean War*, pp. 17-9; Morison, *History*, I, pp. xlvii-liii; 'Foreign Naval Air Services', *JRUSI*, LXXXII (1937), pp. 161-4; Polmar, pp. 71-4; A. Hezlet, 'The Development of U. S. Naval Aviation and the British Fleet Air Arm and Coastal Command between the Wars', *Aerospace Historian*, XVIII (1971), pp. 118-19; A. Turnbull, C. Lord, *A History of United States Naval Aviation* (New Haven, 1949), pp. 284-317.

10 E. van der Porten, *The German Navy in World War II* (London, 1969), pp. 27, 32-3; Polmar, pp. 708-12.

11 D. Mack Smith, *Mussolini's Roman Empire* (London, 1976), p. 179; Polmar, pp. 77, 114, 715-17.

12 Roskill, *War at Sea*, I, pp. 29-30, 38; R. Barker, *The Shipbusters: the Story of the RAF Torpedo-Bombers* (London, 1957), pp. 33-6; Polmar, pp. 74-7, 82; Jackson, pp. 52-5; Roskill, *Naval Policy*, II, pp. 406-12; D. Divine, *Broken Wing* (London, 1966), pp. 200-1; Kemp, pp. 103-12.

13 Roskill, *War at Sea*, I, pp. 39-40; Roskill, *Naval Policy*, I, pp. 407-17; II, pp. 194-212, 392-415; H. M. Hyde, *British Air Policy between the Wars 1918-1939* (London, 1976), pp. 397-403; M. Salewski, *Die deutsche Seekriegsleitung 1935-45* (2 vols., Frankfurt a.M., 1970), I, pp. 252-5; Mack Smith, p. 177; P. Joubert de la Ferté, *The Third Service* (London, 1955), pp. 109-12.

14 W. Medlicott, *The Economic Blockade* (2 vols., HSMO, 1952), I, pp. 23-4.

15 Salewski, I, pp. 213-16, 251-7; Polmar, p. 86; van der Porten, pp. 32-3; Roskill, *War at Sea*, I, p. 326; C. Bekker, *The Luftwaffe War Diaries* (London, 1966), p. 273; C. Bekker, *Hitler's Naval War* (London, 1974), pp. 73-94; K-H. Völker, *Die deutsche Luftwaffe 1933-1939* (Stuttgart, 1967), pp. 90-3.

16 F. H. Hinsley, *Hitler's Strategy* (Cambridge, 1951), p. 167.

17 Ibid., pp. 167-8.

18 J. L. Cate, W. F. Craven, *The Army Air Forces in World in World War II* (7 vols., Chicago,

1948–58), I, pp. 30–2, 44–5; the Baker Board reporting on the position of the various services in 1934 emphasized that the army 'remains the ultimate decisive factor in war'; K. Greenfield, *American Strategy in World War II: a Reconsideration* (Balitmore, 1963), pp. 86–8.

19 K-H. Völker, *Dokumente und Dokumentarfotos zur Geschichte der deutschen Luftwaffe* (Stuttgart, 1968), p. 469, Document 200, 'Luftkriegführung', March 1940.

20 P. Deichmann, *German Air Force Operations in Support of the Army* (New York, 1962), pp. 12–42; G. Förster, *Totaler Krieg und Blitzkrieg* (Berlin, 1967), pp. 155–9; P. Smith, *The Stuka at War* (London, 1971), pp. 13–16.

21 C. Messenger, *The Art of Blitzkrieg* (London, 1976), p. 88; A. Boyd, *The Soviet Air Force since 1918* (London, 1977), pp. 57–8; J. Erickson, *The Soviet High Command* (London, 1962), pp. 350–1; D. Poulain, 'The Role of Aircraft in the Spanish Civil War', *JRUSI*, LXXXIII (1938), pp. 581–6.

22 Boyd, pp. 92–3; E. O'Ballance, *The Red Army* (London, 1964), pp. 114–15.

23 Wilson, pp. 26–33; *AAF*, I, pp. 17–24, 50–2; R. W. Krauskopf, 'The Army and the Strategic Bomber 1930–1939', Part I, *Military Affairs*, XXII (1958), pp. 87–8.

24 Messenger, pp. 91–3; P. Le Goyet, 'Évolution de la doctrine d'emploi de l'aviation française entre 1919 et 1939', *RDGM*, XIX (1969), pp. 15–32; O. Stewart, 'The Air Forces of France', *JRUSI*, LXXXV (1940), pp. 240–1.

25 M. Weygand, 'How France is Defended', *International Affairs*, XVIII (1939), pp. 470–1.

26 *GS*, I, pp. 670–2; J. Slessor, *Air Power and Armies* (Oxford, 1936), pp. 29–30; M. Howard, *The Continental Commitment* (London, 1972), pp. 110-13; Divine, pp. 206-9.

27 See the discussion in Slessor, *Air Power*, pp. 31–60; 'Western Air Plans 1' in C. Webster, N. Frankland, *The Strategic Air Offensive against Germany* (4 vols., HMSO, 1961), I, p. 94 (hereafter cited as *SAOG*).

28 Völker, *Dokumente*, p. 470, document 200, 'Luftkriegführung'.

29 A. Boyle, *Trenchard* (London, 1962), p. 577

30 G. Douhet, *The Command of the Air* (London, 1943), p. 161; on 'Douhetism' see B. Brodie, *Strategy in the Missile Age* (Princeton U. P., 1959), pp. 71–7, 82–3.

31 Hyde, ch. II; Boyle, pp. 448–91; Divine, pp. 156-7, 164-70, 199-204; B. Powers, *Strategy without Slide Rule* (London, 1976), pp. 178–81; G. Dickens, *Bombing and Strategy: the Fallacy of Total War* (London, 1947), pp. 8–9; R. Shay, *British Rearmament in the Thirties* (Princeton U. P., 1977), pp. 36–8.

32 Krauskopf, Part II, *Military Affairs*, XXII (1958), pp. 208–15; *AAF*, I, pp. 40–2.

33 M. Smith, 'The Royal Air Force, Air Power and British Foreign Policy', *Journal of Contemporary History*, XII (1977), pp. 157–8; E. Strauss, 'The Psychological Effects of Bombing', *JRUSI*, LXXXIV (1939), pp. 269–80; *SAOG*, I, pp. 46-7.

34 M. Smith, 'The RAF and Counter-force Strategy before World War II', *JRUSI*, CXXI (1976), pp. 69–71; *SAOG*, I, pp. 63–4; *GS*, I, pp. 550–1.

35 *SAOG*, I, p. 97.

36 Ibid., pp. 93–7; F. H. Hinsley, *British Intelligence in the Second World War: Volume I* (HMSO, 1979), p. 27.

37 *SAOG*, I, pp. 103–4.

38 G. Quester, *Deterrence before Hiroshima* (New York, 1966), p. 128.

39 *AAF*, I, p. 33; H. Hansell, *The Air Plan that Defeated Hitler* (Atlanta, Ga., 1972), pp. 30–48; H. H. Arnold, *Global Mission* (New York, 1949), pp. 155–7; Krauskopf, Part II, pp. 208–15.

40 R. J. Overy, 'From "Uralbomber" to "Amerikabomber": the Luftwaffe and Strategic Bombing', *Journal of Strategic Studies*, I (1978), pp. 157–60; D. Kahn, *Hitler's Spies: German Military Intelligence in World War II* (London, 1978), pp. 382–3.

41 Boyd, pp. 55–8, 68–9; Erickson, pp. 500–1.

42 Poulain, pp. 581–6; W. Murray, 'German Air Power and the Munich crisis' in B. Bond, I. Roy (eds.), *War and Society: I* (London, 1976), pp. 110-11; E. Homze, *Arming the Luftwaffe* (Nebraska U.P., 1976), pp. 169–73.

43 Slessor, *Central Blue*, pp. 203–5; C. Portal, 'Air Force Co-operation in Policing the Empire', *JRUSI*, LXXXII (1937), pp. 343–57; A. Harris, *Bomber Offensive* (London, 1947), pp. 18–23, 29–31; Howard, pp. 112-14. On the assessment of bombing possibilities see H. Allen, *The Legacy of Lord Trenchard* (London, 1972), pp. 78–80; A. Verrier, *The Bombing Offensive* (London, 1968), pp. 8–9.

44 Douhet, *Command*, pp. 14, 20; Brodie, pp. 87–95.

45 Smith, 'The Royal Air Force . . .', pp. 168–70; Smith, 'The RAF and Counter-force Strategy . . .', pp. 71–2; E. Sims, *Fighter Tactics and Strategy 1914–70* (London, 1972), pp. 87–8.

46 Smith, 'The RAF and Counter-force Strategy . . .', pp. 68–9, 71; N. Frankland, *The Bombing Offensive against Germany* (London, 1965), pp. 46–7; Allen, pp. 73–4, 76–8.

47 B. Collier, *The Defence of the United Kingdom* (HMSO, 1957), pp. 26–38; I. Hogg, *Anti Aircraft. A History of Air Defence* (London, 1978), pp. 81–3, 85–9.

48 D. Dempster, D. Wood, *The Narrow Margin: the Battle of Britain and the Rise of Airpower* (London, 1961), pp. 55–8.

49 A. Lee, *The German Air Force* (London, 1946), pp. 206–8.

50 R. Kilmarx, *A History of Soviet Air Power* (London, 1962), pp. 122–4; Mack Smith, pp. 173–4; *AAF*, I, pp. 152–3; *AAF*, VI, pp. 80–4; Le Goyet, pp. 40–1; USSBS Report 62, *Japanese Air Power* (Washington, July 1946), Appdx iv.

51 Le Goyet, pp. 16–17.

52 *AAF*, I, pp. 82–5; Mack Smith, pp. 173–4.

53 *AAF*, VI, p. 80.

54 *AAF*, VI, p. 81.

55 *AAF*, I, pp. 288–92; Hogg, pp. 111–12; Dempster and Wood, pp. 142–3.

56 *AAF*, VI, p. 79, Radio Message of 9.12.1941; see too 'Message to Congress May 16th 1940' in *The Public Papers and Addresses of Franklin D. Roosevelt* (8 vols., London, 1938–45), IV, p. 199.

57 *GS*, I, p. 213; Smith, "The RAF and Counter-force Strategy . . .', p. 159.

58 Howard, pp. 109–11; *GS*, I, pp. 103–6.

59 E. M. Emme, 'Emergence of Nazi Luftpolitik as a Weapon in International Affairs 1933–1935' *Aerospace Historian*, VII (1960); H. S. Dinerstein, 'The Impact of Air Power on the International Scene 1930–1939', *Military Affairs*, XIX (1955), pp. 67–8.; R. Manvell, H. Fraenkel, *Göring* (London, 1962), p. 148; H. Rumpf, *The Bombing of Germany* (London, 1963), p. 37; Quester, pp. 95–100.

60 *GS*, I, pp. 534–7; I. B. Holley, *Buying Aircraft: Materiel Procurement for the Army Air Forces* (Washington, 1964), pp. 223–37; Homze, pp. 155–6; Shay, pp. 170–3.

61 B. Collier, *A History of Air Power* (London, 1974), pp. 100–18.

62 R. J. Overy, 'The German Pre-war Aircraft Production Plans', *English Historical Review*, XC (1975), p. 791; R. Suchenwirth, *The Development of the German Air Force, 1919–1939* (New York, 1968), pp. 123–4.

63 *GS*, I, pp. 532–3, 565–74; Shay, pp. 238–42.

64 British figures calculated from Shay, p. 297; German figures: Bundesarchiv (hereafter cited as BA) R2/21776–81, Reichsfinanzministerium, Abteilung 1, 'Entwicklung der Ausgaben in den Rechnungsjahren 1934–1939', 17.7.1939.

65 Holley, p. 176; *AAF*, VI, pp. 171–2; *Nazi Conspiracy and Aggression* (hereafter cited as NCA), (8 vols., Washington, 1946), III, pp. 892–3, doc. 1301–PS, Blomberg to Göring, 31.8.1936.

66 *AAF*, VI, pp. 9–15; Holley, pp. 169–76; Arnold, pp. 177–9.

67 Kilmarx, pp. 126–9.

68 Overy, 'Pre-war Plans . . .', pp. 782–5.

69 J. Truelle, 'La production aéronautique militaire française jusqu'en juin 1940', *RDGM*, XIX (1969), pp. 92–3.

70 Overy, 'Pre-war Plans . . .', pp. 784–6; M. M. Postan, *British War Production* (HMSO, 1952), pp. 472–3.

71 It should be borne in mind that figures for actual production only tell half the story. They do not necessarily reflect a proportional difference in air strength. In the case of Germany a very large amount of the production was of trainers in the early years of the build-up. and reserves were low since Germany lacked a large stock of aircraft for second-line service because of Versailles. In France and Britain on the other hand a smaller proportion of production was devoted to trainer aircraft, and a much larger reserve of aircraft was available from the older aircraft built during the period of German disarmament. Their military value was perhaps questionable, but they could be used for training and other non-combat purposes, thus releasing current output for more urgent needs.

72 Figures for France from Truelle, p. 102; for Germany from R. Wagenführ, *Die deutsche Industrie im Kriege* (Berlin, 1963), p. 74; for Italy from S. Clough, *The Economic History of Modern Italy* (Columbia U.P., 1964), p. 261; for Japan from R. J. Francillon, *Japanese Aircraft of the Pacific War* (London, 1970), p. 4; for UK from P. Fearon, 'The British Airframe Industry and the State 1918–1935', *Economic History Review*, 2nd Ser., XXVII (1974); P. Masefield, 'The Royal Air Force and British Military Aircraft Production 1934–1940' (paper to the Anglo-French Colloquium, Paris, December 1975, organized by the

Comité international d'histoire de la 2ᵉ guerre mondiale), p. 29; Postan, p. 484; figures for United States from J. Rae, *Climb to Greatness* (Cambridge, Mass., 1968), pp. 49, 81; figures for Russia from Boyd, pp. 36, 98; O'Ballance, p. 127; Erickson, p. 304.

73 W. Baumbach, *Broken Swastika* (London, 1960), p. 34; Lee, pp. 206-8; Hogg, pp. 108-9; H. Schliephake, *The Birth of the Luftwaffe* (London, 1971), p. 47.

74 Collier, *Defence* . . ., pp. 44-8; F. Pile, *Ack Ack: Britain's Defence against Air Attack* (London, 1949), pp. 67-73, 88-92; *GS*, I, pp. 526-682.

75 Hogg, p. 95.

76 Masefield, pp. 52-3.

77 Kilmarx, pp. 153-9.

78 *GS*, I, p. 599.

79 See the conclusions arrived at in Homze, pp. 264-7; Murray, pp. 113-16; Völker, *Die deutsche Luftwaffe* . . . pp. 188-90, 210-14. This fact was attested by German soldiers after the war as well. See for example F. Halder, *Hitler as Warlord* (London, 1950), pp. 3-4; IMT, *Trials of the Major War Criminals* (42 vols., Nuremberg, 1947), IX, pp. 28-9, Bodenschatz evidence.

80 IMT, *Trials*, IX, p. 60, Milch cross-examination.

81 Murray, p. 116; Homze, pp. 242-4; IMT, *Trials*, XXXVII, pp. 443-60, Doc. 043-L.

82 N. Rose, *Vansittart: Study of a Diplomat* (London, 1978), pp. 127-36; S. Roskill, *Hankey: Man of Secrets* (3 vols., London, 1970-74), III, pp. 168-70, 259-65; Christie Papers (Churchill College, Cambridge), 180/1/7, 'Germany Air Sept. 1935'; 180/1/14, 'Notes July 1935'; 180/1/15, 'Organisation of the German Air Force'; Lord Londonderry, *Wings of Destiny* (London, 1943), pp. 167-8; M. Gilbert, *Winston Churchill: Volume V* (London, 1976), pp. 550-9, 623-51; W. Churchill, *The Second World War* (6 vols., London, 1948-54), I, pp. 538-43, 'Statement on the Occasion of the Deputation of Conservative Members . . . to the Prime Minister, 28.7.1936'.

83 See for example PRO FO/ 800-309 5537, Sir Warren Fisher to Chamberlain, 'Air Comparison 2nd April 1938'; *GS*, I, pp. 538-5; Hinsley, *British Intelligence*, pp. 60-1; *Documents on British Foreign Policy*, 3rd Ser., III, pp. 616-17, Henderson to Secretary of State for Air, 12.10.1938; IV, pp. 117-19, Group Captain Vachell to Henderson, 15.2.1939.

84 *GS*, I, pp. 547-51, 584-5; Hinsley, pp. 77-8.

85 Homze, p. 244; W. Schwabedissen, *The Russian Air Force in the Eyes of German Commanders* (New York, 1960), pp. 48-51.

86 Baumbach, pp. 30-1; K. Bartz, *Swastika in the Air* (London, 1956), p. 37; Homze, pp. 244-5.

87 On Czechoslovakia see Homze, pp. 232-3; on reserves see Hinsley, p. 110; K. Gundelach, 'The German Air Force', *Aerospace Historian*, XVIII (1971), p. 88, who claims that the Luftwaffe had virtually no reserves in 1939. German aircraft were, of course, technically superior to many Allied aircraft. Moreover Germany had the advantage of being able to use her large first-line strength against divided air forces. Nevertheless the fact remains that the alleged disparity of forces had disappeared in terms of numbers by 1939.

88 Figures for Germany from Dempster, Wood, p. 478; Hinsley, p. 110; Masefield, Table 1; D. Richards, H. Saunders, *The Royal Air Force 1939-1945* (3 vols., HMSO, 1953), I, p. 410. Bekker, *Luftwaffe*, gives a lower total of 2,775 serviceable front-line aircraft (p. 33); Schliephake, p. 54, also gives a lower figure: 3,441. Figures for Britain from Richards, I, p. 410; *GS*, I, p. 599. Figures for France from Truelle, p. 105; *GS*, I, P. 599. Figures for Poland from Bekker, *Luftwaffe*, p. 467. Figures for Czechoslovakia from M. Hauner, 'Czechoslovakia as a Military Factor in British Considerations of 1938', *Journal of Strategic Studies*, I (1978), p. 209.

89 Overy, 'Pre-war plans', pp. 781-3; Homze, pp. 226-31; IMT, *Trials*, XXXVII, pp. 443-60, Doc. 043-L, 'Organisationsstudie 1950, 2.5.1938'; XXXVIII, pp. 380-5, Doc. 140R, Goering speech to aircraft industry heads, 8.7.1938.

90 Overy, 'Pre-war plans . . . ', p. 796; National Archives (Washington, D.C.) hereafter cited as (NA), T177, Roll 14, frames 3698739-40, 'Mobilisierungsplan 1.9.1939'.

91 IMT, *Trials*, XXXIX, p. 107, Doc 090-TC, Goering interrogation, 29.8.1945; D. Irving, *The Rise and Fall of the Luftwaffe* (London, 1973), p. 72; Manvell, Fraenkel, pp. 151-64.

92 Truelle, pp. 76-7; A.C. Clinton, 'The Trend of Development in Aircraft', *JRUSI*, LXXXII (1937), pp. 113-24; Stewart, pp. 240-1.

93 Wilson, pp. 23-5; Clinton, p. 124; E.J. Bois, *Truth on the Tragedy of France* (London, 1941), pp. 89-92; M. Werner, *The Military Strength of the Powers* (London, 1939), pp. 216-19.

94 U. Bialer, 'The Danger of Bombardment from the Air and the Making of British Air Disarmament Policy 1932-4' in Bond, Roy, *War and Society;* U. Bialer, ' "Humanization"

of Air Warfare in British Foreign Policy on the Eve of the Second World War', *Journal of Contemporary History*, XII (1978), pp. 79–92.

95 Ibid., p.85; Quester, p. 99.

96 Rumpf, p. 18.

97 Bialer, ' "Humanization" . . .', pp. 88–9.

98 *Documents on German Foreign Policy*, Series D 'I, p. 244; German Foreign Minister to Henderson, 4 April 1938.

99 Hitler's Reichstag speech is reproduced in F. Kurowski, *Der Luftkrieg über Deutschland* (Düsseldorf, 1977), p. 45; for the Goering declaration, *Documents on British Foreign Policy*, 3rd Ser., VII, p. 485.

100 Slessor, *Central Blue*, p. 213.

101 Rumpf, pp. 18–19; Quester, p. 106. See J. Butler, *Grand Stategy: Volume II* (HMSO, 1957), pp. 567–8, for the text of the 'Anglo-French Declaration on the Conduct of Warfare, 2.9.1939'.

102 H. M. Hyde, G. R. Nuttall, *Air Defence and the Civil Population* (London, 1937), pp. 150–61; Rumpf, pp. 182–3; J. B. Haldane, *A.R.P.* (London, 1938).

103 L. Gouré, *Civil Defense in the Soviet Union* (Berkeley, 1962), pp. 2–5.

104 Quester, p. 101; Rumpf, pp. 182–3; Hyde, Nuttall, pp. 152–5.

105 Collier, *Defence*, pp. 69–70; T. O'Brien, *Civil Defence* (HMSO, 1955), chs. iii–iv; Quester, p. 101.

Chapter 2

1 H. Trevor-Roper (ed.), *Hitler's War Directives* (hereafter *War Directives*) (London, 1964), pp. 38–40, Directive no. 1; Völker, *Deutsche Luftwaffe* . . . p. 163; Schliephake, pp. 52–3.

2 Völker, *Dokumente*, pp. 460–3, Doc 199, 'Schlussbesprechung des Planspiels des Luftflottenkommandos 2, 13.5.1939; K. Klee, 'The Battle of Britain' in H. Jacobsen, J. Rohwer, *Decisive Battles of World War II: the German View* (London, 1965), pp. 75–6. By the outbreak of war the Luftwaffe had not yet undertaken any map exercises to test the possibilities of air warfare against Britain.

3 *GS*, II, pp. 17–20

4 Ibid., p. 168; *SAOG*, I, pp. 136–7; de la Ferté, *Third Service*, p. 134.

5 *SAOG*, I, pp. 94–102; IV, pp. 99–102, 'Western Air Plans, 1st Sept. 1939'.

6 *GS*, II, pp. 165–71.

7 Postan, *War Production*, pp. 67–9; p. 474 for details of the programme.

8 Truelle, p. 96.

9 BA/RL3 159, Lieferprogramm 15, 1.9.1939 and 16, 28.10.1939.

10 Truelle, p. 102, for French production; *Statistical Digest of the War* (HMSO, 1951), p. 152, for British production.

11 J. McHaight, 'Les négociations relatives aux achats d'avions américains par la France pendant la période qui précéda immédiatement la guerre', *RDGM*, XV (1965); Rae, *Climb to Greatness*, pp. 104–15.

12 G. Feuchter, *Geschichte des Luftkrieges* (Frankfurt a.M., 1964), pp. 112–13; Bekker, *Luftwaffe*, pp. 27–78, 466.

13 *War Directives*, pp. 51–3, Directive no. 7, 18.10.1939, and pp. 56–9, Directive no. 9, 29.11.1939; Rumpf, pp. 19–23; Salewski, I, pp. 250–1.

14 T. K. Derry, *The Campaign in Norway* (HMSO, 1952), pp. 234–5; Bekker, *Luftwaffe*, pp. 103–19; Irving, *Rise and Fall*, pp. 84–8; Richards, I., pp. 77–89

15 Bekker, p. 149; Richards, I, ch. v; L. Ellis, *The War in France and Flanders* (HMSO, 1954), pp. 307–14, 353.

16 Directive to Bomber Command, Slessor to Portal, 13.4.1940, *SAOG*, IV, pp. 109–11; Ellis, pp. 294–5; D. Richards, *Portal of Hungerford* (London, 1977), pp. 148–9, 152–3.

17 Directive to Bomber Command, Douglas to Portal, 20.6.1940, *SAOG*, IV, pp. 115–17; *SAOG*, I, pp. 146–50.

18 *GS*, II, p. 182; *SAOG*, I, p. 145.

19 W. Warlimont, *Inside Hitler's Headquarters* (London, 1964), pp. 110–12; A. Hillgruber, *Hitlers Strategie: Politik und Kriegsführung 1940–41* (Frankfurt a.M., 1965), pp. 157–91, 218–19.

20 GS II, 270.

21 *War Directives*, pp. 74–9, Directive no. 16, 16.7.1940; K. Klee, *Dokumente zum Unternehmen*

Seelöwe (Göttingen, 1959), pp. 305–9, doc. 11, 'Denkschrift des Generalmajors Jodl über eine Landung in England 12.7.1940', and p. 324, 'Vorbereitung des Luftwaffeneinsatzes gegen England, 30.7.1940'.

22 *War Directives*, p. 79, Directive no. 17; see too Klee, *Dokumente*, pp. 355–6, doc. 17.

23 K. Klee, *Das Unternehmen 'Seelöwe'* (Göttingen, 1958), pp. 210–21; R. Wheatley, *Operation Sea Lion* (Oxford, 1958), pp. 52–64.

24 F. Halder, *Kriegstagebuch* (3 vols., Stuttgart, 1962–4), II, pp. 81, 128–9; A. L. Gropmann, 'The Battle of Britain and the Principles of War', *Aerospace Historian*, XVIII (1971); Rumpf, pp. 39–41; H. Allen, *Who Won the Battle of Britain?* (London, 1974), pp. 159–82. Allen's critical view of RAF strategy and performance suffers primarily from the author's failure to evaluate the impact of the Battle of Britain on the Luftwaffe, in particular its declining strength and morale and poor strategic deployment.

25 Luftwaffe Operations Staff Ic, 'Comparative Survey of RAF and Luftwaffe Striking Power, 16.7.1940', reproduced in Dempster and Wood, pp. 106–10.

26 Ibid., p. 115.

27 R. Suchenwirth, *Historical Turning Points in the German Air Force War Effort* (New York, 1959), pp. 66–7; for losses in the Battle of France see R. Jackson, *Air War over France 1939–40* (London, 1974), p. 38. French losses amounted to 914, German losses to 937 for the period 3 September to 1 May.

28 Postan, pp. 116–17, 474, 484; BA/RL3 159, 'Flugzeug-Beschaffungs-Programm Nr. 16, 28.10.1939'; NA, T177, Roll 31, frame 3719681, Luftwaffe mobilization planning, 1.4.1938.

29 Figures for Germany from Dempster and Wood, pp. 248–9, 478–80; Suchenwirth, *Turning Points*, p. 65; A. S. Milward, *The German Economy at War* (London, 1965), p. 38; Bekker, *Luftwaffe*, p. 211; British figures from Dempster and Wood, pp. 461, 463; Richards and Saunders, I, p. 152.

30 Postan, pp. 318–19; E. Fairfax, *Calling All Arms* (London, 1946), p. 25.

31 E. Sims, *Fighter Tactics and Strategy* (London, 1972), pp. 92–3; Dempster and Wood, pp. 196, 471, 474; Suchenwirth, *Turning Points*, pp. 66–71.

32 Warlimont, pp. 115–18.

33 Ibid., pp. 107–9; Wheatley, pp. 77–8, 89.

34 J. Killen, *The Luftwaffe* (London, 1967), p. 148.

35 'German Air Force Operations against Great Britain', address by O. Bechtle in Berlin, 2.2.1944, reproduced in *RAF Quarterly*, XIX (1947/8), pp. 48–56; Wheatley, pp. 78–9; Hillgruber, pp. 173–4; Klee, *Dokumente*, p. 263, 'Seekriegsleitung: Besprechung der Oberbefehlshaber beim Führer. 14.9.1940'; Halder, *Kriegstagebuch*, II, pp. 128, 216.

36 Collier, *Defence of Great Britain*, pp. 256–9, 280–1; Postan, pp. 164–6; C. B. Behrens, *Merchant Shipping and the Demands of War* (HMSO, 1958), pp. 126–42; the quotation is in GS, II, p. 393.

37 Rumpf, pp. 39–41; Overy, ' "Uralbomber" to "Amerikabomber" ', pp. 159–60; on the bombing 'beams' see R. V. Jones, *Most Secret War* (London, 1978), pp. 135–81.

38 Overy, ' "Uralbomber" to "Amerikabomber" ', pp. 156–8.

39 SAOG, IV, pp. 501–4; Bekker, *Luftwaffe*, pp. 232–3.

40 L. Lochner (ed.), *The Goebbels Diaries* (London, 1948), p. 139, entry for 27.4.42.

41 Milward, pp. 40–4; G. Thomas, *Geschichte der deutschen Wehr- und Rüstungswirtschaft 1918–1943/5*, ed. W. Birkenfeld (Boppard am Rhein, 1966), pp. 432–3, 'Führererlass über Steigerung der Rüstung, 28.9.1940'; pp. 438–43, 'OKW betr. Dringlichkeit der Fertigungsprogramme, 7.2.1941'.

42 *War Directives*, p. 103, Directive no. 23, 6.2.1941.

43 Overy, ' "Uralbomber" to "Amerikabomber" ', pp. 163, 174–5.

44 Polmar, pp. 710–15, 744–5; Salewski, I, pp. 213–16 on the mining campaign; Hinsley, pp. 86–9.

45 'The Munitions Situation. Memorandum by the Prime Minister, Sept. 3 1940', Churchill, II, p. 406.

46 SAOG, i, p. 153.

47 GS, II, pp. 412–3; SAOG, I, pp. 155–66; A. Verrier, *The Bomber Offensive* (London, 1968), pp. 125–48.

48 GS, II, p. 411.

49 SAOG, I, p. 169.

50 van der Porten, pp. 174–8; K. Poolman, *Focke-Wulf Condor: Scourge of the Atlantic* (London, 1978); Roskill, *War at Sea*, I, p.p. 500, 613.

51 Ibid., I, p. 60; Salewski, I, pp. 261–7.
52 Roskill, *War at Sea*, I, pp. 459–60; *GS*, II, pp. 400–2; J. R. Butler, *Grand Strategy: Volume III Part II* (HMSO, 1964), pp. 504–7.
53 Polmar, p. 281; Poolman, chs. X–XI.
54 Baumbach, pp. 84, 6–7, 93; *War Directives*, p. 103, Directive no. 23, 6.2.1941.
55 W. Green, *The Air Forces of the World* (London, 1958), p. 173.
56 *GS*, II, p. 298; I.S.O. Playfair, *The Mediterranean and Middle East* (6 vols., HMSO, 1956–62), I, pp. 94–7; Green, *Air Forces*, p. 173.
57 Playfair, I, p. 208.
58 Mack Smith, pp. 177–8; Green, *Air Forces*, p. 174.
59 G. Bignozzi, B. Catalanotto, *Storia degli Aerei d'Italia* (Rome, 1962), pp. 131–2; Clough, p. 263; Mack Smith, pp. 177–8; Feuchter, p. 77.
60 *GS*, II, p. 98; A. Kesselring, *Memoirs* (London, 1955), p. 78.
61 Richards and Saunders, I, p. 242; Playfair, I, p. 95.
62 Polmar, pp. 97, 118–25; Roskill, *War at Sea*, I, pp. 538–9; J. Killen, *A History of Marine Aviation* (London, 1969), pp. 112–23.
63 Playfair, I, pp. 351–69; *GS*, II, pp. 374–5, 385–8, 449–50.
64 Playfair, I, pp. 431–2, 447.
65 Ibid., I, p. 208.
66 Richards and Saunders, I, pp. 247–9; Playfair, I, pp. 194–7.
67 Richards and Saunders, II, pp. 162–7.
68 *War Directives*, p. 116, Directive no. 27, 4.4.1941; pp. 120–1, Directive no. 29, 17.5.1941; Warlimont, pp. 130–2; Kesselring, pp. 116–18.
69 Ibid., pp. 119–29.
70 *War Directives*, p. 134, Directive no. 32, 11.6.1941; BA/RL3 157, Plan 'Elch'.
71 Hinsley, pp. 155–60; J. M. Gwyer, *Grand Strategy: Volume III Part I* (HMSO, 1964), p. 176; Playfair, II, p. 299; Richards and Saunders, I, pp. 274–5, 305–7.
72 Playfair, II, p. 300.
73 R. J. Overy, 'Die Mobilisierung der britischen Wirtschaft während des Zweiten Weltkrieges' in F. Forstmeier, H.-E. Volkmann (eds.), *Kriegswirtschaft und Rüstung 1939–1945* (Düsseldorf, 1977), pp. 287–9.

Chapter 3

1 *War Directives*, p. 97, directive no. 21, 18.12.1940; pp. 102–4, Directive no. 23, 6.2.1941; B. A. Leach, *German Strategy against Russia, 1941* (Oxford, 1973), pp. 129–35; A. Phillipi, F. Heim, *Der Feldzug gegen Sowjetrussland* (Stuttgart, 1962), pp. 26–42; J. Strawson, *Hitler as Military Commander* (London, 1971), pp. 132–6.
2 H. Plocher, *The German Air Force versus Russia* (3 vols., New York, 1965–8), I, pp. 18–20; Schwabedissen, pp. 48–51; A. Lee, *The Soviet Air Force* (London, 1950), pp. 117–18.
3 Boyd, p. 109; Plocher, I, p. 39; Kilmarx, p. 181; A. Seaton, *The Russo-German War 1941–45* (London, 1971), pp. 86–8.
4 *War Directives*, p. 97, Directive no. 21.
5 Halder, *Hitler as Warlord*, pp. 3–4, 20–4; Kilmarx, pp. 172–3; Seaton, pp. 75–6; R. J. Overy, 'Hitler and Air Strategy', *Journal of Contemporary History*, XV (1980), pp. 413–14; Plocher, I, pp. 252–3; R. Hofman, 'The Battle for Moscow 1941' in Jacobsen and Rohwer, p. 146; Suchenwirth, *Turning Points*, pp. 58–9.
6 *The Soviet Air Force in World War II* (ed. R. Wagner, London, 1974), Appendix 3, p. 400; Schwabedissen, p. 36.
7 Boyd, pp. 110, 190–1; Baumbach estimated on the basis of visits to Russia in 1940 that Russian air strength was 15,000 aircraft (p. 120); Lee, *Soviet Air Force*, pp. 118, 128; *Soviet Air Force*, pp. 27–8.
8 Figures from Boyd, pp. 109–11. See too Plocher, I, p. 41; Irving, *Rise and Fall*, p. 123.
9 Bekker, *Luftwaffe*, pp. 288–9; Irving, *Rise and Fall*, p. 144; Suchenwirth, *Turning Points*, pp. 25–6; Plocher, I, pp. 238–48; II, pp. 12–14.
10 Lee, *Soviet Air Force*, pp. 127–8; Kilmarx, p. 183. Halder, *Kriegstagebuch*, III, p. 341, 'Kriegslage 11.12.1941' gives a figure for all aircraft of 1,050. What reduced the figure was the very low level of serviceability which had fallen by 27.12.1941 to only 44 per cent (Klee, *Unternehmen*, p. 177).

11 *SAOG*, IV, pp. 501-4, Appendix XXVIII.
12 *War Directives*, pp. 135-8, Directive no. 32a, 14.7.1941; Thomas, *Geschichte*, pp. 436-7, 'Stellungnahme für Rüstungsfertigung 3.12.1940'; Suchenwirth, *Command and Leadership*, pp. 38-9; Hillgruber, p. 255.
13 Milward, p. 42; Suchenwirth, *Turning Points*, pp. 45-9, 54-5.
14 Overy, 'Hitler and Air Strategy', pp. 406-8; T. Elmhirst, 'The German Air Force and its Failure', *JRUSI*, XCI (1946), p. 504; Warlimont, p. 280.
15 Thomas, *Geschichte*, pp. 448-50; Milward, p. 43; Irving, *Rise and Fall*, pp. 124-6.
16 *Soviet Air Force*, pp. 67-8 on the strategy; figures from Lee, *Soviet Air Force*, p. 127; Boyd, p. 123.
17 Plocher, II, pp. 78-86; Bekker, *Luftwaffe*, pp. 351-3; Seaton, p. 246; Suchenwirth, *Turning Points*, pp. 25-6, 61-3, 73.
18 Plocher, II, p. 67.
19 Plocher, I, pp. 22-3.
20 Ibid., p. 24.
21 Irving, *Rise and Fall*, p. 131.
22 Ibid., pp. 116-17; Suchenwirth, *Command and Leadership*, p. 36.
23 Milch Documents (hereafter cited as MD), vol. LXII, 5165.
24 Irving, *Rise and Fall*, pp. 144-5; Bekker, *Luftwaffe*, pp. 369-70; W. Green, *Warplanes of the Third Reich* (London, 1970), pp. 229-30, 343.
25 Bekker, *Luftwaffe*, p. 370.
26 Ibid., p. 353.
27 Boyd, pp. 92-3, 114, 142-6; Erickson, *Soviet High Command*, p. 602; Kilmarx, pp. 175-80; K. Uebe, *Russian Reactions to German Air Power in World War II* (New York, 1964), pp. 29-31.
28 Boyd, p. 146; Uebe, p. 31; *Soviet Air Force*, pp. 103, 110, 117.
29 Boyd, p. 142; Kilmarx, pp. 176-9; Lee, *Soviet Air Force*, pp. 50-2.
30 *Soviet Air Force*, pp. 127-8.
31 Boyd, p. 147 (RAB—Raion aviatsionnovo bazirovaniya); Schwabedissen, pp. 252-3; Lee, *Soviet Air Force*, pp. 54-5, 145-6.
32 *Soviet Air Force*, pp. 383-4; Boyd, pp. 142-3.
33 Uebe, pp. 41-2; Schwabedissen, pp. 369-71, 373.
34 *Soviet Air Force*, pp. 106, 117.
35 Ibid., pp. 380, 383-4.
36 Boyd, pp. 155-60; Kilmarx, p. 185; Lee, *Soviet Air Force*, p. 133.
37 Seaton, pp. 273-4; Boyd, pp. 159-60; J. Erickson, *The Road to Stalingrad* (London, 1975), pp. 340-1; G. Zhukov, *Marshal Zhukov's Greatest Battles* (London, 1969), pp. 115-20.
38 Kilmarx, p. 185; Plocher, II, pp. 184-206 for details on the Luftwaffe attack on Sevastopol; Lee, *Soviet Air Force*, pp. 113-14.
39 Kilmarx, p. 187; Lee, *Soviet Air Force*, pp. 133-5; Collier, *Air Power*, pp. 250-1.
40 A. Galland, *The First and the Last* (London, 1955), pp. 123-4.
41 J. Fischer, 'Über den Entschluss zur Luftversorgung Stalingrads', *Militärgeschichtliche Mitteilungen*, VI (1969); Bekker, *Luftwaffe*, pp. 355-8, 369; Kilmarx, p. 186; Boyd, pp. 161-4; Manvell, Fraenkel, *Göring*, p. 196; Collier, *Air Power*, pp. 255-6.
42 *Soviet Air Force*, pp. 104, 117.
43 Ministry of Foreign Affairs, USSR, *Stalin's Correspondence with Churchill, Attlee, Roosevelt and Truman 1941-1945* (London, 1958), p. 16, 'Personal Message from Mr. Churchill to M. Stalin, 28.7.1941'. See too p. 22, Churchill to Stalin 6.9.1941, 'there is in fact no possibility of any British action in the West, except air action, which would draw German forces from the East . . .'.
44 F. Loewenheim, H. B. Langley, M. Jones, *Roosevelt and Churchill: their Secret Wartime Correspondence* (London, 1975), p. 151, doc. 67, Churchill to Roosevelt 25.7.1941.
45 *GS*, III (II), p. 526; Erickson, *Road to Stalingrad*, p. 398.
46 *Stalin's Correspondence*, p. 42, Churchill to Stalin, 21.3.1942.
47 M. Howard, *Grand Strategy: Volume IV* (HMSO, 1972), p. 264.
48 *SAOG*, II, pp. 295-6.
49 E. Stettinius, *Lend-Lease: Weapon for Victory* (New York, 1944), pp. 174-9, 187-92; Kilmarx, pp. 206-13; M. Matloff, E. Snell, *Strategic Planning for Coalition Warfare* (2 vols., Washington, 1953-9), I, pp. 341-6.
50 Seaton, pp. 436, 527; Boyd, pp. 180-2; Kilmarx, pp. 188-92; Lee, *Soviet Air Force*, pp. 140-1.

51 Baumbach, p. 213; Green, *Warplanes*, pp. 396–7; Bekker, *Luftwaffe*, pp. 379–81.
52 A. Speer, *Inside the Third Reich* (London, 1971), p. 266; for Goering's political position at the time see Manvell, Fraenkel, *Göring*, pp. 200–3.
53 Irving, *Rise and Fall*, pp. 263–72; Milward, pp. 141–2; Speer, p. 332; MD, vol. LVI, pp. 2701–13, report on formation of the *Jägerstab*.
54 *Soviet Air Force*, p. 117.
55 J. Alexander, *Russian Aircraft since 1940* (London, 1975), pp. 8, 93, 304–8; Boyd, pp. 69–73; Kilmarx, pp. 177–8; *Soviet Air Force*, pp. 13–14.
56 Kilmarx, pp. 193–4; *Soviet Air Force*, pp. 385–6; K. Craven, *The Story of Soviet Aviation* (London, 1945), pp. 14–19.
57 *Goebbels Diaries*, p. 139; Suchenwirth, *Turning Points*, pp. 76–90.
58 NA, T177, Roll 4, frame 3698645, RLM report 19.8.1941; BA/RL3 18, File 1, Kurzbericht, 21.9.1941.
59 MD, vol. LI, MD 479; MD, vol. LXII, MD 5204; Overy, ' "Uralbomber" to "Amerikabomber" ', pp. 163–5.
60 Speer, pp. 281–3.
61 A. Hillgruber *et al.*, *Kriegstagebuch des Oberkommandos der Wehrmacht* (4 vols., Frankfurt a.M., 1961–5), III (Part II), p. 1598; Green, *Warplanes*, pp. 345–6; Plocher, III, pp. 223–9; Boyd, pp. 177–8; F. Ziemke, *Stalingrad to Berlin* (New York, 1968), p. 123.
62 Irving, *Rise and Fall*, p. 216.
63 P. Wykeham, *Fighter Command* (London, 1960), pp. 210–15; Richards and Saunders, I, pp. 382–7; J. Bushby, *The Air Defence of Great Britain* (London, 1973), pp. 151–3.
64 Matloff, Snell, I, pp. 29–31; R. M. Leighton, R. W. Coakley, *Global Logistics and Strategy* (2 vols., Washington, 1955–68), I, pp. 36–9; *AAF*, VI, pp. 267–71; F. C. Pogue, *George C. Marshall: Ordeal and Hope 1939–1942* (London, 1968), pp. 67–9; H. D. Hall, *Studies of Overseas Supply* (HMSO, 1955), pp. 29–31.
65 Postan, pp. 173–4; H. D. Hall, *North American Supply* (HMSO, 1955), pp. 170–3.
66 Matloff, Snell, I, pp. 25–31; J. Winant, *A Letter from Grosvenor Square* (London, 1947), pp. 35–6; R. Payne, *General Marshall* (London, 1952), pp. 129–33.
67 On Roosevelt's enthusiasm for air power, which developed throughout the 1930s and was confirmed by the events of 1940, see Quester, p. 129; Arnold, p. 265; *AAF*, VI, pp. 14–15; K. Greenfield, *American Strategy in World War II: a Reconsideration* (Baltimore, 1963), pp. 88–9. See too *The War Messages of Franklin D. Roosevelt*, (Washington, 1943), p. 32, 'Report to Congress, 7.1.1943'. On Stimson see E. E. Morison, *Turmoil and Tradition: a Study of the Life and Times of Henry L. Stimson* (Boston, 1960), pp. 504, 542.
68 *AAF*, I, pp. 131, 139–44.
69 Hansell, Appendix IV, 'Extracts from AWPD-1', pp. 298–309; *AAF*, I, pp. 146–50.
70 Hansell, pp. 94–9, 107–11. On Marshall's attitude to air power see Pogue, pp. 86–8.
71 Hansell, pp. 100, 102–3. The argument was incorporated into the text of AWPD-42.
72 Greenfield, pp. 89–90; *AAF*, I, pp. 66–71, 257–67; VI, pp. 48–57.
73 Ibid., VI, pp. 48–9; I, pp. 253–7; I. Jacob, 'The High Level Conduct and Direction of World War II,' *JRUSI*, CI (1956), pp. 366–7.
74 Matloff, Snell, I, pp. 43–4. The US forces were to be required to reduce 'Axis economic power to wage war by blockade, raids and a sustained air offensive'.
75 *AAF*, I, pp. 237–41, 558–62; Arnold, pp. 276–88; T. Higgins, *Winston Churchill and the Second Front 1940–1943* (New York, 1957), pp. 66–9; *Roosevelt-Churchill Correspondence*, p. 19.
76 GS, III (II), pp. 523–4; Leighton, Coakley, I, pp. 275–6; *AAF*, I, pp. 567–9; Slessor, *Central Blue*, pp. 404–5; Matloff, Snell, I, pp. 248–9.
77 S. E. Morison, *American Contributions to the Strategy of World War II* (London, 1958), pp. 20–4; M. Howard, *The Mediterranean Strategy in the Second World War* (London, 1968), pp. 28–36; Matloff, Snell, I, pp. 198–216.
78 *AAF*, I, pp. 607–9, 628–39; *SAOG*, I, pp. 354–9.
79 H. Arnold, *Second Report of the Commanding General of the United States Army Air Forces to the Secretary of War* (HMSO, 1945), pp. 8–9; GS, III (II), p. 525; *SAOG*, I, pp. 214–5; Richards and Saunders, II, p. 153.
80 H. Trevor-Roper, *Hitler's Table Talk* (London, 1973), p. 70, discussion of 17.10.1941. See too p. 479, conversation of 13.5.1942, 'and, as we have no interests in the Mediterranean . . .'.
81 Mack Smith, pp. 226–8, 234.
82 *War Directives*, p. 164, Directive no. 38, 2.12.1941.

83 Ibid., pp. 163-4.
84 Hinsley, pp. 155-60; Baumbach, pp. 132-3; Polmar, p. 124; Playfair, III, p. 188. By the end of May 1942 Fliegerkorps II was down to a strength of only 91 serviceable aircraft. British figures from Polmar, pp. 749-50. A total of 764 aircraft were ferried to Malta of which 718 were safely delivered.
85 *Table Talk*, p. 573, discussion of 9.7.1942.
86 A. Tedder, 'Air, Land and Sea Warfare', *JRUSI*, XCI (1946), pp. 62-7; A. Tedder, *Air Power in War* (London, 1948), pp. 38-40; Churchill ordered on 7.10.1941 that 'The Army Commander in Chief will specify to the Air Officer Commander in Chief the targets and tasks which he requires to be performed and it will be for the Air Officer Commander in Chief to use his maximum force for these objects in the manner most effective' (Slessor, *Central Blue*, p. 422).
87 P. R. Drummond, 'The Air Campaign in Libya and Tripolitania', *JRUSI*, LXXVIII (1943), pp. 265-6; T. Elmhirst, 'Mobile Air Forces', *JRUSI*, XCVI (1951), pp. 457-61; Richards and Saunders, II, pp. 161-2.
88 H. Lloyd, 'Allied Air Power in the Mediterranean 1940-1945', *JRUSI*, XCII (1947), pp. 554-63; *GS*, IV, pp. 62-4; Richards and Saunders, II, ch. X; for details of losses see Playfair, IV, pp. 78, 101.
89 *GS*, III (II), p. 530.
90 Ibid., pp. 220-2; A. Bryant, *The Turn of the Tide* (London, 1957), pp. 194-5; de la Ferté, *Third Service*, pp. 207-9.
91 A. Coningham, 'The Development of Tactical Air Forces', *JRUSI*, XCI (1946), pp. 211-22; Playfair, IV, pp. 306-13; *AAF*, II, pp. 136-45, 161-5.
92 R. Owen, *Tedder* (London, 1952), pp. 198-202.
93 *AAF*, II, p. 137; III, pp. 806-7.
94 Greenfield, pp. 107-8; *AAF*, II, pp. 205-6.
95 Kesselring, *Memoirs*, pp. 104-8; Hinsley, p. 160.
96 Kesselring, ch. XIV; Playfair, III, pp. 177-93; Tedder, *Air Power*, pp. 46-7; Bekker, *Luftwaffe*, p. 298; Suchenwirth, *Turning Points*, pp. 90-9.
97 Bartz, p. 129; on one occasion 18 out of 20 Me 323 'Gigant' transport aircraft were destroyed on a single operation; see Playfair, IV, pp. 415-16. Total transport losses were 432 aircraft from 5-22 April 1943; see Richards and Saunders, II, p. 269.
98 Green, *Air Forces*, pp. 174-5.
99 Roskill, *War at Sea*, II, pp. 344, 432.
100 Richards and Saunders, I, ch. XII; Roskill, *War at Sea*, I, pp. 413-15, 459-62.
101 Greenfield, p. 99; E. J. King, *Fleet Admiral King: a Naval Record* (New York, 1952), pp. 451-9; *AAF*, I, pp. 538-53, on the formation of the Anti-Submarine Command; Morison, *Turmoil and Tradition*, pp. 572-7.
102 Greenfield, p. 100; King, p. 459; Morison, *Two Ocean War*, pp. 122-9.
103 *SAOG*, I, pp. 321-2, 326-7; *GS*, IV, p. 21; de la Ferté, *Third Service*, pp. 155-7.
104 Roskill, *War at Sea*, II, pp. 79-81.
105 *GS*, III (II), pp. 538-40; Slessor, *Central Blue*, pp. 482-3, 488-95; *AAF*, II, pp. 384-92; Churchill, IV, pp. 111-15.
106 Polmar, pp. 294-9; Roskill, *War at Sea*, II, pp. 366-8; III, Part I, pp. 34-6.
107 *GS*, pp. 302-8; 'Coastal Command Review, December 1943', reproduced in Slessor, *Central Blue*, pp. 472-80, esp. p. 474; *AAF*, II, pp. 387-8.
108 Slessor, *Central Blue*, pp. 511-17; Roskill, *War at Sea*, II, p. 371; Richards and Saunders, III, pp. 48-50; G. Hartcup, *The Challenge of War: Scientific and Engineering Contributions to World War II* (Newton Abbot, 1970), pp. 57-60.
109 Hinsley, p. 206; Salewski, II, pp. 297, 302-3; Richards and Saunders, III, pp. 53-4; Bekker, *Luftwaffe*, pp. 331-2.
110 *GS*, IV, pp. 311-15; K. Dönitz, *Memoirs* (London, 1959), pp. 312-13.
111 Roskill, *War at Sea*, II, pp. 352-3.
112 Slessor, *Central Blue*, p. 514; Roskill, *War at Sea*, III, Part I, pp. 15-34.
113 *GS*, IV, pp. 242-64; Hansell, pp. 149-56; *AAF*, II, pp. 295-307; Matloff, Snell, II, pp. 27-9, 70-2.
114 *GS*, IV, p. 315.
115 *AAF*, II, pp. 280, 282, 288-95; Matloff, Snell, II, p. 28.
116 *AAF*, II, p. 278. for Arnold's strategic views see *SAOG*, II, pp. 42-3.
117 *SAOG*, II, p. 13.

118 *GS*, IV, pp. 318–19; Hansell, pp. 158–71; *SAOG*, II, pp. 10–21; *AAF*, II, pp. 355–66.

119 *SAOG*, II, p. 25; 'The Combined Bomber Offensive from the United Kingdom as approved by the Chiefs of Staff, 14 May 1943', *SAOG*, IV, Appendix XXIII, pp. 273–83; *AAF*, II, pp. 348, 370–5.

120 Postan, pp. 308–16; Holley, pp. 240–1; *GS*, IV, pp. 567–8; *AAF*, II, pp. 290–1; pp. 560–74 (on establishment of XV AAF in Italy), pp. 725–6.

121 J. Ehrman, *Grand Strategy: Volume V* (HMSO, 1956), pp. 6–8; *SAOG*, II, p. 31; *AAF*, II, pp. 727–8; quotation in D. Richards, *Portal of Hungerford* (London, 1977), p. 313.

122 *GS*, V, p. 296; *Report of the Supreme Commander to the Combined Chiefs of Staff on the Operations in Europe* (HMSO, 1946), pp. 19–20; Hansell, pp. 184–8.

123 *GS*, V, pp. 291–5, 297; *AAF*, II, pp. 733–44, 751–6; III, pp. 79–83, 108–21; D. D. Eisenhower, *Crusade in Europe* (London, 1948), pp. 243–5; Hansell, pp. 232–9.

124 *AAF*, III, pp. 30–66, 149–62; *SAOG*, III, pp. 32–3, 88; USSBS, *Effects of Strategic Bombing on German Transportation*, Report 200, pp. 1–3; Bekker, *Luftwaffe*, pp. 443–6.

125 *AAF*, III, pp. 562–73.

126 Ibid., p. 591.

127 German figures from Postan, Appendix 2 (i), p. 471; *SAOG*, IV, Appendix 49 (xxiii), p. 496; Bartz, p. 203. Losses of fighter aircraft were particularly high for the Luftwaffe. Average monthly losses of fighter aircraft rose from 20 per cent in 1941 to 42 per cent in 1943 and 73 per cent in 1944. United States losses by contrast were 6.5 per cent in 1943 and 22 per cent in 1944 (USSBS, *The Defeat of the German Air Force*, Report 59, pp. 7–8). British figures from *Statistical Digest*, p. 152; Bartz, p. 203; Richards and Saunders, II, p. 372; III, p. 402; American figures from *AAF*, VI, p. 423.

128 Arnold, *Second Report*, p. 36; Arnold, *Third Report of the Commanding General of the United States Army Air Forces to the Secretary of War* (HMSO, 12.11.1945), p. 7; Bartz, p. 187; Richards and Saunders, III, pp. 112–13, 209–10; *AAF*, III, pp. 194–6. For details of the air fighting see *AAF*, III, pp. 672–711; L. F. Ellis, *Victory in the West* (2 vols., HMSO, 1962–8), I, pp. 188–90.

129 The obvious exception was the jet aircraft. Even here, however, the lead was not all that great as the performance of the Me 262, under difficult battle conditions, did not reach the Luftwaffe's expectations.

130 Overy, ' "Uralbomber" to "Amerikabomber" ', pp. 161–3; Irving, *Rise and Fall*, pp. 224, 239; on the production plans, BA/RL3 167, Plan 222; RL3 177, Plan 224/1.

131 Overy, 'Hitler and Air Strategy', p. 413; D. Irving, *Hitler's War* (London, 1977), pp. 685–6, 727–8; Galland, p. 175, who quotes General Koller (Luftwaffe Chief of Staff) as saying, 'Hitler conducted every operation and almost every battle without reserves'.

132 Lee, *German Air Force*, p. 172.

133 Overy, 'Hitler and Air Strategy', pp. 416–18.

134 Hogg, pp. 110–11; Galland, pp. 138–40; Richards and Saunders, II, pp. 288–90; Baumbach, pp. 151–2; Bekker, *Luftwaffe*, pp. 264–7, 272–3; Bartz, pp. 105–16 on General Kammhuber; Suchenwirth, *Turning Points*, pp. 110–13.

135 Galland, pp. 138–41.

136 Bekker, *Luftwaffe*, pp. 422–4, 440; Galland, pp. 156–7, 192–3.

137 Ibid., pp. 158, 189.

138 Richards and Saunders, III, pp. 279–93; Galland, pp. 189–90, 200–1.

139 *Goebbels Diaries*, p. 347, entry for 10.9.1943.

140 The proportion of fighters to bombers was 1:1 in 1940, 2:1 in 1943 and 12:1 in 1944. See Bekker, p. 481, Appendix 13; Tedder, *Air Power*, pp. 42–5.

141 USSBS, Report 59, p. 8.

142 Tedder, *Air Power*, pp. 47–8; Suchenwirth, *Turning Points*, pp. 25–6.

143 Calculated from Bekker, *Luftwaffe*, p. 485, Appendix 16.

144 Bekker, pp. 456–7; Galland, pp. 170–1; Manvell, Fraenkel, pp. 215–17, 227–8; Suchenwirth, *Command and Leadership*, pp. 193–202.

145 Irving, *Hitler's War*, pp. 703, 708; Speer, p. 408; H. Trevor-Roper (ed.), *The Goebbels Diaries: the Last Days* (London, 1978), pp. 89–90, 106–7, 112–13, 126–8; *The Collapse Viewed from within: the Memoirs of General Koller, the German Chief of Air Staff*, ADI/K Report no. 348/1945 (Imperial War Museum Library), pp. 3–8.

146 Irving, *Hitler's War*, p. 729; W. Dornberger, *V2* (London, 1954), pp. 100–5; Hinsley, pp. 230–1, 236–8; Killen, *Luftwaffe*, pp. 285–8.

147 Dornberger, p. 105.

148 Bartz, pp. 191-7, on the collapse of the Luftwaffe in 1945; see Killen, *Luftwaffe*, pp. 292-4, on the suicide squadrons or 'Raubvögel Gruppe' formed in April 1945 for the final defence of the Reich.

Chapter 4

1 R. Butow, *Tojo and the Coming of War* (Princeton U.P., 1961); C. Argyle, *Japan at War* (London, 1970); I. Nish, 'Japan and the Outbreak of War in 1941' in A. Sked, C. Cook (eds.), *Crisis and Controversy: Essays in Honour of A. J. P. Taylor* (London, 1976).
2 J. Morley (ed.), *Deterrent Diplomacy: Japan, Germany and the USSR 1935-1940* (New York, 1976), p. 131.
3 S. W. Kirby, *The War against Japan* (5 vols., HMSO, 1957-69), V, 382.
4 R. F. C. Jones, *Japan's New Order in East Asia* (Oxford, 1954), pp. 295-6.
5 A. D'Albas, *Death of a Navy* (London, 1957), p. 17.
6 Jones, pp. 293-4; A. Iriye, 'The Failure of Military Expansionism' in J. Morley (ed.), *Dilemmas of Growth in pre-war Japan* (Princeton U.P., 1971), pp. 130-6; N. Ike, *Japan's Decision for War: Records of the 1941 Policy Conferences* (Stanford, 1967); J. B. Crowley, 'A New Asian Order: some Notes on Fre-war Japanese Nationalism' in B. Silberman, H. Havooturian (eds.), *Japan in Crisis* (Princeton U.P., 1974), pp. 290-2.
7 C. Browne, *Tojo: the Last Banzai* (London, 1967), pp. 106-9; M. Ito, *The End of the Imperial Japanese Navy* (London, 1962), pp. 34-5.
8 Iriye, pp. 130-1; P. S. Dull, *A Battle History of the Imperial Japanese Navy 1941-1945* (Cambridge, 1978), pp. 5-8; D'Albas, pp. 18-21.
9 B. Collier, *The War in the Far East* (London, 1969), p. 490.
10 J. Goette, *Japan Fights for Asia* (London, 1945), pp. 62-3; R. J. Francillon, *Japanese Aircraft of the Pacific War* (London, 1970), pp. 32, 40-1.
11 Ibid., p. 31; Horikoshi, Okumiya, *Zero Fighter*, p. 121.
12 Francillon, p. 4; J. B. Cohen, *Japan's Economy in War and Reconstruction* (Minnesota U.P., 1949), p. 210.
13 *AAF*, I, pp. 137-9, 235-6; C. Thorne, *Allies of a Kind: the United States, Britain and the War against Japan 1941-1945* (London, 1978), pp. 66-78; *GS*, II, pp. 504-6; III (II), pp. 280-3.
14 *AAF*, I, p. 198; *GS*, II, p. 298; Collier, *Far East*, p. 105; Arnold, *Global Mission*, pp. 268-9.
15 *AAF*, I, p. 191.
16 Ibid., I, pp. 153-5.
17 Ibid., I, pp. 171, 288-92, 298-9; Hogg, *Anti-Aircraft*, pp. 111-13.
18 *AAF*, I, pp. 174-6.
19 Ibid., I, p. 177; Collier, *Far East*, pp. 100-1; Richards and Saunders, II, pp. 2-12; Matloff, Snell, I, pp. 69-70.
20 Collier, *Far East*, pp. 108-9; *GS*, II, pp. 350-1.
21 Richards and Saunders, II, p.5.
22 Ibid., II, pp. 6-8, 11.
23 S. Sakai, *Samurai* (London, 1959), pp. 10-13.
24 Kirby, V, pp. 394-5; Dull, pp. 103-11; Argyle, pp. 28-32; Polmar, pp. 169-79; Potter, pp. 149-51; D'Albas, pp. 62-3.
25 Thorne, pp. 155-7; Argyle, pp. 33-4; Potter, pp. 139-58; Francillon, p. 43.
26 Kirby, V, pp. 407-9; Richards and Saunders, III, pp. 299-300; by December 1942 there were 1,443 aircraft in India, the air force increasing from 5 to 26 squadrons. See too *GS*, III (II), pp. 475-6, 482-4, 489-92.
27 *AAF*, I, pp. 236-9; Matloff, Snell, I pp. 20-3; *GS*, III (II), pp. 669-72, Appendix 1, 'Washington War Conference Memo by the US and British Chiefs of Staff'.
28 'Second Report to the Secretary of the Navy' in E. J. King, *US Navy at War 1941-1945: the Official Reports to the Secretary of the Navy* (Washington, 1946), p. 162; King, *Fleet Admiral*, pp. 213-15, 247-65.
29 *AAF*, I, pp. 213-13, 330-1; VII, pp. 46-55; Roosevelt, *Public Papers, VI, pp. 108-9*.
30 *AAF*, I, pp. 361-2; VII, pp. 8-18.
31 Kirby, V, pp. 412-14; *AAF*, IV, pp. 405-34.
32 Ibid., VII, pp. 114-51; V, pp. 58-91; G. Grimsdale, 'The War against Japan in China', *JRUSI*, XCV (1950), pp. 260-7; on Japanese planning see USAF Far East (hereafter cited as USAFFE), *Air Operations in the China Area* (Japanese Monographs no. 76, December 1956), esp. pp. 107-8, 143-57.

33 'First Report to the Secretary of the Navy', 23.4.1944, in King, *US Navy*, pp. 15, 39; Leighton, Coakley, I, pp. 133–4.

34 Ito, pp. 13–69; Polmar, pp. 194–235;.Dull, pp. 115–29, 145–68; D'Albas, pp. 91–9; Collier, *Far East*, pp. 451–6.

35 Cohen, p. 233.

36 Kirby, V, pp. 399–401; USSBS, *Japanese Air Power*, Report 62, pp. 9–12.

37 Morison, *American Contributions*, pp. 63–70; Dull, pp. 303–10, 313–19; D'Albas, pp. 166–7.

38 'Third Report to the Secretary of the Navy', 8.12.1945, in King, *US Navy*, pp. 233–4, 287; Polmar, p. 753.

39 'Second Report', 27.3.1945, p. 146.

40 Kirby, V, p. 398; Morison, *American Contributions*, p. 47.

41 B. Martin, *Deutschland und Japan im Zweiten Weltkrieg* (Göttingen, 1969), pp. 129–51.

42 Cohen, pp. 210, 226–7.

43 Ibid., p. 210.

44 Ibid., p. 211.

45 Strength figures from Cohen, p. 233. Total United States naval air strength was 36,721 in mid-1944 and 41,272 by VJ-Day; see Turnbull, Lord, pp. 319, 322. Figures for losses from USSBS, *Summary Report Pacific War*, p. 9; Cohen, p. 233; USSBS, *Japanese Air Power*, Report 62, Exhibits B. C.

46 Argyle, pp. 174–5; USSBS, *Japanese Air Weapons and Tactics*, Report 63, pp. 1–4, 8; Francillon, pp. 5–6.

47 USSBS, Report 62, Exhibit P 'Japanese Fighters Assigned to Defence of Japan'.

48 BIOS JAP PR 932, *The Aluminium Industry of Japan*, pp. 2–3; Cohen, p. 231.

49 Polmar, p. 474, who claims that 70 per cent of Japanese aircraft broke down before entering service by late 1944. On aluminium see USSBS, *Effects of Strategic Bombing on Japan's War Economy*, Report 53, p. 25; Cohen, pp. 230–1.

50 Cohen, p. 231; USSBS, Report 62, pp. 44–5, Appendix iii, Tables B, C.

51 King, 'First Report', pp. 63–9, 'Second Report', p. 109.

52 Horikoshi, Okumiya, pp. 163–4; USSBS, Report 63, p. 10. See too Morison, *History* III, p. 24: 'We are striving to reach a superhuman degree of skill and perfect fighting efficiency' (Japanese Naval Dept. 1937).

53 T. Kase, *Eclipse of the Rising Sun* (London, 1951), p. 139; USSBS, Report 62, p. 12; Cohen, p. 215.

54 Polmar, pp. 470–2.

55 *AAF*, pp. 470–504.

56 King, 'Third Report', pp. 181–9; *AAF*, V, pp. 685–6.

57 Ibid., V, pp. 233–51, 275–469; Morison, *American Contributions*, pp. 52–4, 62–3; Kirby, V, pp. 409–16.

58 *AAF*, V, pp. 13–19; IV, pp. 422–43.

59 Ibid., V, pp. 105–6; W. Koenig, *Over the Hump: Airlift to China* (London, 1972), pp. 63–6, 112–17.

60 Arnold, 'Second Report AAF', pp. 64–72; Matloff, Snell, II, pp. 328–30; *AAF*, VI, pp. 208–9.

61 Matloff, Snell, II, pp. 87–8, 136–7.

62 G. Grimsdale, 'The War against Japan in China', *JRUSI*, XCV (1950), pp. 261–6; Matloff, Snell, II, pp. 442–50.

63 *AAF*, V, pp. 28–9, 133.

64 USAFFE, *Air Operations in China Area*, pp. 157–80; *AAF*, V, pp. 215–24.

65 Greenfield, pp. 118–19.

66 *AAF*, p. 552; H. Feis, *The Atomic Bomb and the End of World War II* (Princeton U.P., 1966), pp. 6–8.

67 *AAF*, V, pp. 575–6, 608–14.

68 USSBS, Report 62, p. 26; *AAF*, V, p. 643.

69 USSBS, Report 62, pp. 3, 26, 45–6; USSBS, Report 63, p. 4.

70 R. Inoguchi, T. Nakajima, R. Pineau, *The Divine Wind: Japan's Kamikaze Force in World War II* (London, 1959), pp. 169–71.

71 Kirby, V, p. 404; C. W. Nimitz, E. Potter, *The Great Sea War* (London, 1961), pp. 454–5; Ito, pp. 184–99; USSBS, Report 62, Appendix V. American intelligence estimated that some 90 ships would be sunk during the projected Japanese invasion, a small fraction of those available for the operation.

72 R. Nagatsaku, *I was a Kamikaze* (London, 1973), pp. 183–9.

73 USSBS, Report 11, *Final Report Covering Air-Raid Protection and Allied Subjects in Japan*, p. 200; on the fire-bombing campaign see *AAF*, V, ch xx.
74 Ibid., V, pp. 626-7, LeMay to Norstad, 25.4.1945.
75 King, 'Third Report', p. 190; *AAF*, V, pp. 646-62; Quester, pp. 165, 168.
76 *AAF*, V, pp. 663-4; E. A. Johnson, *Mines against Japan* (White Oak, Md., 1963), pp. 21-39.
77 *AAF*, V, pp. 728-30, 756; Quester, p. 171; Feis, pp. 190-4.
78 *War Directives*, p. 105, Directive no. 24, 5.3.1941.

Chapter 5

1 Overy, ' "Uralbomber" to "Amerikabomber" ', pp. 155-6.
2 Suchenwirth, *Command and Leadership*, p. 77; Irving, *Rise and Fall*, p. 65; Suchenwirth, *Turning Points*, pp. 29-31, 36-7.
3 *SAOG*, I, pp. 36-7, note.
4 MD, vol. LXV, 7320, 7409-10. Baumbach, p. 51, records Goering's claim on 8 Nov. 1943 that 'At the start of the war Germany was the only country in the world to have a strategic air force with machines that were absolutely modern.'
5 Boyd, pp. 55-69. Both Tupolev and Petlyakov were interned in the mid-1930s after their successful heavy-bomber designs were superseded by the medium-bombers for close support which Stalin personally favoured.
6 R. Worcester, *The Roots of British Air Policy* (London, 1966), pp. 24-6.
7 Prime Minister to Secretary of State for Air, 20.10.1940, in Churchill, II, pp. 603-4; *SAOG*, IV, Directive to Bomber Command, 21.9.1940, pp. 124-5.
8 Prime Minister to Trenchard, 4.9.1942, in Churchill, IV, p. 496.
9 T. A. Wilson, *The First Summit* (London, 1969), pp. 134-5; R. E. Sherwood, *The White House Papers of Harry L. Hopkins* (2 vols., London, 1949), II p. 586; Morison, *Turmoil and Tradition*, p. 542.
10 Wilson, *First Summit*, pp. 134-5, 252-5; *AAF*, VI, pp. 270-1, on Churchill's influence on Roosevelt to create an American heavy-bomber force.
11 M. P. Schoenfeld, *The War Ministry of Winston Churchill* (Iowa State U.P., 1972), pp. 92-3; Quester, p. 141.
12 Prime Minister to Minister of Aircraft Production, 8.7.1940, in Churchill, II, 567.
13 *White House Papers*, II, p. 585.
14 *Stalin's Correspondence*, p. 16, Churchill to Stalin, 28.7.1941, and p. 22, Churchill to Stalin, 6.9.1941; H. Feis, *Churchill, Roosevelt, Stalin* (Princeton U.P., 1957), pp. 80-4; Higgins, pp. 66-9.
15 *AAF*, IV, 438-40; V, p. 21; Thorne, pp. 427-8; Arnold, pp. 422-3; Quester, p. 164.
16 For a general discussion see Frankland, *Bombing Offensive*, M. Dean, *The Royal Air Force and Two World Wars* (London, 1979), pp. 254-97; Verrier, *Bomber Offensive*, esp. Part IV.
17 See General Spaatz's conclusion that 'Strategic Air Power could not have won this war without the surface forces'; C. Spaatz, 'Strategic Air Power—Fulfilment of a Concept', *Foreign Affairs*, no. 24 (1945-6), p. 395; Dickens, pp. 33-7; M. Howard, *Studies in War and Peace* (London, 1970), pp. 141-5; *AAF*, III, p. 804.
18 GS, III (II), p. 525; Richards, *Portal*, p. 305; *SAOG*, IV, pp. 135-7, Directive to Bomber Command, Bottomley to Peirse, Appendix A, 'for approximately ¾ of each month it is only possible to obtain satisfactory results by heavy, concentrated and continuous area attacks of large working-class and industrial areas . . .'.
19 GS, II, pp. 483-4.
20 Hansell, pp. 85, 104-5.
21 *AAF*, V, p. 610.
22 *SAOG*, I, pp. 144-65.
23 Hansell, pp. 80-3, 105-6.
24 Ibid., Appendix IV, AWPD-I, p. 299.
25 *SAOG*, I, pp. 147-8, 294-5, 351-2.
26 *War Directives*, p. 134, Directive no. 32, 11.6.1941: 'the "Siege of England" must be resumed with the utmost intensity by the Navy and Air Force after the conclusion of the campaign in the East'; *Goebbels Diaries*, p. 139.
27 Dickens, pp. 39-40; Higgins, pp. 66-9, 98-9; J. Slessor, 'Air Power and the Future of War', *JRUSI*, XCIX (1954), pp. 344-5; Quester, pp. 146-7.
28 Arnold, p. 235.

29 Hansell, p. 299.
30 *SAOG*, II, pp. 10–11; *GS*, IV, pp. 253–5, 262–4.
31 *SAOG*, II, pp. 24–30.
32 Ibid., II, pp. 64–7; Richards, *Portal*, pp. 307–8, 312–16, 318–19.
33 *GS*, IV, pp. 25–7; Churchill, IV, p. 609; Richards, *Portal*, pp. 258–60; Arnold, pp. 396–7; *AAF*, II, pp. 298–300, 302–3.
34 Hinsley, p. 27; *SAOG*, I, p. 97.
35 Hinsley, pp. 28–30.
36 D. Kahn, *Hitler's Spies* (London, 1979), pp. 382–4.
37 Hinsley, pp. 101–2; *SAOG*, I, pp. 260–7.
38 Ibid., I, pp. 178–9, 247; Richards, *Portal*, pp. 302–3; Verrier, pp. 128–31.
39 *SAOG*, I, pp. 353–63; Richards, *Portal*, pp. 312–17; A. Harris, *Bomber Offensive* (London, 1947), p. 264, who claimed 'we never had sufficient information about German industry to offer any certainty of success.'
40 Hansell, pp. 49–50.
41 Ibid., pp. 51–2.
42 Ibid., pp. 52–3.
43 Ibid., pp. 105, 108.
44 Ibid., pp. 148–9.
45 Ibid., pp. 195–7; *AAF*, III, pp. 790–1; D. McIsaac, *Strategic Bombing in World War Two* (London, 1976), for a general discussion of the establishment and activities of the bombing surveys.
46 Richards, *Portal*, pp. 312–13; Harris to Air Ministry, 7.12.1943, in *SAOG*, II, pp. 54–7; *SAOG*, III, p. 21.
47 Ibid., III, pp. 302–3; II, pp. 47–9; Verrier, pp. 320–2.
48 Overy, ' "Uralbomber" to "Amerikabomber" ', pp. 167–8.
49 Ibid., pp. 168–71; E. Heinkel, *He 1000* (London, 1954), pp. 220–34. The actual production of heavy bombers in Germany was 251 in 1942, 491 in 1943 and 516 in 1944. Britain was producing over 5,000 a year by 1944.
50 *GS*, I, pp. 550–1; *AAF*, I, pp. 65–71; Spaatz, p. 389; M. M. Postan, D. Hay, J. D. Scott, *Design and Development of Weapons* (HMSO, 1964), pp. 78–9, 125.
51 *AAF*, V, pp. 6–10.
52 *SAOG*, II, pp. 20–1; Verrier, p. 46; Arnold, pp. 261–4.
53 Matloff, II, p. 70; *AAF*, III, pp. 9–12; *SAOG*, II, pp. 79–82; Hansell, pp. 253–4.
54 MD, vol. LXII, 5208; vol. LXIII, 5859–61.
55 *SAOG*, I, pp. 225–6, 252–3, 391–3. Portal wrote in 1940 'We have not yet reached the stage of desiring to burn down a whole town, but when this stage is reached we shall do it by dropping a large quantity of incendiaries first and then a sustained attack with High Explosive to drive the fire-fighters underground and let the flames get a good hold . . .' (Richards, *Portal*, p. 165).
56 *AAF*, III, ch. VI; *GS*, V, pp. 286–7; on LeMay's arguments for the move from precision bombing see *AAF*, V, p. 612. According to LeMay's intelligence reports no more than 17 per cent and sometimes as little as 0–1 per cent of bombs were within 3,000 feet of the precise target.
57 Jones, pp. 396–9; Verrier, pp. 146–7, 211–12; Harris, pp. 124–8, 170–2.
58 Richards, *Portal*, p. 189.
59 Prime Minister to Chief of Air Staff, 7.10.1941, in Churchill, III, pp. 451–2.
60 *GS*, III (I), p. 37. On Churchill's disillusionment with bombing see Schoenfeld, pp. 93–4.
61 A. J. P. Taylor, *Beaverbrook* (London, 1972), pp. 402–3, 510; Beaverbrook also favoured the idea of a separate army air force, *GS*, II, p. 349.
62 M. Foot, *Aneurin Bevan* (2 vols., London, 1962), I, p. 374.
63 See for example G. E. Hopkins, 'Bombing and the American Conscience during the Second World War', *Historian*, XXVIII (1966).
64 Bryant, *Turn of the Tide*, p. 322.
65 Slessor, *Central Blue*, pp. 494–5, discusses the reluctance of the air forces to assist in naval work. General Arnold claimed later: 'The Army Air Force from the start never did really want to continue the anti-submarine patrol work . . .' (*Global Mission*, p. 363). On Harris's resistance see *SAOG*, IV, pp. 239–44, 'Note by Air Marshal Sir Arthur Harris . . . on the Role of Work of Bomber Command, 28.6.1942'.
66 *GS*, IV, pp. 19–21; III, pp. 528–9; *SAOG*, II, pp. 48–9, 97–8, 269.

67 Hansell, p. 299.
68 Harris, pp. 192-3, 263; *SAOG*, II, pp. 35-6, 47-8; *GS*, V, pp. 289-96; Quester, pp. 146-7.
69 *AAF*, V, pp. 9-10; Quester, pp. 165-8.
70 *SAOG*, IV, pp. 164-5, Directive to Bomber Command, 17.2.1944; pp. 167-70, Directive by the Supreme Commander USSTAF and Bomber Command for Support of Overlord, 17.4.1944; A. Bryant, *Triumph in the West* (London, 1959), pp. 143-4; Hansell, pp. 204-9; N. Bottomley, 'The Strategic Bomber Offensive against Germany,' *JRUSI*, XCIII (1946), pp. 228-33; on Eisenhower's concern at the bomber's capabilities see Eisenhower, *Crusade*, pp. 71-2; *GS*, V, pp. 286-8.
71 *SAOG*, III, p. 22; Eisenhower, p. 72.
72 *GS*, V, p. 296.
73 Quester, p. 133; USAFFE, *Air Operations*, p. 180; Kirby, V, pp. 382-7.
74 Galland, pp. 158, 189; Warlimont, p. 280, who wrote 'Up to August 1943 the German Supreme Headquarters had treated the air offensive more or less as a routine matter . . .'.
75 Irving, *Hitler's War*, p. 574.
76 Overy, ' "Uralbomber" to "Amerikabomber" ', pp. 161-2.
77 MD, vol. LXIII, 6216, 5862-3; vol. LIII, 732, Goering to Milch, 12.10.1943; Galland, pp. 171-2; Quester, pp. 144-6; Suchenwirth, *Turning Points*, pp. 110-11; Salewski, II, p. 303 on Jeshonnek's directive to drop at least 'one bomb on London every night if possible . . .'.
78 Hinsley, *Hitler's Strategy*, pp. 167-8; Warlimont, p. 228.
79 Tedder, *Air Power*, diagram 5; *SAOG*, IV, p. 496; *Statistical Digest*, p. 152; *AAF*, VI, p. 352.
80 W. Boelcke, *Deutschlands Rüstung im Zweiten Weltkrieg: Hitlers Konferenz_n mit Albert Speer 1942-45* (Frankfurt a.M., 1969), p. 468; Green, *Warplanes*, pp. 53-4. The Arado bomber was produced but it was used as a high-level reconnaissance aircraft.
81 Irving, *Hitler's War*, p. 729; Killen, *Luftwaffe*, pp. 245-7, 263-4.
82 Thomas, *Geschichte*, pp. 414-15, 425-6, 433 for documents on anti-aircraft gun priority; *Hitler's Table Talk*, p. 669; MD, vol. LXII, 5167-75; Irving, *Hitler's war*, pp. 703, 708; Speer, p. 408.
83 Suchenwirth, *Command and Leadership*, p. 272; Baumbach, p. 52.
84 Irving, *Rise and Fall*, pp. 224, 244, 287; Speer, pp. 349-51.
85 Ibid., p. 351; Galland, pp. 206, 219-22.
86 Ibid., p. 206.
87 Warlimont, p. 280; L. Moseley, *The Reich Marshal* (London, 1974), pp. 290-1; W. Frischauer, *The Rise and Fall of Hermann Göring* (London, 1950), pp. 234-5; *Goebbels Diaries: the Last Days*, pp. 89-90, 106-7.
88 Speer, pp. 397-8; R. Manvell, H. Fraenkel, *Doctor Goebbels* (London, 1960), pp. 211-14; D. Orlow, *The History of the Nazi Party* (2 vols., Newton Abbot, 1973), II, pp. 463-4, 468-71; Manvell, Fraenkel, *Göring*, pp. 227-8.
89 R. Wagenführ, *Die deutsche Industrie im Kriege* (Berlin, 1963), p. 78.
90 *SAOG*, IV, pp. 321-40, Speer's reports to Hitler on fuel situation, 30.6.1944 to 19.1.1945; III, pp. 115-40.
91 R. J. Overy, *German Aircraft Production 1939-1942* (unpublished Ph.D. thesis, Cambridge University, 1978), pp. 214-19; Milward, pp. 92-3.
92 Interrogation of Speer, 30.5.1945 in *SAOG*, IV, p. 377; Speer estimated the number engaged on repair of war damage at 1-1.5 million by mid-1944. Interrogation of Albert Speer, 18.7.1945 in *SAOG*, IV, p. 383; Tedder, *Air Power*, p. 103; Arnold, 'Third report', p. 10.
93 Milward, pp. 101-18; Verrier, p. 321; *SAOG*, II, pp. 247-54; III, pp. 302-3.
94 BA/RL3 157, 'Elch-Programm', 13.8.1941; RL3 146, 'Göring-Flugzeug-Lieferplan', 15.9.1941. A programme of 3,000 aircraft a month was first planned in mid-1942; BA/RL3 156, 'Flugzeug-Programm 22E', 19.8.1942.
95 BA/RL3 237, Studie 1036. Output was planned to rise to 7,100 a month by 1946. According to Speer fighter output was 50 per cent lower than capacity in 1944-5; Arnold, 'Third Report', p. 10.
96 Irving, *Rise and Fall*, p. 125; Speer, p. 112; MD, vol. LXII, 5221, 5237; BA/RL3 244, minutes of Industrierat meeting, 26.10.1942.
97 Overy, *Aircraft Production*, pp. 145-6.
98 Ibid., pp. 219-21, 202-5.
99 USSBS, Report 4, *Aircraft Division Industry Report*, p. 32; USSBS, *Aircraft Division Air Frames Report no. 6*, Appendix I, pp. 1-4, Appendix II, pp. 1-5; Ibid., Report 9, pp. 9-12. There are many other examples.

100 USSBS, Report 4, pp. 24, 26; the 27 main aircraft plants were to be broken up in 1944 into 729 smaller ones; *SAOG*, III, pp. 222–3; Overy, *Aircraft Production*, pp. 283–6.
101 USSBS, Report 4, p. 20.
102 Ibid., pp. 25–6; Overy, *Aircraft Production*, pp. 212–12.
103 R. J. Overy, 'The Luftwaffe and the European Economy 1939–1945', *Militärgeschichtliche Mitteilungen*, XXI (1979), pp. 57–65.
104 *SAOG*, II, pp. 292–3; Overy, 'European Economy', pp. 66–9.
105 *SAOG*, IV, p. 494; BA/RL3 244 Milch conference, 10.12.1942; RL3 245, 71–6 Junkers-Studie 177; MD, vol. LVI, Milch conference on dispersal 11.11.1942.
106 Overy, 'European Economy', pp. 64–5; *SAOG*, III, pp. 225–72; on Polish aircraft capacity see J. Cynk, *Polish Aircraft 1893–1939* (London, 1971), pp. xix–xx.
107 USSBS, report 63, pp. 8, 12.
108 Morison, *Turmoil and Tradition*, pp. 633–6.
109 Arnold, 'Third Report', pp. 36–40, interrogation of Premier Hagishi-Kuni; *SAOG*, III, pp. 221–4; Kase, pp. 139–40, Greenfield, p. 113.
110 *AAF*, V, pp. 710–11.
111 Kase, pp. 214, 217; Arnold, p. 564. Prince Konoye maintained after the surrender that 'Fundamentally the thing that brought about the determination to make peace was the prolonged bombing by the B-29's'. Prince Suzuki, Prime Minister during the summer of 1945, concluded that 'on the basis of the B-29 raids . . . the cause was hopeless'; see *AAF*, V, p. 741 for both quotations.
112 H. Truman, *Year of Decision, 1945* (New York, 1955), pp. 346–50. Truman believed that Japan would not be defeated until November 1946 by conventional means despite all the evidence that Japanese resistance was about to end because of the bombing campaign.

Chapter 6

1 For an interesting introduction to this theme see A. Perlmutter, 'Military Incompetence and Failure: A Historical, Comparative and Analytical Evaluation', *Journal of Strategic Studies*, I (1978), pp. 121–36.
2 There are few studies of air force administration. See C. Grey, *Luftwaffe* (London, 1944), pp. 133–7, 208–10; C. Grey, *A History of the Air Ministry* (London, 1940); on the AAF see *AAF*, VI, chs. I–II.
3 F. A. Johnson, *Defence by Committee: The British Committee of Imperial Defence 1885–1959* (Oxford, 1960), pp. 1–8, 288–303, 349–74; Jacob, pp. 365–6; H. Sprout, 'Trends in the Traditional Relation between Military and Civilian', *Proceedings of the American Philosophical Society*, XCII (1948); Command Paper Cmd 6351, *The Organization for Joint Planning* (HMSO, 1942), pp. 2–4; Dean, pp. 82–98; E. R. May, 'The Development of Politico-Military Consultation in the United States', *Political Science Quarterly*, LXX (1955), pp. 171–3.
4 Schoenfeld, chs. ii–iii, pp. 91–4; Dean, pp. 180–6.
5 H. L. Stimson, McG. Bundy, *On Active Service in Peace and War* (New York, 1947), pp. 524, 538–9.
6 Mack Smith, pp. 176–9; one under-secretary at the Air Ministry claimed never to have seen Mussolini at the Ministry building; R. Klibansky (ed.), *Mussolini's Memoirs 1942–43* (London, 1949), p. 237.
7 W. Carr, *Hitler: a Study in Personality and Politics* (London, 1978), pp. 78–80; Rumpf, pp. 35–6.
8 Warlimont, pp. 75, 280.
9 Baumbach, p. 50; Elmhirst, 'German Air Force', p. 504; Overy, *Aircraft Production*, ch. III.
10 Overy, 'Hitler and Air Strategy', p. 408.
11 Suchenwirth, *Command and Leadership*, pp. 138–9; Baumbach, p. 84, who records Hitler's view in the middle of the war that the Luftwaffe was 'the most effective strategic weapon. . .'; even in May 1944 Hitler was prepared to tell Goering that 'in the final analysis it was always the Luftwaffe which had turned the scales in his campaigns. . .' (Irving, *Rise and Fall*, p. 279).
12 Suchenwirth, *Command and Leadership*, pp. 274–8; A. Nielsen, *The German Air Force General Staff* (New York, 1959), pp. 139–40, 143–5, 151–4.
13 Ibid., p. 147.
14 Dornberger, pp. 103–4; Halder, *Warlord*, pp. 15–16.
15 Speer, pp. 407–8; Hitler concluded a stormy meeting on 10 August 1944 by shouting, 'I want

no more planes produced at all. The fighter arm is to be dissolved. Stop aircraft production!'.
On Hitler and the problem of jet aircraft see Suchenwirth, *Turning Points*, pp. 124–6; Irving,
Rise and Fall, pp. 275–89.

16 Koller, *Collapse. . .*, p. 8.

17 *Goebbels Diaries: the Last Days*, p. 126, entry for 26 March 1945.

18 de la Ferté, *Third Service*, pp. 107–17 on the political crisis of the 1930s; Hyde, *British Air
Policy*, pp. 98–150; Slessor, *Central Blue*, pp. 144–84; Powers, pp. 174–86; Dean, pp. 69–73.
On United States experience in the 1930s see Turnbull, Lord, pp. 186–92.

19 Morison, *Turmoil and Tradition*, pp. 504, 542. Stimson maintained that 'Air power. . . has
decided the fate of nations. . .'; *AAF*, I, p. 116.

20 Ibid., I, p. 152–3.

21 Ibid., VI, p. 25.

22 Pogue, pp. 290–1.

23 *AAF*, VI, pp. 27–30.

24 Ibid., I, pp. 66–71, 257–67; II, pp. 205–6; VI, pp. 48–57; Greenfield, pp. 89–90, 96–107.

25 Boyd, pp. 92–3, 142–6; Kilmarx, pp. 176–9; Lee, *Soviet Air Force*, pp. 35–6.

26 Nielsen, p. 123.

27 Ibid., pp. 21–3; Homze, pp. 46–55.

28 USSBS, Report 62, pp. 1–2; Francillon, pp. 29–33.

29 USSBS, Report 62, Appendix 1, p.59.

30 Slessor, *Central Blue*, pp. 419–22, on the clash between army and RAF views of strategy; *GS*,
III (II), pp. 530–7; Churchill, III, p. 728; Greenfield, pp. 98–9, 101.

31 On Germany see Wagenführ, pp. 29–30, 73; Homze, p.228; Overy, 'Pre-war plans', pp.
790–1.

32 Postan, pp. 304–6.

33 de la Ferté, *Third Service*, pp. 109–11, 115; T. Taylor, *The Breaking Wave* (London, 1967),
pp. 83–4.

34 Jacob, p. 365; E. Devons, *Planning in Practice. Essays in Aircraft Planning in Wartime*
(Cambridge, 1950), pp. 2–15; Dean, pp. 82–98.

35 *AAF*, VI, pp. 32–3, 38–9; Sprout, pp. 265–8; Greenfield, p. 89.

36 *AAF*, VI, pp. 36–8.

37 Arnold, 'Third Report', pp. 63–5; by 1945 over 500,000 civilians were employed by the AAF
in the technical and maintenance sectors. *AAF*, VI, pp. 38–40; May, pp. 171–3.

38 Lee, *Soviet Air Force*, p. 35.

39 Ibid., pp. 54–5.

40 Boyd, pp. 90–2; Lee, pp. 42–5, 136.

41 Richards and Saunders, I, pp. 404–5; II, pp. 368–9; III, pp. 396–7.

42 *Soviet Air Force*, p. 125.

43 H. Hermann, *The Rise and Fall of the Luftwaffe* (London, 1944), pp. 84–94; Lee, *Goering*,
p. 205; H. Herlin, *Udet: a Man's Life* (London, 1960), pp. 106–53; Kesselring had spent time
in sanatoria in the 1920s for morphine addiction.

44 Baumbach, pp. 20–1; Nielsen, pp. 23, 27, 41–3; A. Price, *Luftwaffe Handbook 1939–1945*
(London, 1977), pp. 91–100; Jeschonnek (Chief of Staff, 1938–43), Korten (Chief of Staff,
1943–4) and Kreipe (Chief of Staff, 1944) were all from the infantry or cavalry and joined
the Luftwaffe late in their careers. Stumpff, Kesselring and Kammhuber were all ex-army
officers. Only Koller and Sperrle had uninterrupted air force experience. Suchenwirth, *Turning
Points*, pp. 14–15.

45 Nielsen, pp. 138–9; Suchenwirth, *Turning Points*, pp. 8–9; out of the 42 main office-holders
in the Luftwaffe technical organization only two were noble (MD, vol. LVI, list of GL
personnel, Feb. 1939).

46 Nielsen, pp. 26, 145; Irving, *Rise and Fall*, pp. 68–9; Suchenwirth, *Command and Leadership*,
pp. 274–5.

47 Hermann, pp. 66–7; NA, T177, Roll 37, frame 3727564–5, Tank to Kesselring 13.6.1942;
Kesselring, p. 109; Herlin, p. 202; Völker, *Die deutsche Luftwaffe*, p. 126; Völker, *Dokumente*,
pp. 152–64, documents 59–62; Irving, *Rise and Fall*, pp. 67–9.

48 Nielsen, pp. 46–8. Out of 331 Luftwaffe General Staff officers some 87 were killed or captured.
Galland, pp. 173–4.

49 Ibid., pp. 48–9; H. Conradis, *Design for Flight* (London, 1960), 'The causes of the defeat of
the German Luftwaffe 1939–45. Memorandum of Kurt Tank', p. 208.

50 Figures for Germany from *OKW Kriegstagebuch*, III (ii), pp. 1576, 1597. Figures for United

States from *AAF*, VI, p. 427; R. F. Weigley, *History of the United States Army* (London, 1968), p. 435. Figures for Britain from *Statistical Digest*, p. 9. Figures for USSR from Seaton, p. 527.

51 The best discussion of pilot recruitment and training programmes is in *AAF*, VI, chs. xvi-xvii; see too Lee, *Soviet Air Force*, pp. 56–71; Lee, *German Air Force*, pp. 29–40.

52 *AAF*, VI, pp. 429–30; Greenfield, p. 90.

53 *AAF*, VI, pp. 523–4.

54 Nagatsuka, pp. 12–37.

55 Boyd, p. 96; Kilmarx, p. 131.

56 P. Meier-Benneckenstein, *Wehrhaftes Volk* (Berlin, 1939), pp. 307–26.

57 Boyd, pp. 94–5; Lee, *Soviet Air Force*, pp. 56–9; Kilmarx, pp. 132–3.

58 Dempster and Wood, pp. 67, 74; B. Philpott, *Challenge in the Air* (Hemel Hempstead, 1971), p. 11.

59 *AAF*, VI, pp. 445–6.

60 Postan, pp. 316–22; in the Russian case the factories actually trained the service engineers: see *Soviet Air Force*, p. 19.

61 P. Joubert de la Ferté *The Forgotten Ones: the Story of the Ground Crews* (London, 1961); Schwabedissen, pp. 252–3; Boyd, pp. 147, 206–7; Richards and Saunders, II, pp. 62–3; Roskill, *War at Sea*, II, p. 85; *Soviet Air Force*, pp. 128, 206–7; CIOS, XXV–45, *German Aircraft Maintenance* (HMSO, 1946); CIOS, XXVII–64, *German Aircraft Maintenance and Overhaul Methods* (HMSO, 1946).

62 USSBS, Report 62, Appendix 1, p. 30; *AAF*, III, p. 591; *SAOG*, IV, pp. 501–4; Klee, *Unternehmen*, p. 177.

63 *AAF*, VI, pp. 503–8.

64 USSBS, Report 62, Appendix 1, p. 28, Appendix 2, p. 36.

65 For general details on training see Kilmarx, pp. 132–41; Boyd, pp. 95–6; Schliephake, pp. 56–7; L. Pattinson, 'The Training of a Royal Air Force Pilot', *JRUSI*, LXXXIII(1938), pp. 11–19.

66 Lee, *German Air Force*, pp. 267–75, on the special position enjoyed by air force recruits; see the discussion in R. F. Toliver, T. J. Constable, *Horrido! Fighter Aces of the Luftwaffe* (London, 1968).

67 Horikoshi, Okumiya, pp. 62–3.

68 Inoguchi, *Divine Wind*, pp. 175–6; Goette, pp. 62–3.

69 Nagatsuka, pp. 22–7, 176–7.

70 USSBS, Report 62, Appendix 2, p. 35; *AAF*, I, pp. 79–80.

71 USSBS, Report 62, pp. 11–12.

72 Bekker, *Luftwaffe*, Appendix 2, p. 466.

73 *GS*, II, pp. 38–9.

74 'The Empire Air Training Scheme', *RAF Quarterly*, XVI (1944/5), pp. 80–8; Slessor, *Central Blue*, p. 33; Richards and Saunders, I, pp. 72–4; III, p. 371.

75 *GS*, II, p. 39.

76 Richards and Saunders, I, p. 72; *GS*, II, p. 414.

77 *AAF*, VI, pp. 428–34; USSBS, Report 62, p. 2.

78 *AAF*, VI, pp. 520–1.

79 Boyd, pp. 16–19; Lee, *Soviet Air Force*, pp. 59–65; *Soviet Air Force*, pp. 124–5.

80 USSBS, Report 62, pp.2, 11–12; Appendix 2, pp. 34–6; *AAF*, I, pp. 80–2.

81 USSBS, Report 62, p. 36; Inoguchi, pp. 92–3; Nagatsuka, pp. 146–8.

82 USSBS, Report 62, p. 2.

83 Nielsen, p. 188.

84 Bekker, *Luftwaffe* p. 485, Appendix 16.

85 Suchenwirth, *Turning Points*, pp. 22, 25–6; Galland, pp. 174–5.

86 Lee, *German Air Force*, pp. 31–4; Price, *Luftwaffe Handbook*, 63–4; USSBS, Report 59, p. 3; Suchenwirth, *Turning Points*, p. 28; Elmhirst, 'German Air Force', p. 515.

87 *SAOG*, II, pp. 74–6, 194–6; III, pp. 293–4; Verrier, pp. 194–204.

88 *Soviet Air Force*, pp. 124–5, 148–9.

89 *Soviet Air Force*, pp. 22–3.

90 M. Messerschmidt, *Die Wehrmacht im NS-Staat* (Hamburg, 1969), pp. 264–76; Suchenwirth, *Turning Points*, pp. 14–15; Lee, *German Air Force*, pp. 270–1. Hitler was reported by Halder as saying that volunteers would not 'want to go into a conservative army, but to where the spirit is National Socialist, to the SS or the Air Force' (Halder, *Warlord*, pp. 6–7).

91 Nielsen, pp. 187-8. The SS was more successful in its bid for some control over aircraft production: see Speer, pp. 372-3.
92 Suchenwirth, *Command and Leadership*, pp. 289-90.
93 Nielsen, pp. 185-7; Koller, *Collapse Viewed from Within*, pp. 3-8, 19-20; Irving, *Hitler's War*, pp. 689-728.
94 Nagatsuka, pp. 18-20.
95 Kase, p. 139.
96 On Japan USSBS, Report 62, Appendix 5, pp. 60-1, interrogation of General Kawabe. Yakovlev observed the exhortation to German soldiers displayed in all the German air force establishments that his Russian deputation visited in 1939: see A. Yakovlev, *Notes of an Aircraft Designer* (Moscow, 1961), p. 132.
97 USSBS, Report 62, p. 24; Ito, pp. 184-99.
98 N. Ike, 'War and Modernization' in R. E. Ward (ed.), *The Political Development of Modern Japan* (Princeton U. P., 1968); R. J. Smethurst, *A Social Basis for Pre-war Japanese Militarism* (Berkeley, 1974). On the suicide pilots, Inoguchi, pp. 82-91.

Chapter 7

1 Figures for United States from G. Simonson, 'The Demand for Aircraft and the Aircraft Industry,' *Journal of Economic History*, XX (1960); *AAF*, VI, pp. 352-3. Figures for USSR from Alexander, p. 4; Boyd, pp. 98, 191-2, 199. Figures for Britain from *Statistical Digest*, pp. 152-4. Figures for Commonwealth calculated from D. Mellor, *Australia in the War of 1939-1945 V: the Role of Industry and Science* (Canberra, 1958), pp. 385-413; J. Kennedy, *History of the Department of Munitions and Supply* (2 vols., Ottawa, 1950), I, p. 31; Hall, *North American Supply*, p. 424. Figures for Germany from *SAOG*, IV, pp. 494-6; USSBS, Report 4, p. 96, fig. vi-2, vi-11, vi-12. Figures for Japan from Francillon, p. 4; USSBS, Report 15, *Aircraft Division: the Japanese Aircraft Industry*, p. 155; USSBS, Report 53, *The Effects of Strategic Bombing on Japan's War Economy*, p. 222; Cohen, p. 210. Figures for Italy are estimates based on Clough, p. 261; Green, *Air Forces*, pp. 174-5.
2 Figures for percentage of world manufacture from Clough, p. 262. Figures for vehicle output from Society of Motor Manufacturers and Traders, *The Motor Industry of Great Britain* (London, 1951), p. 21. Other figures from League of Nations, *Statistical Year Book* (annually 1937-40); *Statistiches Jahrbuch für das Deutsche Reich* (Berlin, annually 1939-1941); Cohen, pp. 128, 163, 174; Clough, pp. 261-2; A. Nove, *An Economic History of the USSR* (London, 1969), p. 225; U.S. Department of Commerce, *Statistical Abstract of the United States* (Washington, 1941); N. Jasny, *Soviet Industrialization* (Chicago U.P., 1961), pp. 310-11; Political and Economic Planning, *The British Fuel and Power Industry* (London, 1947), p. 154; S. Pollard, *The Development of the British Economy 1914-1967* (London, 1969), p. 99; C. Feinstein, *Statistical Tables of National Income, Expenditure and Output of the U.K. 1855-1965* (Cambridge, 1976), Table 57; C. D. Long, *The Labour Force under Changing Income and Employment* (Princeton U.P., 1958), p. 286; Wagenführ, p. 21; B. Klein, *Germany's Economic Preparations for War* (Harvard U.P., 1959), p. 74.
3 Suchenwirth, *Command and Leadership*, pp. 251-2; Suchenwirth, *Turning Points*, pp. 23-4, 45-9.
4 J. Rae, 'The Financial Problems of the American Aircraft Industry 1906-1940', *Business History Review*, XXXIX (1965), pp. 99-103; P. Fearon, 'The British Airframe Industry and the State 1918-1935', *Economic History Review*, 2nd Ser., XXVII (1974), pp. 245-8.
5 For a general discussion of these problems see Devons, *Planning in Wartime* and Holley, *Buying Aircraft*.
6 Hinsley, pp. 227-8; Postan, *War Production*, pp. 68-9.
7 *AAF*, VI, p. 263.
8 'Message to Congress May 16th 1940', Roosevelt, *Public Papers*, IV, p. 202; 'Fireside Chat on National Defense May 20th 1940', Ibid., IV, p. 234; Holley, *Buying Aircraft*, pp. 169-76; *AAF*, VI, pp. 263-6, 277-8.
9 Rae, *Climb to Greatness*, p. 142; *AAF*, VI, p. 278.
10 Beasley, *Knudsen*, pp. 309-10; King, 'Second Report', p. 146.
11 *AAF*, VI, pp. 277-80.
12 Ibid., *VI*, pp. 283-9; Hansell, pp. 61-2, on the Victory programme and its background; Postan,

War Production, pp. 40-1; R. Higham, 'Government Companies and National Defense: British aeronautical experience 1918-1945 as the basis of a broad hypthesis', *Business History Review*, XXXIX (1965), pp. 330-1.

13 Suchenwirth, *Turning Points*, pp. 23-4; Overy, 'Pre-war Plans', pp. 790-1; Homze, pp. 222-5; Irving, *Rise and Fall*, p. 67.

14 Overy, *German Aircraft Production*, pp. 12-42.

15 Overy,'Hitler and Air Strategy', pp. 406-9; Lee, *Goering*, p. 73.

16 BA/RL3 146 Plan 20 'Göring-Flugzeug-Lieferplan', 15.9.1941; RL3 156, Flugzeug-Programm 22E, 19.8.1942; Irving, *Rise and Fall*, p. 279.

17 Klein, pp. 198-9; Jeschonnek is also credited with the remark 'I cannot find hangars for more than 400 to 500 fighters'. See Baumbach, p. 52.

18 On the failure in planning see Overy, *German Aircraft Production*, p. 31a. Production in 1940 was only 86 per cent of the last peace-time plan, no. 15. On the war economy see Klein, pp. 85-103, 173-205; Milward, pp. 28-53; B. A. Carroll, *Design for Total War* (The Hague, 1968), pp. 179-90.

19 Horikoshi, Okumiya, pp. 193-4; Cohen, pp. 226-7.

20 Cohen, p. 74. It should be added that Japan did not have the necessary resources to build this many aircraft. There certainly existed sufficient slack in the economy, however, to allow a considerable increase over actual output.

21 Scott, Hughes, pp. 291-4, 415-24, 457-65.

22 Devons, pp. 3-14; Scott, Hughes, pp. 410-25; Chester, pp. 5-13.

23 'Executive Order no. 9024 16.6.1942' in *Public Papers*, VI, pp. 54-6; *AAF, VI*, pp. 272-3.

24 P. C. Koistinen, 'Mobilizing the World War II Economy: Labour and the Industrial Military Alliance', *Pacific Historical Review*, XLII (1973), pp. 443-50, 477; O. Franks, *Central Planning and Control in War and Peace* (London, 1947), pp. 10, 27-8; *AAF, VI*, pp. 292-5; the remark by Churchill is in House of Commons Debates 368, column 259, 22.1.1941.

25 Yakovev, pp. 142-67.

26 *Mussolini's Memoirs*, p. 237.

27 Cohen, p. 59.

28 Conradis, 'Causes of Defeat . . .', p. 207; Wagenführ, p. 74; Suchenwirth, *Command and Leadership*, pp. 68-75, 28-33.

29 Devons, pp. 165-89.

30 *AAF*, VI, p. 291.

31 Leighton, Coakley, p. 795; Jacob, pp. 365-7; Franks, pp. 27-8; S. M. Rosen, *The Combined Boards of the Second World War* (Columbia U.P., 1951).

32 Irving, *Rise and Fall*, pp. 119-20, 134; Overy, *German Aircraft Production*, p. 87.

33 USSBS, Report 62, pp. 28-9; Cohen, pp. 58, 74-9; Francillon, pp. 6-7; T. Bisson, *Japan's War Economy* (New York, 1945), pp. 110-29, 136-7.

34 Milward, pp. 82-9, 142-50; MD, vol. LVI, 5701-13, memorandum by Milch on establishment, of 'Fighter Staff', n.d.; Klein, pp. 220-5.

35 Baumbach, pp. 50-4; Irving, *Rise and Fall*, pp. 288-90; Milward, pp. 159-60.

36 R. Sarti, *Fascism and the Industrial Leadership in Italy 1919–40* (Berkeley, 1971), pp. 131-2 for the attitude of big business. On Mussoloni's reforms FIAT Final Report 240, *Italian Aircraft Developments* (HMSO, 1945), p. 2.

37 Koistinen, pp. 443-50; B. Stein, 'Labor's Role in Government Agencies during World War II', *Journal of Economic History*, XVII (1957); Chester, pp. 19-20, 24; Overy, 'Mobilisierung . . .', pp. 294-6; H. J. Cooper, 'War and the Businessman', *JRUSI*, LXXXIV (1940), pp. 457-8; R. Higham, 'Quantity vs Quality: the Impact of Changing Demand on the British Aircraft Industry 1900-60', *Business History Review*, p. 437.

38 Stein, p. 407; Polenberg, p. 10-11, who records Nelson's desire 'to establish a set of rules under which the game could be played the way industry said it wanted it to be played'; *AAF*, VI, p. 297; I. Holley, 'Un organisme de guerre économique; le comité de coordination des industries aéronautiques', *RDGM*, XX (1970).

39 Polenberg, pp. 10-13; K. E. Bailey, *Technology and Society under Lenin and Stalin* (Princeton U.P., 1978), pp. 218-21, 292; E. Zaleski, 'Planning for Industrial Growth' in V. Treml (ed.), *The Development of the Soviet Economy* (New York, 1968), pp. 55-77.

40 B. K. Marshall, *Capitalism and Nationalism in Pre-war Japan* (Stanford, 1967), pp. 104-7; Ike, 'War and Modernization', pp. 205-7; Nish, p. 143; Francillon, p. 3; Cohen, pp. 33-46.

41 USSBS, Report 4, pp. 37-9; Wagenführ, p. 75.

42 Conradis, 'Causes of Defeat', p. 207; Overy, *German Aircraft Production*, pp. 235-42.

43 IMT, XXXVIII, pp. 380–97, Goering address to aircraft manufacturers 8.7.1938; Homze, pp. 228–32; Carroll, p. 133.
44 W. Ashworth, *Contracts and Finance* (HMSO, 1953), p. 250; BA/RL3 46, Chart 1, 'Investitionen, Zellenbau'.
45 W. Hornby, *Factories and Plant* (HMSO, 1958), pp. 218–22; Command Paper 5295, 'Note on the Policy of His Majesty's Government in Relation to the Production of Aero-engines' (HMSO, 1936); Postan, *War Production*, pp. 14–23, 68.
46 Boyd, pp. 187–90, 200; Kilmarx, p. 202. Production was concentrated in 20 airframe and 11 aero-engine factories.
47 Cohen, pp. 49–51; Goering in particular is alleged to have discounted American production potential. See Manvell, Fraenkel, *Göring*, p. 196.
48 G. Simonson (ed.), *History of the American Aircraft Industry* (MIT Press, 1968), pp. 124–30.
49 *AAF*, VI, pp. 304, 318.
50 USSBS, Report 4, p. 18a. Total German floorspace was 41 m. sq. ft. but this included a large amount of dispersed production and was capable of much less efficient utilization than American or British floorspace. On Britain see C. Kohan, *Works and Buildings* (HMSO, 1952), pp. 311–25.
51 *AAF*, pp. 320–1.
52 Rae, *Climb to Greatness*, pp. 143–4, 157–61; *AAF*, VI, p. 324.
53 Rae, *Climb to Greatness*, p. 157; Simonson, *History*, pp. 121–3; *AAF*, VI, pp. 322–3, 327–8.
54 R. J. Overy, *William Morris, Viscount Nuffield* (London, 1976), pp. 118–21.
55 Hornby, pp. 254–7, 395.
56 Hornby, pp. 218–22. It should be added that Britain also had the advantage of being able to disperse production to the Empire. Canada provided over 16,000 aircraft and large quantities of components, as did Australia, New Zealand and South Africa. See Kennedy, I, pp. 25–31, 468–9; Hall, *North American Supply*, p. 424.
57 BIOS Overall Report 21, *The Motor Car Industry in Germany 1939–1945*, pp. 7, 10–12; USSBS, Report 77, *German Motor Vehicles Industry Report*, pp. 7–11; R. J. Overy, 'Transportation and Rearmament in the Third Reich', *Historical Journal*, XVI (1973), pp. 407–8; MD, vol. LXV, 7107–8, 'Besprechungspunkte Opel, 10.10.1941'; on the Volkswagen plant see K. Hopfinger, *Beyond Expectation: the Volkswagen Story* (London, 1954), pp. 131–2.
58 Kilmarx, p. 202; on the evacuation see Yakovlev, pp. 145–9; Alexander, pp. 2–3; Boyd, pp. 187–9.
59 Cohen, pp. 296–9; Francillon, pp. 14–15 on dispersal, pp. 18–28 on details of aircraft firm ownership.
60 On Britain Ashworth, pp. 250–1; Hornby, p. 223. On Germany Overy, *German Aircraft Production*, pp. 143–4.
61 R. W. Lindholm, 'German Finance in World War II', *American Economic Review*, XXXVII (1947), pp. 121–7; Pollard, pp. 322–7; E. L. Hargreaves, M. M. Gowing, *Civil Industry and Trade* (HMSO, 1952), p. 648; Wagenführ, p. 173; Cohen, pp. 85–97.
62 *AAF*, VI, pp. 314–16; Ashworth, p. 250. Fixed capital expenditure by MAP reached a peak in 1940–1.
63 On American experience *AAF*, VI, p. 319. On Germany Overy, *German Aircraft Production*, pp. 144–6.
64 USSBS, Report 4, pp. 25–32.
65 USSBS, Report 15, p. 126.
66 Ibid., pp. 31, 34–59; Cohen, pp. 81–2.
67 Leighton, Coakley, II, p. 798. The McCoy Board and the Richards Committee both concluded that too much material was being produced. *AAF*, VI, pp. 316–17.
68 Cohen, p. 219. See also USSBS, Report 4, Fig. vi–12; Holley, *Buying Aircraft*, p. 560.
69 Postan, *War Production*, p. 315; BA/RL3 252, 202–3 'Voraussetzungen für die Durchführung des "Göring-Programms" ' 18.10.1941; Speer Collection FD 4355/45 vol. 5, 'Leistungssteigerung in der Fertigung von Luftwaffengerät, 15.8.1941'; RLM Industrierat, *Leistungssteigerung in der Luftwaffenfertigung* (Berlin, 1943).
70 Postan, *War Production*, p. 391.
71 Hornby, p. 397.
72 Boyd, pp. 192–3. This figure was only achieved in the last months of war.
73 Hornby, p. 388; Kohan, pp. 312–13; Postan, p. 391; for Junkers Speer Collection FD 5665/45, File V, Labour Statistics for Dec. 1944 and FD 5504/45 Motor Plants File, Chart B.

74 Hornby, p. 388.
75 J. F. Heath, 'American War Mobilization and the Use of Small Manufacturers 1939–1945', *Business History Review*, XLVI (1972).
76 Rae, *Climb to Greatness*, pp. 145–6; Simonson, *History*, pp. 135–8; *AAF*, VI, pp. 332–7.
77 Simonson, 'Demand', p. 372.
78 Alexander, p. 5; Craven, p. 23; Postan, *War Production*, pp. 390–1; J. Jewkes, 'Is British Industry Inefficient?', *Manchester School*, XIV (1946); Hornby, pp. 242–50, 395–403.
79 See above pp. 122–5.
80 BIOS Final Report 537, *Investigation of Production Control and Organisation in German Factories* (HMSO, 1946), pp. 1–8; Report 537, Appendix i, 'Production Control in the Heinkel Aircraft Organisation', pp. 1–28; BIOS Final Report 881, *Conditions in German Aircraft Instruments Industry* (HMSO, 1947), pp. 3, 6, 9; Overy, *Aircraft Production*, pp. 151–63.
81 Ibid., p. 274. The Luftwaffe was allowed 200,000 tons of aluminium in 1941 and produced 11,776 aircraft. In 1942 15,409 were produced from 185,000 tons.
82 USSBS, Report 63, p. 3.
83 Postan, pp. 164–6; C. M. Sharp, *D.H. An Outline of de Havilland History* (London, 1960), p. 182.
84 BIOS Overall Report 21, pp. 11–12; Overy, *German Aircraft Production*, pp. 284–5; H. Block, 'European Transportation under German Rule', *Social Research*, XI (1944), pp. 235–6.
85 Kilmarx, p. 202; Simonson, 'Demand', p. 377: USSBS, Report 15, p. 158; USSBS, Report 4, p. 19; F. Walton, *Miracle of World War II* (New York, 1956), p. 365; Rae, *Climb to Greatness*, p. 149; *Statistical Digest*, p. 20; Boyd, p. 98; Overy, *German Aircraft Production*, p. 206; Cohen, p. 302.
86 *AAF*, VI, p. 317; P. Inman, *Labour in the Munitions Industry* (HMSO, 1957), pp. 210–14.
87 Rae, *Climb to Greatness*, pp. 149–51; Long, p. 16; *AAF*, VI, pp. 345–7.
88 Boyd, p. 195; Lee, *Soviet Air Force*, p. 93; Bailey, pp. 218–21, 292.
89 Wagenführ, p. 139. Female employment was 14.6 million in 1939 and actually fell to 14.4 million by 1942, rising to 14.8 million in the last full year of war. Long, pp. 470–1.
90 H. Pfahlmann, *Fremdarbeiter und Kriegsgefangene in der deutschen Kriegswirtschaft 1939–1945* (Darmstadt, 1968), pp. 131–2; E. Homze, *Foreign Labor in Nazi Germany* (Princeton U.P., 1967), pp. 232–7.
91 Overy, 'Luftwaffe and European Economy', pp. 56–7.
92 NA T177, Roll 3, frame 3684346, RLM to armaments inspectorates, 6.9.1939; Milward, pp. 46–7; Klein, pp. 136–8.
93 Boyd, p. 98; Kilmarx, p. 104. Russian factories operated on a continuous three-shift basis. On British experience: Inman, pp. 419–28; H. M. Parker, *Manpower* (HMSO, 1957), pp. 422–4.
94 Cohen, pp. 219–20, 225–6, 296–302. By 1945 women made up approximately 30 per cent of the workforce.
95 Cohen, p. 302.
96 Rae, *Climb to Greatness*, pp. 152–3.
97 Simonson, 'Demand', p. 372; G. Ince, 'The Mobilisation of Manpower in Great Britain in the Second World War', *Manchester School*, XIV (1946); Inman, pp. 27–34, 48–68; Parker, pp. 279–98 on female employment.
98 This applied equally to the Luftwaffe itself as well as to the aircraft industry: see Conradis, 'Causes', pp. 207–8; Ludwig, pp. 288–300; Homze, *Arming the Luftwaffe*, pp. 237–44. On the high dependence on skilled men see BIOS Report 881, pp. 8–9; Overy, *German Aircraft Production*, pp. 158–60, 211–13.
99 Boyd, p. 189.
100 T. Mason, 'Labour in the Third Reich', *Past & Present*, no. 33 (1966).
101 M. Sumiya, 'Les ouvriers japonais pendant la deuxième guerre mondiale', *RDGM*, XXIII (1973); Cohen, pp. 327–47.
102 BIOS Final Report 881, p. 9. For a general discussion see G. Bry, *Wages in Germany* (Princeton U.P., 1960), pp. 233–65, 315–22.
103 Inman, pp. 315–27; Parker, pp. 392–447 on conditions and wages.
104 *AAF*, VI, p. 301. Hourly earnings increased 50 per cent over the period 1941–4, while consumer prices rose only 20 per cent.
105 Homze, *Foreign Labour*, pp. 231–48.
106 Alexander, p. 5; Kilmarx, p. 202; Horikoshi, Okumiya, pp. 197–8.
107 J. Hurstfield, *The Control of Raw Materials* (HMSO, 1953), pp. 346–9.

108 *AAF*, VI, pp. 342–5.
109 USSBS, Report 20, *Light Metal Industry of Germany*, pp. 11, 17a, 22a; Overy, *German Aircraft Production*, pp. 195–203; on Italy see BIOS Final Report 308, *The Production of Aluminium in Italy* (HMSO, 1946); on Japan see BIOS JAP PR 932, *The Aluminium Industry of Japan* (HMSO, n.d.), pp. 2–3; Overy, 'European Economy', pp. 61–2, 66.
110 Irving, *Rise and Fall*, p. 126; USSBS, Report 20, p. 13.
111 Cohen, pp. 207–8.
112 *Statistical Digest*, pp. 110–111.
113 USSBS, Report 4, p. 86; Overy, *German Aircraft Production*, pp. 214–19; Cohen, pp. 220–1, 225; USSBS, Report 53, p. 201. The peak of Japanese machine-tool production was 1938.
114 Boyd, pp. 194, 196–7; Alexander, pp. 4–5. In fact only one new design, the Tu 2, was put into mass production during the war.
115 Higham, 'Quantity vs Quality', pp. 451–6; Postan, Hay, *Design and Development*, pp. 91–5; *AAF*, VI, pp. 217–20.
116 Walton, pp. 249–52; Rae, *Climb to Greatness*, pp. 147–9; *AAF*, VI, pp. 335–6.
117 Postan, Hay, *Design and Development*, pp. 159–74.
118 Clough, pp. 263–4; Bognozzi, Catalanotto, pp. 124–6; J. W. Thompson, *Italian Civil and Military Aircraft* (London, 1963).
119 Cohen, p. 212; *AAF*, VI, pp. 353–4.
120 Horikoshi, Okumiya, pp. 201–2.
121 Ibid., pp. 101, 103, 193–5; USSBS, Report 62, Appendix 1, p. 28; Cohen, pp. 76, 78–81.
122 Cohen, pp. 212–14.
123 Baumbach, pp. 25–6, 42–3, 46–7; Conradis, 'Causes . . .', pp. 207–8; Overy, *German Aircraft Production*, pp. 108–12.
124 Bartz, p. 78; USSBS, Report 4, p. 88; Baumbach, p. 47; Suchenwirth, *Command and Leadership* pp. 75–7; Irving, *Rise and Fall*, pp. 75–7. The designer-managers included Tank of Focke-Wulf, Heinkel, and Messerschmitt.
125 Green, *Warplanes, passim*; Baumbach, pp. 48–9; USSBS, Report 4, pp. 45–6.
126 The problem involved the heavy bomber and the 'Bomber B', the replacement for the standard medium-bomber. Irving, *Rise and Fall*, pp. 147–53; Overy, *German Aircraft Production*, pp. 186–8.
127 Speer Collection FD 3210/45 Report from Wirtschaftsgruppe Luftfahrtindustrie to all aircraft firms, 1.1.1945.
128 Milward, pp. 143–7; Arnold, 'Third Report', p. 8.
129 Overy, *German Aircraft Production*, pp. 156–8.
130 A. van Ishoven, *Messerschmitt* (London, 1975), pp. 156–64.
131 Polenberg, pp. 10–12; J. S. Dupré, W. E. Gustafson, 'Contracting for Defense: Private Firms and the Public Interest', *Political Science Quarterly*, LXXVII (1962). Arnold favoured investing in 20 state-run plants to turn out 1,200 aircraft each per year but the plan was vigorously resisted by private business; *AAF*, VI, p. 305; Higham, 'Government Companies', pp. 327–8, 342–3.
132 Ashworth, pp. 88–90.
133 Ashworth, pp. 66–94, 118–72; J. Steindl, 'Economic Incentive and Efficiency in War Industry' in *Studies in War Economics* (Oxford, 1947), pp. 390–403; G. Worswick, 'A Survey of War Contract Procedure' in ibid., pp. 375–81.
134 Ashworth, p. 120.
135 Ibid., p. 90.
136 Ibid., p. 91. Actual percentage profit on companies' capital was calculated as follows: 1941 18.5 per cent, 1942 20.4 per cent, 1943 19.0 per cent, 1944 29.7 per cent. This situation benefited private capital substantially as costs were higher in state firms and operating profit was calculated on the basis of state firms' costs rather than those of private companies. See Higham, 'Government Companies', pp. 326–7.
137 P. Andrews, E. Brunner, *The Life of Lord Nuffield* (Oxford, 1955), pp. 227–31; Hornby, pp. 390–1.
138 *AAF*, VI, pp. 305–6, 320–3.
139 G. T. White, 'Financing Industrial Expansion for War; the Origin of the Defense Plant Corporation Leases', *Journal of Economic History*, IX (1949), p. 157; Rae, *Climb to Greatness*, pp. 120–1; *AAF*, VI, p. 306; Simonson, 'Demand', p. 376.
140 Polenberg, p. 19; White, pp. 157–66; *AAF*, VI, p. 307; Simonson, 'Demand', p. 372.
141 Walton, pp. 263–6; Simonson, 'Demand', p. 376.

142 Rae, *Climb to Greatness*, p. 155; *AAF*, VI, p. 347; President's Air Policy Commission, *Survival in the Air Age* (Washington, 1948), p. 54.

143 White, p. 166; the Wright company got a large plant by the end of the war for the cost of the original farm land on which it was built; Rae, *Climb to Greatness*, pp. 153-6; Simonson, 'Demand', p. 372; Rae, 'Financial Problems', pp. 99, 111-12.

144 Marshall, pp. 104-11; on profits see Cohen, pp. 509-10, 'Financial Position of 17 Holding Companies'.

145 Bisson, pp. viii-x.

146 A. Speer, 'Selbstverantwortung in der Rüstungsindustrie', *Der Vierjahrsplan*, VII (1943); USSBS, Report 4, p. 16; Overy, *German Aircraft Production*, pp. 124-5, 173-7.

147 Ibid., pp. 177-88; MD, vol. LXII, 5277-315, Goering's speech to heads of aircraft industry, 13.9.1942.

148 MD, vol. LI, 451 Milch to Goering, 21.9.1938; MD, vol. LXV, 7429, Goering conference in Berlin, 29.11.1938.

149 *SAOG*, IV, p. 500, Appendix 49 (xxvii); USSBS, Report 62, Exhibits C, D.

Chapter 8

1 Scott, Hughes, pp. 33-40; Yakovlev, pp. 72-108; V. Bush, *Modern Arms and Free Men* (New York, 1949), pp. 23-6; Homze, *Arming the Luftwaffe*, pp. 22-39; Suchenwirth, *Development*, pp. 21-6.

2 R. W. Clark, *Tizard* (London, 1965), pp. 116-73; *GS*, I, pp. 594-5; S. Zuckerman, *Scientists and War* (London, 1966), pp. 114-15; R. W. Clark, *The Rise of the Boffins* (London, 1962), p. 49; P. M. Blackett, *Studies of War: Nuclear and Conventional* (London, 1962), pp. 101-3.

3 Homze, *Arming the Luftwaffe*, pp. 209-16.

4 Hartcup, pp. 22-4; Clark, *Boffins*, pp. 158-9; Roskill, *Hankey*, III, pp. 487-93.

5 R. V. Jones, 'Winston S. Churchill', *Biographical Memoirs of Fellows of the Royal Society*, XII (1966), pp. 69, 75; Cherwell claimed of Churchill that he had 'always looked upon Mr WSC as a scientist who had missed his vocation'. On their relationship see R. F. Harrod, *The Prof: a Personal Memoir of Lord Cherwell* (London, 1959); Lord Birkenhead, *The Prof in Two Worlds* (London, 1961), pp. 262-8.

6 Blackett, pp. 104-5. Dowding had been Air Member for Research and Development from 1930-36, Tedder Director General of Research and Development from 1938-40.

7 A. D. Beyerchen, *Scientists under Hitler* (Yale U. P., 1977); Hartcup, pp. 29-30; S. Goudsmit, *ALSOS: the Failure in German Science* (London, 1947), pp. 14-56, 187-95; C. Ramsauer, 'Eingabe an Rust 20.1.1942' reprinted in *Physikalische Blätter*, I (1947), pp. 43-4; Ramsauer, 'Zur Geschichte der deutschen Physikalischen Gesellschaft in der Hitlerzeit', ibid., I (1947); Ludwig, pp. 241-5, 257-9.

8 Beyerchen, pp. 168-73; J. Haberer, *Politics and the Community of Science* (New York, 1969), pp. 121-55. For a list of prominent intellectual émigrés see D. Fleming, B. Bailyn (eds.), *The Intellectual Migration: Europe and America 1930-60* (Harvard U.P., 1968), pp. 675-718.

9 Goudsmit, pp. 142, 187, 190.

10 Ibid., p. 188; J. P. Baxter, *Scientists against Time* (MIT Press, 1946), pp. 8-9; Ludwig, pp. 288-300; Bush, pp. 207-8.

11 Goudsmit, pp. 191-3; Ludwig, pp. 241-5.

12 Goudsmit, p. 158. The remark was made by Ramsauer of AEG at the end of a lecture in 1943.

13 Baxter, pp. 12-19; Hartcup, pp. 26-7; *AAF*, VI, pp. 235-6, 239-42.

14 Ibid., VI, pp. 231-5; A. V. Hill, *The Ethical Dilemma of Science and Other Writings* (New York, 1960), pp. 276-82; Blackett, pp. 102-6; Zuckerman, pp. 16-19; C. P. Snow, *Science and Government* (Oxford, 1961), pp. 53-66; Scott, Hughes, pp. 363-82; J. Burchard, *Q.E.D. MIT in World War II* (New York, 1948), pp. 217-36; Arnold, 'Third Report', pp. 69-70.

15 C. A. Waddington, *O.R. in World War 2* (London, 1973); Blackett, pp. 103-9, 207-30; de la Ferté, *Third Service*, pp. 261-3, Appendix V, 'The Service Outlook Towards Operational Research'.

16 Zuckerman, pp. 114-16; *SAOG*, I, pp. 251, 312-13; *AAF*, II, pp. 342-3; III, p. 237; Clark, *Boffins*, p. 221; Bottomley, pp. 234-5.

17 *AAF*, II, pp. 225, 348-70; Hansell, pp. 148-56 on the founding and early development of the Committee of Operations Analysts; *AAF*, VI, pp. 40-41.

18 Hartcup, p. 30; A. P. West, 'The Design and Production of Japanese Military Aircraft', *JRAeS*, L (1946), pp. 532–4, 537.
19 Baxter, p. 10; USSBS, Report 62, p. 26.
20 L. Simon, *German Research in World War II* (New York, 1947), pp. 69–81; Goudsmit, pp. 147–8, 155–6.
21 Baxter, pp. 8–9; Goudsmit, p. 146; Bush, p. 207; Conradis, 'Causes of Defeat of the German Luftwaffe', pp. 206–10.
22 Simon, p. 77; R. Smelt, 'A Critical Review of German Research on High-Speed Airflow', *JRAeS* L (1946), pp. 926–7; Conradis, pp. 122–7.
23 Heinkel, pp. 220–3; MD, vol. LVI, 2432–44, A. Bäumker, 'Organisation der Luftfahrtforschung' 10.1.1942; Speer Collection FD 4335/45 vol. 5, pp. 48–52, Messerschmitt to Udet 'Zweckforschung und reine Forschung im Kriege', 22.1.1940; Conradis, pp. 113–20.
24 See the discussion in Zuckerman, pp. 9–11.
25 C. Gibbs-Smith, *Aviation: an Historical Survey* (London, 1970), pp. 180–204.
26 Lee, *Soviet Air Force*, pp. 72–3; Russia also obtained material from Germany on the very eve of war, including the models Ju 88, Me 109E and Me 110 (Boyd, p. 164); F. Brockway, F. Mullally, *Death Pays a Dividend* (London, 1945), pp. 107–16; Homze, *Arming the Luftwaffe*, pp. 19–29.
27 Okumiya, pp. 9–13; Argyle, p. 174; Bush, p. 53.
28 USSBS, Report 63, pp. 5–6; Cohen, p. 217.
29 G. C. Herring, *Aid to Russia 1941–1946* (New York, 1973), pp. 71–3, 116–19; Stettinius, pp. 176–7, 187–90.
30 The most successful example was the 'Tizard Mission' in 1940. See Hartcup, pp. 28–9; Hall, *Studies in Overseas Supply*, 104–5. For other collaboration see *AAF*, VI, pp. 237–9.
31 See the general discussions in Jones, *Most Secret War*; B. Johnson, *The Secret War* (London, 1978); G. Pawle, *Secret War* (London, 1956).
32 Zuckerman, pp. 8–9.
33 Simon, pp. 54–60, 64–81; Homze, pp. 212–16; USSBS, Report 63, pp. 1–4.
34 Baxter, pp. 5–8; Suchenwirth, *Turning Points*, pp. 49–53; NCA, VII, pp. 588–9, doc. EC-606.
35 A. Price, *Instruments of Darkness* (London, 1967), pp. 271, 274; Bush, pp. 50–2.
36 Hartcup. pp. 91–2.
37 Kilmarx, pp. 112–15; Alexander, pp. 5–8.
38 Postan, Hay, *Design and Development*, pp. 6–7.
39 Rae, *Climb to Greatness*, p. 147; *AAF*, VI, p. 229.
40 Ibid., VI, pp. 229–30; Postan, Hay, *Design and Development*, pp. 7–9.
41 Ludwig, pp. 231–2; USSBS, Report 4, p. 43; Heinkel, pp. 221–2, 260–1; Irving, *Rise and Fall*, pp. 130–1 on Messerschmitt's continuation of jet research in the face of ministry proscription.
42 Baumbach, pp. 24–9, 42–3; Irving, *Rise and Fall*, pp. 124–41; Herlin, pp. 226–44; Udet was credited with the remark 'I don't understand anything about production. I understand even less about big aeroplanes' (Heinkel, p. 185).
43 Suchenwirth, *Command and Leadership*, pp. 138–9; MD, vol. LIII, 764–86, Wirtschaftsgruppe Luftfahrtindustrie to Goering, 2.11.1942; perhaps the best example was the unfortunate history of the He 177 heavy bomber. See Overy, ' "Uralbomber" to "Amerikabomber" ', pp. 168–71.
44 This was particularly the case with jet aircraft. See Irving, *Rise and Fall*, pp. 251–4, 280–3.
45 This was particularly the case with the Ju 88, Me 210 and the Fw 190; M. Caidin, *Me 109* (London, 1969), pp. 112–13; van Ishoven, pp. 132–3, 158–64.
46 MD, vol. LIII, 798–818, 'Denkschrift über Entwicklung und Entwicklungsplanung in der deutschen Luftrüstung' 15.1.1942. A similar letter had been sent by Tank to Goering in July 1941 pointing out the fact that new projects took at least four years to develop; Tank to Goering, 7.7.1941 in Conradis, pp. 141–2.
47 *AAF*, VI, p. 232. On American jet research see Rae, *Climb to Greatness*, pp. 164–7; Arnold, 'Second Report', pp. 75–6.
48 Hartcup, pp. 24–5.
49 Postan, Hay, *Design and Development*, pp. 140–2.
50 C. M. Sharp, *D.H. An Outline of De Havilland History* (London, 1960), pp. 179–86.
51 J. L. Nayler, E. Owen, *Aviation: its Technical Development* (London, 1965), p. 149; R. Miller, D. Sawers, *The Technical Development of Modern Aviation*, pp. 18–21.
52 Burchard, pp. 215–36; Postan, Hay, *Design and Development*, pp. 96–120.

53 D. Irving, *The Virus House* (London, 1967), p. 110, 268–9; M. M. Gowing, *Britain and Atomic Energy 1939–1945* (London, 1964), pp. 367–8; Bush, pp. 206–7.
54 Dornberger, p. 105.
55 Suchenwirth, *Turning Points,* pp. 124–6; Killen, pp. 266–74.
56 Gowing, pp. 45–54.
57 Ibid., p. 368; Truman, p. 350.
58 F. Whittle, *Jet* (London, 1953); Postan, Hay, *Design and Development,* pp. 212–20.
59 Ibid., p. 226.
60 Hartcup. pp. 236–8; Bush, pp. 53, 77–8; Baxter, pp. 5–6.
61 USSBS, Report 15, Appendix xx.
62 Hansell, pp. 49–50.
63 IWM Collection, Luftwaffe Führungsstab *Die Kriegsflugzeuge der Feindmächte* B/2/43; RLM Planungsamt *Flugzeuge, Flugausrüstung und Waffen der sowjetischen Luftwaffe* (May, 1942).
64 Hinsley, pp. 11–12, 284.
65 Ibid., ch. ix; Dempster and Wood, pp. 117–20.
66 Kahn, pp. 386–7.
67 Ibid., p. 385.
68 G. Perrault, *The Red Orchestra* (London, 1967); R. A. Haldane, *The Hidden War* (London, 1978), pp. 76–99.
69 Hinsley, pp. 77–9; Quester, pp. 82, 85–6. See above pp. 22–3.
70 Hinsley, pp. 61, 299–301; Collier, *Defence,* p. 231, who reports the British claim that the Lufwaffe would have '14,000' aircraft ready to attack Britain in the spring of 1941. See too 'Estimated British and German Air Strengths, December 9, 1940' in Churchill, III, pp. 694–6.
71 Dempster and Wood, pp. 101–13; Halder, *Kriegstagebuch,* II, pp. 128–9.
72 Schwabedissen, pp. 9–11, 49; Baumbach, pp. xx.
73 Overy, *German Aircraft Production,* p. 49.
74 Kahn, pp. 386–7; *SAOG,* IV, p. 498, Appendix 49, xxv. The margin of error was wide at the beginning and end of the war. In the first half of 1941 Air Intelligence estimated German monthly production at 1,575 when the true figure was 880. In the first half of 1944 the intelligence figure was 1,870 when actual production had risen to 2,811 a month.
75 See Hansell, esp. chs. iii–vii; *SAOG,* III, pp. 320–3.
76 J. Masterman, *The Double-X System* (London, 1972), pp. 178–82.
77 Zuckerman, pp. 114–16.
78 Kahn, p. 386; Galland, pp. 180–1, 187–93.
79 Masterman, pp. 60–185; Kahn, pp. 13–26.
80 Schwabedissen, pp. 8–10; Plocher, I, pp. 16–17.
81 J. Piekalkiewicz, *Secret Agents, Spies and Saboteurs* (Newton Abbot, 1974), pp. 176–7; Irving, *Rise and Fall,* pp. 174–5; Kilmarx, p. 211.
82 See Jones, *Most Secret War, passim;* M. R. D. Foot, *Resistance* (London, 1976), pp. 305–10.
83 Kahn, p. 387; Dempster and Wood, pp. 103–5; P. Leverkuehn, *German Military Intelligence* (London, 1954), p. 70. 'Beppo' Schmid, the head of Luftwaffe intelligence from its inception in 1937, could speak no foreign language.
84 D. Kahn, 'Le rôle du décryptage et du renseignement dans la stratégie et la tactique des Alliés', *RDGM,* XXVIII (1978); Kahn, *The Codebreakers* (New York, 1967), pp. 459–60; Johnson, *Secret War,* pp. 345–96; Hinsley, p. 268; G. Bertrand, *Enigma* (London, 1972).
85 USSBS, Report 63, p. 12.
86 A. J. Brookes, *Photo Reconnaissance* (London, 1975), pp. 88–9; Kahn, *Hitler's Spies,* pp. 123–6.
87 C. Babington-Smith, *Evidence in Camera* (London, 1958), pp. 250–2; Brookes, pp. 90, 167–9.
88 Ibid., pp. 169–70.
89 Ibid., pp. 170–2; Kahn, *Hitler's Spies,* pp. 125–35.
90 Brookes, p. 173; Green, *Warplanes* pp. 53–5.
91 Jackson, *Fall of France,* p. 37; Hinsley, pp. 27–30, 148–9; Brookes, pp. 48–9; Russia, too, began the war with poor aerial reconnaissance: see Boyd, pp. 48–9.
92 Brookes, pp. 49–87; Hinsley, pp. 28–30, 278–82, 496–9; Babington-Smith, pp. 24–38; F. Winterbotham, *Secret and Personal* (London, 1969), pp. 126–30.
93 Babington-Smith, pp. 167–98; Hinsley, pp. 169–70.
94 Brookes, pp. 130–67; *AAF,* VI, pp. 616–21; Richards and Saunders, III, pp. 71–5, 92–3; on Russia: Lee, *Soviet Air Force,* p. 50; Babington-Smith pp. 145–66.

95 Price, *Instruments of Darkness*, pp. 60–1; Hogg, pp. 86, 108–9; Kahn, *Hitler's Spies*, pp. 201–7.

96 Price, *Instruments of Darkness*, pp. 61–9, 72; Dempster and Wood pp. 56–9; *SAOG*, I.

97 Burchard, pp. 215–36; on the general development of radar see Postan, Hay, *Design and Development* pp. 378–430.

98 Price, *Instruments of Darkness*, pp. 244–5; Bush, p. 52; Hartcup, pp. 28, 107. A centralized office for radar research was not set up in Germany until July 1943.

99 Hartcup, p. 108; Jones, *Most Secret War*, pp. 389–90, 392.

100 Bush, pp. 51–2; Price, *Instruments of Darkness*, pp. 235–7, 245.

101 Brookes, p. 185; Jones, *Most Secret War*, pp. 400–12; *SAOG*, III, pp. 150–1.

102 USSBS, Report 62, p. 3; V. Haughland, *The AAF against Japan* (New York, 1948), p. 452.

Chapter 9

1 Letter, Roosevelt to Stimson, 4.5.1941 reproduced in Beasley, *Knudsen*, p. 309.

2 Roosevelt, *War Messages*, p. 32, 'Report to Congress, January 7th 1943'.

3 *NCA*, VII, pp. 852–3, doc. L-79.

4 Baines, p. 393.

5 Ibid., pp. 391–3.

6 A. Nevins, *This is England Today* (New York, 1941), p. 42. A Gallup Poll in London late in the Blitz found that 47 per cent of respondents disapproved of vengeance bombing, 45 per cent approved.

7 Boelcke, *Secret Conferences*, pp. 338–9, conference of 10.3.1943; pp. 341–3, conference of 13.3.1943.

8 R. Benedict, *The Chrysanthemum and the Sword* (London, 1947), p. 25.

9 Rumpf, pp. 54–65; *AAF*, V, pp. 754–5.

10 Ikle, pp. 198–9; A. Calder, *The People's War* (London, 1971), ch. IV.

11 Richards, *Portal*, p. 167. 'The loss of life, which amounted to some 600,000 killed, was purely incidental' (from an Address to Winchester College, 1945).

12 C. Bewley, *Hermann Göring in the Third Reich* (New York, 1962), p. 306. General Kawabe, who led the 'kamikaze' pilots, made an almost identical statement to his captors in 1945: 'Right up until the end, we believed we could outweigh your material and scientific superiority by the force of our moral and spiritual convictions' (Nagatsuka, p. 7). See too Benedict, pp. 22–3.

13 Polenberg, p. 12.

Bibliography

The following bibliography is not an exhaustive list of books on the air war but is an extensive list of the books and articles used in the writing of this book. I have left out some books of a more popular kind, many of which are largely fiction, and also more general books which have helped me in establishing perspectives on the air war but which are not themselves related directly to the subject. Apart from the published documents and sources I have made extensive use of the German records deposited at the Imperial War Museum in London, where I was able to consult the originals before their restitution to Germany in the early 1970s. The most important German records are the records of the air ministry (RLM), the Milch records, records of the Luftwaffe general staff and the records of private firms. Of these last the largest collections are those of Junkers, Messerschmitt and Focke-Wulf. I have also used the German material available on microfilm at the National Archives, Washington D.C., and the so-called 'Speer Collection' of records on the German wartime economy and administration, also available on microfilm at the War Museum. Detailed references to all these collections can be found in the notes. I have relied for the British and American evidence on the official histories and published documents, details of which appear below. The official histories provide in most cases excellent and detailed references for anyone anxious to pursue the evidence further. Russian records are confined to the documents published from time to time by the Soviet government. Material on Japan and Germany is also available in the bombing surveys. The USSBS is particularly useful and I have been able to use the survey collection at the War Museum. The published intelligence reports of CIOS and BIOS also provide a wealth of neglected material. Details of both sources are provided below. Finally I have consulted a number of miscellaneous collections housed at Churchill College, Cambridge. The most useful have been the Christie papers for material on Britain and Germany, the Weir papers, the Swinton papers and the papers of Lord Thurso. References to these collections, and to British parliamentary debates and papers can be found in the footnotes.

A: Official Publications and Published Documents

Aircraft Industries Association, *Aviation Facts and Figures 1945* (New York, 1945).

Air Ministry, *Bomber Command* (HMSO, 1941).

Air Ministry, *Roof over Britain* (HMSO, 1943).

H. H. Arnold, *Second Report of the Commanding General of the United States Army Air Forces to the Secretary of War* (HMSO, 1945).

H. H. Arnold, *Third Report of the Commanding General of the United States Army Air Forces to the Secretary of War* (HMSO, 12.11.1945).

O. Bechtle, 'German Air Force Operations against Great Britain: address in Berlin 2.2.1944' in *RAF Quarterly* XIX (1947/8).

H. Blood-Ryan (ed.), *The Political Testament of Hermann Goering: a selection of important speeches and articles* (London, 1940).

W. Boelcke (ed.), *Deutschlands Rüstung im Zweiten Weltkrieg: Hitlers Konferenzen mit Albert Speer* (Frankfurt a. M., 1969).

W. Boelcke (ed.), *The Secret Conferences of Dr. Goebbels* (London, 1970).

U. Cavallero, *Comando Supremo: Diario 1940-43* (Bologna, 1948).

Documents on German Foreign Policy 1918-45 Series D, (13 vols., HMSO. 1949-64).

F. Gilbert (ed.), *Hitler Directs his War* (New York, 1950).

F. Halder, *Kriegstagebuch* (3 vols., Stuttgart, 1962-64).

H. Heiber (ed.) *Hitlers Lagebesprechungen* (Stuttgart, 1962).

A. Hillgruber et al. *Kriegstagebuch des Oberkommandos der Wehrmacht* (4 vols., Frankfurt a. Main, 1961-5).

Home Office, *Air Raid Precautions Handbook* (HMSO, 1937),

N. Ike, *Japan's Decision for War: Records of the 1941 Policy Conferences* (Stanford, 1967).

International Military Tribunal, *Trial of the Major War Criminals* (42 vols., Nuremberg, 1947).

H. Jacobsen, *Dokumente zum Westfeldzug 1940* (Göttingen, 1960).

Jahrbuch . . ., *Jahrbuch der deutschen Luftwaffe* (Berlin, annually from 1936).

E. J. King, *U.S. Navy at War 1941-1945. The Official Reports to the Secretary of the Navy* (Washington, 1946).

K. Klee, *Dokumente zum Unternehmen Seelöwe* (Göttingen, 1959).

R. Klibansky (ed.), *Mussolini's Memoirs 1942-1943* (London, 1949).

G. Koller, *The Collapse Viewed from Within* (IWM Library, ADI(K) Report no. 348/1945).

League of Nations, *Armaments Year Book* (Geneva, annually 1933-40).

League of Nations, *Statistical Year Book* (Geneva, annually 1937-40).

L. Lochner (ed.), *The Goebbels Diaries* (London, 1948).

F. Loewenheim, H. B. Langley, M. Jones, *Roosevelt and Churchill: their Secret Wartime Correspondence* (London, 1975).

'Marshal . . .', 'Marshal of the Royal Air Force Viscount Dowding's Despatch on the Battle of Britain to Secretary of State for Air, 20.8.1941' *RAF Quarterly* XVIII (1946/7).

Ministry of Foreign Affairs, U.S.S.R., *Stalin's Correspondence with Churchill, Attlee, Roosevelt and Truman 1941-1945* (London, 1958).

M. Muggeridge (ed.), *Ciano's Diary* (London, 1947).

Nazi . . ., *Nazi Conspiracy and Aggression* (8 vols., Washington, 1946).

President's Air Policy Commission, *Survival in the Air Age* (Washington, 1948).

The Public . . ., *The Public Papers and Addresses of Franklin D. Roosevelt* (8 vols., London, 1938-1945).

Reichsluftschutzbund, *Luftschutz Taschenkalender 1941* (Berlin, 1940).

Report . . ., *Report of the Supreme Commander to the Combined Chiefs of Staff on the Operations in Europe* (HMSO, 1946).

E. Roosevelt (ed.), *The Roosevelt Letters* (3 vols., London, 1949-52).

F. D. Roosevelt, *The War Messages of Franklin D. Roosevelt* (Washington, 1943).

Statistisches Reichsamt, *Statistisches Jahrbuch für das Deutsche Reich* (Berlin, annually).

G. Thomas, *Geschichte der deutschen Wehr- und Rüstungswirtschaft 1918-1943/45* (ed. W. Birkenfeld, Boppard-am-Rhein, 1966).

H. Trevor-Roper (ed.), *The Goebbels Diaries* (London, 1978).

H. Trevor-Roper (ed.), *Hitler's Table Talk 1941-1944* (London, 2nd ed., 1973).

H. Trevor-Roper (ed.), *Hitler's War Directives* (London, 1964).

USAF Far East, *Air Operations in the China Area July 1937-Aug. 1945* (Japanese Monographs no. 76, Dec. 1956).

K-H. Völker (ed.), *Dokumente und Dokumentarfotos zur Geschichte der deutschen Luftwaffe* (Stuttgart, 1968).

The following BIOS and CIOS reports are the most useful though the list by no means exhausts the number available on aircraft industry and related topics.

BIOS/JAP/PR 82, *Activities of the Research Institute of Light Metals for Aviation.*

BIOS/JAP/PR 89, *Structural Requirements and Techniques in the Design of Japanese Aircraft.*

BIOS/JAP/PR 131, *Flight-Testing Methods of the Japanese Navy.*

BIOS/JAP/PR 173, *Woods and Glues on Japanese Aircraft.*

BIOS/JAP/PR 816, *Report on the Magnesium Industry of Japan.*

BIOS/JAP/PR 902-3, *The Raw Aluminium Industry of Japan: Parts I and II.*

BIOS/JAP/PR 932, *The Aluminium Industry of Japan.*

BIOS/JAP/PR 1353, *The Light Metals Control Association.*

BIOS Final Report 170, *Visits in American and French Zones, Aircraft and Aircraft Engines.*

BIOS 308, *The Production of Aluminium in Italy.*

BIOS FR 537, *Investigation of Production Control and Organisation in German Factories.*

BIOS Overall Report 21, *The Motor Car Industry in Germany during the Period 1939-1945.*

CIOS XVII-1, *German Activities in the French Aircraft Industry.*

CIOS XXV-42, *Survey of Production Techniques Used in the German Aircraft Industry.*

CIOS XXVII-64, *German Aircraft Maintenance and Overhaul Methods.*

CIOS XXX-94, *Administration, Plastics, Production Tooling, Spare Parts and Servicing in the German Aircraft Industry.*

FIAT 240, *Italian Aircraft Developments.*

FIAT, *Review of German Science 1939-1945* (Wiesbaden, 1948).

The United States Strategic Bombing Survey provides much useful material on a wide number of topics. Those listed below are the most useful. References to a number of more minor reports can be found in the footnotes. The Reports were published in Washington between 1945 and 1949. I have been able to make use of the collection in the IWM Library.

USSBS Report 3, *The Effects of Strategic Bombing on the German War Economy.*

USSBS Report 4, *Aircraft Division Industry Report (European Theater).*

USSBS Report 11, *Final Report Covering Air-Raid Protection and Allied Subjects in Japan.*

USSBS Report 15, *Aircraft Division: The Japanese Aircraft Industry.*

USSBS Report 20, *Light Metal Industry of Germany.*

USSBS Report 53, *The Effects of Strategic Bombing on Japan's War Economy.*

USSBS Report 59, *The Defeat of the German Air Force.*

USSBS Report 62, *Japanese Air Power.*

USSBS Report 63, *Japanese Air Weapons and Tactics.*

USSBS Report 77, *German Motor Vehicles Industry Report.*

USSBS Report 200, *The Effects of Strategic Bombing on German Transportation.*

B: Official Histories

W. Ashworth, *Contracts and Finance* (HMSO, 1953).

J. A. Brown, *Eagles Strike: the Campaigns of the SAAF 1941–43* (Capetown, 1974).

J. R. Butler, *Grand Strategy II: Sept. 39–June 41* (HMSO, 1957).

J. R. Butler, *Grand Strategy III, Part II: June 41–Aug. 42* (HMSO, 1964).

J. L. Cate, W. F. Craven, *The Army Air Forces in World War II* (7 vols., Chicago, 1948-1958).

B. Collier, *The Defence of the United Kingdom* (HMSO, 1957).

J. G. Crowther, *Science at War* (HMSO, 1947).

J. Ehrman, *Grand Strategy V: Aug. 43–Sept. 44* (HMSO, 1956).

J. Ehrman, *Grand Strategy VI: Oct. 44–Aug. 45* (HMSO, 1956).

L. F. Ellis, *Victory in the West* (2 vols., HMSO, 1962–68).

L. F. Ellis, *The War in France and Flanders 1939–40* (HMSO, 1954).

N. Gibbs, *Grand Strategy I: Rearmament Policy* (HMSO, 1976).

K. R. Greenfield, *Command Decisions* (Washington, 1960).

J. M. Gwyer, *Grand Strategy III, Part I: June 41–Aug. 42* (HMSO, 1964).

H. D. Hall, *North American Supply* (HMSO, 1955).

H. D. Hall, C. Wrigley, *Studies in Overseas Supply* (HMSO, 1956).

W. Hancock, M. Gowing, *The British War Economy* (HMSO, 1949).

J. Herington, *Air Power over Europe 1944-1945* (Canberra, 1963).

J. Herington, *Air War against Germany and Italy 1939–1943* (Canberra, 1954).

F. H. Hinsley, *British Intelligence in the Second World War: Vol. 1* (HMSO, 1979).

I. B. Holley, *Buying Aircraft; Materiel Procurement for the Army Air Forces* (Washington, 1964).

W. Hornby, *Factories and Plant* (HMSO, 1958).

M. Howard, *Grand Strategy IV: Aug. 42–Sept. 43* (HMSO, 1972).

P. Inman, *Labour in the Munitions Industry* (HMSO, 1957).

J. Kennedy, *History of the Department of Munitions and Supply* (2 vols., Ottawa, 1950).

S. W. Kirby, *The War Against Japan* (5 vols., HMSO, 1957–69).

C. M. Kohan, *Works and Buildings* (HMSO, 1952).

R. M. Leighton, R. W. Coakley, *Global Logistics and Strategy* (2 vols., Washington, 1955–68).

N. Macmillan, *The Royal Air Force in the World War* (4 vols., HMSO, 1949–50).

H. J. Martin, N. Orpen, *Eagles Victorious: the SAAF 1943–1945* (Capetown, 1977).

M. Matloff, E. Snell, *Strategic Planning for Coalition Warfare* (2 vols., Washington, 1953–9).

W. W. Medlicott, *The Economic Blockade* (2 vols., HMSO 1952–59).

D. P. Mellor, *Australia in the War of 1939–1945 V: the role of Science and Industry* (Canberra, 1958).

S. E. Morison, *The History of the United States Naval Operations in World War II* (15 vols., Boston, 1947–62).

T. H. O'Brien, *Civil Defence* (HMSO, 1955).

H. Parker, *Manpower* (HMSO, 1957).

I. S. O. Playfair, *The Mediterranean and Middle East* (6 vols., HMSO, 1956-62).

M. M. Postan, *British War Production* (HMSO, 1952).

M. M. Postan, D. Hay, J. D. Scott, *Design and Development of Weapons* (HMSO, 1964).

D. Richards, H. Saunders, *The Royal Air Force 1939–1945* (3 vols., HMSO, 1953).

S. W. Roskill, *The War at Sea 1939–1945* (4 vols., HMSO, 1954–61).

J. M. Ross, *Royal New Zealand Air Force* (Wellington, 1955).

R. S. Sayers, *Financial Policy* (HMSO, 1956).

J. Scott, R. Hughes, *The Administration of War Production* (HMSO, 1955).

Soviet . . ., *The Soviet Air Force in World War II* (ed. R. Wagner, London, 1974).

Statistical . . ., *Statistical Digest of the War* (HMSO, 1951).

C. Webster, N. Frankland, *The Strategic Air Offensive against Germany* (4 vols., HMSO, 1961).

C: Memoirs and Contemporary Accounts

H. H. Arnold, *Global Mission* (New York, 1949).

Lord Avon, *The Eden Memoirs: Facing the Dictators* (London, 1962).
W. Baumbach, *Broken Swastika* (London, 1960).
Lord Brabazon of Tara, *The Brabazon Story* (London, 1956).
V. Bush, *Modern Arms and Free Men* (New York, 1949).
H. C. Butcher, *Three Years with Eisenhower* (London, 1946).
W. S. Churchill, *The Second World War* (6 vols., London, 1948-54).
P. Clostermann, *The Big Show* (London, 1951).
J. R. Deane, *The Strange Alliance* (London, 1947).
W. Dornberger, *V2* (London, 1954).
H. Dowding, *Twelve Legions of Angels* (London, 1946).
D. D. Eisenhower, *Crusade in Europe* (London, 1948).
A. Fredborg, *Behind the Steel Wall: Berlin 1941-43* (London, 1944).
A. Galland, *The First and the Last* (London, 1955).
P. Groves, *Behind the Smoke Screen* (London, 1934).
H. Guderian, *Panzer Leader* (London, 1952).
W. A. Harriman, E. Abel, *Special Envoy to Churchill and Stalin 1941-46* (New York, 1975).
A. Harris, *Bomber Offensive* (London, 1947).
E. Heinkel, *He 1000* (London, 1956).
C. Hull, *The Memoirs of Cordell Hull* (2 vols., London, 1948).
P. Joubert de la Ferté, *Birds and Fishes: the Story of Coastal Command* (London, 1960).
P. Joubert de la Ferté, *The Third Service* (London, 1955).
W. Keitel, *The Memoirs of Field Marshal Keitel* (London, 1965).
A. Kesselring, *Memoirs* (London, 1955).
I. Konev, *Years of Victory* (Moscow, 1969).
L. Kuter, *Airman at Yalta* (New York, 1955).
W. D. Leahy, *I Was There* (London, 1950).
Lord Londonderry, *Wings of Destiny* (London, 1943).
A. Longmore, *From Sea to Sky* (London, 1946).
H. Macmillan, *The Blast of War* (London, 1977).
E. von Manstein, *Lost Victories* (London, 1958).
W. Mitchell, *Winged Defense* (New York, 1925).
B. Montgomery, *Memoirs of Field Marshal Montgomery* (London, 1958).
A. Nevins, *This is England Today* (New York, 1941).
C. W. Nimitz, E. Potter, *The Great Sea War* (London, 1961).
F. Pile, *Ack Ack: Britain's Defence against Air Attack during the Second World War* (London, 1949).
H. U. Rudel, *Stuka Pilot* (Dublin, 1952).
R. E. Sherwood, *The White House Papers of Harry L. Hopkins* (2 vols., London, 1949).
N. Shute, *Slide Rule: the Autobiography of an Engineer* (London, 1954).
J. Slessor, *The Central Blue* (London, 1956).
A. Speer, *Inside the Third Reich* (London, 1971).
H. L. Stimson, McG. Bundy, *On Active Service in Peace and War* (New York, 1947).
H.-G. von Studwitz, *While Berlin Burns: the Diary of Hans-Georg von Studwitz* (London, 1963).
Lord Tedder, *Air Power in War* (London, 1948).
Lord Tedder, *With Prejudice* (London, 1966).
H. S. Truman, *Year of Decision, 1945* (New York, 1955).
W. Warlimont, *Inside Hitler's Headquarters* (London, 1964).
F. Whittle, *Jet* (London, 1953).
J. G. Winant, *A Letter from Grosvenor Square* (London, 1947).
A. Yakovlev, *Notes of an Aircraft Designer* (Moscow, 1961).
S. Yoshida, *The Yoshida Memoirs: the Story of Japan in Crisis* (London, 1961).
G. Zhukov, *Marshal Zhukov's Greatest Battles* (London, 1969).

D: Secondary Sources

I. GENERAL

J. Alexander, *Russian Aircraft since 1940* (London, 1975).

G. Barclay, *The Rise and Fall of the New Roman Empire* (London, 1973).

V. E. Blunt, *The Use of Airpower* (London, 1942).

B. Bond, I. Roy (eds.), *War and Society: I* (London, 1976).

G. Bowman, *War in the Air* (London, 1956).

D. Brown, *Carrier Operations in World War II* (2 vols., London, 1974).

M. Caidin, *Air Force* (New York, 1957).

B. Collier, *A History of Air Power* (London, 1974).

A. Coningham, 'The Development of Tactical Air Forces' *JRUSI* XCI (1946).

H. Cooper, O. Thetford, *Aircraft of the Fighting Powers* (7 vols., London).

T. Elmhirst, 'Some Aspects and Lessons of Air Warfare 1939-1945' *RAF Quarterly* XIX (1947/8).

C. Falls, *The Nature of Modern Warfare* (London, 1941).

G. Feuchter, *Geschichte des Luftkrieges* (Frankurt am Main, 1964).

G. Förster, *Totaler Krieg und Blitzkrieg* (Berlin, 1967).

J. Fuller, *The Second World War* (London, 1948).

C. H. Gibbs-Smith, *The Aeroplane* (London, 1960).

A. Goldberg (ed.), *A History of the United States Airforce 1907-1957* (New York, 1957).

W. Green, *The Air Forces of the World* (London, 1958).

K. Greenfield, *American Strategy in World War II: a Reconsideration* (Baltimore, 1963).

P. R. Groves, *Our Future in the Air* (London, 1935).

B. L. Hart, *A History of the Second World War* (London, 1970).

B. L. Hart, *The Revolution in Warfare* (London, 1946).

R. Higham, *Air Power: a Concise History* (London, 1972).

A. Hillgruber (ed.), *Probleme des Zweiten Weltkrieges* (Cologne, 1967).

F. H. Hinsley, *Hitler's Strategy* (Cambridge, 1951).

H. Hinton, *Air Victory* (New York, 1948).

I. V. Hogg, *Anti-Aircraft. A History of Air Defence* (London, 1978).

M. Howard, *Studies in War and Peace* (London, 1970).

M. Howard (ed.), *The Theory and Practice of War* (London, 1974).

R. Jackson, *Strike from the Sea* (London, 1970).

H. A. Jacobsen, J. Rohwer (eds.), *Decisive Battles of World War II: the German View* (London, 1965).

J. Johnson, *Full Circle* (London, 1964).

J. Killen, *A History of Marine Aviation* (London, 1969).

E. Kingston-McCloughrey, *War in Three Dimensions* (London, 1949).

K. Knorr, *The War Potential of Nations* (Princeton, 1956).

W. Laqueur (ed.), *Fascism* (London, 1976).

A. Lee, *Air Power* (London, 1955).

A. M. Low, *Modern Armaments* (London, 1939).

N. Macmillan, *The Royal Air Force in the World War* (4 vols., London, 1942-50).

H. Michel, *The Second World War* (London, 1975).

R. Miller, D. Sawyers, *The Technical Development of Modern Aviation* (London, 1969).

F. Morison, *War on Great Cities* (London, 1937).

S. E. Morison, *American Contributions to the Strategy of World War II* (London, 1958).

S. E. Morison, *The Two-Ocean War* (Boston, 1963).

J. Nayler, E. Owen, *Aviation: its Technical Development* (London, 1965).

N. Polmar, *Aircraft Carriers* (London, 1969).

E. van der Porten, *The German Navy in World War II* (London, 1969).

G. H. Quester, *Deterrence Before Hiroshima* (New York, 1966).

S. W. Roskill, *The War at Sea 1939-1945* (London, 1960).

A. P. de Seversky, *Air power: Key to Survival* (London, 1952).

E. Sims, *Fighter Tactics and Strategy 1914-1970* (London, 1972).

A. Sked, C. Cook, *Crisis and Controversy: Essays in Honour of A. J. P. Taylor* (London, 1976).

J. Slessor, *Air Power and Armies* (London, 1936).

J. Slessor, 'Air Power and the Future of War', *JRUSI* XCIX (1954).

J. Slessor, 'The Past Development of Air Power', *JRUSI* XCIV (1949).

P. M. Smith, *The Air Force Plans for Peace 1943-5* (Baltimore, 1970).

J. Spaight, *Air Power and the Cities* (London, 1930).

J. Spaight, *Air Power in the Next War* (London, 1938).

F. Sternberg, *The Military and Industrial Revolution of our Time* (London, 1959).

P. H. Sumner, *Aircraft: Progress and Development* (London, 1935).

F. Swanborough, *United States Military Aircraft since 1919* (London, 1963).

E. C. Talbot-Booth, *The Air Forces of the World* (London, 1939).

Lord Tedder, 'Air, Land and Sea Warfare', *JRUSI* XCI (1946).

O. Thetford, *Aircraft of the Royal Air Force 1918-1957* (London, 1957).

J. Tompkins, *The Weapons of World War II* (London, 1967).

E. Wilson, *Air Power for Peace* (New York, 1945).

W. Winter, *Warplanes of the Nations* (London, 1944).

G. Wright, *The Ordeal of Total War* (New York, 1968).

II Preparations for War

S. Aster, *1939: the Making of the Second World War* (London, 1973).

U. Bialer, 'The Danger of Bombardment from the Air and the Making of British Air Disarmament Policy 1932-4' in B. Bond, I. Roy (eds.) *War and Society* I (London, 1976).

U. Bialer, ' "Humanization" of Air Warfare in British Foreign Policy on the Eve of the Second World War', *Journal of Contemporary History* XIII (1978).

R. Burlingham, *General Billy Mitchell* (New York, 1952).

J. Bushby, *The Air Defence of Great Britain* (London, 1973).

R. A. Chaput, *Disarmament in British Foreign Policy* (London, 1935).

L. E. Charlton, G. Garrett, R. Fletcher, *The Air Defence of Britain* (London, 1938).

J. B. Cynk, *Polish Aircraft 1893-1939* (London, 1971).

H. S. Dinerstein, 'The Impact of Air Power on the International Scene 1930-1939', *Military Affairs* XIX (1955).

D. Divine, *Broken Wing: a Study in the British Exercise of Air Power* (London, 1966).

G. Douhet, *The Command of the Air* (London, 1943).

E. M. Eddy, 'Britain and the Fear of Aerial Bombardment', *Aerospace Historian* XV (1968).

E. M. Emme, 'Emergence of Nazi Luftpolitik as a Weapon in International Affairs 1933-35', *Aerospace Historian* VII (1960).

R. Frankenstein, 'A propos des aspects financiers du réarmement français 1935-1939', *RDGM* XXVI (1976).

L. Gouré, *Civil Defence in the Soviet Union* (Berkeley, 1962).

J. B. Haldane, *A.R.P.* (London, 1938).

B. L. Hart, *The Defence of Britain* (London, 1939).

M. Hauner, 'Czechoslovakia as a Military Factor in British Considerations of 1938', *Journal of Strategic Studies* I (1978).

A. Hezlet, 'The Development of U.S. Naval Aviation and the British Fleet Air Arm and Coastal Command between the Wars', *Aerospace Historian* XVIII (1971).

E. Homze, *Arming the Luftwaffe* (Nebraska U.P., 1976).

M. Howard, *The Continental Commitment* (London, 1972).

H. M. Hyde, G. Nuttall, *Air Defence and the Civil Population* (London, 1937).

H. M. Hyde, *British Air Policy between the Wars 1918-1939* (London, 1976).

H. A. Jones, W. Raleigh, *The War in the Air* (2 vols., HMSO, 1969).

F. X. Kane, 'French Airpower in the Thirties', *Aerospace Historian* XIII (1966).

H. Klotz, *Germany's Secret Armaments* (London, 1934).

R. W. Krauskopf, 'The Army and the Strategic Bomber 1930-1939', *Military Affairs* XXII (1958).

P. Le Goyet, 'Evolution de la doctrine d'emploi de l'aviation française entre 1919 et 1939', *RDGM* XIX (1969).

W. B. Leach, 'Obstacles to the Development of American Air Power', *Annals of the American Academy of Political and Social Science* CCXIXC (1955).

Luftschutz durch Bauen (Berlin, 1939).

P. Masefield, 'The Royal Air Force and British Military Aircraft Production 1934 to 1940', Comité international d'histoire de la 2ᵉ Guerre Mondiale, Anglo-French Colloquium, Dec. 1975.

G. Meinck, *Hitler und die deutsche Aufrüstung 1933-1937* (Wiesbaden, 1959).

C. Messenger, *The Art of Blitzkrieg* (London, 1976).

W. Murray, 'German Air Power and the Munich Crisis' in B. Bond, I. Roy (eds.) *War and Society* I (1976).

R. J. Overy, 'The German pre-war aircraft production plans', *English Historical Review* XC (1975).

C. Portal, 'Air Force Co-operation in Policing the Empire' *JRUSI* LXXXII (1937).

S. Possony, *Tomorrow's War* (London, 1938).

B. Powers, *Strategy without Slide Rule* (London, 1976).

B. Ranft, *Technical Change and British Naval Policy 1860-1939* (London, 1977).

W. J. Reader, *Architect of Air Power: the Life of the First Viscount Weir of Eastwood* (London, 1968).

E. M. Robertson, *Hitler's Pre-war Policy and Military Plans* (London, 1963).

E. M. Robertson, *Mussolini as Empire-Builder* (London, 1977).

W. R. Rock, *British Appeasement in the 1930s* (London, 1977).

N. Rose, *Vansittart: Study of a Diplomat* (London, 1978).

S. Roskill, *Naval Policy between the Wars* (2 vols., London, 1968-76).

H. Schliephake, *The Birth of the Luftwaffe* (London, 1971).

R. Shay, *British Rearmament in the Thirties* (Princeton U.P., 1977).

C. Sims, *The Royal Air Force: the First Fifty Years* (London, 1968).

M. Smith, 'The Royal Air Force, Air Power and British Foreign Policy', *Journal of Contemporary History* XII (1977).

M. Smith, 'The RAF and Counter-Force Strategy before World War II', *JRUSI* CXXI (1976).

F. Sternberg, *Germany and a Lightning War* (London, 1938).

O. Stewart, 'The Air Force of France', *JRUSI* LXXXV (1940).

R. Suchenwirth, *The Development of the German Air Force 1919-1939* (New York, 1968).

A. J. P. Taylor, *The Origins of the Second World War* (London, 1961).

J. Truelle, 'La production aéronautique militaire française jusqu'en juin 1940', *RDGM* XIX (1969).

K-H. Völker, *Die deutsche Luftwaffe 1933-1939* (Stuttgart, 1967).

K-H. Völker, *Die Entwicklung der militärischen Luftfahrt in Deutschland 1920-1933* (Stuttgart, 1964).

M. Werner (pseud.), *The Military Strength of the Powers* (London, 1939).

M. Weygand, 'How France is Defended', *International Affairs* XVIII (1939).

T. Wintringham, *New Ways of War* (London, 1940).

III EUROPEAN AIR WAR

R. Absolon, *Die Wehrmacht im Dritten Reich* (Boppard am Rhein, 1969).

H. Adler, *Ein Buch von der neuen Luftwaffe* (Stuttgart, 1938).

H. Allen, *Who Won the Battle of Britain?* (London, 1974).

W. Ansel, *Hitler Confronts England* (Duke U.P., 1960).

G. Barclay, *The Rise and Fall of the New Roman Empire* (London, 1973).

K. Bartz, *Swastika in the Air* (London, 1956).

C. Bekker, *Hitler's Naval War* (London, 1974).

C. Bekker, *The Luftwaffe War Diaries* (London, 1966).

R. de Belot, *The Struggle for the Mediterranean 1941–1945* (Princeton U.P., 1951).

G. Bignozzi, B. Catalanotto, *Storia degli Aerei D'Italia* (Rome, 1962).

E. Bishop, *The Battle of Britain* (London, 1961).

B. Bond, *France and Belgium 1939–40* (London, 1975).

Λ. Boyd, *The Soviet Air Force since 1918* (London, 1977).

L. Broad, *The War that Churchill Waged* (London, 1960).

Λ. Bryant, *Triumph in the West* (London, 1959).

Λ. Bryant, *The Turn of the Tide* (London, 1957).

P. Carell, *Hitler's War on Russia* (2 vols., London, 1964).

W. Carr, *Arms, Autarky and Aggression* (London, 1972).

B. Λ. Carroll, *Design for Total War: Arms and Economics in the Third Reich* (The Hague, 1968).

B. Collier, *The Battle of Britain,* (London, 1962).

B. Collier, *Battle of the V-Weapons* (London, 1964).

R. Collier, *Eagle Day* (London, 1966).

Comité d'Histoire de la 2ᵉ Guerre Mondiale, *La Guerre en Méditerranée 1939–1945* (Paris, 1971).

M. Cooper, *The German Army* (London, 1978).

K. Craven, *Soviet Aviation* (London, 1945).

P. Deichmann, *German Air Force Operations in Support of the Army* (New York, 1962).

D. Dempster, D. Wood, *The Narrow Margin: the Battle of Britain and the Rise of Airpower* (London, 1961).

I. Deutscher, *Stalin* (London, 1949).

J. P. Dournel, 'L'armée de l'air en 1946', *RDGM* XXVIII (1978).

P. R. Drummond, 'Air Campaigns in Libya and Tripolitania', *JRUSI* LXXVIII (1943).

T. C. Elmhirst, 'The German Air Force and its Failure', *JRUSI* XCI (1946).

T. C. Elmhirst, 'Mobile Air Forces', *JRUSI* XCVI (1951).

J. Erickson, *The Road to Stalingrad* (London, 1975).

E. C. Fay, 'Air Strength of the United States', *Annals of the American Academy of Political and Social Science* CCXCIX (1955).

J. Fischer, 'Uber den Entschluss zur Luftversorgung Stalingrads', *Militärgeschichtliche Mitteilungen* VI (1969).

C. Fitzgibbon, *The Blitz* (London, 1970).

P. Fleming, *Invasion 1940* (London, 1957).

W. Green, *Warplanes of the Third Reich* (London, 1970).

C. Grey, *Luftwaffe* (London, 1944).

A. L. Gropman, 'The Battle of Britain and the Principles of War', *Aerospace Historian* XVIII (1971).

K. Gundelach, 'The German Air Force Yesterday and Today', *Aerospace Historian* XVIII (1971).

H. Hansell, *The Air Plan that Defeated Hitler* (Atlanta, Ga., 1972).

Hauptmann Hermann (pseud.), *The Rise and Fall of the Luftwaffe* (London, 1944).

G. C. Herring, *Aid to Russia 1941–1946* (New York, 1973).

Λ. Hezlet, *Aircraft and Seapower* (London, 1970).

T. Higgins, *Winston Churchill and the Second Front 1940–1943* (New York, 1957).

K. Hildebrand, *The Foreign Policy of the Third Reich* (London, 1973).

A. Hillgruber, *Hitlers Strategie: Politik und Kriegsführung 1940–1941* (Frankfurt am Rhein, 1965).

F. H. Hinsley, *Hitler's Strategy* (Cambridge, 1951).

M. Howard, *The Mediterranean Strategy in the Second World War* (London, 1968).

D. Irving, *Hitler's War* (London, 1977).

D. Irving, *The Rise and Fall of the Luftwaffe* (London, 1973).

R. Jackson, *Air War over France 1939-1940* (London, 1974).

R. Jackson, *The Red Falcons* (Brighton, 1970).

M. Jullian, *The Battle of Britain* (London, 1967).

P. K. Kemp, *The Fleet Air Arm* (London, 1954).

J. Killen, *The Luftwaffe: a History* (London, 1967).

R. Kilmarx, *A History of Soviet Air Power* (London, 1962).

J. D. Langer, 'The Harrison-Beaverbrook Mission and the Debate over Unconditional Aid for the Soviet Union, 1941', *Journal of Contemporary History* XIV (1979).

B. Leach, *German Strategy against Russia 1939-1941* (Oxford, 1973).

Λ. Lee, *The German Air Force* (London, 1946).

Λ. Lee, *The Soviet Air Force* (London, 1950).

B. H. Liddell Hart, *The Other Side of the Hill* (London, 1948).

H. Lloyd, 'Allied Air Power in the Mediterranean 1940-1945', *JRUSI* XCII (1947).

J. Lukacs, *The Last European War* (London, 1976).

R. Lukas, *Eagles East: the Army Air Forces and the Soviet Union* (Florida State U.P., 1970).

C. B. Macdonald, *The Mighty Endeavour: American Armed Forces in the European Theatre in World War II* (Oxford, 1969).

D. Mack Smith, *Mussolini's Roman Empire* (London, 1976).

F. Morzik, *German Air Force Airlift Operations* (New York, 1961).

E. O'Ballance, *The Red Army* (London, 1964).

R. J. Overy, 'Hitler and Air Strategy', *Journal of Contemporary History* XV (1980).

R. Owen, *The Desert Air Force* (London, 1948).

Λ. Phillipi, F. Heim, *Der Feldzug gegen Sowjetrussland* (Stuttgart, 1962).

H. Plocher, *The German Air Force versus Russia* (3 vols., New York, 1965-1968).

K. Poolman, *Focke-Wulf Condor: Scourge of the Atlantic* (London, 1978).

R. D. Potts, 'The Foundation of Soviet Air Power: an Historical and Managerial Interpretation', *AAAPSS* CCXCIX (1955).

Λ. Price, *Luftwaffe* (London, 1970).

Λ. Price, *Luftwaffe Handbook 1939-1945* (London, 1977).

C. Rawnsley, R. Wright, *Night Fighter* (London, 1957).

M. Salewski, *Die deutsche Seekriegsleitung 1939-1945* (2 vols., Frankfurt am Main, 1970).

G. Santoro, *L'Aeronautica Italiana nella Seconda Guerra Mondiale* (2 vols., Rome, 1957).

W. Schwabedissen, *The Russian Air Force in the Eyes of German Commanders* (New York, 1960).

Λ. Seaton, *The Russo-German War 1941-1945* (London, 1971).

S. Sears, H. McFarland, *Air War against Hitler's Germany* (London, 1964).

P. C. Smith, *The Stuka at War* (London, 1971).

R. Stockwell, *Soviet Air Power* (New York, 1956).

J. Stroud, *The Red Air Force* (London, 1943).

R. Suchenwirth, *Historical Turning Points in the German Air Force War Effort* (New York, 1959).

T. Taylor, *The Breaking Wave* (London, 1967).

T. Taylor, *The March of Conquest* (New York, 1958).

J. W. Thompson, *Italian Civil and Military Aircraft* (London, 1963).

H. Trevor-Roper, *The Last Days of Hitler* (London, 1947).

K. Uebe, *Russian Reactions to German Air Power in World War II* (New York, 1964).

J. Ulrich, *Der Luftkrieg über Österreich 1939-1945* (Vienna, 1967).

R. E. Vintras, 'The German Air Force', *JRUSI* XCII (1947).

A. Werth, *Russia at War* (London, 1964).

R. Wheatley, *Operation Sea Lion* (Oxford, 1958).

C. Wilmot, *The Struggle for Europe* (London, 1952).

R. Wright, *Dowding and the Battle of Britain* (London, 1969).

P. Wykeham, *Fighter Command* (London, 1960).

F. Ziemke, *Stalingrad to Berlin* (New York, 1968).

IV AIR WAR IN THE FAR EAST

A. d'Albas, *Death of a Navy* (London, 1957).

L. Allen, *The End of the War in Asia* (London, 1976).

C. Argyle, *Japan at War 1937-1945* (London, 1976).

J. Baldwin, 'Air Aspects of the Operations in Burma', *JRUSI* XÇ (1945).

R. Butow, *Japan's Decision to Surrender* (Stanford, 1954).

R. Butow, *Tojo and the Coming of War* (Princeton U.P., 1961).

M. Caidin, *A Torch to the Enemy* (London, 1960).

R. Callahan, *Burma, 1942-1945* (London, 1978).

W. Chamberlin, *Japan over Asia* (London, 1938).

B. Collier, *The War in the Far East* (London, 1969).

A. Dubinsky, *The Far East in the Second World War* (Moscow, 1972).

P. S. Dull, *A Battle History of the Imperial Japanese Navy 1941-1945* (Cambridge, 1978).

H. Feis, *The Atomic Bomb and the End of World War II* (Princeton U.P., 1966).

H. Feis, *The Road to Pearl Harbor* (Princeton, 1950).

R. J. Francillon, *Japanese Aircraft of the Pacific War* (London, 1970).

J. Goette, *Japan Fights for Asia* (London, 1945).

G. Grimsdale, 'The War against Japan in China', *JRUSI* XCV (1950).

R. J. Harden, 'The Use of Allied Air Power in the War against Japan', *RAF Quarterly* XVII (1945/6).

V. Haughland, *The AAF against Japan* (New York, 1948).

J. Horikoshi, M. Okumiya, *The Zero Fighter* (London, 1958).

R. Inoguchi, T. Nakajima, R. Pineas, *The Divine Wind: Japan's Kamikaze Force in World War II* (London, 1959).

A. Iriye, 'The Failure of Military Expansionism' in J. Morley (ed.), *Dilemmas of Growth in Pre-war Japan* (Princeton U.P., 1971).

M. Ito, *The End of the Imperial Japanese Navy* (London, 1962).

E. A. Johnson, D. A. Katcher, *Mines against Japan* (White Oak, Maryland, 1973).

F. C. Jones, *Japan's New Order in East Asia 1937-1945* (Oxford, 1954).

T. Kase, *Eclipse of the Rising Sun* (London, 1951).

E. J. King, *Fleet Admiral King: a Naval Record* (New York, 1952).

W. Koenig, *Over the Hump: Airlift to China* (London, 1972).

W. L. Langer, *The Undeclared War 1940-41* (New York, 1953).

B. K. Marshall, *Capitalism and Nationalism in Pre-war Japan* (Stanford, 1967).

J. Meskill, *Hitler and Japan: the Hollow Alliance* (New York, 1967).

J. Morley (ed.), *Deterrent Diplomacy: Japan, Germany and the U.S.S.R. 1935-40* (New York, 1976).

R. Nagatsuka, *I was a Kamikaze* (London, 1973).

J. D. Potter, *Admiral of the Pacific: the Life of Yamamoto* (London, 1960).

W. W. Russell, *Forgotten Skies* (London, 1945).

B. Silberman, *Japan in Crisis* (Princeton U.P., 1974).

R. J. Smethurst, *A Social Basis for Pre-war Japanese Militarism* (Berkeley, 1974).

E. Speyer, 'Japan's Air Strength', *JRUSI* LXXXVII (1942).

D. A. Thomas, *Japan's War at Sea* (London, 1978).

C. Thorne, *Allies of a Kind: the United States, Britain and the War against Japan 1941–1945* (London), 1978).
A. D. Turnbull, C. L. Lord, *History of United States Naval Aviation* (New Haven, 1949).
R. E. Ward (ed.), *Political Development of Modern Japan* (Princeton U.P., 1968).

V BOMBING

H. R. Allen, *The Legacy of Lord Trenchard* (London, 1972).
R. Barker, *The 1000 Plan* (London, 1965).
G. Bonacina, *Comando Bombardieri* (Milan, 1975).
N. Bottomley, 'The Strategic Bomber Offensive against Germany', *JRUSI* XCIII (1948).
A. Boyle, *Trenchard* (London, 1962).
G. Dickens, *Bombing and Strategy: the Fallacy of Total War* (London, 1947).
N. Frankland, *Bomber Offensive* (London, 1969).
N. Frankland, *The Bombing Offensive against Germany* (London, 1965).
R. A. Freeman, *The Mighty Eighth* (London, 1970).
L. Giovanni, F. Fried, *The Decision to Drop the Bomb* (London, 1965).
G. E. Hopkins, 'Bombing and the American conscience during World War II', *Historian* XXVIII (1966).
D. Irving, *The Destruction of Dresden* (London, 1963).
D. Irving, *The Mare's Nest* (London, 1964).
N. Jones, *The Origins of Strategic Bombing* (London, 1973).
J. Kurowski, *Der Luftkrieg über Deutschland* (Düsseldorf, 1977).
P. Lewis, *The British Bomber since 1914* (London, 1967).
D. McIsaac, *Strategic Bombing in World War Two* (London, 1976).
R. J. Overy, 'From Uralbomber to Amerikabomber: the Luftwaffe and Strategic Bombing', *Journal of Strategic Studies* I (1978).
A. Price, *Battle over the Reich* (London, 1973).
H. Rumpf, *The Bombing of Germany* (London, 1963).
H. Rumpf, 'Die Industrie im Bombenkrieg', *Wehrwissenschaftliche Rundschau* III (1953).
R. Saundby, *Air Bombardment: the Story of its Development* (London, 1961).
R. Saundby, 'Bomber Command', *JRUSI* LXXXIX (1944).
W. S. Schoenberger, *Decision of Destiny* (Ohio U.P., 1969).
M. Smith, 'The Strategic Bombing Debate: the Second World War and Vietnam', *Journal of Contemporary History* XII (1977).
C. Spaatz, 'Strategic Air Power—Fulfilment of a Concept', *Foreign Affairs* no. 24 (1945/6).
J. Spaight, *Bombing Vindicated* (London, 1944).
J. Spaight, 'Strategic Air Bombardment', *RAF Quarterly* XVIII (1946/7).
O. Stewart, 'Strategic Bombing', *JRUSI* LXXXI (1936).
E. B. Strauss, 'The Psychological Effects of Bombing', *JRUSI* LXXXIV (1939).
S. M. Ulanoff (ed.), *Bombs Away!* (New York, 1971).
A. Verrier, *The Bombing Offensive* (London, 1968).

VI LEADERSHIP, ORGANIZATION AND TRAINING

S. E. Ambrose, *The Supreme Commander: the War Years of General Dwight D. Eisenhower* (London, 1969).
A. Andrews, *The Air Marshals* (London, 1970).
K. E. Bailey, *Technology and Society under Lenin and Stalin* (Princeton U.P., 1978).
E. Baker, *Fighter Aces of the RAF* (London, 1962).
R. Benedict, *The Chrysanthemum and the Sword* (London, 1967).

C. Bewley, *Hermann Goering in the Third Reich* (New York, 1962).

A. Brown, *Ground Staff* (London, 1943).

C. Browne, *Tojo: the Last Banzai* (London, 1967).

W. Carr, *Hitler. A Study in Personality and Politics* (London, 1978).

M. Dean, *The Royal Air Force and Two World Wars* (London, 1979).

J. Erickson, *The Soviet High Command* (London, 1962).

H. Feis, *Churchill, Roosevelt and Stalin* (Princeton U.P., 1957).

M. Foot, *Aneurin Bevan* (2 vols., London, 1962).

M. Gilbert, *Winston Churchill: Volume V* (London, 1976).

W. Görlitz, *The German General Staff* (New York, 1953).

C. Grey, *A History of the Air Ministry* (London, 1940).

R. Grunberger, *A Social History of the Third Reich* (London, 1971).

F. Halder, *Hitler as Warlord* (London, 1950).

H. Herlin, *Udet* (London, 1960).

I. Jacob, 'The High Level Conduct and Direction of World War II', *JRUSI* CI (1956).

F. A. Johnson, *Defence by Committee: the British Committee of Imperial Defence 1885–1959* (Oxford, 1960).

H. Knoke, *I Flew for the Führer* (London, 1953).

A. Lee, *Goering: Air Leader* (London, 1972).

R. Manvell, H. Fraenkel, *Göring* (London, 1962).

E. R. May, 'The Development of Politico-Military Consultation in the United States', *Political Science Quarterly* (1955).

M. Messerschmidt, *Die Wehrmacht im NS-Staat* (Hamburg, 1969).

L. E. Morison, *Turmoil and Tradition: a Study of the Life and Times of Henry L. Stimson* (Boston, 1960).

L. Moseley, *The Reich Marshal* (London, 1974).

A. Nielsen, *The German Air Force General Staff* (New York, 1959).

R. Owen, *Tedder* (London, 1952).

L. A. Pattinson, 'The Training of a Royal Air Force Pilot', *JRUSI* LXXXIII (1938).

R. Payne, *General Marshall* (London, 1952).

B. Philpott, *Challenge in the Air* (Hemel Hempstead, 1970).

F. C. Pogue, *George C. Marshall: Ordeal and Hope 1939–1942* (London, 1968).

D. Richards, *Portal of Hungerford* (London, 1977).

S. Sakai, *Samurai* (London, 1957).

M. P. Schoenfeld, *The War Ministry of Winston Churchill* (Iowa State U.P., 1972).

P. Schramm, *Hitler. The Man and the Military Leader* (London, 1972).

E. Sims, *American Aces of World War II* (London, 1958).

E. Sims, *The Fighter Pilots* (London, 1967).

H. Sprout, 'Trends in the Traditional Relation between Military and Civilian', *Proceedings of the American Philosophical Society* XCII (1948).

J. Strawson, *Hitler as Military Commander* (London, 1971).

R. Suchenwirth, *Command and Leadership in the German Air Force* (New York, 1969).

A. J. P. Taylor, *Beaverbrook* (London, 1972).

A. J. P. Taylor, *The Warlords* (London, 1977).

R. F. Toliver, T. J. Constable, *Horrido! Fighter Aces of the Luftwaffe* (London, 1968).

R. F. Weigley, *History of the United States Army* (London, 1968).

K. Young, *Churchill and Beaverbrook* (London, 1966).

VII The Aircraft Economies

C. F. Andrews, *Vickers Aircraft since 1918* (London, 1969).

P. Andrews, E. Brunner, *The Life of Lord Nuffield* (Oxford, 1955).

N. Beasley, *Knudsen: a Biography* (New York).

T. Bisson, *Japan's War Economy* (New York, 1945).

D. N. Chester (ed.), *Lessons of the British War Economy* (Cambridge, 1951).

S. Clough, *The Economic History of Modern Italy* (Columbia U.P., 1964).

J. B. Cohen, *Japan's Economy in War and Reconstruction* (Minnesota U.P., 1949).

H. Conradis, *Design for Flight* (London. 1960).

H-J. Cooper, 'War and the Businessman', *JRUSI* LXXXIV (1940).

E. Devons, *Planning in Practice. Essays in Aircraft Planning in Wartime* (Cambridge, 1950).

M. Dobb, *Soviet Economy and the War* (London, 1941).

J. S. Dupré, W. E. Gustafson, 'Contracting for Defense: Private Firms and the Public Interest', *Political Science Quarterly* LXXVII (1962).

D. Eichholtz, *Geschichte der deutschen Kriegswirtschaft 1939-45: Vol. I* (Berlin, 1969).

P. Façon, 'Aperçus sur la collaboration aéronautique franco-allemande 1940-1943', *RDGM* XXVII (1977).

E. Fairfax, *Calling All Arms* (London, 1946).

P. Fearon, 'The British Airframe Industry and the State 1918-1935', *Economic History Review* 2nd Ser. XXVII (1974).

P. Fearon 'The Vicissitudes of a British Aircraft Company: Handley Page between the Wars', *Business History* XX (1978).

F. Forstmeier, H-E. Volkmann (eds.), *Kriegswirtschaft und Rüstung 1939-1945* (Düsseldorf, 1977).

F. Forstmeier, H-E. Volkmann (eds.), *Wirtschaft und Rüstung am Vorabend des Zweiten Weltkrieges* (Düsseldorf, 1975).

O. Franks, *Central Planning and Control in War and Peace* (London, 1947).

D. Gordon, R. Dangerfield, *The Hidden Weapon. The Story of Economic Warfare* (New York, 1947).

J. Mc. Haight, 'Les négociations relatives aux achats d'avions américains par la France pendant la période qui précéda immédiatement la guerre', *RDGM* XV (1965).

A. Hara, 'L'économie japonaise pendant la deuxième guerre mondiale', *RDGM* XXIII (1973).

R. Higham, 'Government Companies and national defense: British aeronautical experience 1918-1945 as the basis of a broad hypothesis', *Business History Review* XXXIX (1965).

R. Higham, 'Quantity vs Quality: the Impact of Changing Demand on the British Aircraft Industry 1900-1960', *Business History Review* XLII (1968).

I. B. Holley, 'Un organisme de guerre économique; le comité de co-ordination des industries aéronautiques', *RDGM* XX (1970).

E. Homze, *Foreign Labour in Nazi Germany* (Princeton, 1967).

G. Ince, 'The Mobilisation of Manpower in Great Britain in the Second World War', *Manchester School* XIV (1946).

A. van Ishoven, *Messerschmitt* (London, 1975).

E. Janeway, *The Struggle for Survival. A Chronicle of Economic Mobilization in World War II* (New Haven, 1951).

G. Janssen, *Das Ministerium Speers; Deutschlands Rüstung im Krieg* (Frankfurt a.M, 1968).

N. Kaldor, 'The German War Economy', *Manchester School* XIV (1946).

B. H. Klein, *Germany's Economic Preparations for War* (Harvard U.P., 1959).

P. C. Koistinen, 'Mobilizing the World War II Economy: Labour and the Industrial-Military Alliance', *Pacific Historical Review* XLII (1973).

J. Kuczynski, *Germany: Economic and Labour Conditions under Fascism* (New York, 1945).

K. Lachmann, 'War and Peace Economics of Aviation', *Social Research* VII (1940).

C. D. Long, *The Labor Force under Changing Income and Employment* (Princeton U.P., 1958).

K-H. Ludwig, *Technik und Ingenieure im Dritten Reich* (Düsseldorf, 1974).

T. Mason, 'Labour in the Third Reich' *Past & Present,* No. 33 (1966).
T. Mason, 'The Primacy of Politics—Politics and Economics in National-Socialist Germany' in S. Woolf (ed.) *The Nature of Fascism* (London, 1968).
A. S. Milward, 'The End of the Blitzkrieg', *Economic History Review,* 2nd. Ser. XVI (1963/4).
A. S. Milward, *The Fascist Economy in Norway* (Oxford, 1972).
A. S. Milward, *The German Economy at War* (London, 1965).
A. S. Milward, *The New Order and the French Economy* (Oxford, 1970).
M. Murphy, *The British War Economy 1939–1943* (New York, 1943).
A. Nove, *An Economic History of the U.S.S.R.* (London, 1969).
R. J. Overy, 'The Luftwaffe and the European Economy', *Militärgeschichtliche Mitteilungen* XXI (1979).
R. J. Overy, 'Transportation and Rearmament in the Third Reich', *The Historical Journal* XVI (1973).
R. J. Overy, *William Morris, Viscount Nuffield* (London, 1976).
Oxford Univ. Institute of Statistics, *Studies in War Economics* (Oxford, 1947).
R. Polenberg, *War and Society: the United States 1941–1945* (New York, 1972).
S. Pollard, *The Development of the British Economy 1914–1967* (London, 1969).
J. Rae, *Climb to Greatness* (Cambridge, Mass., 1968).
J. Rae, 'The Financial Problems of the American Aircraft Industry 1906–1940', *Business History Review* XXXIX (1965).
A. J. Robertson, 'The British Airframe Industry and the State in the Inter-War Period: a Comment', *Economic History Review,* 2nd. Ser. XXVIII (1975).
S. M. Rosen, *The Combined Boards of the Second World War* (Columbia U.P., 1951).
R. Sarti, *Fascism and the Industrial Leadership in Italy 1919–1940* (Berkeley, 1971).
C. T. Saunders, 'Manpower Distribution 1939–1945: some international comparisons', *Manchester School* XIV (1946).
C. M. Sharp, *D.H. An Outline of de Havilland History* (London, 1960).
C. M. Sharp, M. J. F. Bowyer, *Mosquito* (London, 1967).
G. Simonson, 'The Demand for Aircraft and the Aircraft Industry 1907–1958', *Journal of Economic History* XX (1960).
G. Simonson, *History of the American Aircraft Industry* (MIT Press, 1968).
M. Smith, 'The Air Ministry, the Aircraft Industry and the Building of the Bomber Force', *Business History Review* LIII (1979).
R. E. Smith, 'La mobilisation économique', *RDGM* XVII (1967).
B. Stein, 'Labor's Role in Government Agencies During World War II', *Journal of Economic History* XVII (1957).
E. R. Stettinius, *Lend-Lease: Weapon for Victory* (New York, 1944).
M. Sumiya, 'Les ouvriers japonais pendant la deuxième guerre mondiale', *RDGM* XXIII (1973).
V. G. Treml (ed.), *The Development of the Soviet Economy* (New York, 1968).
R. Wagenführ, *Die deutsche Industrie im Kriege* (Berlin), 1963.
F. Walton, *Miracle of World War II* (New York, 1956).
G. T. White, 'Financing Industrial Expansion for War: the Origin of the Defense Plant Corporation Leases', *Journal of Economic History* IX (1949).
D. O. Woodbury, *Battlefronts of Industry. Westinghouse in World War II* (New York, 1948).

VIII Science and Intelligence

E. B. Addison, 'The Radio War', *JRUSI* XCII (1947).
C. Babington-Smith, *Evidence in Camera* (London, 1958).
J. P. Baxter, *Scientists Against Time* (Cambridge, Mass., 1968).
J. Bernal, *The Freedom of Necessity* (London, 1949).
A. D. Beyerchen, *Scientists under Hitler* (Yale U.P., 1977).

Lord Birkenhead, *The Prof. in Two Worlds* (London, 1961).

P. Blackett, *Military and Political Consequences of Atomic Energy* (London, 1948).

A. J. Brookes, *Photo Reconnaissance* (London, 1975).

J. Burchard, *Q.E.D. MIT in World War II* (New York, 1948).

R. W. Clark, *The Birth of the Bomb* (London, 1961).

R. W. Clark, *The Rise of the Boffins* (London, 1962).

J. G. Crowther, *Soviet Science* (London, 1936).

J. Erasmus, *Der geheime Nachrichtendienst* (Göttingen, 1955).

D. Fleming, B. Bailyn (eds.), *The Intellectual Migration: Europe and America 1939–60* (Harvard U.P., 1968).

B. Ford, *German Secret Weapons* (London, 1972).

S. A. Goudsmit, *ALSOS: the Failure in German Science* (London, 1947).

M. Gowing, *Britain and Atomic Energy 1939–1945* (London, 1964).

W. Green, *Rocket Fighter* (London, 1971).

L. R. Groves, *Now It Can Be Told* (London, 1963).

J. Haberer, *Politics and the Community of Science* (New York, 1969).

F. Hahn, *Deutsche Geheimwaffen 1939–1945* (Heidenheim, 1963).

R. F. Harrod, *The Prof. A Personal Memoir of Lord Cherwell* (London, 1959).

G. Hartcup, *The Challenge of War. Scientific and Engineering Contributions to World War II* (Newton Abbot, 1970).

W. Heisenberg, *Physics and Beyond. Encounters and Conversations* (London, 1971).

A. V. Hill, *The Ethical Dilemma of Science and Other Writings* (New York, 1960).

D. Irving, *The Virus House* (London, 1967).

B. Johnson, *The Secret War* (London, 1978).

R. V. Jones, *Most Secret War. British Scientific Intelligence 1939–1945* (London, 1978).

R. V. Jones, 'Scientific Intelligence', *JRUSI* XCII (1947).

R. V. Jones, 'Winston Churchill', *Biographical Memoirs of Fellows of the Royal Society* XII (1966).

R. Jungk, *Brighter than a Thousand Suns* (London, 1958).

D. Kahn, *The Codebreakers* (New York, 1967).

D. Kahn, *Hitler's Spies* (London, 1979).

D. Kahn, 'Le rôle du décryptage et du renseignement dans la stratégie et la tactique des Alliés', *RDGM* XXVIII (1978).

P. Leverkuehn, *German Military Intelligence* (London, 1954).

R. B. Lindsay, *The Role of Science in Civilisation* (New York, 1963).

I. Lloyd, *Rolls-Royce: the Merlin at War* (London, 1978).

R. Lusar, *German Secret Weapons of the Second World War* (London, 1960).

R. Manvell, H. Fraenkel, *The Canaris Conspiracy* (London, 1969).

J. C. Masterman, *The Double-Cross System 1939–1945* (London, 1972).

G. Pawle, *Secret War* (London, 1956).

G. Perrault, *The Red Orchestra* (London, 1967).

W. G. Perring, 'A Critical review of German Long-Range Rocket Development', *JRAeI* L (1946).

J. Piekalkiewicz, *Secret Agents, Spies and Saboteurs* (Newton Abbot, 1974).

R. Pocock, *German Guided Missiles of the Second World War* (London, 1967).

A. Price, *Instruments of Darkness* (London, 1967).

C. Ramsauer, 'Zur Geschichte der deutschen Physikalishen Gesellschaft in der Hitlerzeit', *Physikalische Blätter* I (1947).

S. W. Roskill, *Hankey, Man of Secrets* (3 vols., London, 1970–74).

A. P. Rowe, *One Story of Radar* (Cambridge, 1948).

Science . . ., *Science in War* (London, 1940).

L. Simon, *German Research in World War II* (New York, 1947).

R. Smelt, 'A Critical Review of German Research on High-Speed Airflow', *JRAeI* L (1946).

G. G. Smith, *Gas Turbines and Jet Propulsion for Aircraft* (London, 4th edn., 1946).
C. P. Snow, *Science and Government* (Oxford, 1961).
O. G. Sutton, *The Science of Flight* (London, 1949).
H. Tizard, 'Science and the Services', *JRUSI* XCI (1946).
C. H. Waddington, *Operational Research in World War 2* (London, 1973).
O. H. Wansborough-Jones, 'Science in War', *JRUSI* XCIX (1954).
R. Watson-Watt, *Three Steps to Victory* (London, 1958).
R. Weeks, *Organisation and Equipment for War* (Cambridge, 1950).
A. P. West, 'The Design and Production of Japanese Military Aircraft', *JRAeI* L (1946).
M. Ziegler, *Rocket Fighter* (London, 1961).
S. Zuckerman, *Scientists and War* (London, 1966).

IX Air War and Society

R. Aron, *The Century of Total War* (New York, 1954).
H. Bardua, *Stuttgart im Luftkrieg* (Stuttgart, 1968).
A. Calder, *The People's War* (London, 1971).
R. Collier, *The City that Wouldn't Die* (London, 1959).
J. L. Davies, *Air Raid* (London, 1938).
K. S. Davis, *The American Experience of War 1939-1945* (London, 1967).
K. S. Davis, *The Hero. Charles A. Lindbergh* (London, 1960).
M. J. B. Davy, *Air Power and Civilisation* (London, 1941).
E. M. Eddy, 'Britain and the Fear of Aerial Bombardment', *Aerospace Historian* XIII (1966).
N. Farson, *Bomber's Moon. London in the Blitzkrieg* (London, 1941).
V. Gollancz, *Shall our Children Live or Die?* (London, 1942).
E. Hampe, *Der zivile Luftschutz im 2. Weltkrieg* (Frankfurt a.M., 1963).
T. Harrison, *Living Through the Blitz* (London, 1976).
J. Hersey, *Hiroshima* (London, 1946).
F. C. Iklé, *The Social Impact of Bomb Destruction* (Norman, Okla., 1958).
B. J. Johnson, *The Evacuees* (London, 1968).
L. Kessler, *The Great York Air Raid* (London, 1979).
M. Seydewitz, *Civil Life in Wartime Germany* (New York, 1945).
C. Shore, C. Williams, *Aces High; the Fighter Aces of the British and Commonwealth Air Forces in World War II* (London, 1960).
E. Spetzler, *Luftkrieg und Menschlichkeit* (Göttingen, 1956).
M. Steinert, *Hitlers Krieg und die Deutschen* (Düsseldorf, 1970).
M. J. Yavenditti, 'The American People and the Use of the Atomic Bomb on Japan: the 1940s', *Historian* XXXVI (1974).

Index

ABC-1 Staff talks, 61, 63-4, 104

Abwehr (German counter-intelligence), 199

Abysinnian crisis, 18-19, 206

Academy of Aeronautical Research (Germ.), 187

Adam Opel company, 165

Aeronautical Research Institute (Jap.), 147

Afrika Korps, 65

Air-basing regions (U.S.S.R.), 53

Air Corps (U.S.), 14, 16, 28, 63, 111, 135, 153, 196

Air Council (U.K.), 135

Aircraft:
  Germany, Arado-234, 121, 200; Do-17Z, 113; FW-190, 55; FW-200, 37, 39-40; He-111, 113; He-177, 59, 112-13; He-274, 113; Hs-129, 57; Ju-86, 41, 200; Ju-87, 57; Ju-88, 103, 112, 113; Me-109, 55; Me-262, 195;
  Japan, 'Fugako' heavy bomber, 125; Mitsubishi A6 (Zero), 89;
  U.K., Blenheim, 200; Halifax, 113; Hurricane, 21, 56; Lancaster, 113, 178; Meteor, 195; Mosquito, 113, 193; Spitfire, 21, 163, 169, 178, 200; Stirling, 113;
  U.S.A., B-17, 112, 113, 114; B-24, 113, 114, 164, 170, 178; B-29, 92, 97-8, 100, 105, 113, 114, 125, 198; B-36, 113; P-51 (Mustang), 178;
  U.S.S.R., I-16, 49; I-53, 49; Il-4, 55; LaGG-3, 49; MiG-3, 49, 55; Pe-2, 55; Pe-8, 55; Su-2, 55; Yak-4, 55

Aircraft carriers, 6-8, 39-40, 42, 71, 93

Aircraft industry; and aircraft contracts, 181-2; and aircraft modification, 178; attacks on German, 124-4; and dispersal policies, 167; and efficiency, 152, 168-71; expansion of in U.S.A., 163-4; German, 162; German entrepreneurs and, 179; industrial mobilization, 162-7; inefficiency of Axis, 170-1; investment in, 166-7; labour conditions in, 174-5; and labour problems, 171-5; and managerial conservatism, 168; managerial efficiency in, 180; and mobilization of women, 172; rationalization of, 168-70; and shadow factory plans, 162-3; skilled labour in, 173-4; Soviet, 163; and state ownership, 183

Aircraft maintenance, 42-3, 140-1; in 'Overlord' campaign, 76; in Russia, 51-3

Aircraft Modification Committee, 178

Aircraft production, 2, 27-8, 45; and American plans, 153-4; and Battle of Britain, 32-3; bomber output, 120; British, 61; and conversion of car industry, 164-5; and finance, 181-3; German and bombing, 123-5; and German plans, 154; German production crisis, 50-1; industrial mobilization and, 162-7; Japanese, 93-4; and Japanese planning, 154-5; and labour, 171-5; and machine tools, 176; in Mediterranean campaign, 70; organization of, 155-9; and planning, 152-3; product selection, 177-80, 194-5; 'production miracle', 80; Soviet, 49; wartime production figures, 150

Aircraft Production Board (U.S.), 156

Aircraft Resources Control Office (U.S.), 157

Aircraft Scheduling Unit (U.S.), 157, 176

Air Defence Cadet Corps (U.K.), 140

Air intelligence; Allied on Germany, 197-8; Barbarossa, 49; in Battle of Britain, 32, 197; and bombing, 110-12; and course of war, 197-8; German on Russia, 198-9; in Germany, 79; photographic intelligence, 199-200; pre-war, 22-3; pre-war organization, 196-7; radar, 200-2

Air Member for Supply, (U.K.), 21

Air rearmament, 18-22

Air Support Controls (U.K.), 67
Air Targets Sub-Committee (U.K.), 14, 110
Air training, 81, 138-9, 141-5
Air Transport Command (U.S.), 91
Air War Plans Division (U.S.), 62, 111
Allied Expeditionary Air Forces, 76
Aluminium supplies, 56, 175-6
Anti-aircraft defences, 20-1, 121, 122
Anti- U-Boat Warfare Committee, 71
Arcadia Conference, 65, 90
Ardennes offensive (1944), 77
Army-Navy-British Purchasing Commission, 61
Arnold, Gen. H. H., 16, 63, 74-5, 76, 97-9, 108, 125, 132, 135, 142, 192, 196
Arnold-Slessor Agreement, 64
Aschenbrenner, Col. H., 197
Assistant Secretary of War for Air (U.S.), 63, 135
Atlantic, Battle of the, 38-40, 64-5, 70-3, 116
Atomic weapons, 2, 100, 125-6, 194, 195, 203, 211
Austin, H., 165
Automotive Committee for Air Defense, 164
AWPD-1, 62, 107, 117, 143
AWPD-42, 62

'Baedeker' air raids, 120
Baldwin, S., 21
'Baptism of Fire', 206
Bastico, Gen., 69
Battle Lessons Committee (Jap.), 87
Beaverbrook, Lord, 57, 105, 116, 160, 192
Bevan, A., 116
'Big Week' attack, 76
Bismarck battleship, 70
Blitz, 34-6, 83, 103, 106, 108, 110, 112, 114, 118, 119-20, 171, 204
Blockade strategy, 8, 30-1, 36-7, 95-6, 100
Bomber Command (RAF), 16, 34, 37, 104, 112, 115, 119, 120, 122; and bombing policy, 106-8; and early bombing attacks, 109; and oil attacks, 38; and opening of offensive, 30; and target selection, 110; and use of intelligence, 198
Bombing, 1-2; and Allied strategy, 116-18; atomic attacks, 125-6; and attacks on economy, 107; and Blitz, 34-6; and bomb tonnages, 120; bombing of Japan, 97-100; bombing technology, 112-15; bombs, 114; and British offensive, 37-8;

at Casablanca, 74-6; and casualties, 208; daylight and night, 108-9; and defeat of Japan, 125; firestorms, 114; German, 102-3; and German economy, 122-4; and German offensive, 120-1; Joint Directive on, 65; results of, 118-9; in Russian campaign, 58-60; tactical, 11 *See also* Atomic weapons, Bomber Command, Combined Bomber Offensive
Britain, Battle of, 31-4, 38, 45, 66, 197, 204, 206
British Air Ministry, 89, 135, 155, 163
Brooke, Field Marshal A., 116
Bush, Prof. V., 187
Butt Report, 110, 115

Cabinet Advisory Board (Jap.), 158
Casablanca Conference, 56, 73-4, 108
Castle Bromwich aircraft factory, 165, 169
Cavallero, Marshal U., 69
Cavity magnetron, 191
Central Planning Board (Germ.), 158
Chain Home radar stations, 15
Chamberlain, N., 21, 24, 104
Chennault, Maj.-Gen. C. L., 91, 97
Cherwell, Lord, 110, 115, 186
Chiang Kai-shek, 91, 97, 105
Chiefs of Staff (U.K.), 24, 46, 89, 108
China Air Task Force, 91,
Churchill, W. L. S., 22, 34, 38, 63, 64, 108, 112, 156, 207; and aid to Russia, 55-6; and attitude to science, 186-8; and bombing, 104-5; and committee system, 129; and doubts about bombing strategy, 115-16; and U-Boat war, 71
'Circus' operations, 65
Civil defence, 24-5, 26
Coastal Command (RAF), 37, 39-40, 71
Combined Bomber Offensive, 75, 79, 98, 111, 117, 198
Combined Chiefs of Staff, 63, 75, 108, 116, 118, 135
Combined Fleet (Jap.), 142
Commissar system, 146
Commissariat for Aviation Industry (U.S.S.R.), 156
Commission du Conseil supérieur de la Guerre, 11
Committee for Air Defence (U.K.), 186
Committee of Operations Analysts (U.S.), 97-8. 111
Communist Party (U.S.S.R.), 136, 209
Compton, Prof. K. T., 187
Controlled Materials Plan (U.S), 176

Coral Sea, Battle of, 92, 203
'C' schools (Germ.), 145

Dahlerus, B., 24
D-Day, 77, 79
Death-ray, 195
Demyansk airlift, 49, 145
Deputy Directorate of Intelligence (U.K.), 196
Director of Intelligence (U.K.), 196
Directorate of Management Control (U.S.), 135
Directorate of Operations and Intelligence (U.K.), 196
Directorate of Planning, Programmes and Statistics (U.K.), 157
Disarmament, 24
Dönitz, Admiral K., 72
Dornberger, Gen. W., 81, 194
Douglas aircraft corporation, 182
Douhet, Gen. G., 11-12, 16, 17, 33, 36
Douhetism, 129
Dunkirk evacuation, 30

Eaker, Gen. I., 117
East African campaign, 41-2
Eden, A., 24, 116
Eighth Air Force (AAF), 109
Eisenhower, Gen. D. D., 76, 83, 118
Empire Air Training Scheme, 143
English Electric Company, 165
Excess Profits Tax, 181-2

Fighter Command (RAF), 15, 16, 31, 33
Fighter Staff (Jägerstab), 80, 158, 159, 198
First World War, 5, 177, 185, 187, 202, 209
Five-Year-Plans (U.S.S.R.), 136, 160, 163, 172
Fleet Air Arm (U.K.), 39
Ford Motor Company, 164, 178
France, Battle of, 29-30, 32, 34, 45, 200
French air force; and Battle of France, 29-30; pre-war, 23-4; wartime planning of, 27-8
Fujihara, G., 155, 158

Galland, Gen. A., 80
Gas bombing, 206
Gauleiter, 122, 146, 159
'Gee' bombing aid, 115
Genda, Commander M., 6, 86
General Electric Company, 165

General Headquarters Air Force (U.S.), 63
German Air Ministry (RLM), 22, 50, 124, 167, 169, 189, 193, 195
German Army, 26, 50, 82, 133, 204
German Education Ministry, 186
German Navy, 37, 40, 83
Goebbels, J., 58, 122, 131, 207
Goering, Marshal H., 19, 21, 23, 24, 26, 36, 39, 46, 55, 59, 60, 108, 119, 134, 146, 151, 159, 183, 209; and aircraft production, 157-8; and anti-aircraft defences, 121; and Battle of Britain, 31; Blitz, 36; and bombing, 103; and collapse of Luftwaffe, 132-3; and exploitation of Europe, 124; and failure of leadership, 129-31; and fire-bombing, 114; and flying training, 145; and German car industry, 165; and hostility to navy, 39-40, 72-3; and independence of Luftwaffe, 132-3; and industry, 162; and intelligence, 196-7; miscalculates impact of bombing, 120; and officer corps, 137; and production crisis, 50-1; and rockets, 194-5; and science, 186-7; and Stalingrad airlift, 58; and technological change, 192-3
Goering-Programme, 164
Graziani, Marshal R., 40, 42
Great Crash, 182
Ground-crews, 140-1
G2 Office (U.S.), 196
Guadalcanal, Battle of, 74, 92, 95
Guernica, 206

Hankey, Lord, 186
Harris, Marshal A., 71, 73, 75, 109, 110, 115; and area bombing, 110-11; and bombing strategy, 116-17
Harrogate Programme (U.K.), 28
Hawaiian Air Force, 88
Heinkel aircraft company, 179, 193
Himmler, H., 146
Hiroshima, 100
Hitler, A., 1, 13, 18, 19, 22, 23, 30, 31, 37, 64, 69, 70, 83, 104, 105, 108, 109, 117, 119, 132, 144, 145, 148, 156, 183, 197, 201, 209; and administrative failure, 129-31; and aircraft production, 151-4; and Battle of Atlantic, 71-3; and Blitz, 34-6; and bombing, 103; and bombing in Russia, 59-60; and collapse of Luftwaffe, 78-81; and development of weapons, 192-3; and disarmament, 24;

and fire-bombing, 114; and invasion of Russia, 47-9; and Japan, 101; and Luftwaffe staff, 138; and Mediterranean campaign, 65-6; and naval power, 8; and North African campaign, 42-3; plans to disband Luftwaffe, 130-1; and Polish campaign, 26-8; and renewed German strategic bombing, 119-21; and rocket research, 194-5; and scientific research, 186-7; views on air strategy, 204-5; views on reserves, 79
Hopkins, H. H., 105
H₂S bombing aid, 115

Industrial Councils (Germ.), 124
Industry; see aircraft industry, aircraft production
Intelligence; see air intelligence
Italian Air Force (Regia Aeronautica), 40-1; and production, 41; and strength in Mediterranean, 44, 66
Italian Army, 41
Iwo-Jima, 96, 99

Japanese Army, 86, 90; competition with navy, 94; in Philippines, 93; and war with China, 86-7
Japanese Army Air Forces, 87; and defence against B-29s, 98-9; and defence of Japan, 94-5; and links with army, 133; problem of maintenance in, 141; strength and losses, 94; and training, 142
Japanese Imperial General Headquarters, 86, 93, 133
Japanese Naval Air Forces; and destruction of U.S. fleet, 90; and maintenance personnel, 141; and Pacific battles, 92-3; prepare for war, 87; and relations with navy, 133; strength and losses, 94; and training, 142, 144; and 11th air fleet, 89
Japanese Navy, 85, 86, 204; competes with army, 94; losses, 96
Jeschonnek, Gen. H., 37, 121, 137, 146, 154
Jet aircraft, 189, 192, 193, 194, 195
Joint Aircraft Board, 158
Joint Intelligence Committee (U.S.), 111
Joint Purchasing Commission, 158
Junkers aero-engine company, 163
Junkers aircraft company. 169, 179
Jutland, Battle of, 6

Kaganovich, M. M., 156, 206
'Kamikaze' attacks, 99, 147

Kammhuber Line, 79
Keitel, Field Marshal W., 31
Kesselring, Field Marshal A., 66, 69, 134
'Kindergarten' staff, 130
King, Fleet Admiral E. J., 71, 74, 90, 92-3
Klinov aero-engines (U.S.S.R.), 163
Knudsen, W. S., 156, 164
Koga, Admiral M., 92
Kondor aircraft, 37, 39-40

Labour; see aircraft industry, aircraft production, trades unions
Leigh-Mallory, Marshal T., 76
LeMay, Gen. C., 98-100, 114, 125
Lend-Lease, 56, 190
Leyte Gulf, Battle of, 92
Lindemann; see Cherwell, Lord
'Little Blitz', 115
Lovett, R. A., 135, 192
Luftflotte 3, 77, 79
Luftwaffe; Air Administrative Districts of, 51; and air defence, 79-80; and aircraft production, 154; aircraft production of in Europe, 124-5; and aluminium production, 176; and army co-operation, 10; and Atlantic Battle, 70-2; and Battle of Britain, 32-4; and 'Big Week', 76; in Blitz, 34-6; and blockade strategy, 36-7; bombing plans, 103; and bombing plans in Russia, 59-60; and collapse of morale, 81; failure of in Russia, 58-60; Fliegerkorps II, 66; Fliegerkorps X, 42, 44; and home defence, 121-2; intelligence of, 196-7; and invasion of Britain, 30-1; links with Abwehr, 199; maintenance of in Russia, 51-2; and naval co-operation, 8; and new weapons, 194-5; in North African campaign, 42-3; officer corps of, 137-8; and Polish campaign, 28-9; pre-war strength of, 22-3; and radar, 201; and rearmament, 20; renewed bombing offensive of, 119-21; in Scandinavian campaigns, 29; science and, 186, 189; serviceability in, 140-1; Special Duty Staffs in, 51; and Stalingrad battle, 55; strength of, 77; target selection, 110; and threat of disbandment, 130-1; training in, 142, 144-5; and views on tactical bombing, 11; and war at sea, 39-40; weapons selection in, 192-3
Luftwaffe Director of Training, 145
Lusser, Dr. R., 193

Macarthur, Gen. D., 96

Maintenance; *see* aircraft maintenance
Maintenance Group (RAF), 42–3
Malenkov, G. M., 53
Malkin Committee (U.K.), 24
Malta, Battle of, 66, 70
Marshall, Gen. G. C., 61, 71, 132, 192
Massachusetts Institute of Technology, 187
'Matterhorn' operation, 92, 97–8
Meister (master-craftsmen), 170, 173
Messerschmitt aircraft company, 179
Midway, Battle of, 92, 95
Milch, Field Marshal E., 22, 23, 52, 57,
    58, 80, 121, 130, 137, 154, 157, 158–9,
    161, 166, 170, 176, 179, 193
Mine-laying, 37
Ministry of Aircraft Production (U.K.),
    155, 168, 169, 172, 173, 193, 195
Ministry of Economic Warfare (U.K.),
    110, 112
Ministry of Home Security (U.K.), 35
Ministry of Information (U.K.), 38
Ministry of Production (U.K.), 155
Mitchell, Gen. W., 7, 13, 14, 104
Mitsubishi aircraft factories, 167
Modification Centres (U.S.), 178
Mölders, W., 54
Morale, 13; in air war, 145–8; and bomb-
    ing, 106–7, 207–8; in Japan, 147; in
    Luftwaffe, 122
Munich crisis, 18, 19, 23
Munitions Ministry (Jap.), 155, 158, 160,
    179, 182–3
Mussolini, B., 7, 16, 69, 148, 156, 159;
    leadership qualities of, 129; and Medi-
    terranean campaign, 40–1

Nagasaki, 100
Nagumo, Admiral C., 90
Nakajima aircraft factories, 167
National Advisory Committe for Aeronau-
    tics (U.S.), 187
National Aircraft War Production Council
    (U.S.), 160
National Defense Advisory Council (U.S.),
    156
National Socialism, 146, 187
Naval Bureau of Aeronautics (U.S.), 91
Nazi party, 81, 122, 146
Nazi Party Air Corps (NSFK), 139
Nazi-Soviet pact, 198
Nelson, D., 153
Neutrality Ban, 28
New Developments Division (U.S.), 193
Novikov, Marshal A. A., 53

Nuclear weapons; *see* atomic weapons
Nuffield, Viscount, 33, 165
Nuffield Organisation, 163

'Oboe' bombing aid, 115
Office of Production Management (U.S.),
    156
Office of Scientific Research and Devel-
    opment (U.S.), 187
Okinawa, 96, 99, 100, 147
Operation 'Olympic', 96
Operation 'Sealion', 48, 77, 104
Operation 'Torch', 69
Operational Research (U.K.), 140, 188,
    198
Operations Analysis (U.S.), 188
Organizational Planning and Statistical
    Control (U.S.), 135
Osenberg, Prof. W., 187
Osoaviakhim, 139–40
'Overlord', 75–7, 79, 111, 115, 117, 198,
    201

Pearl Harbour, 7, 63, 87, 89, 92, 132, 153,
    206
Philippine Sea, Battle of, 92, 95
Photographic Development Unit (U.K.),
    200
Photo-reconnaissance, 199-200, 202
'Planned Flying and Maintenance' (U.K.),
    140
'Pointblank' operation, 75, 109, 117
Polish Air Force, 28
Polish campaign, 26–9, 142
Porro, General, 42
Portal, Marshal C., 30, 76, 106, 109, 115,
    208
Pound, Admiral D., 71
Production Efficiency Board (U.K.), 168
Production Executive (U.K.), 155
'Production miracle' (Germ.), 80, 158
Propaganda, 206–7
Prussian tradition, 137, 202

Quadrant Conference, 75

Rabaul, 92
Radar, 194, 200-2; British, 15, 201; cen-
    timetric, 72, 191, 201; German, 16, 192,
    200–1; Japanese, 133, 202; Russian,
    200; United States, 88–9
Raeder, Admiral E., 8, 39, 66, 120
Rearmament; *see* air rearmament
Red Air Force; *see* Soviet Air Force
Red Army; *see* Soviet Army

Reich Air Defence League, 25
Reichsforschungsamt, 187
Reichsluftfahrtministerium (RLM); *see* German Air Ministry
Reichswehr, 137
Renegotiation Act, 182
Re-orientation Plan (U.K.), 15
Research and development, 2-3; atomic, 195; duplication of, 191; German lead in, 194; and involvement of science, 186-8; selection procedure in, 191-3
Ribbentrop, J., 24
Rocket research, 194-5
Rolls-Royce Ltd., 165
Rommel, Field Marshal E., 43, 65-7, 69, 87
Roosevelt, F. D. R., 18, 24, 28, 56, 62, 63, 75, 125, 132; and aid to Britain, 61; and aircraft production, 153; and bombing, 104-5; and China policy, 105; and recruitment of science, 188; and style of leadership, 129; and US rearmament, 19; views on air power, 205
Rote Kapelle spy ring, 197, 199
Royal Air Force; and area bombing, 110; and army support, 11; attacks German fighter force, 107; and Battle of Atlantic, 70-3; and Battle of Britain, 31-4; and Battle of France, 29-30; in Blitz, 35-6; bombing doctrine of, 12-14; bombing policy of, 74-5, 105-8; and Burma campaign, 90; co-operation with AAF, 68-9; co-operation with army, 68; defence doctrine of 14-15; evolution of air staff, 135; failure of early bombing, 108; ideas of on heavy bomber, 112-13; independence of, 131; and North African campaigns, 65-8; and onset of bombing, 37-9; and OR, 185; pre-war strength, 23; radar in, 201; and rearmament, 20-1; relations of with army, 116; Scandinavian campaign and, 29; strategy of in 1941, 46; strength of, 77; strength of in Middle East, 41; and training programmes, 143; wartime plans of, 27-8
Royal Navy, 71

Schmid, Col. J., 32
Schulze-Boysen, H., 199
Science; and air war, 185-96; co-operation with military, 188-9; mobilization of for war, 186-8; scientific co-operation, 190-1, 209
Scientific Advisory Committee (U.K.), 186

Scientific Intelligence, 200-2
Section de la Défense nationale du Cabinet, 11
Seidel, Gen. H., 52
Serviceability, 140-1
Shadow aircraft factories, 162-3
Simon, Sir J., 24
South African Air Force, 41
Soviet Air Force; achieves air superiority, 57; and 'air offensive', 54; and aircraft production, 49; in Battle for Moscow, 49-50; and co-operation with army, 10; establishment of ADD and PVO, 53; maintenance in, 52-3; operational independence of, 132; pilot training in, 144; quality of aircraft in, 177; repair facilities of, 140-1; Stalingrad and, 55; and strategic bombing, 58; strength in 1941, 48
Soviet Army, 49, 54, 57, 60
Soviet Supreme Command (Stavka), 53, 54
Spaatz, Gen. C., 117
Spanish Civil War, 14
Special attack groups (Tokubetsu Kogeki-tai), 147
Speer, A., 58, 59, 120-1, 122, 124, 158, 161, 167, 180; and self-responsibility of industry, 183
S.S., 146, 186
Stalin, J., 10, 47, 55, 56, 58, 82, 116, 128, 206; bombing policy of, 104-5; and morale, 146; and purges, 136
Stalingrad, Battle of, 58, 73
Stamp Survey (U.K.), 181
State Aircraft Factories (U.S.S.R.), 166
Stilwell, Gen., J. W., 91, 97
Stimson, H., 61, 64, 104, 125, 129, 132, 210
Strategic Bombing Surveys, 123
Suez Canal, 41, 64
Supreme Allied Commander, 76; *see* Eisenhower, D. D.
Suzuki, Gen. T., 86
Synthetic Oil Industry Law (Jap.), 86

Takoradi supply route, 42
Taranto, Battle of, 42, 86
Tedder, Marshal A., 69, 76
Telecommunications Research Establishment, 193
Tizard Committee, 186
Todt, F., 166
Tojo, Gen. H., 148, 158
Trades Unions, 173, 174-5

Trenchard, Lord, 12, 104, 106
Trident Conference, 97
Tuchachevski, Marshal M. N., 10
Tupolev, A. N., 58

Udet, Col. E., 50, 54, 158, 161, 176, 179, 192
Underground factories, 167
United Nations, 81
United States Army, 62-3, 96, 104
United States Army Air Forces; aircraft production plans of, 62; and anti-submarine Command, 71; and Atlantic Battle, 71; and attack on German fighter force, 107, 109; and atomic attacks, 100; and AWPD-1, 62; and bombing of Japan from China, 97-8; and bombing from Pacific bases, 98-100; bombing plans of, 106-8; bombing policy of, 74-5; co-operation with ground army, 69; and co-operation with RAF, 68-9; and creation of AAF, 63; and development of administration, 135-6; and heavy bomber, 112-13; and intelligence organization, 196; maintenance in, 76; and Pacific supply routes, 91; pilot training in, 143; and precision bombing, 111; and preparations in Pacific, 88-9; and Rainbow 5 Plan, 61-2; recruitment policies of, 139; relations of with surface forces, 132; in south-west Pacific, 96; strength of, 77; and supply of China theatre, 97-8; and Xth Air Force, 91
United States Joint Staffs, 63
United States Navy, 71-2, 85, 88; and campaign in Pacific, 94-6

United States Secretary of the Navy, 91
United States Strategic Bombing Survey (USSBS), 111, 123

V1, 81, 195
V2 rocket, 81, 130
'V' weapons, 118, 121, 198
Vansittart, Lord, 22
Vickers Ltd., 165
Vickers Supermarine Company, 178
'Victory' production programme, 64
Vinson-Trammell Act (U.S.), 182
Volkswagen, 165

Wallace Clark Company, 135
War Department (U.S.), 10, 62-3, 92, 111, 128, 193, 196
'War Potential' programme (U.K.), 23
War Production Board (U.S.), 153, 156, 176
Washington Conference (Jan. 1942), 64, 91
Washington Naval Agreement, 6
Wehrmacht, 161
Western Air Plans, 27
Westinghouse corporation, 165
Wever, Col. W., 103
Weygand, Gen. M., 11
Whitehall, 159
Willow Run aircraft factory, 164, 170

Yakovlev, A., 156
Yamamoto, Admiral T., 86, 90, 92

Zaibatsu (Japanese industrial trusts), 160, 162, 166; and profits, 182-3

R. J. OVERY taught for many years at Cambridge University and is now a lecturer at King's College, University of London. The author of numerous articles on the Nazi economy and the Luftwaffe, Dr. Overy is now working on a political biography of Goering.